SO-BGH-985

Principles of
Law Enforcement

Law Enforcement Code of Ethics

As a Law Enforcement Officer, my fundamental duty is to serve mankind; to safeguard lives and property; to protect the innocent against deception, the weak against oppression or intimidation, and the peaceful against violence or disorder; and to respect the Constitutional rights of all men to liberty, equality and justice.

I will keep my private life unsullied as an example to all; maintain courageous calm in the face of danger, scorn, or ridicule; develop self-restraint; and be constantly mindful of the welfare of others. Honest in thought and deed in both my personal and official life, I will be exemplary in obeying the laws of the land and the regulations of my department. Whatever I see or hear of a confidential nature or that is confided to me in my official capacity will be kept ever secret unless revelation is necessary in the performance of my duty.

I will never act officiously or permit personal feelings, prejudices, animosities or friendships to influence my decisions. With no compromise for crime and with relentless prosecution of criminals, I will enforce the law courteously and appropriately without fear or favor, malice or ill will, never employing unnecessary force or violence and never accepting gratuities.

I recognize the badge of my office as a symbol of public faith, and I accept it as a public trust to be held so long as I am true to the ethics of the police service. I will constantly strive to achieve these objectives and ideals, dedicating myself before God to my chosen profession . . . law enforcement.

Principles of
Law Enforcement

Second Edition

Edward Eldefonso

Supervisor, County of Santa Clara
Juvenile Probation Department;
Instructor, Department of Law Enforcement
and Criminal Justice,
De Anza College

Alan Coffey

Director, Staff Development,
County of Santa Clara
Juvenile Probation Department;
Instructor, Department of Social Science,
De Anza College

Richard C. Grace

Associate Professor,
Department of Criminal Justice,
California State University,
Los Angeles, California

HV
8031
.E5
1974
west

John Wiley & Sons

New York   London   Sydney   Toronto

Copyright © 1968, 1974, by John Wiley & Sons, Inc.

All rights reserved. Published simultaneously in Canada.

No part of this book may be reproduced by any means,
nor transmitted, nor translated into a machine language
without the written permission of the publisher.

Library of Congress Cataloging in Publication Data:

Eldefonso, Edward
  Principles of law enforcement.

  Includes bibliographies.
  1. Police. I. Coffey, Alan, joint author.
II. Grace, Richard C., joint author. III. Title.
HV8031.E5 1974   363.2   74-1275
ISBN 0-471-23501-6

Printed in the United States of America

10 9 8 7 6 5 4 3 2 1

This book is dedicated
to
The Memories of America's
Twentieth-Century Leaders in Law Enforcement
AUGUST VOLLMER
WILLIAM H. PARKER
ORLANDO WINFIELD WILSON
JOHN EDGAR HOOVER

Preface

Although the authors have made some significant changes in the second edition of *Principles of Law Enforcement,* the original format was still maintained. In other words, this book still fulfills the philosophy of "total involvement on an introductory level." *This book introduces the student to all facets of Law Enforcement.* It presents history and theory along with the human and scientific aspects of police work. Thus it deals with many general topics instead of a few topics in great depth. The book truly *introduces* the student to the principles of law enforcement.

Also, in keeping with the academic philosophy of providing opportunities for expanded research, the student will find references (annotated) at the conclusion of each chapter which will enhance the possibilities of further reading in a given area of police work.

Since enforcement of the laws of society has become increasingly controversial and scientific in recent years, the authors have made some changes in the second edition to "reflect police work in the 70's." Each chapter has been expanded to include *technological, legal,* and *humanistic* changes. Therefore, in keeping with the aforementioned changes of police work in the 70's, the authors—aside from updating and expanding the original twelve chapters (particularly those dealing with Police-Community Relations and

Career Opportunities)—have added six relevant chapters. The contents of these new chapters, although significant to police work, do not appear in other books of this nature and add a new dimension to *Principles of Law Enforcement*. These chapters are: The Fragmented Criminal Justice System; Leadership in Law Enforcement; Organized Crime; Ethics; "Victimless" Crime?; and Crime Prevention.

Furthermore, along with the original *Appendix* dealing with the history of law enforcement (outline), the authors have included other Appendices such as: Criminal Process and Court Structure; Purpose of the District Attorney's Office; Laboratory of Criminalistics; Glossary of Legal Terms; and Pertinent United States Supreme Court Decisions.

Both the original and new chapters take into consideration that sciences are only a part of law enforcement. *People* staff law enforcement agencies. *People* provide the support that enables these agencies to function effectively. And, of course, people break the laws of society. Law enforcement, then, is people interacting with people—a very human process. This book discusses human relations as an important, necessary concern of any law enforcement organization.

The material is divided into three parts. Part One deals with fragmentation of the criminal justice system as well as historical, theoretical, and legal aspects of law enforcement and crime. Part Two discusses opportunities for employment in the criminal justice system, the organization and administration of various functions and services of law enforcement, (i.e., introduction to specific techniques of police work such as patrol, investigation, and criminalistics). Part Three introduces the student specialized topics such as: Organized Crime, Crime "Without Victims," Arrest Procedures, Crime Prevention, Ethics in Police Work, and, Police Relationship With the Community.

Much more could be said, of course, about each of these topics; in fact, the student will be taking separate courses in most of the areas discussed in this book. Our aim here, however, is to show the student how the individual segments are related, and how they depend on each other for success. We have also attempted to indicate the many opportunities available in our profession. We hope that this book will be the starting point for a successful and rewarding career in law enforcement.

Edward Eldefonso
San Jose, California   *Alan Coffey*
Los Angeles, California   *Richard C. Grace*

Acknowledgments

With the usual proviso that they cannot be held accountable for either errors of omission or commission, the authors express their gratitude to the following agencies for their assistance in completing the revision of the first edition: The International Association Chiefs of Police; The Commission on Peace Officers' Standards and Training (POST); The Federal Bureau of Investigation; The Childrens Bureau, U.S. Dept. of Health, Education and Welfare; The California Association of Administration of Justice Educators and *The Administration and Staff of the County of Santa Clara (California) Juvenile Probation Department—specifically Mr. Richard Bothman, Chief Juvenile Probation Officer and his assistant, Michael Kuzirian.*

Beyond the assistance of many who aided in shaping the second edition of *Principles of Law Enforcement* is the thoughtful advice of B. Earl Lewis, Professor of Law Enforcement and Criminal Justice, De Anza College (California); Richard Cox and Len Pacheco, Office of Public Information, County of Santa Clara—particularly for their assistance in obtaining some of the photographs utilized in this second edition; James Geary, Sheriff, County of Santa Clara; Peter J. Pitchess, Sheriff, County of Los Angeles (California); Edward M. Davis, Chief of Police, Los Angeles Police Department; David B. Michael, Chief of Police, Anaheim Police Department.

X   ACKNOWLEDGMENTS

A deep feeling of appreciation and personal gratitude is expressed to the following friends, colleagues and associates: Melvin H. Miller, Professor Emeritus of Law Enforcement and Criminal Justice, California State University, San Jose, California; Doctor David Chapman, Professor of Law Enforcement and Criminal Justice, California State University, Los Angeles, California; G. Douglas Gourley, Chairman, Department of Criminal Justice, California State University, Los Angeles, California; Clarence M. Coster, Associate Administrator, United States Department of Justice; and the late O. W. Wilson, a long-time friend and mentor of Professor Grace; for their stimulating guidance, support and suggestions without which the task of updating, revising and expanding to this second edition could not have been accomplished.

Finally for reasons possibly clear only to those who have attempted to reduce a "mountain of material" to a single volume, we offer our deepest gratitude to *Mildred Ann Eldefonso, Beverly May Coffey,* and *Doris Jane Grace.*

Contents

PART ONE
HISTORY, THEORY AND EVOLUTION OF LAW ENFORCEMENT   1

CHAPTER ONE
Law Enforcement and the Fragmented Criminal Justice System   3

Criminal Justice Processes   5

Criminal Justice Process Description and Organization   5

Law Enforcement Process   7

  Crime Prevention and Suppression   7

  Law Enforcement: Investigation and Apprehension   10

Judicial Process   11

  Juvenile Judicial Process   13

Correctional Process   14

Problems of the Criminal Justice System and Due Process of Law   16

Administration of Criminal Justice: A Complicated Process   18

  Due Process of Law   19

xi

Fragmentation of the Criminal Justice System   20

Summary   23

Annotated References   24

Notes   24

CHAPTER TWO
Scope of Policemen and the Crime Problem   **26**

Definitions of Policemen and Police Power   27

  The Public View   29

  Awareness of the Police Role   31

The Social and Psychological Control Role of Law Enforcement   31

  Coercive Control: "The Cop"   33

  Persuasive Control: The Policeman   35

Scope and Nature of the Crime Problem   37

  Limitations on the Measurement of Crime and Delinquency   39

  FBI Crime Report and the U.S. Children's Bureau Statistical Series   41

  Extent of Juvenile Crime   42

  Extent of Adult Crime   46

Summary   49

Annotated References   51

Notes   52

CHAPTER THREE
Philosophy and History of Enforcing Laws   **54**

Philosophy of Enforcing Laws   55

  Personal Safety   55

  Property, Security, and Freedom   56

  Laws to Control Behavior   57

  Punishment   57

  American Philosophy   58

History of Enforcing Laws   59

  Ancient History   59

  Modern History   61

Development of American Law Enforcement   63

Summary   65

Annotated References   66

Notes   67

CHAPTER FOUR
Leadership in Law Enforcement   68

Sir Robert Peel   68
Allan Pinkerton   72
August Vollmer   75
Orlando Winfield Wilson   79
John Edgar Hoover   84
William H. Parker   89
Leonarde Keeler   92
Quinn Tamm   94
Summary   96
Annotated References   97

CHAPTER FIVE
Theories of Crime and Delinquency   98

Myths and Misunderstanding   100
Theoretical Approaches to Criminal Behavior   101
    Sociological Factors   102
    Psychological Factors   106
    Physiological Factors   108
Multiple Causation: An Eclectic Approach   110
Summary   111
Annotated References   113
Notes   113

CHAPTER SIX
Legal Aspects of Law Enforcement   115

The Legal System   116
    Criminal Law   116
    Criminal Court   117
    Civil Liability   123
Posting Bail and Bond   125
Summary   126
Annotated References   127
Notes   128

PART TWO

CAREER OPPORTUNITIES AND TECHNICAL ASPECTS OF LAW ENFORCEMENT: PROCEDURES AND PROBLEMS   131

CHAPTER SEVEN

Careers in Law Enforcement   133

Is There a Need for Police Personnel?   134
  Emphasis on Education and Training   135
Selection for Appointment and Minimum Standards   139
  Good Moral Character   141
  Psychological Testing   142
  Physical-Agility Tests   142
  Oral Board   143
  Probationary Period   144
  Police Salaries   147
  Advantages and Disadvantages of Law Enforcement as a Career   149
  Employment Opportunities   153
Women in Police Work   155
Job Opportunities with Related Agencies   159
  Corrections Today   160
  Employment Opportunities   162
  Advantages and Disadvantages of Correction Work as a Career   165
Summary   170
Annotated References   171
Notes   172

CHAPTER EIGHT

Police Organization   174

Analysis of Organization   175
Lines of Control and Communication   175
Small Police Agencies   176
Characteristics of an Organization   180
Principles of Organization   181
Analysis of Police Services   181
Specialization   182

Problems in Specialization   184
Primary Police Services   188
Ancillary Services   189
Administrative Services   191
Rank of Supervisors and Description of Organizations   192
Summary   194
Annotated References   195
Notes   196

CHAPTER NINE

Police Administration   197

Administrative Leadership   203
  Setting Policy   203
  Fiscal Budget Policy   206
  Selective Enforcement Policy   207
  Public Opinion   207
  Morale   210
  Discipline   211
  Administrative Control   212
Summary   214
Annotated References   215
Notes   216

CHAPTER TEN

Police Patrol   217

Evolution of Patrol   218
Importance of Police Patrol   220
Objectives of the Patrol Force   220
Types of Patrol   221
  Foot Patrol   222
  Horse Patrol   224
  Bicycle Patrol   225
  Automobile Patrol   226
  Patrol with Scooters and Motorcycles   226

Canine Patrol 227
Aircraft Patrol 229
Marine Patrol 231
Special Types of Patrol 232
Saturation Patrol 233
Team Patrol 234
Plainclothes Patrol 235
Patrol Through Electronics 236
Private Police and Security Services 237
Activities and Responsibilities of Patrol 238
Routine Calls and Services 238
Crime Prevention 238
Public Disorders and Disasters 240
Traffic Law Enforcement 242
Summary 243
Annotated References 244
Notes 245

CHAPTER ELEVEN

Investigation **246**

The Investigative Process 247
Investigative Techniques 251
Interviews and Interrogations 252
Undercover Work 255
Surveillance 256
Methods of Identification 257
Scientific Field Aids 259
Physical Evidence 260
Summary 261
Annotated References 261
Notes 262

CHAPTER TWELVE

Criminalistics **263**

History of Criminalistics 264
First Uses 264
Pioneers in the Field 264

Need for Criminalistics   264

Purpose of Criminalistics   265

Crime Laboratory   266

Local Laboratory   267

Regional Laboratory   267

Laboratory Personnel   267

Areas of Investigation and Analysis   268

  Firearms Examination   268

  Fingerprint Examination   269

  Spectrographic Examination   269

  Serological Examination   271

  General Chemical and Toxicological Examination   272

  Fiber and Hair Examination   272

  Metallurgical and Petrographic Examination   272

  Neutron-Activation Analysis   273

  Radiological Examination   274

  Uses of Photography   274

  Questioned Documents   275

  Polygraphic Examination   276

  Voiceprint Identification   278

Future of Criminalistics   279

Summary   280

Annotated References   280

Notes   281

PART THREE

CRIME IN AMERICA
AND POLICE-COMMUNITY RELATIONS

283

CHAPTER THIRTEEN

Organized Crime

285

Historical Background   285

Organization and Membership   287

  Internal Structure   290

Purposes of Organized Crime   293

  Implications   294

Types of Illegal Activity   296

Corruption of Public Officials   299

Control of Organized Crime   300
Summary   306
Annotated References   307
Notes   308

CHAPTER FOURTEEN
"Victimless" Crime?   **310**

History   311
Scope of Victimless Crime   312
Types of Victimless Crime   313
  Gambling   313
  Narcotics and Dangerous Drugs   318
  Prostitution   323
  Homosexuality   326
  Pornography   328
  Alcohol   332
Vice Law Enforcement   336
Vice Enforcement and the Legal System   339
Summary   343
Annotated References   343
Notes   344

CHAPTER FIFTEEN
Arrest Procedures   **346**

Legal Procedure   347
  Manner of Making Arrests   347
Exemptions from Arrest   348
Arrest by Peace Officers without Warrant   349
Arrest by Peace Officers with Warrant   350
Arrests by Private Persons   352
Special Statutes Authorizing Arrest without Warrant   355
Arrest Techniques   356
Human Factors   356
  Confidence   357
  Knowledge of the Job   357
  Personality   357

Psychology   358
Human Failures   359
Arrests with Warrants   359
Arrests without Warrants   361
Proper Methods of Approach   363
  On Street   363
  In Residence or Building   364
  In Vehicle   365
Special Problems   367
  Constitutional Rights   367
  Selected Problems   369
Summary   370
Annotated References   371
Notes   371

CHAPTER SIXTEEN
Crime Prevention   **373**

Prevention as a Concept   373
Police and Crime Prevention   374
  Police and Corrective Prevention   377
  Police and Mechanical Prevention   379
Summary   385
Annotated References   385
Notes   386

CHAPTER SEVENTEEN
Ethics   **387**

Law Enforcement Code of Ethics   390
Canons of Police Ethics   390
FBI Pledge for Law Enforcement Officers   393
General Rules of Official Conduct   394
Ethics and Employment Policies   396
Summary   396
Annotated References   397
Notes   397

CHAPTER EIGHTEEN
Police-Community Relations   **398**

Human Relations Defined   400
Human Relations and Ethics   402
Rewarding Misbelief   404
Human-Relations Programs   405
Human Relations with ''Precriminals''   407
Public Support   409
Summary   411
Annotated References   412
Notes   412

APPENDICES

Criminal Process and Court Structure   414
History of Law Enforcement   426
Pertinent United States Supreme Court Decisions   429
Glossary of Legal Terms   432
Laboratory of Criminalistics   441
Purpose of the District Attorneys' Office   443

INDEX   **449**

Principles of
Law Enforcement

PART ONE

History, Theory, and Evolution of Law Enforcement

CHAPTER ONE

Law Enforcement and the Fragmented Criminal Justice System

The "enforcers" of the criminal justice—POLICE, COURTS, and CORREC-TIONAL apparatus—where viewed as individual agencies organized to carry out their mission "are an improbable, quixotic army" [1].

> The major elements of war-time planning are knowledge of the status of friendly forces and knowledge of the strength and intent of the enemy. Military analogies frequently fail in the war on crime. However, the need is clear to catalog the organization, condition, status, and deployment of resources of society to combat crime [2].

This chapter is intended to fulfill the need which spelled out succinctly is: Describing the method our rapidly changing society has devised to cope with crime. The American method of dealing with crime is commonly referred to as the CRIMINAL JUSTICE SYSTEM.

Studies [3] have long ago learned that most crime is inseparable from the social context in which it is found. This social context includes attitudes, prejudices, and knowledges. Crime also is inseparable from economy, education, politics, and morality. As a result the criminal justice system is a small but integral part of the social system in which we live. That criminality which we perceive daily must be duly controlled by a system which is yet only

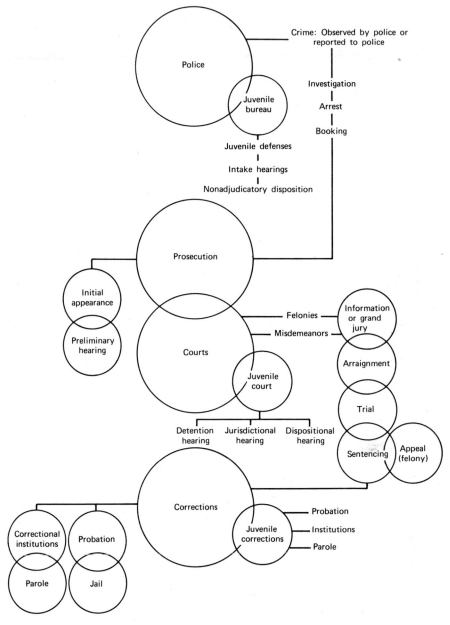

FIGURE 1.1. *A general view of the criminal justice system. Source: Adapted from:* The Challenge of Crime in a Free Society, *President's Commission on Administration of Criminal Justice, 1967, pp. 8–9.*

a *diverse and loosely knit series of agencies which includes the police, courts, and corrections* [4]

Before moving further, however, into describing the incohesive and fragmented criminal justice system [5], it would appear appropriate at this time to introduce the mechanics of the criminal justice processes [6].

CRIMINAL JUSTICE PROCESSES

Any criminal justice system—or the processes within the system—is an apparatus society uses to cope with crime. There has never been a civilized society that did not find itself continually coping with crime. It can be said that great differences exist between the crime philosophies of various societies, and between the criminal theories and activities from culture to culture. But it cannot be said that any society, including the United States, has devised any method to *avoid* coping with crime on a continuing basis. This section separates the criminal justice system into a collection of individual processes.

Criminal justice in the United States is a composite of many complex factors including formally constituted agencies at all levels as well as informal groups which provide additional resources. This diverse assortment leads to some difficulty in defining or understanding the system [7].

The system works by apprehending, prosecuting, convicting, and sentencing those members of the community who violate the basic rules of group existence. The action taken against law-breakers is designed to serve three purposes beyond the immediate punitive one. It removes dangerous people from the community; it deters others from criminal behavior; and it gives society an opportunity to attempt to transform law-breakers into law-abiding citizens. What most significantly distinguishes the system of one country from that of another is the extent and form of protections it offers individuals in the PROCESS of determining guilt and imposing punishment. "Our system of justice deliberately sacrifices much efficiency and effectiveness in order to preserve local autonomy and to protect the individual. Sometimes it may seem to sacrifice too much [8]."

CRIMINAL JUSTICE PROCESS
DESCRIPTION AND ORGANIZATION

Traditional usage has divided the criminal justice system into three (four if prosecution and defense counsel are separated from the court process) functional components: *Law enforcement,* the *courts,* and *corrections.* While providing a *useful* starting point, this tripartite breakdown does not go far enough; separate functions are clearly evident in these categories and thus additional refinements have to be made.

First, it is necessary to recognize the large scope of law enforcement activities outside the spectrum of work connected with specific crimes. The *law enforcement* component logically breaks down into the *crime prevention/suppression function* and the *investigation/apprehension function.* The former includes those processes which directly tend to prevent or suppress acts which are both injurious to the public safety and legally prohibited. The latter refers to those processes of investigation of the particulars of an alleged or actual criminal incident.

Second, in dealing with the *court system,* the law currently separates *adjudication of juveniles* from *adjudication of adults.* Hence, the court function must be broken down into the judicial process which involves the adjudication of adult criminality and the juvenile judicial process which involves the adjudication of juvenile delinquency and dependency.

Third, a similar distinction is recognized in both the law and the practice of *corrections.* Thus, the correctional function is divided into both *adult corrections and juvenile corrections.* But, there is an additional correctional distinction which must also be made. The custodial and rehabilitative processes supporting the correctional function are usually applied to adjudicated adults and juveniles. To provide clarification, preadjudication custody or rehabilitative activities should be separated into their own separate categories. And two additional functions, *unsentenced custody/correctional processes* for both adults and juveniles, have been developed as part of the organizational format.

This leads to an eight part functional breakdown of the criminal justice system and these have been organized in a way which is based partly on sequence and partly on client group. Thus, the *first two parts of the law enforcement functions of crime prevention/suppression and investigation/apprehension.* The *next three parts all pertain to subsequent processes involved with adults: Judicial process, adult corrections, and unsentenced custody/correctional processes for adults.* While this latter category is sequentially prior to the judicial process, its present place in the organizational framework represents both its smaller relative size and its close material compatibility with the correctional function. *The final three categories are the juvenile judicial process, juvenile corrections, and unadjudicated custody/correctional processes for juveniles.*

Since the basic breakdown of the criminal justice system into eight parts is based upon function, it is important to point out that several agencies may be involved in each category. Thus, the police and sheriff's departments, and the State Highway Patrol, are involved in the two law enforcement functions; and the functions of corrections and unadjudicated custody/correctional processes are performed not only by probation, parole, and prison agencies but also by police and sheriff departments. And the two parts related to the judicial function encompass many agencies in addition to the courts such as public defenders, district attorneys, probation departments, law enforcement officers, bail projects, court staffs, and county clerks. Most of the time, however, those agencies participating in criminal justice functions are limited in this format to public agencies.

LAW ENFORCEMENT PROCESS

As previously stated, the police agency is one of three basic social processes utilized by modern administration of criminal justice. Since its inception in England in 1829, the police mission has had two *primary* functions: (a) Investigation of crime, and (b) apprehension of criminals. Although, as pointed out in this chapter, the aforementioned functions are separated into different categories (i.e., work activities), the police mission still consists of:

. . . investigating crime and apprehending criminals. To fulfill the duty, they are given authority to invoke the criminal process—to arrest, to prosecute and seek a conviction. As important as this function is, however, the average police officer spends a relatively small part of his time investigating and prosecuting serious criminal offenses. Most of his day is spent in keeping order, settling disputes, finding missing children, helping drunks, directing traffic, and monitoring parking meters [9].

The work of law enforcement is divided into two functions—*crime prevention/suppression and investigation/apprehension.* The former function pertains to all the activities of law enforcement agencies which do not involve a specific crime situation. The processes which relate to this function can be grouped into four sections: (a) Community and personal contact, (b) preventive patrol, (c) maintenance of public order, and (d) movement/control of traffic.

Crime Prevention and Suppression

It will be seen that the processes listed in each group are logically distinct from the processes in other groups except for the fact that all are concerned with prevention/suppression activities of a general nature. However, the particular process to which an officer may be assigned should not be confused with what he actually ends up doing.

It is also noted that some of the contact processes may generate record inquiries with the criminal justice information record system and all contact processes require report preparation.

Community and Personal Contact.   Initially service incorporates those police processes involving community and personal contact of a general nature. Each type of contact serves a distinct purpose. The normal process of stopping, questioning, and inspecting is a prelude to the investigation function, while personal or community assistance, such as giving directions to a motorist, pertains to the service aspect of law enforcement work. Community relations is defined as providing specific crime prevention techniques and information to community groups and individuals.

Preventive Patrol.   This category of processes, completed by officers on patrol, has two purposes—that of observing the public and that of being on view for a deterrent effect. The basic forms of preventive patrol, all of which are covered in Chapter Thirteen, are motorized patrol, patrol using vehicles other than automobiles, and foot patrol. If the patrol activity involves providing an escort for security purposes, it is separated out as a security escort. Furthermore, the examination of structures for the purpose of assuring that they have not been the scene of a criminal or delinquent act is included in this work activity under the heading of security inspections because of its basic similarity to other preventive patrol processes.

Maintenance of Public Order.   These are the processes applied to the preservation of public peace or compliance with the law while a portion of the public engages in special or unusual activities. Here, the processes are categorized according to the major types of activities where such services are provided—special events and civil disturbances.

Movement/Control of Traffic.   The fourth work activity grouping relates to the regulation of movement of vehicles, ships, and persons which involves traffic patrol and accident investigation. These two processes are given a broader description than other processes described under this function. They include investigation and apprehension related to traffic laws which could also belong to the investigation/apprehension function. However, it is desirable to distinguish traffic crimes from the more serious offenses dealt with in the processes of the investigation/apprehension function. Nevertheless, although traffic patrol may become involved in apprehension or investigation

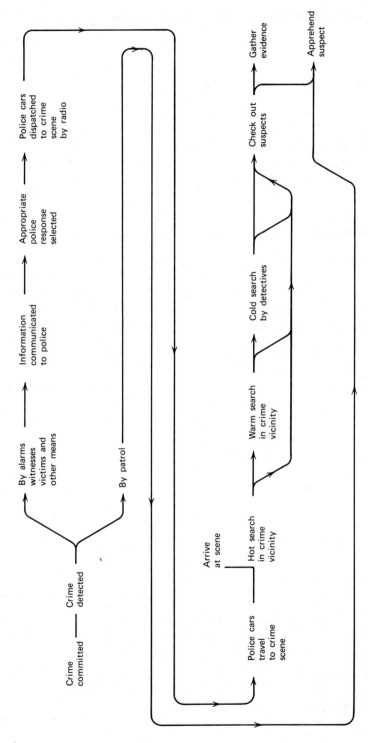

FIGURE 1.2. *A general view of an alarm response. Source: The Challenge of Crime in a Free Society, A Report by the President's Commission on Administration of Criminal Justice System, 1967, pp. 246–247.*

of traffic law violations, other criminal incidents related to the use of vehicles such as auto theft, drunk driving, or transporting contraband, etc., are included under the investigation/apprehension section.

The investigation/apprehension functions are discussed in Chapters Eleven and Fifteen involve inquiring into the particulars of a criminal incident in order to learn the elements of the incident which could in turn lead to the arrest of one or more persons considered to be responsible for the criminal incident. The processes which compose the function can be divided into two categories: (*a*) General programs and (*b*) special programs.

Law Enforcement: Investigation and Apprehension

While some of the processes which make up these two work categories are classified according to the kind of work which they involve (as with the crime prevention/suppression processes), others depend on the underlying offense which leads to the process. As with the crime prevention/suppression processes, actual work by a law enforcement officer rather than formal assignment determines which process is invoked, and report preparation where applicable is distinguished as a separate process.

General Programs.   The general program encompasses those processes typically associated with investigation *and* apprehension work. Four processes classify investigation or apprehension by offense category. Crimes against persons and crimes against properties refer to those offenses traditionally placed in these categories. Vice/organized crime refers to narcotics, prostitution, liquor law violations, gambling, etc. A category of miscellaneous offenses against the public and peace and order involves drunkenness, disturbing the peace, public nuisances, and the like. It is distinguished from the process of maintaining public order at civil disturbances since the latter involves a group of persons as opposed to one or two individuals.

A fifth process pertains more to the activity involved rather than the underlying offense. This is alarm response—that process of sending a unit to a location where an electronic/mechanical signaling device has been activated.

Special Programs.   Where investigation and apprehension activities are of a distinct character and are not covered by the general program categories, they are classified as special programs. The principal process in this work activity group are the serving of arrests and/or subpoenas and booking, which is defined as including all activities performed in carrying out the usual booking operation.

JUDICIAL PROCESS [10]

The function of judicial processes is to initiate and carry out the adjudication of crime [refer to Appendix A]. The processes which compose this function are organized into five work activity groups: (1) Initiation of Prosecution; (2) Proceedings Prior to Trial; (3) Trial Proceedings; (4) Post-Trial proceedings; and (5) Habeas Corpus.

Arrest to First Judicial Appearance.   Many States and the Federal courts require appearance "without unnecessary delay." Depending on the circumstances, a few hours—or less—may be regarded as "unnecessary delay." Compliance with this standard may require extension of court operating hours and the continual availability of a magistrate.

First Judicial Appearance to Arraignment.   Standards here are complicated because: (*a*) a shorter period is appropriate for defendants in jail than for those released; (*b*) preliminary hearings are waived in many cases and the formality and usefulness of the hearing varies; (*c*) formal charge in some cases is by grand jury indictment, while in others by prosecutor's information—usually the right to indictment can be waived by the defendant; and (*d*) in many jurisdictions proceedings through preliminary hearing in felony cases are in one court while grand jury charge and subsequent proceedings are in another. While in all cases these steps should take no more than 17 days, in most cases it should be possible to accomplish them in substantially less time.

Arraignment to Trial.   Many of the increasing number of motions require the judge to hear and decide factual issues. Discovery orders may require time for the assembling and screening of documents. The recommended standard would allow slightly more than 5 weeks for these steps and would allow a total of 9 weeks between arraignment and trial. Where complicated motions are not involved, the period before trial should be shortened.

Trial to Sentence.   During this period a presentence investigation should be completed.

Sentence to Appellate Review.   This standard is based on the time periods of the proposed Uniform Rules of Federal Appellate Procedure. Many jurisdictions would have to change existing practices concerning printing and preparation of records to meet this standard [11]. Source adapted from: *The Challenge of Crime in a Free Society.* A Report by The President's Commission on Law Enforcement and the Administration of Justice. U.S. Govt. Printing Office, Wash., D.C., 1967. pp. 155–156.

The processes applicable to each of these activity groups are arranged for the most part in the sequence they take in the adjudication of an individual criminal defendant. *Habeas Corpus* which can occur at any time an individual is confined is placed at the final listing. Furthermore, the individual process listings distinguish between felony and misdemeanor adjudication in Superior, Municipal, and Justice Courts. This refinement facilitates determination of such issues as the cost con-

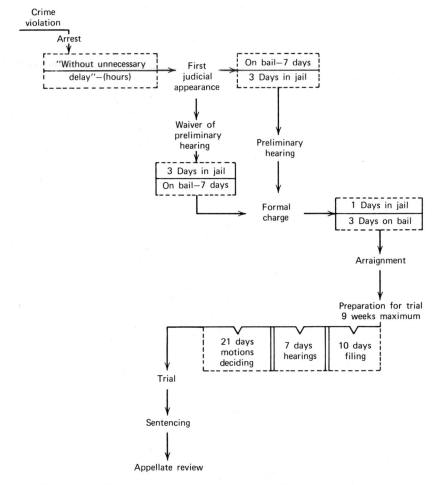

FIGURE 1.3. *Timetable for felony cases (model). Source:* The Challenge of Crime in a Free Society, *President's Commission on Law Enforcement and the Administration of Justice, 1967, pp. 155–156.*

sequences of *plea bargaining* and procedural changes in the adjudication sequence.

Initiation of Prosecution. Those processes which provide a transition from law enforcement activity (the investigation/apprehension function) to judicial activity are grouped under initiation of prosecution. The two main processes in this category are *charging* and *indicting.* The former includes all work by district attorneys (including investigation) in preparing complaints and information; the latter comprises all grand jury activities in issuing an indictment.

Bail and Own Recognizance.   Release activities are also included in this activity group as part of the releasing from custody processes. While technically, these actions may occur both before and after a court appearance, they are included in the prior category because no judicial time is allocated to this process; only the staffs who support these programs are included.

Proceedings Prior to Trial.   Those processes which occur before trial either necessarily or at the defendant's option are grouped as proceedings prior to trial. This activity group includes arraignment and pre-trial proceedings for both mis-demeanors and felonies as well as felony preliminary examination. Hearings based on petitions to higher courts are separated from other pre-trial hearings because of their frequency and significance.

Trial Proceedings.   Those processes which lead to a determination of guilt or innocence are listed under trial proceedings. The trial confirmation process includes both the calendar hearings under a master calendar system and the pre-trial or trial confirmation conference which some courts adopt. The trial process includes both court and jury trials. A further category, trials on transcript, is defined as a felony court trial disposed of on the record of the preliminary hearings (although other evidence may also be introduced by either party).

Post-Trial Proceedings.   This fourth activity group encompasses those proc-esses which either must occur prior to conviction or which may occur at any stage in adjudication prior to sentencing. The included processes are *insanity and civil commitment hearings, post-trial hearings, sentencing/probation revoca-tion hearings,* and *appeals to higher courts.* The civil commitment hearings concern alleged narcotic addicts and mentally disordered sex offenders who have been convicted of some offense. Sentencing and probation revocation hearings are dealt with as a single category, even though some courts may conduct them as separate calendars, because of their essential similarity.

Habeas Corpus.   As already noted, the fifth activity group is concerned with habeas corpus hearings and appeals.

Juvenile Judicial Process

The function of the juvenile judicial process is to initiate and carry out the adjudica-tion of juvenile delinquency or dependency. The processes which compose this function are divided into four work activity groups: (1) Initiation of Juvenile Pro-ceedings; (2) Detaining Juveniles; (3) Proceedings to Declare a Minor a Ward or Dependent Child of the Court; and (4) Other Hearings Related to Juveniles.

As indicated, the juvenile judicial process includes the adjudication of the dependency status. Although this is not technically a part of crime-related judicial activity, it is included because of its procedural similarity and relevance. Other proceedings involving non-delinquent youth, such as adoption and guardianship are not, however, included in this function. As in the case of the judicial process, the processes are arranged sequentially and preparation time for all participants involved in each process is allocated to the process itself.

Initiation of Juvenile Proceedings.   That process which provides a transition from law enforcement activity (the investigation/apprehension function) to entry in the juvenile justice system is probation intake. In order to maintain analogy with the activity group entitled initiation of prosecution, the aspect of the intake function dealt with is limited to the screening of minors to determine subsequent action. In this, probation officers function analogously to district attorneys.

Detaining Juveniles.   Detaining juveniles is limited to processes involved in the judicial determination of whether to detain—*detention hearings* and rehearings. The custodial aspects of juvenile detention are included in another functional process.

Proceedings to Declare a Minor a Ward or Dependent Child of the Court. This function is composed of judicial activities leading to a determination of whether wardship or dependency will be declared. Because of the bifurcated juvenile proceedings, jurisdictional and dispositional hearings are two separate processes. Where these hearings are conducted by a referee, there may be a rehearing before a juvenile court judge. Appeals may be made, as in the judicial process,

Other Hearings Related to Juveniles.   This function includes processes dealing with three different situations. The *first* is subsequent changes in the case of a minor who has been declared a ward or dependent child of the juvenile court. These range from new hearings because of a change of circumstances or discovery of new evidence and hearings on supplemental petitions which involve custodial change to other hearings or modifications of court orders, annual review of dependency cases, and hearings on petitions for the sealing of police, probation, and court records.

The *second* situation is the process whereby the juvenile court reviews a probation officer's decision not to file a case which has been referred.

Finally, for certain offenses, adjudicatory proceedings may take place which do not lead to a declaration of wardship. The most prominent example is the traffic hearing.

CORRECTIONAL PROCESS

Many people tend to think of the administration of justice in terms of the criminal trial alone because this is part of the process which occurs in the local community, but, more than that, because it is infused with the human element; it is exciting, colorful, and dramatic. This is why the movies and television have given so much time to criminal trials [12].

The actual trial is not the whole of the administration of criminal justice.

The total process is a deadly serious business that begins with an arrest, proceeds through a trial, and is followed by a judgment and a sentence to a term of confinement in a prison or other institution. The administration of criminal justice in any civilized country must embrace the ideas of rehabilitation of the guilty person as well as the protection of society [13].

Contemporary society utilizes *corrections* as a means of dealing with officially identified law-breakers. The correctional apparatus is a system of diversely organized agencies. As originally stated, corrections is responsible for administering the assigned penalties (i.e., assigned penalties through the judicial process).

The correctional process, as we know it today, developed in the nineteenth century as a result of significant modifications and changes in the penalty system. Initially, the seventeenth and eighteenth centuries were eras which were primarily concerned with retribution and punishment. Sentences such as death, mutilation, and banishment were not unusual. Supposedly, these harsh penalties eliminated the law violator from the community or branded him permanently as a criminal. Needless to say, the administration of such penalties were dispensed without great expense or personnel; all that was required was the hangman and the keeper of the jail where offenders were held for trial and execution. It was during the nineteenth century that one of many reforms which reflected a new evaluation of human life was the substitution of the restrictive and punitive punishments mentioned. Instead, the penalties were in the area of time, status, and restriction. Since the type of penalties were drastically modified, a different kind of administrative personnel and an expanded agency structured to supervise those periods of restricted status was necessary to keep track of this "budding bureaucratic system."

The modifications in the nineteenth century not only required a different type of administrative structure and personnel but it introduced the idea of treatment. Initial rehabilitative efforts were concerned primarily with working with the offender in an institution and returning him to his "normal" status in the community at the end of his period of restriction. This, however, produced a great deal of concern and anxiety about the possibility of further misbehavior on the part of the "rehabilitated" offender. Due to the increased knowledge brought about by the behavioral sciences, it is felt that an individual somehow could be reformed or corrected while residing within a particular community. It is felt that this individual can be observed and controlled along with efforts made to produce changes in his lawless behavior. The increased knowledge about the dynamics of human behavior and how it is modified, soon became available to penologists in the twentieth century and, therefore, it was possible to give a great deal of attention to the rehabilitation of the offender. Thus, it can be said, that the correctional process has undergone a change of meaning and definition; from a punitive, restrictive, and meaningless incarceration, the correctional process has come to mean the administration of the penalty in such a way that the offender is "corrected" (i.e., in other words, the offender's current behavior is maintained within acceptable limits at the same time that his life-style adjustment is modified).

Corrections is therefore a social process by which society maintains legally identified offenders as members of the community in temporarily handicapped status. The necessities of this task require both control over the behavior of the offender during the period of his penalty and services designed to help him achieve a less socially dangerous mode of participation in the community [14].

The modern correctional process is administered through a system of operating agencies which are a part of the formal system of social control and are authorized to use, under limitations, the force of the state to protect the community against the unlawful acts which might be performed by the offenders under their care. They are primarily governmental agencies, established by legislation which authorizes their activities and which makes the service mandatory for both agent and client [15].

PROBLEMS OF THE CRIMINAL JUSTICE SYSTEM AND DUE PROCESS OF LAW

As long as it can be remembered, there has been a great deal of dissatisfaction with the administration of justice and discontent has an ancient and unbroken pedigree [16]. A noted author and barrister once wrote:

The Anglo-Saxon laws continually direct that justice is to be done equally to rich and to poor, and the King exhorts that the peace must be kept better than has been wont, and that men of every order readily submit . . . each to that law which is appropriate to him. . . . In the 18th Century it was complained that the Bench was occupied by legal monks, probably ignorant of human nature and the affairs of men. In the 19th Century vehement criticism of the reform movement needs only to be mentioned. In other words, as long as there has been laws and lawyers, conscientious and well-meaning men have believed that laws were mere arbitrary technicalities, and that attempts to regulate the relations of mankind in accordance with them resulted largely in injustice. But we must not be deceived by this innocuous and inevitable discontent with all law into overlooking or underrating the real and serious dissatisfaction with courts and lack of respect for law which exists in the United States today [17].

The socioeconomic and cultural changes exert great pressures which make effective law enforcement in our society extremely difficult. This is typically pointed out in the following quotation:

In the days of Daniel Boone, there would be little point in a traffic light at a crossing of foot trails. Today, we accept the interference with our liberty represented by traffic signals because we know that without them all of us would be snarled in hopeless traffic jams.

When a generation ago, a farm boy on a spring day yelled, ran, picked up a rock and threw it—who cared? He was a boy. But today—with perhaps no more basic motivation than the animal spirits which moved his rural grandfather—this same conduct would almost inevitably produce a police call and a police statistic.

In earlier days few people would be bothered by the bitter and violent words uttered by a pioneer and a few companions around a camp fire, but in today's hot summer city streets, words of equal violence addressed to a Ku-Klux-minded crowd in St. Augustine, or to a Muslim-minded crowd in Philadelphia, would prove to be a major public hazard [18].

The examples provided by Edwards serves to remind us that contemporary law enforcement differs significantly from law enforcement in a community not undergoing rapid change. The special conditions of large urban centers tend to interfere with efficient law enforcement and the administration of criminal justice. Members of our society today reside in large metropolitan areas, where the urban dweller is not familiar with his neighbor nor does he especially desire to "become involved." Therefore, there is a rapid trend towards relinquishing to the police officer numerous functions which were once carried out by an individual and his family.

Today the policeman's tour of duty is full of radio-gut-runs which require him to correct the conduct of children, mediate family quarrels, determine the right-of-way between over-eager drivers, care for the injured on the streets, protect our homes at night and our persons in the day-time—all, hopefully, with the concern of a social worker, the wisdom of a Solomon, and the prompt courage of a combat soldier [19].

Along with the rapid societal transition, we have the problem of each state, each county, each municipality, each court, each prosecutor, each police organization, each correctional agency, going its independent course, with little or no regard for what the other is doing. It is not unusual, as a matter of fact, for state and federal prosecuting agencies or judicial officers to cross each other's paths and to interfere with each other's operations. The frequency of clashes between state and federal enforcement agencies is not unusual and when municipal, state, and federal agencies have concurrent powers, they seldom concur in any effective cooperation. Where there is but one jurisdiction involved, police, public prosecutor, and coroner may proceed with parallel investigations, or with investigations that cross each other or may even hamper each other, as the exigencies of politics, quest for publicity, or zeal for the public service may dictate [20].

ADMINISTRATION OF CRIMINAL JUSTICE: A COMPLICATED PROCESS

As previously stated, modern administration of criminal justice utilizes three social processes: *(a) Law enforcement,* which is concerned with the collection of evidence about reported offenses and with the detection and arrest of suspected offenders; *(b) the courts,* including prosecution and defense or the preparation and presentation of criminal cases before the court; the court, or better yet, the judicial process is concerned with the legal determination of guilt and assignment of penalties; and *(c) corrections,* which is responsible for administering the assigned penalties. Although each of these processes has distinct tasks, they are by no means independent. The courts must deal, and can only deal, with those whom the police arrest. The business of corrections is with those delivered to it by the courts. How successful corrections rehabilitates the offender determines whether they will once again become police business and influences the sentences the judges pass; police activities are subject to court scrutiny and are often determined by court decision—decisions such as Mapp, Mallory, Gideon, Gault, and Miranda—the more recent and significant decisions are discussed throughout this volume. As Chief Justice Warren E. Burger of the United States Supreme Court stated in a Commencement Address delivered at Ripon College on May 21, 1967:

Our system of criminal justice, like our entire political structure was based on the idea of striking a fair balance between the needs of society and the rights of the individual. In short, we tried to establish order while protecting liberty. It is from this we derive the description of the American system as one of ordered liberty. To maintain this ordered liberty we must maintain a reasonable balance between the collective need and the individual right, and this requires periodic examination of the balancing process as an engineer checks pressure gauges on his boilers.

Furthermore, as pointed out by the President's Commission on Law Enforcement and Administration of Justice, the criminal process, the method by which the system deals with individual cases, is not a hodge-podge of random action. It is rather, a continuum—and an orderly progression of events—some of which, like arrest and trial, are highly visible, and some of which, though of no great importance, occur out of public view. *A study of the system must begin by viewing it as a whole.*

Due Process of Law

The *administration of criminal justice* is a term which seeks to describe a *complicated process* designed by our society to engage and deal with the problem of crime and delinquency and its threat to the larger community. Some of the implications of this term become apparent when one considers the large number of formal agencies which exist to deal with different aspects of the problem of crime and delinquency. The police, the courts (prosecutor and defense), and corrections are formally organized to operate within the process of justice. In addition, large numbers of unofficial agencies or community organizations are also organized to give assistance to the process.

Justice, therefore, is not easily achieved. Each of the agencies—official or unofficial—which takes part in the process of administering criminal justice may have either a functional or *dysfunctional* effect upon the entire system. The task of one agency may be assisted or hampered by the politics and procedures of another agency. The actions of any one of the agencies may have unintended consequences for the planned programs and goals of another agency, or of the process as a whole. In the United States, it is assumed that the courts will occupy the dominant position in the administration of justice. It is the courts, in particular the appellate courts, which interpret the meaning and scope of such principles as due process of law, the presumption of innocence, the reasonableness of such a procedure, etc. Few of our citizens, however, come into any direct contact at *any* time during their lives with our appellate courts. If citizens are to have dealings with any of the agencies of justice, then this contact for most of them will come about as a result of their dealings directly with lower, magistrate courts, or with the police.

Justice, for the most part, can be measured by the actual contact which the average citizen may have with the police or lower courts. Pronouncements of the higher courts notwithstanding, the content of justice, the real meaning of justice, is determined by the types of relationships the individual can consistently expect to receive when he deals with these two lower-level agencies. If the average citizen—one without personal power or influence—can reasonably expect to receive fair and sympathetic treatment from the police and from the lower courts, then justice to him is both smooth and sympathetic. If he cannot expect this treatment, then to him justice is neither fair nor sympathetic. It is for these reasons, therefore, that the operating policies and procedures of the police are of crucial importance. Contacts with the police, more than any other matter, determines citizen evaluation of the administration of criminal justice as a whole. Justice, in fact, consists of those rights which the average citizen enjoys "out on the street."

FRAGMENTATION OF THE CRIMINAL JUSTICE SYSTEM

Improving police efficiency in the administration of due process, is, of course, just one aspect of the task ahead. After the arrest, the next step is the judicial process—including prosecution and defense—and deficiencies in that process as well as deficiencies in the correctional process can also contribute to increased disenchantment with the entire criminal justice system as well as increasing criminal activities.

The fragmentation of the criminal justice system is a direct result of the amount and type of crime, as well as the ability of law enforcement agencies to control lawlessness in our free society. The administration of criminal justice in America is extremely overburdened and can hardly deliver more than a similarity of expected justice. It has been pointed out by practitioners in the field that the system (criminal justice) is really a nonsystem in which the police are unable to apprehend criminals; the courts, because of their propensity to delay prosecution (thus criminal court dockets continue to lengthen), are unable to afford immediate trial; and the "rehabilitation facilities" are unable to do their jobs.

Each town, county, city, and state has its own criminal justice system, and there is a Federal system as well. All of them operate somewhat alike—no two of them operate precisely alike.

A perceptive observer and practitioner in the field of corrections offers as an example the juvenile and criminal justice system of the State of California as a *model* of fragmentation [21]:

Juvenile and criminal justice system of California offers perhaps the ultimate model of disjointed, multi-faceted fragmentation of a governmental process. The process that deals with offender groups is housed at three different levels of government and consists of 450 police agencies, 391 courts, 60 probation departments, and two State correctional agencies. This entire structure is then duplicated in each function by the Federal system. Probably no other function of government is so fragmented, and, hence, so dependent on the intermeshing of so many bureaucratic entities. While created by and operating under a common statutory law, each administrative unit has its own power base, funding source, and developmental tradition.

The system's incohesive fragmentation contributes to dysfunctional quality in several important aspects:

The Police-Court and Police-Corrections interlock in most cases and represent a kind of uneasy alliance with frequently conflicting objectives and missions. Intermittently, the sand in the inter-meshing gears sparks out mutual recriminations. Only occasionally do good, largely personal relations result in a breath of perspective and understanding that creates mutually supportive effort.

Even superficial analysis of court and probation operations reveals wide discrepancies in policies relating to who is detained, who is charged, or who is committed. Commitment rates to State institutions vary widely, even from areas of apparent socioeconomic composition.

The kind of referral systems between public agencies that could tap significant support resources for the offender's rehabilitation is poorly developed. It is safe to say that the $23 million per year that the Federal government is pumping into some 15 different manpower and development programs is available to probationer and parolee only intermittently and haphazardly.

Inexperienced practitioners could attest to many other failures of communication and coordination between corrections and schools, and from different units and levels of the correctional apparatus itself.

Indeed, some students of the governmental process raise serious questions as to the capacity of bureaucratic structures to force meaningful and viable coordinating mechanism. At all levels of government there is evidence of failure to achieve such coordination. Such failure may be more typical of the correctional bureaucracy than others. Perhaps the general sense of isolation with which society cloaks the identified offender gets transmitted to the correctional practitioner as well, leaving him more comfortable in operating exclusively within his immediate bureaucratic domain.

It is not surprising therefore that the President's Commission on Law Enforcement and Administration of Justice reported that there is a drastic need for reorganization and coordination between the three basic arms of criminal justice—police, courts, and corrections. Furthermore, according to the aforementioned report, there is also a need to coordinate the activities between the allied agencies and the three primary agencies of the criminal justice system.

The system, quite obviously, needs organization and manpower.

The process of justice is indeed more time-consuming than it was a decade ago. Rather than one trial, a case now often involves many "trials" in which the issue is not whether the accused is innocent or guilty, but whether he has been treated in accordance with recent Supreme Court rulings. . . . The system plainly needs more of everything—more patrol cars and more policemen might catch more suspects; more courtrooms and more judges would unclog more dockets; more legal-aid lawyers and assistant prosecutors would ensure that more cases would be prepared in time to go to trial. But the more urgent question is quality, not quantity. Many states have no mandatory standards for selecting policemen; some require little or no legal experience for judges; many jurisdictions give little financial support to prosecutors and court-appointed attorneys, many offer no training programs for jail and prison guards. . . . More serious is the shortage of talented defense attorneys—especially those who serve the indigent. Overburdened and underpaid, public defenders and legal-aid attorneys sometimes seem more interested in keeping the courts moving than in representing their clients. . . . Correctional officers are the step-children of the system: the average prison guard earns less than $6,000 a year. And most inmates need psychiatric help; there are only 50 full-time psychiatrists or psychologists working directly with adults in all state and Federal prisons—one for every 4,400 prisoners. That jails and prisons are graduate schools of crime has become a truism. Yet, only 20% of all correctional officers work at rehabilitation [22].

In sum, America's system of criminal justice is overcrowded and overworked, undermanned, underfinanced, fragmented, and very often misunderstood. It needs more information and more knowledge. It needs more technical resources. It needs more coordination among its many parts. It needs more public support. It needs the help of community programs and institutions in dealing with offenders and potential offenders. It needs, above all, the willingness to re-examine old ways of doing things, to reform itself, and to experiment. The criminal justice system, in other words, could use more "system." On the positive side, during the last five years, there has been more progress toward centralization. Eighteen states now have substantially unified court systems; thirty-five have a central court administrator. Because of political resistance, consolidation of local police departments has been more difficult [23].

The Federal government has led the efforts to coordinate all the various parts of the criminal justice system. In order to receive Federal aid from the Law Enforcement Assistance Administration, a criminal-justice planning agency must be created within the applying state. The criminal-justice planning agency has the responsibilities of mediating between various elements of the criminal justice system and of providing assistance in funding and budget problems. Other applications for similar aid are being processed now.

The District of Columbia Crime Commission engaged the International Association of Chiefs of Police to study the organization of the District's Police Department, and received in return a thoughtful and constructive report. Federal assistance has been extended and is now available to enable local criminal justice agencies obtain the kind of evaluation that was so helpful in Washington, D.C.

SUMMARY

Chapter One "sets the pace" for the rest of the book. It describes the method by which the American society deals with criminal behavior. This method as pointed out in Chapter One is commonly referred to as the CRIMINAL JUSTICE PROCESS. The "enforcers" of criminal justice—POLICE, COURTS, and CORRECTIONS—are viewed as an integral part of any civilized society that finds itself confronted with criminal behavior. Furthermore, regardless of differing philosophies, each civilized society finds it necessary to devise a method of *continually* coping with crime.

The criminal justice system in the United States is a composite of many complex factors and involve formal and informal groups which provide additional resources. The system operates by *apprehending, prosecuting,* and *rehabilitating* the law violator. The fragmentation of the aforementioned process is directly attributed to the multifaceted intermeshing of fifty such bureaucratic entities. Also, while created by and operating under a common statutory law, each administrative unit has its own power base, funding source, and developmental tradition. The authors write that the fragmentation of the criminal justice system in the United States impinges upon the ability of law enforcement agencies to control crime in a free society.

This chapter also describes the functional components of the criminal justice system and separates these functions into the following work groups:

Law Enforcement	**Court**
Crime prevention/suppression function	Adjudication of juveniles
Investigation/apprehension function	Adjudication of adults

Corrections

Adult corrections	Unsentenced custody (juveniles and adults)
Juvenile corrections	Correctional processes

ANNOTATED REFERENCES

Barnes, H. E., and N. K. Teeters, *New Horizons in Criminology,* 3rd ed., Prentice–Hall, Englewood Cliffs, N.J., 1959. Chapter 18 gives a generally good background for discussing law enforcement.

Block, H. A., and G. Geis, *Man, Crime and Society,* Random House, New York, 1962. Covers overall relationships of criminal justice as presented in Chapter 1 to society.

Burger, W. E., "Paradoxes in the Administration of Criminal Justice," *Jour. Crim. Law, Crim., Pol. Sci.,* Vol. 58, No. 4, Dec. 1967. Chief Justice Burger describes the complexities of a criminal trial and the impact of sentencing on the offender and society.

Challenge of Crime in a Free Society, A Report by the President's Commission on Law Enforcement and Administration of Justice, U.S. Government Printing Office, Washington, D.C., 1967. An excellent overview of the dimensions of human dynamics in police problems.

Edwards, G., "Due Process of Law in Criminal Cases," *Jour. Crim. Law, Crim., Pol. Sci.,* Vol. 57, No. 2, June 1966, p. 131. The author discusses the problems confronting law enforcement in contemporary society and as compared to a community *not* undergoing rapid change.

Eldefonso, E., A. Coffey, and J. Sullivan, *Police and the Criminal Law,* Goodyear, Pacific Palisades, Ca., 1972. Chapters 4 and 10 discuss the judicial process (i.e., preliminary hearings, arraignments, juvenile proceedings, etc.) as outlined in this chapter.

Kerper, H. B., *Introduction to the Criminal Justice System,* West, St. Paul, Minn., 1972. The author discusses the police mission in judicial and correctional apparatus in a democratic society. Mr. Kerper discusses the criminal justice system in nontechnical language.

Rubin, S., *Crime and Juvenile Delinquency: A Rational Approach to Penal Problems,* Oceanic Press, New York, 1970. Amplifies the institutional problems as discussed in Chapter 1.

Tappan, P. W., *Crime, Justice and Correction,* McGraw–Hill, New York, 1960. Chapters 10–13 orient enforcement of law in the legally defined judicial process.

NOTES

1. California Council on Criminal Justice, *The California Criminal Justice System,* Sacramento, California, 1971, p. 5.

2. *Ibid.*

3. *Ibid.*

4. *Ibid.*

5. H. Ohmart, "The Challenge of Crime in a Free Society," *Youth Authority Quarterly,* Vol. 21, No. 3, Fall, 1968, pp. 2–12.

6. For a complete analysis of the criminal justice process refer to: *California Criminal Justice,* Public Systems Inc., Sunnyvale, Ca., 1971.

7. California Council on Criminal Justice, *op. cit.,* p. 9.

8. Ohmart, *op. cit.,* pp. 1–7.

9. H. B. Kerper, *Introduction to the Criminal Justice System,* p. 418.

10. W. Hartinger, E. Eldefonso, and A. Coffey, *Corrections: A Component of the Criminal Justice System,* Goodyear, Pacific Palisades, Ca., 1973, pp. 23–26.

11. *The Challenge of Crime in a Free Society,* President's Commission on Law Enforcement and Administration of Justice, 1967, pp. 155–156.

12. W. E. Burger, "Paradoxes in the Administration of Criminal Justice," p. 430.

13. *Ibid.*

14. E. Studt, *Education for Social Workers in the Correctional Field,* Council on Social Work Education, N.Y., 1959, p. 7.

15. *Ibid.,* pp. 7–8.

16. Much of this information is handled in greater depth in another publication by the authors: *The Impact and Process of Criminal Justice,* Glencoe, Beverly Hills, Ca., 1974. See also: J. D. Lohman, and G. E. Misner, *The Policeman in the Community: The Dynamics of Their Relationship in a Changing Community,* Vol. 1, Sections I and II. A Report for the President's Commission on Law Enforcement and the Administration of Justice, U.S. Government Printing Office, Washington, D.C., Oct. 1966, pp. 132–33.

17. "The Causes of Popular Dissatisfaction with the Administration of Justice," a paper read by Rosco Pound of Lincoln, Nebraska, at the Twenty-Ninth Annual Meeting of the American Bar Association, held at St. Paul, August 29, 1906. Taken from *Crime and Delinquency,* Vol. 10, No. 4, Oct. 1964, pp. 355–56.

18. G. Edwards, "Due Process of Law in Criminal Cases," p. 131.

19. *Ibid.*

20. Ohmart, *op. cit.,* pp. 325–26.

21. *Ibid.,* pp. 3–4.

22. "Justice on Trial," *Newsweek,* March 18, 1971, pp. 44–45.

23. *Ibid.*

CHAPTER TWO

Policemen and Scope of the Crime Problem

Every society in every age has experienced the perplexing problem of crime. The presence of crime, developing from a combination of personal inadequacies and a cultural environment conducive to criminality, has served to encourage man to develop a society less likely to produce criminals.

Crime cannot exist in an environment occupied by only one person for there would be no victim. Crime can be perpetrated only where men join together to form a society. Therefore it is not contradictory to state that the structure, relationships, and goals of organized society serve both to produce and to control criminal behavior. A blind defense of an economic, legal, or social system can be of no value in the search for a solution to enigmatic crime. What is needed now is a realistic evaluation of the assets and liabilities of these systems to determine our current ability to combat crime within their framework. Action follows appraisal [1].

We have inherited our present legal, economic, and social systems. If this particular way of life generates crime, we agree to pay "the price," for the liability of criminality is far less than our assets of individual liberty. The task that confronts law enforcement is not one of attempting to shape the system according to the mechanical measure of police efficiency, but rather that of developing peak efficiency within the boundaries established by our mores.

26

The broad interpretation of criminal behavior holds that the behavior is not in and of itself the "problem" but that it is a manifestation and result of various social and psychological disturbances. Just as certain maladjusted persons turn to alcohol, narcotics, or suicide, others manifest symptoms of their disorganization through behavior that brings loss or injury to others. Research projects reveal that some individuals in all societies and in all classes of society respond to pressures by committing crimes. Economic necessity, or problems fostered by racial, religious, or national prejudice, may lie at the base of such criminal behavior [2].

Therefore many law enforcement agencies are designed to deal with the crime problem by giving due consideration to the underlying causes. The police cannot ignore the causes of crime, but in performing their appointed task of law enforcement, police officers often must dismiss many causative factors.

For the police, the "problem" of crime is one of minimizing those known crime-breeding conditions and opportunities, or identifying and apprehending those who violate the law.

DEFINITIONS OF POLICEMAN AND POLICE POWER

The basic philosophy relating to law enforcement responsibilities specifies that the police are charged with the protection of lives and property, the safety and well-being of all citizens through the detection and apprehension of criminals, the prevention of crime, and limited control of nonviolent conduct.

The police responsibility to the people of the community involves taking aggressive and technically competent action to solve crimes whether the perpetrators be adults or juveniles. Similarly, in connection with the investigating and solving of crime, police are expected to prevent the people from potentially dangerous situations; *prevention* of crime, regardless of age, is an important police function.

One of the questions that often comes up during a discussion of *police power* concerns the degree of force that the police may use to overcome resistance or to subdue violence. The only acceptable standard for the application of force by an officer in effecting an arrest or protecting himself, others, or even the violator from harm, *is that quantum sufficient to overcome resistance or to subdue violence and no more.*

The policeman's role in an integrated system is, by definition and by law, explicitly concerned with: *control, apprehension,* and *support.* To elaborate:

If you violate the law, you can expect to be arrested but if you go along peacefully, you can, unless a special circumstance dictates otherwise, expect to be treated reasonably.

Furthermore, in the course of controlling one member of society, the policeman often provides indirect support to the other. For example, when the arresting officer apprehends, and thus controls a wife-beating husband, he supports the wife, just as, in a reverse situation, the physician controls the behavior of those attending a patient when he prescribes rest and sympathy. Finally, besides latent support, the policeman often accords direct assistance to people in various types of difficulties. In so doing, the balance between support and control has shifted, and he is acting overtly as a supportive agent and only covertly in his controlling role. He has at the same time changed from a *professional* to an *amateur* [3].

The responsibility of protecting society is an obligation that varies in difficulty and method with the political and cultural intensity and stability of the area. Dedicated to the preservation of the status quo, law enforcement interprets its duty to protect society as that of maintaining order and safe-guarding life and property. When a society is in a stage of rapid transition, persons and groups encroach on each other in many ways—politically, socially, economically, morally, and physically. The protection of life, property, and social order in a changing culture necessitates accommodation to a multitude of pressures, some conflicting, emerging from political, societal, economic, and personal values. The law enforcement officer, because of his personality structure and emotional needs, sometimes is deprived of his flexibility—flexibility necessary to make the aforementioned accommodations. It is this interaction (often conflicting) of historical, social, psychological, and cultural pressures and forces, which the law cannot exactly define, that creates the dilemmas in law enforcement [4].

There is a wide discrepancy between what the people expect the police to do and what the police are permitted to do under the law. And there is confusion as to why this is so. It appears, however, that such confusion can be attributed to two sources of antagonism toward the police. The first concerns the responsibility of the police for enforcing traffic laws and regulations. The police often are used as scapegoats by "law-abiding" citizens who are stopped by the police for traffic violation, that is, such violators often blame the police rather than themselves. No one likes to admit he is wrong. The second source of antagonism toward the police is the tendency to blame the police for a high incidence of crime instead of recognizing that there are many crime causes, such as slum conditions, narcotic addiction, lack of parental care, unemployment, cultural inequalities, and other social factors over which the police have no influence or control.

Under our democratic system, then, there are certain functions for which the police are responsible and certain limits or boundaries within which the police are expected to discharge these responsibilities. For instance, the police are obliged to arrest law violators, but the unnecessary or excessive use of force by police is not tolerated and officers may be disciplined for utilizing it. Why? For the simple reason that it is wrong under the basic tenets of the philosophy of good law enforcement. Similarly, although it is incumbent upon the police to present to the courts those charged with crimes, to detain them in jail without complying with certain procedural safeguards against abuse would be in violation of their due process. The *primary function* of law enforcement is to enforce the law; to protect the life, limb, and property of citizens; to prevent crime; and to provide certain limited direction and control for behavior that is not criminal. When a crime is committed, the police are expected to investigate, using all the techniques at their disposal. They must locate the perpetrator, charge him with the offense, and along with all the available evidence, submit the case to the court [5].

> The enactment of laws, the judging and the treating of offenders are outside the scope of police agencies. The basic function of the police is to give meaning and force to law—that is, to assume that the extent of violations is held to a minimum. Where compliance is not achieved the police must gather facts and persons for presentation to the proper evaluative body—the Court [6].

There is a separation of powers as applied to law enforcement. Such a division limits the matters that may reasonably be classified as being within the proper sphere of police interest and responsibility.

Although the foregoing may hold true in most law enforcement agencies, the reader should be cognizant of one important factor: The specific assignments that any community demands of its police may pass beyond the strict boundaries of the legalistic setting simply because the community believes the individuals within the force have the capabilities and interest for a specific task [7]. Police administrators, however, believe that the assumption of non-police tasks, particularly those associated with judging and treating juveniles, should be avoided. But the police administrator takes the position that such an opinion must not deter his obligation to the community for assisting in stimulating the creation or expansion of a proper agency or facility essential to proper services for the community [8].

The Public View

Public criticism of law enforcement and its tactics is a favorite American pastime. This criticism, however, lacks validity and is comparable in some respects to reprimanding a doctor for his inability to save the life of a patient whose heart has been punctured by a lethal weapon. In this analogy, there are biological and physiological factors that play an important part in determining the patient's expiration, over which the physician has little control [9]. The police are in a similar position. They are exposed in their ongoing battle against antisocial behavior, to cultural, social, and psychological forces over which they, as law enforcement officers, have little or no control. The social forces usually stem from the political structure of the community which includes: The efficiency and reliability of elected and appointed officials; the patterns of coercion, leadership, and responsibility of and between police officials and the political leaders; the capabilities, training, and experience of policemen; the attitudes and behavior of citizens toward the police; and the particular conditions or set of circumstances under which these forces interact [10].

The *public's view* toward police, in general, is still rated high. According to a 1970 survey by Louis Harris ("The Harris Survey") published by the *Chicago Tribune,* December 29, 1970:

> Despite widespread fear over rising crime and disenchantment about the way the law enforcement system is working, solid majorities of the American people give high marks to law enforcement officials on the local, state and federal levels. . . . Only small minorities of the entire public singled out negative words to describe law enforcement officials: "Not too bright," "cynical," "corrupt," "incompetent," "lazy," "violent," and "sadistic." Thus, by any measure, it is easy to see that a sizable majority of the American people stand rather firmly behind their law enforcement officials at all levels.

As indicated by the Harris Survey, the public in general characterize most law enforcement officers in a highly favorable manner, relating that the job being done by the local officers is good to excellent, 64–33%; by the state police, 63–30%; and 60–30% recorded for the federal law enforcement officials—all positive ratings.

There is, however, one significant drawback—a definite lack of *support* found among black and white youths. According to Harris, the local, state, and federal police officials retain a much more favorable image among white people than the black citizenry. With the exception of federal law enforcement officials, the black community paints an extremely negative image of *all* law enforcement personnel.

Thus law enforcement officers are double cursed. On the one hand they are public servants, and on the other they are forced by occupation to have contacts with the public that cannot be entirely pleasant. Public hostility and abuse has resulted, in turn, in an almost universal phenomenon: Peace officers have banded together in condemnation of everyone who levels criticism at them.

Awareness of the Police Role

A community has so many faces that it is not possible to view them all with any degree of clarity. It follows then that the opinion of the community regarding law enforcement officers will be so varied and diverse as to stagger the imagination.

In a recent survey conducted regarding law enforcement in the metropolitan Los Angeles Area, the general lack of understanding displayed by the public was appalling. The survey points out in one instance that [11]:

Fewer than half of all respondents displayed even a reasonably correct understanding of the structure and function of the Sheriff's Department.

It is small wonder that peace officers feel they must unite against those who have little understanding of their functions. That the police will never find themselves in the position of favor enjoyed by many other occupations must be recognized by potential police officers if law enforcement is ever to overcome those difficulties within its power to correct. A vital requirement for proper community-police relations is that both the normal, law-abiding citizens and the police recognize the modern-day, restrictive boundaries of government, which place the police in the position they occupy.

THE SOCIAL AND PSYCHOLOGICAL CONTROL ROLE OF LAW ENFORCEMENT

There can be no doubt that the last half century has seen a marked change in the character of society in the United States. *Perhaps the greatest change has been the diminution of respect for authority.* But this new factor creates no unusual problems for law-enforcement agencies throughout the United States. It affects all those whose business it is to uphold authority—educational facilities, parents, playgrounds, and "the particular neighborhood," among others. Certainly, lack of respect has had a significant impact on industrial discipline. Greater prosperity and extensive employment have weakened the authority of the employer, who no longer can rely on the threat of "firing." Therefore, managers, foremen, and union arbitrators have had to learn new techniques of industrial leadership to achieve favorable results. To this extent, the remedy is in their own hands.

The police, however, do not have the remedy in their hands. It is not part of their function, as it is that of parents and teachers and religious institutions, to exhort and to persuade. This duty is left for others to discharge. The *enforcement* of discipline differs from the teaching of self-discipline to members of a society.

Another factor affecting the social and psychological role of the police is the increasing complexity of society. Criminal law has changed drastically—gone is the simplicity of criminal law. A half century ago the police were confronted with men who would not or could not accept the restraints that society placed on the individual. Not all criminals, however, were dangerous men who enjoyed committing antisocial acts. These individuals were men who merely were against the law. But now we have a vast number of social regulations that have become "law enforcement problems." According to Devlin [12], those who violate these laws are better referred to as "offenders."

. . . for in the bulk—though one must make exceptions for a few very bad cases—they are not real criminals but generally law-abiding members of society. This change in function of the police has profoundly affected their relations with the public.

Devlin further states:

The shepherd and the sheepdog are no longer employed simply to beat off the wolves. The sheep are no longer allowed to graze freely wherever they will. Their grazing is now strictly controlled and those that stray are harried by the sheepdog. The sheepdog is no longer seen simply as the benevolent protector; and some sheep—no doubt the more troublesome ones—begin to have a sneaking sympathy for the wolf.

What are some of the social and psychological consequences of the police role? The most obvious one, of course, is the impact of *power*. The law enforcement officer embodies the law so visibly and directly that neither the police officer nor the public finds it easy to differentiate between the law and the enforcement of such law [13]. The public is confused and unable to recognize the broad concept of the police officer. As Smith pointed out [14]:

Relatively few citizens recall ever having seen a judge; fewer still, a prosecutor, coroner, sheriff, probation officer or prison warden. The patrolman is thoroughly familiar to all. His uniform picks him out from the crowd so distinctly that he becomes the living symbol of the law—not always of its majesty, but certainly of its power. Whether the police like it or not, they are forever marked men.

Any officer of the law is partly a *symbol,* and law enforcement work consists to some extent in the creation of illusions based on symbolic attributes. Thus an unoccupied police vehicle can slow down turnpike traffic or "motivate" drivers to make complete stops at designated intersections, and the presence of half a dozen officers can control a large crowd [15].

The uniform of a police officer is viewed as a symbolic license to judge and to punish. It does so not only by representing the right to arrest, but also by connoting the role of a disciplinarian. Unfortunately, it is for this reason, for instance, that children may be threatened by means of pointed references to policemen. Needless to say, the "punishing role" does not lend itself to the promotion of any social role other than an "enforcer" [16].

According to a noted author, Toch, in "Psychological Consequences of the Police Role," it is the broader connotations of police actions rather than their direct impact that may promote most of the antagonism on the part of society. Although these connotations probably can be ameliorated (via police courtesy and stronger emphasis on sensitivity, public relations, and so forth), they can hardly be completely eradicated. Ultimately, the social and psychological control role of law enforcement is regulated to one in which there is essentially "one-way" communication against a backdrop of latent power.

If limited to this type of contact, the police role as a controlling agent within the community will be damaged. Furthermore, such a one-way contact ultimately will prove to be psychologically harmful to the police as well as to the public. In this respect, the police officer loses his feeling of communality with the public. He exaggerates the prevalence of apathy and projects hostility even where there is none. He interprets public antagonism as an indication of his inevitable separation from the "mainstream" of the community [17].

Coercive Control: "The Cop" [18]

The police, particularly in the central urban community, is the most significant agency of social control. Law enforcement agencies, historically, have been concerned primarily with coercive control. Such control emanates from agencies concerned with law (including government bureaus) and is accomplished via force or threat of force [19].

The power and authority of the policeman is transferred to symbols: uniform, badge, sidearm, handcuffs, and nightstick. The aforementioned necessities take on functional elements of legal authority [20]:

Pillars of the middle-class community feel safe with the knowledge that this type of control protects their neighborhoods, while the lower-class person more frequently views the coercive powers of the police as a threat.

Contrary to the belief of most people, however, there is evidence to support the view that coercive powers of law enforcement are more effective with those individuals who have internalized controls over their own behavior. Coercive control, then, is most effective with those who are capable of self-discipline and need such control the least [21].

It is unavoidable and out of necessity that all law enforcement agencies utilize coercion as a function of their respective police systems. More important, however, is the need (particularly in urban communities) for *persuasive control* functions of the police. Middle-class citizens are educated in the etiology of "we should obey the laws" and "the policeman is our friend," but direct contact is almost nil. As a consequence, middle-class cultures have little firsthand knowledge of behavioral patterns associated with the police role [22].

On the other hand, in the inner city, many youngsters come into contact with the police more frequently than their own fathers or other important relatives [23].

The same children lack much of the informal social controls taught by and expected of the middle class. Young persons in lower class communities see policemen breaking up family fights, taking drunks and derelicts off the street, raiding a prostitute's flat or a gambling house, picking up some of the local boys for interrogation, knocking on the door because a disturbance had been reported, breaking up a game of pitching coins or shooting dice on the street, checking locked doors of merchant neighbors, evicting slum residents, asking questions pertaining to rat control, transporting patients to mental hospitals, beating others and being beaten, taking bribes and arresting bribers, and numerous other behaviors associated with police systems.

Within this context the maturing youngster from the lower class develops attitudes and forms his impressions toward the police. These attitudes and demeanor are then transferred to the larger adult world and its system of social control. It is within this environment, states Derbyshire, that the youth gains meaningful information relating to law, rights, duties, privileges, loyalties, and many other items necessary for adulthood. Such items, in many cases, are developed from impressions received from the policeman, one of the few representatives of the social control system with whom he has had direct contact [24].

The function of the police, in these communities, is integrated into the child's knowledge even before he is cognizant of the role of teachers. Persuasive control is of great importance in the central urban communities as a "tool" for controlling antisocial behavior. Lower-class youngsters will respond favorably to a stable, steady, and friendly person. If these youngsters can be persuaded to control their own behavior because they want to and not because they are afraid of force, the "battle" is won.

Persuasive Control: The Policeman [25]

To ensure effective persuasive control, a law enforcement officer selected to work with slum families must have the personality, the interest, the time, the fortitude, and, above all, the training. He should be specifically and adequately trained for his role and commensurately rewarded. "An emulative image must be presented consistently so that the children, the adolescents, young and old adults alike, will look to him for guidance in areas other than crime control" [26].

Incidents of complete disrespect for the law have shown a sharp increase over the last ten years. Illustrative are the headlines that appeared in the San Francisco newspapers expounding on incidents such as: "Young Toughs Attack Cops," "Defiant Jeers and Violence Greet the Law Today," and, "Policeman Set Upon by Youths in an Outburst of Violence on Nob Hill." Furthermore, it is not unusual to pick up the newspaper and read "Police officer beaten while citizens watch," "Gun taken from policeman while citizens cheer," "Police officers mobbed while attempting to make an arrest at a football game," and so on. Why is it members of urban communities stand by passively while policemen are physically abused? In most cases such irresponsible behavior can be attributed to a total disinterest in and disrespect for laws that have little meaning to them, and a lack of identification with persons who enforce these laws, persons for whom they have little respect. To state, however, that any apathy or disrespect for law enforcement agencies is due to the law, its enforcing agency, or the slum dweller would not be completely accurate [27]:

Responsibility for this type of behavior can be identified as the result of the interaction of these variables and a social system that permits inequities and irregularities in law, stimulates poverty and inhibits initiative and motivation of the poor, and regulates low social and economic status to the police while concomitantly giving them more extraneous non-police duties than adequately can be performed.

What can be done to ameliorate this problem? What measures must be initiated to ensure a more positive perspective of the control role of law enforcement agencies? Day [28], advocates different measures that could be initiated or expanded on the local level to encourage better law observance which indirectly affects the social and psychological control role of law enforcement.

Community Education

This particular program deserves a great deal of attention. In order to arouse public cognizance of its responsibilities in keeping communities as good places in which to reside, the assistance of organizations whose objectives embrace community education must be solicited. Such organizations should spearhead educational programs on the community level to enlighten people about the laws of arrest and court procedures, and to emphasize the citizen's duty to actively support his local law enforcement agencies.

Public Apathy

This is an enigma that law enforcement finds increasingly prevalent in almost every segment of our society. The term "public apathy" characterizes the attitudes of the public, including officials and educators, toward the selection and training of prospective police officers as well as those officers practicing law enforcement. The public needs to become better informed about the role of law enforcement and to accept the fact that law enforcement, in one form or another, is an essential arm of government and that its personnel must measure up to the tasks assigned.

Arrest Laws

Revision of the antiquated arrest laws of the past century is a must. Such laws are not practical or adequate—in an age of atom, hydrogen, and cobalt bombs, and astronauts or AGENA rockets—for effective dealings with the criminal who utilizes the most recent advances of science for his own nefarious purposes.

SCOPE AND NATURE OF THE CRIME PROBLEM

Although crime and delinquency are major problems in our society, it is impossible to determine just how significant recent increases in the problem may be. In order to evaluate these increases, we are forced to rely on statistics. While statistics show that there are more crimes committed in proportion to the increasing population than heretofore, they are available for only the past 15–20 years. Statistical evaluation of crime and delinquency are thus relatively new, and there is not enough evidence to say with certainty that the overall problem is *actually* increasing.

It is also probable that two other factors have strongly influenced the upward trend of recent years. *The first factor,* which has been mentioned before,

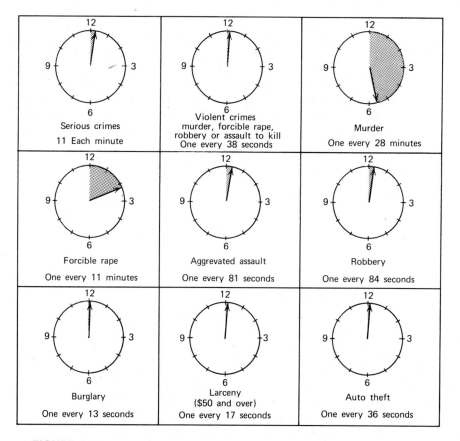

FIGURE 2.1.   *Crime clocks, 1972. Source:* Uniform Crime Reports, *Aug. 1973, p. 30.*

is the fact that the police are apprehending more law violators and as adult crime increases, juvenile crime also tends to rise. The *second factor,* which is most important in interpreting crime statistics, is that the police are arresting people today for behavior that was not even considered criminal in previous years. Law enforcement in a rapidly changing community where maximum freedom of movement and choice is permissible as long as it is consistent with the law and the maintenance of a lawful society. An article by Edwards cites some vivid examples of the differences between law enforcement in a rural society and law enforcement in our modern transitional, urban society [29]:

> . . . Most of America today lives in metropolitan areas, where millions of people who do not know one another nevertheless live and work in close proximity, with greater increased chances of conflict. At least partly out of necessity—and frequently without recognizing what we have done—we have turned over to the police officer of our big cities many functions which used to be among the most important duties of the individual and the family.

According to Beattie, a noted authority on criminal statistics, one of the first realizations necessary in the field of statistical crime reporting is the fact that crime is not just one kind of antisocial behavior, but a complex of many kinds and types of human behavior [30]. Crime, therefore, is not a homogeneous phenomenon and cannot be measured with a single yardstick. The tendency for one type of criminal or delinquent behavior to increase

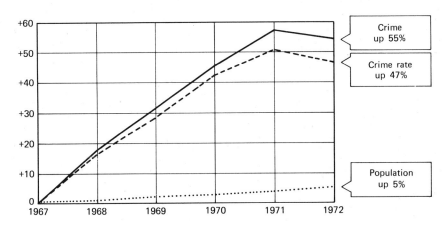

FIGURE 2.2. *Crime and population, 1967–1972. Crime-crime index offenses. Crime rate-number of offenses per 100,000 inhabitants. Source:* Uniform Crime Reports, *Aug. 1973, p. 2.*

or decrease may have no relationship whatever to other types of criminal or delinquent behavior that are also changing in volume.

> The first requirement generally stated for a system of criminal statistics is to know the amount and extent of crime, and the number and kinds of criminals. Crimes can be accounted for only through those special agencies set up to enforce criminal law. Thus has come the general axiom that crimes can be counted best in terms of the known offenses reported to police agencies. Obviously, no one will ever know actually how many criminal offenses are committed. The number and extent of unknown offenses may be a subject of speculation, but not of measurement [31].

In truth, we have no precise measure of crime and delinquency in a nation. Present data on crime and delinquency give *indications, not measurements.*

Limitations on the Measurement of Crime and Delinquency

Most people probably have some general idea of what the term "crime" means, but few realize what a really broad word it is and what it encompasses. Crime, presumably, is to be defined as acts of human behavior, prohibited by law, which carry the possibility of conviction and punishment for persons engaged in such acts. Historically, almost every form of human behavior has been at some time defined as crime. Ordinarily, acts such as homicide, robbery, assault, theft, rape, burglary, arson, and kidnapping are thought of as crimes. Of those just named, most involve overt acts, easily identified, which harm either an individual or his property and are usually reported to local law enforcement authorities.

There are many other types of human behavior also defined as crimes that bear covert criminal characteristics, particularly in the fields of vice, morals, and drug and liquor use. Many such crimes, for example, drug use and sale of drugs, are consensual in nature and not often reported to the police since the victim (the adult and youthful offender included) and offender mutually benefit by concealing the joint act.

Further, within any set of acts defined as criminal, there is a problem of degree of seriousness. Certainly overt acts that are harmful and of a serious degree will be reported with high frequency; but as the degree of seriousness of an act lessens, the probability of reporting that act also lessens. Obviously, the theft of an object having little value or use is *not reported* with the same degree of frequency as the theft of an item with a high value.

Crime is defined by laws of the sovereign state. The legal institutions created to control the defined problem are authorized by the same authority. Basically, law enforcement at its primary level is provided through municipal police departments and county sheriff's offices or, in some states, state police, who perform this service outside incorporated cities. The basic procedures these agencies utilize to enforce their criminal codes are:

1. To learn of crimes either through observation or reports from citizens and to investigate them as to their actuality
2. To seek out and to take into custody alleged offenders
3. To perform general surveillance in the community that restricts, as far as possible, the incidence of criminal acts

FIGURE 2.3.   *Police agencies learn of criminal activities when alert citizens report unusual activities in their neighborhood. Courtesy Police Department, Los Angeles, Ca.*

4. To seek out those law violators that are generally not reported by victims and witnesses through special investigative units which combat consensual illegal activities.

It follows, therefore, that the knowledge available on the amount of crime and the offender involved is basically a matter of what the primary enforcement agencies know and record. Obviously, any measurement of crime is dependent upon the *collection, assemblage, storage, and presentation of data.* Those agencies with limited facilities and personnel for the purpose of classifying, recording, and counting criminal events generally reflect *low crime rates.* The more sophisticated record-keepers trained in crime classifications report more complete and accurate data, and they *suffer from their own exactness by comparison.*

In the United States there are over 8000 primary law enforcement agencies. The fact that so many separate agencies are involved in these reporting procedures, coupled with the fact that crime reporting in its initial stages is never entirely complete, inevitably lead to reporting *inconsistencies.* Whether crime is even to be counted depends on the local agency's interpretation of standard instructions, as well as the particular laws governing this type of crime in the respective state.

FBI Uniform Crime Report and the U.S. Children's Bureau Statistical Series

As previously stated, there are two agencies that compile statistics on crime and delinquency in the United States. These two agencies—the Federal Bureau of Investigation and the U.S. Children's Bureau (a subsidiary of the Department of Health, Education, and Welfare)—report to other agencies and the general public about crime and delinquency in the United States.

During the year 1930, by act of Congress, the Federal Bureau of Investigation was given the responsibility of carrying on the collection of data. This collection has continued without interruption to the present and is published annually in the FBI's widely known "Uniform Crime Reports." While changing little in content during the past 25 years, the Uniform Crime Reports have gradually increased in coverage so that, for the year 1973, approximately 5500 city and county law-enforcement agencies serving 125.5 million persons were submitting data to the FBI. In collecting data for these reports, the crime count is limited to seven categories. The seven major offenses are *willful homicide* (which includes murder and manslaughter, but excludes deaths arising from vehicular type of accidents), *forcible rape, robbery, aggravated assault, burglary, larceny,* and as a special category, *auto theft.* The general larceny category has been limited in the national collection to thefts of over $50, which are counted as major offenses, as opposed to lesser crimes under $50. Although the Uniform Crime Reports are fairly accurate (accurate, that is, for a statistical series), it is known that the statistical reporting in the area of juvenile delinquency is somewhat weak.

There is an agency, however, which collects rather accurate though limited statistics pertaining to juvenile crime. This agency, the U.S. Children's Bureau of Social and Rehabilitation Service, reports annually on delinquent activities in "Juvenile Court Statistics." The purpose of this service is to furnish information which will be of value to professionals in the field of law enforcement. The bureau feels that the collection and publication of such information is essential to law enforcement agencies in evaluating their programs and achieving full understanding of the crime situation and how it is handled in any given area.

Extent of Juvenile Crime

According to the Children's Bureau, the *extent* of the delinquency problem in 1973 is quite significant. Nearly 1 million juvenile delinquency cases (excluding traffic offenses) were handled by juvenile courts in the United States in this year. The estimated number of children involved in the cases was lower, however, since in some instances the same child was referred more than once during the year. These children represent almost 16% of all children aged 10–17 in the country [32].

Nationally, according to the bureau, there was a 10.4% increase in boys' cases and an 11.6% increase in girls' cases. Among the different types of courts, however, there was no consistent pattern; in urban and rural courts girls' cases increased more than boys', but in suburban courts the reverse was true.

The statistics cited here are useful mainly as an indication of how frequently the minor is referred to the juvenile court and how often a petition is filed. Do juvenile court cases adequately reflect *trends* in the extent of juvenile delinquency? Would not police arrests of juveniles be a better indicator than court statistics, since arrest data does not have some of the limitations of juvenile court data? The Children's Bureau has found that both sources of data—police arrests of juveniles reported by the FBI and juvenile court delinquency cases reported here—show a remarkable similarity in their trends

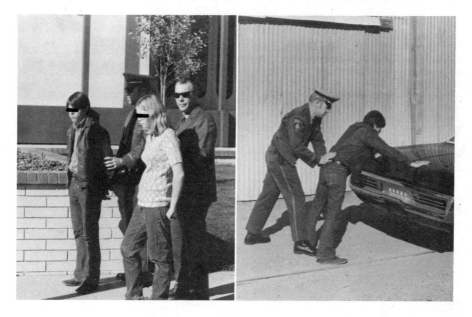

FIGURE 2.4. *Courtesy Michael Johnson, Santa Clara County Juvenile Probation Department and Campbell Police Department, Sgt. Furtaw, Campbell, Ca.*

over a long period of time despite their differences in definitions, units of count, extent of coverage, and so on. Both figures surged upward during World War II, fell off sharply in the immediate postwar years, and then began to climb again. The trend has been steadily upward since 1949, with the exception of the slight decrease in court cases in 1961. In 1973 the increases were similar—10.7% in delinquency court cases, and 9.7% in police arrests of juveniles.

In juvenile court delinquency data, each offense has an equal weight. Since juvenile delinquency cases cover a wide variety of offenses—from the relatively trivial to the very serious—and since the offenses are not weighted, might the upward trend merely reflect an increase in the occurrence of minor offenses? In replying to this question, one needs to rely on the data on police arrests of juveniles reported by the FBI which, unlike the juvenile court data, includes data on the types of arrests and the types of offenses committed. In the 1973 edition of the Uniform Crime Reports, the FBI reported that arrests of juveniles under 18 years of age, for all types of offenses, increased

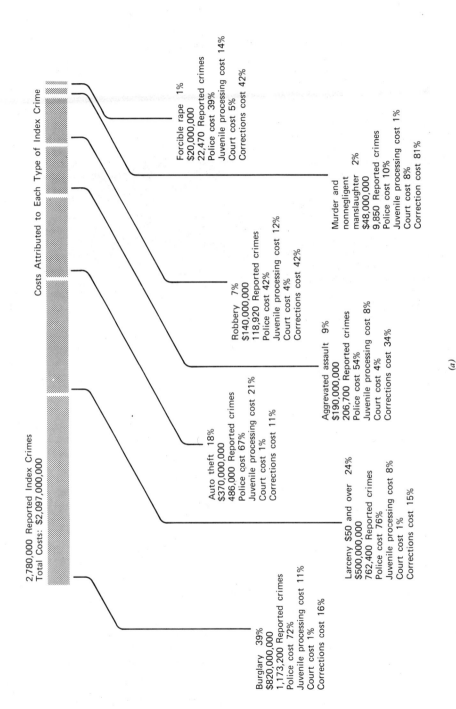

2,780,000 Reported Index Crimes
Total Costs: $2,097,000,000

Costs Attributed to Each Type of Index Crime

Forcible rape   1%
$20,000,000
22,470 Reported crimes
Police cost 39%
Juvenile processing cost 14%
Court cost 5%
Corrections cost 42%

Murder and
nonnegligent
manslaughter   2%
$48,000,000
9,850 Reported crimes
Police cost 10%
Juvenile processing cost 1%
Court cost 8%
Correction cost 81%

Robbery   7%
$140,000,000
118,920 Reported crimes
Police cost 42%
Juvenile processing cost 12%
Court cost 4%
Corrections cost 42%

Auto theft 18%
$370,000,000
486,000 Reported crimes
Police cost 67%
Juvenile processing cost 21%
Court cost 1%
Corrections cost 11%

Aggravated assault   9%
$190,000,000
206,700 Reported crimes
Police cost 54%
Juvenile processing cost 8%
Court cost 4%
Corrections cost 34%

Burglary   39%
$820,000,000
1,173,200 Reported crimes
Police cost 72%
Juvenile processing cost 11%
Court cost 1%
Corrections cost 16%

Larceny $50 and over 24%
$500,000,000
762,400 Reported crimes
Police cost 76%
Juvenile processing cost 8%
Court cost 1%
Corrections cost 15%

FIGURE 2.5. (a) *Estimated criminal justice system direct operating costs for United States index crimes in 1965. Total cost for 2,780,000 reported index crimes was $2,097,000,000.*

(a)

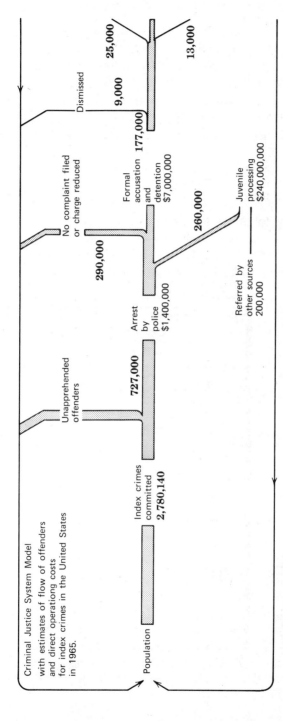

Numbers in boldface indicates estimated flow of persons arrested for index crimes.
Numbers in regular type indicate estimated costs incurred at processing stages.

FIGURE 2.5. (b) *Criminal justice system model with estimates of flow of offenders and direct operating costs for index crimes in the United States for 1965. Source:* The Challenge of Crime in a Free Society, *President's Commission on Administration of the Criminal Justice System, 1967, pp. 264–265.*

39% between 1968 and 1973. For a group of serious offenses selected as being most reliably reported (criminal homicide, forcible rape, burglary, robbery, aggravated assault, larceny, and auto theft), the combined increase between 1968 and 1973 was 31%. It cannot be assumed, therefore, that the upward trend in juvenile delinquency as determined from police arrest data is due primarily to an increase in minor offenses. All groups of offenses seem to be increasing, with the most serious ones showing substantially greater increases.

Extent of Adult Crime

"It's still a 'field day' for the criminal element," the late FBI Director, J. Edgar Hoover, stated in an interview with the noted columnist, Henry J. Taylor in 1972 prior to his death. The late director informed Taylor that at least 1.1 million full-time criminals exist in the United States and the cost to the

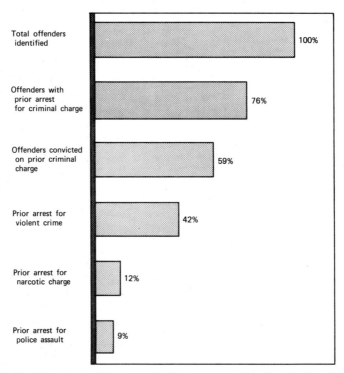

FIGURE 2.6. *Criminal history of 1084 persons identified in the killing of law enforcement officers, 1963–1972. Source:* Uniform Crime Reports, *Aug. 1973, p. 49.*

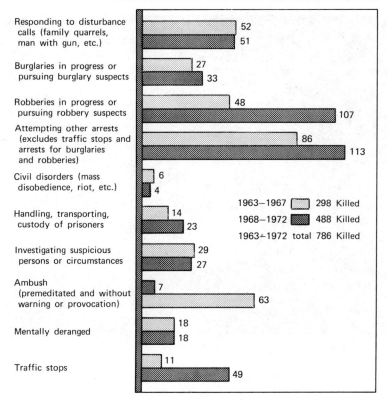

FIGURE 2.7. *Types of activities during which law enforcement officers were killed, 1963–1972. Source:* Uniform Crime Reports, *Aug. 1973, p. 48.*

Administration of Criminal Justice System is vividly pointed out in Figure 2–5. Hoover was also reported to have stated:

. . . "highly specialized" pickpockets are making about $15,000 a year. Burglars steal about $300 million; embezzlers take $300 million; rail and air cargo thieves 1½ billion. Stock fraud promoters around $500 million. Self employed professional men—accountants, physicians, etc.—criminally cheat the tax collector of about $5 billion a year . . . fake arthritis remedies alone were $200 million.

The Uniform Crime Reports (1973) related that in 1972, 66% of homicides committed nationwide involved the use of firearms. More Americans have been killed by guns on our native grounds than in all the wars the United States have been involved in. In 1972 the same report indicated that 18,500 murders were committed in the United States. It is also reported that during the period 1963–1972, 786 officers were slain; 1084 offenders were identified,

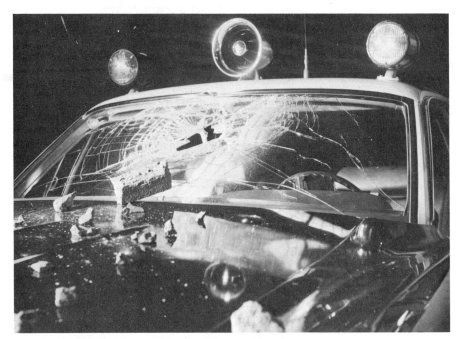

FIGURE 2.8. *Courtesy Police Department, Los Angeles, Ca.*

nearly 80% had been previously arrested. Nearly 60% had been previously convicted. A review of the 1963–1973 figures tells a shocking story (refer to Figures 2.6 and 2.7).

Recently, September 1973, the FBI reported on criminal activities during the first part of 1973. Although the FBI was optimistic about the slight decrease over the same period in 1972 (the first decrease in 11 years), there were other, less comforting, statistics such as the overall increase in violent crimes with the number of murders increasing 5% (numerical increase of 890).

Although crime statistics should be reviewed with caution, a great deal has been done toward their improvement under the auspices of specialists and such able government leaders as J. Edgar Hoover of the FBI and I. R. Pearlman, U.S. Children's Bureau. Potential law enforcement officers—as well as the public—should be cognizant of the fact that if we are to handle our job with more proficiency and confidence, we cannot be misled by the frequently uncritical use of statistical data. In spite of the "pitfalls" in crime statistics, such information still serves a useful purpose. Our most informative statistics, when interpreted by experts, may be of considerable value to the criminologist [33].

Although the FBI publishes data provided by local law enforcement agencies, recognition is accorded to the variability in the completeness and correctness of the statistical data provided them, and although the Bureau has found that the accuracy of such reports continues to improve, they print a notice each year:

In publishing the data sent in by chiefs of police in different cities, the FBI does not vouch for their accuracy. They are given out as current information which may throw some light on problems of crime and criminal law enforcement.

Because of inaccurate reporting on minor crime, the FBI in the past has secured and recorded statistical information from local law enforcement agencies about *crimes known* to the police and listed the classes of major felonies in the accompanying figures. The FBI also publishes data on crimes *cleared by arrest* for all types of offenses except traffic violations. These reports provide limited information on the age, sex, and race of apprehended offenders [34].

It is desirable to point out, once again, that there is no way of determining the total number of crimes committed. Many criminal acts occur which are not reported to official sources. In light of this fact, the best source for obtaining a count of crime is the next logical universe, namely, crimes that come to police attention. *The crimes used in the Crime Index are those considered to be most consistently reported to police and the computations of crime trends and crime rates are prepared using this universe—offenses known to police.*

SUMMARY

Chapter Two discusses the limitations relating to the measurement of delinquent activity in the United States. One major limitation in regard to the increase in juvenile crime is imposed by the fact that statistical evaluation of crime and delinquency is relatively new—approximately 15–20 years old. Therefore, since earlier statistics are not available, it is impossible to make a definitive statement regarding the significance of the increase in this problem. Another factor relating to the increase in delinquent activity—and all statistical information points to a definite increase when compared to the growth of the youth population—is the fact that police are apprehending and taking into custody more law violators. The third factor is that police are arresting adults and juveniles today for activities that were not considered serious in previous years.

The policeman's role in an integrated system is, by definition and by law, explicitly concerned with: *Control, apprehension,* and *support.*

There is a wide discrepancy between what the people expect the police to do and what the police are permitted to do under law. Such confusion can be attributed to two sources of antagonism against the police: (*a*) Responsibility of the police for enforcing traffic laws and regulations, and (*b*) the tendency to blame the police for the high incidence of crime instead of recognizing that there are many factors that cause crime over which the police have no influence or control.

Measures such as community education, discouraging public apathy, and revision of antiquated arrest laws should be initiated to encourage better

FIGURE 2.9. *Property crimes run into millions of dollars in the U.S.—particularly during riots. Courtesy Police Department, Berkeley, Ca.*

law observance which indirectly affects the social and psychological control role of law enforcement.

Most of the criminal statistics in the United States are compiled by the FBI. This data is published periodically in the FBI's Uniform Crime Reports. Although the Uniform Crime Reports are fairly accurate in reporting the number of crimes committed and other pertinent data pertaining to juvenile crime, they do not report on court dispositions. Actual court appearances and dispositions are reported by the Department of Health, Education, and Welfare in the form of an annual report submitted by the Children's Bureau of Social and Rehabilitation Service.

The final area covered in this chapter concerns the impact of adult and juvenile crime on law enforcement agencies throughout the United States. It is generally accepted that most law enforcement agencies have found it necessary to increase their staff and provide specialized services to handle the increase.

ANNOTATED REFERENCES

Barnes, H. E., and N. K. Teeters, *New Horizons in Criminology,* 3rd ed., Prentice–Hall, Englewood Cliffs, N.J., 1959. Chapter 15 affords a particularly good commentary on police history and Chapter 18 gives a generally good background for discussing law enforcement.

Cressey, D. R., "The State of Criminal Statistics," *NPPA Jour.,* Vol. 3, No. 3, July 1957. Concerns the positive and negative aspects of statistical information relating to crime.

Cumming, E., I. Cumming, and L. Edell, "Policeman as Philosopher, Guide and Friend," *Social Problems,* Vol. 12, No. 3, Winter 1965. Excellent coverage on responsibilities and role of police.

Day. F. D., "Criminal Law Enforcement and a Free Society," *Jour. Crim. Law, Crim., Pol. Sci.,* Vol. 54, No. 3, Sept. 1963. Scope of problems confronting law enforcement in a democratic society.

Derbyshire, R. L., "The Social Control Role of the Police in Changing Urban Communities," *Excerpta Criminologica,* Vol. 6, No. 3, May–June 1966. Explores police power, and definition of role.

Devlin, P. A., "The Police in a Changing Society," *Jour. of Crim. Law, Crim., Pol. Sci.,* Vol. 57, No. 2, June 1966. An excellent discussion of impact of social change on traditional law-enforcement roles.

Griffin, J. I., *Statistics Essential for Police Efficiency,* Thomas, Springfield, Ill., 1958. An excellent presentation of departmental essentials in police statistical data.

NOTES

1. G. W. O'Connor, and N. A. Watson, *Juvenile Delinquency and Youth Crime: The Police Role,* International Association of Chiefs of Police, Washington, D.C., 1964, p. 1.

2. *Ibid.,* p. 14.

3. E. Cumming, I. Cumming, and L. Edell, "Policeman as Philosopher, Guide and Friend," p. 277.

4. V. Fox, "Dilemmas in Law Enforcement," *Police,* Sept.–Oct. 1964, p. 2.

5. O'Connor and Watson, *op. cit.,* p. 33.

6. *Ibid.,* p. 32.

7. *Ibid.*

8. *Ibid.*

9. R. L. Derbyshire, "The Social Control Role of the Police in Changing Urban Communities," p. 315.

10. *Ibid.*

11. W. W. Jenssen, "Preliminary Image Assessment, Los Angeles County Sheriff's Department," Los Angeles, April 24, 1961 (unpublished report).

12. P. A. Devlin, "The Police in a Changing Society," p. 124.

13. H. H. Toch, "Psychological Consequences of the Police Role," *Police,* Vol. 10, No. 1, Sept.–Oct. 1965, p. 22.

14. B. Smith, "Municipal Police Administration," *Annals of the American Academy of Police and Social Sciences,* Vol. 40, No. 5, p. 22.

15. Toch, *loc. cit.*

16. *Ibid.*

17. *Ibid.,* p. 23.

18. For a clear, provocative analysis of "Coercive Control: 'The Cop' " and "Persuasive Control: The Policeman," see Derbyshire, *op. cit.*

19. *Ibid.,* p. 318.

20. *Ibid.*

21. *Ibid.*

22. *Ibid.*

23. *Ibid.,* p. 319.

24. *Ibid.*

25. *Ibid.*

26. *Ibid.*

27. *Ibid.*

28. F. D. Day, "Criminal Law Enforcement and a Free Society," pp. 364–65.

29. G. Edwards, "Due Process of Law in Criminal Cases," *Jour. Crim. Law, Crim., Pol. Sci.,* Vol. 57, No. 2, June 1966, p. 131.

30. H. Beattie, "Problems of Criminal Statistics in the United States," *Jour. Crim. Law, Crim., Pol. Sci.,* 46, No. 2, July 1955, p. 178.

31. *Ibid.*

32. *Juvenile Court Statistical Series,* Department of Health, Education and Welfare, U.S. Government Printing Office, Washington, D.C., 1972, pp. 1–11.

33. D. R. Taft, *Criminology,* 3rd ed. MacMillan, New York, 1956, p. 63.

34. *Ibid.,* pp. 36–37.

CHAPTER THREE

Philosophy and History of Enforcing Laws

Against the background of criminal justice fragmentation that was presented in Chapter One, concern is now directed toward the philosophy of enforcing law, and the historical evolution of this philosophy. This concern will be discussed within the following context:

> Whatever else future historians may say of the mid 1960's, it is likely that they will recognize these years as the period when the problems of police operations in a modern society finally became matters of direct interest to practically all segments of that society [1].

The total society, then, is the context within which enforcement of law, and the philosophy of enforcing law is considered.

Many years ago a student of nature stated that to isolate a small child from human society would likely produce a hairy man that walked on all fours and had no intelligible language. This statement was made by the Swedish naturalist Linnaeus, who used the term *Homo ferus* for a human so independent of society. Cases recorded from time to time seem to prove Linnaeus correct. But in terms of the philosophy of enforcing laws, the individual human should be thought of as a talking member of society who walks upright like his brother men and who depends on his society for survival and for law and order (i.e., a reduction of the crime discussed in the preceding chapter).

Entire volumes have been devoted to elaborating the variety of ways in which the individual depends on society for survival. One of the more obvious ways concerns society's regulation of human behavior. The relationship between such regulation and the philosophy of enforcing laws might be illustrated by an example. The biblical Cain's assault on his brother Abel posed (at least from Abel's point of view) an urgent need for society to regulate behavior in order for Abel to survive. To say the least, the absence of such regulation proved grossly unfortunate for Abel. The modern criminal's willingness to use violence or deceit to achieve goals of course continues to necessitate regulation of behavior.

An individual's relationship to his society then is one of dependence. Although crime as reviewed in Chapter Two seems to argue the contrary, the individual is, or should be, motivated to accept his dependence on regulation of behavior in exchange for society providing *personal safety*. Rarely in history has personal safety not depended at least in part on regulations set up by the society. In this sense, society is an enforcer, although in a slightly broader perspective than the *enforcement* concepts that were used in Chapter One. And because humans present such great variations in their willingness to accept regulation of behavior (in spite of the motivation to gain personal safety), the enforcement function of society becomes necessary for society to exist.

PHILOSOPHY OF ENFORCING LAWS

Personal Safety

Regulating behavior is necessary because individuals striving for survival and other needs tend to jeopardize each other's personal safety. How striving for survival might jeopardize personal safety might be illustrated by the activities of an imaginary tribe of mythical "cavemen." Younger cavemen striving to survive and meet other needs by slaying saber-toothed tigers might have little patience and perhaps open hostility toward older, less agile cavemen—particularly when the older hunters sought division of hunting rewards without corresponding hunting effort. But society "recognizing" the combat wisdom of these older survivors of earlier tiger fights would likely protect the personal safety of the tribe's elders by "regulating" the behavior of the younger cavemen. In short, this prehistoric society's very existence probably depends on enforcing a rule that older men offer leadership and share fighting secrets with younger men in exchange for protection, skins, or meat, and, of course, women. In return for observing these rules, society offers personal safety.

Likely as not, enforcement of these rules would fall to the most respected young club wielders that the older tribe members could recruit. The cavemen enforcing the rules would have to be *respected* for two reasons. First, their ability to enforce rules would have to be respected in order for them to be *effective*. Second, they would have to be respected as impartial lest the other cavemen come to feel that the enforcers and not the rules were important.

As discussed in the preceding chapter, society's enforcement problems in the atomic age are considerably more complicated than enforcement problems of this mythical, prehistoric tribe. But society nevertheless continues to require the most respected young men to enforce its rules and for precisely the same reasons.

Property, Security, and Freedom

Another consideration in the philosophy of enforcing laws concerns the freedom permitted the individual by society. Personal safety is provided by all societies to individuals who observe the rules (although some rules in certain societies appear virtually impossible to observe). But in those societies permitting great freedom, individuals usually are permitted to the right of property. This differs from a society in which the state retains all property rights. Control of property rights is a matter of degree rather than kind, inasmuch as no society actually retains *all* property rights but many societies attempt to control all *significant* properties.

From a law enforcement consideration, the rules governing the relatively "free" society's property become far more complicated. For, unlike the society having the state as the single source of property rights, the free society has as many potential property violations as there are property owners (not to mention as many types of violations as there are types of property in the particular society).

Of course, no society permits the individual *complete* freedom, nor is any state completely *without* freedom. Consideration of property rights, however, is one way to distinguish between a *relatively* free society and other societies. *Personal safety* is offered to "conformers" in either society. But *property security* is available only in the society offering freedom to acquire property rights and then only to the degree that the society permits. Put another way, the individual's conformity to the rules "obligates" any society to provide him with personal safety, but further obligates a free society to provide property security as well. As was noted earlier, enforcement of the free society's rules is necessarily more complicated. Chapter Eighteen will discuss how enforcing these more complicated rules is made still more difficult by various considerations dealing with individual freedom.

Laws to Control Behavior

Still another aspect of the philosophy of enforcing law deals with what laws are and what laws do. Chapter Six deals with specific categories of law and provides definitive legal information. From a philosophical point of view, however, the law might be thought of as being society's formal regulation of behavior. To be most effective, it must be enforced impartially. In terms of individual freedom, law restricts behavior either in an effort to protect the freedom of others or for the sake of retaining control over the individual. In both cases, impartiality is necessary to convince the individual that a relationship exists between conformity and personal safety. Regardless of individual freedom, however, the main function of law is to maintain the state as an ongoing operation. This brings into consideration all the philosophies of man's will and the power needed by the state [2]. Most of what is called the "Wisdom of the Ages" deals with various aspects of these two considerations.

Punishment

Law enforcement philosophy, at least the philosophy of maintaining *law and order,* must incorporate of course the concept of *punishment.* The very term *enforcement* implies the possibility of *punishment.* Laws regulating behavior customarily specify sanctions that are intended to be punishing. Of course, the punishing aspects of legally specified sanctions differ from the punishment involved in arrest in that a sanction is designed to be punishing. It nevertheless is worth noting that arrest can be at least as punishing as the specified sanction. But since the society must be stable to function properly, it might be said that punishing the failure to conform is necessary to maintain the society—regardless of whether or not the punishment has been "specified." Even very "free" societies then must punish behavior that threatens the personal safety and property security of conforming individuals. Were this not so, the society could provide individuals little motivation to conform.

Although law and order remain the philosophical basis of society's sanctions, the particular goals of punishment vary. Society can seek through punishment any or all of the following: *Retaliation* (retribution); *justice; deterrence* (example); or *rehabilitation* (treatment). These goals, however, are *theoretically* unrelated to police practices in a society that distinguishes between laws enforced through apprehending violators (a presumed police function) and laws enforced through imposing punishment on those apprehended (a court function). Some believe that American society makes this very distinction almost to the point of minimizing the mutual responsibility of both police and court to *prevent* law violations. Be this as it may, law enforcement customarily is identified with the police function or "apprehending half" of the overall law-enforcing "system."

American Philosophy

American society, of course, demands this distinction between police and court. Nevertheless, various problems related to this distinction, along with other special problems, are discussed elsewhere in this book. Insofar as the philosophy of law enforcement is concerned, it appears noteworthy that this distinction has not been made consistently throughout the world's history of regulating human behavior. Yet in America, except for limited situations involving justices of the peace, the distinction between police and court has prevailed historically throughout a complete change from agricultural to industrial society. And it has prevailed with all of the accompanying variations in distributing the influence, prestige, and wealth of a growing nation.

The philosophy of enforcing American law as discussed in this chapter then includes the obligations imposed on any free society by those who conform to the rules: To provide in an impartial manner personal safety and property security. The term *law enforcement* in this connection takes into account the "law-enforcing" aspects of the court, but remains associated with "policing" personal safety and property security. In this fundamental sense, all regulated behavior from family activities to vehicle speed are functions of American law enforcement. Indeed, modern American police activities, in providing personal safety and property security, complex though they are, are simply discharging this fundamental responsibility.

HISTORY OF ENFORCING LAWS

Ancient History

Various college subjects such as psychology and sociology sometimes are said to have "long pasts, but short histories." By this is meant there seems to be evidence that these subjects were studied through many phases of history even though the actual collection of related information is comparatively new. Law enforcement to some degree is in a similar situation. But unlike other college subjects, law enforcement can draw on history to show not only considerable study through the ages, but evidence of considerable law enforcement activities as well.

Archeologists and anthropologists bring little information to bear on the ancient and prehistoric past of enforcing laws. In spite of this lack of corroborative data, a body of "speculative interpretation" seems to have considerable validity.

As an example, earliest prehistoric man has been pictured as a member of small family groups remaining together for mutual protection from the environment [3]. These family groups merged into tribes that appointed the most reliable men available to protect the interests of the clan. These tribal interests included waging war on hostile clans, but they also included the duty of enforcing various regulations developed by the tribe. Combining the military and police functions tended to regulate violators of tribal law to the unfortunate position of "enemy" and perhaps accounts in part for the brutal sanctions devised by early man.

Another view of equal validity pictures the head of the clan delegating police function to clansmen in general rather than to a particular group. Without a specific police force, the clan functioned as a group to administer justice in the case of rule violation. The military function of dealing with hostile tribes or clans also remained a group responsibility [4].

Still another view conceives of primitive man as attributing violations of tribal rules to the influence of evil spirits which in turn were placated by tribal punishment of the offender. Social revenge evolved from this practice and many feel lent itself to the later contradictory view of crime as voluntary willful acts against the tribe if called *crime* and against God if called *sin.* Blood feuds between tribes removed rule violations still further from evil spirit responsibility with the development of the *lex talionis:* The principle of "an eye for an eye and a tooth for a tooth"—enforcible by the entire tribe. Perhaps all three of these notions regarding prehistoric law enforcement are valid "roots" of modern police work. The earliest recorded indication, however, that ancient man felt the need to organize and standardize control of human behavior dates back to about 2000 years before Christ.

With the rise of kings and potentates in the Middle East, the Sumerian rulers Lipitishtar and Eshnunna standardized what would constitute an offense. Some hundred years later, the Babylonian king Hammurabi standardized for his kingdom not only the offenses but also codified the accompanying penalty. Although the penalties remained as brutal as those specified by the unwritten *lex talionis,* the very fact that the relationship between offense and penalty was *standardized* is considered significant by criminologists [5]. The Mosaic Code was still over 1000 years in the future when these laws were written.

Enforcing these and other codes of the time became the function of officials appointed by the particular king that created the code involved. Such enforcement operated within the limitation the king might impose. Several hundred years passed before courts resembling what is known today evolved in Egypt. The laws enforced by appointed officials and early Egyptian courts probably represent the embryo of the complex codes of the twentieth century. The Egyptian codes incorporated statutes and penalties for offenses far more subtle than those implied in the ancient *lex talionis.*

Criminologists credit Cesare Bonesana, Marchese di Beccaria of Italy, and Jeremy Bentham of England with the "classical" school of criminology that emerged in the mid 1700's [6]. "Classical" criminology in essence held that the punishment must "fit" the crime. A more serious offense then would require a more serious penalty which would in turn "deter" crime. Actually, the underlying philosophy of the ancient *lex talionis* created possibly 4000 years earlier appears somewhat similar. Indeed, hundreds of years before the Roman emperors, the Greek philosopher Plato conceived of punitive sanctions as serving more purpose than retaliation.

Significant to the history of enforcing law was the decision by the Roman emperor Augustus to remove military duties from an elite segment of legionnaires and assign them the task of policing Caesar's personal safety and property security [7]. These *praetorian guards* in many respects bear resemblance to contemporary police in Western civilization. Another Roman variation known as the *vigiles* also bears considerable resemblance to contemporary forces.

Following the decline of the Roman Empire (which occurred in the first three centuries A.D.), enforcing law appears to have lost historical pattern until the era associated with the "feudal" system. Developments in France in this period have definite bearing on the history of enforcing law, but it is to feudal England that American police trace their heritage.

Modern History

Historical developments (refer to Appendix B) of English police have been divided into three eras: (*a*) Prior to 1829, (*b*) the 27 years following the *Metropolitan Police Act of 1829,* (*c*) the period following the *Obligatory Act of 1956* [8].

Before 1829

Early Anglo-Saxon England was divided into four counties known as *shires.* A group of ten families was known as a *shire tything* and ten tythings understandably were known as a *hundred.* The present-day English cities in many cases were at one time *tuns* (i.e., towns) or parishes formed by combination of these hundreds [9].

The king appointed to each county or shire a judge responsible for maintaining law and order as well as serving as a judge. This judge of the *shire* was called a *reeve* which became, of course, *"shire-reeve"*—later "sheriff."

Actual enforcement of the king's law was the responsibility of each man and his own tything. This responsibility was explicit to the point of holding a neighbor responsible for any offense not brought to the attention of the shire-reeve. As a remedy to the hardships of this responsibility, the hundreds adopted a system of annually assigning specific tything men with the responsibility of enforcing the king's law. Substitutes could be hired to serve instead of the tything man appointed, and thereby evolved a tradition of paying for police services. King George II levied taxes in 1737 to pay those serving as police rather than requiring householders and merchants to pay police salaries. King George III in 1777 went still further in establishing the tradition of paying for police services by prescribing wages and equipment.

Increasing church influence evolved a somewhat different system of enforcing law in the less populated areas. In these rural districts, one tything man was appointed annually as the *parish constable.*

Various other historical developments had impact on English law enforcement. William the Conqueror's 1066 invasion of England led to a division of the police and judicial aspects of law enforcement—a rather significant consideration in view of the philosophy discussed earlier in this chapter. William relieved the shire-reeves of their judicial responsibilities and assigned judges, known as *vicecombs*. King Henry I in 1116 defined *felony* and *misdemeanor* and divided England into thirty specific districts to deal with these categories of crime. Henry II later developed the jury system and Richard I introduced the appointment of specific knights to enforce law. These knights later became known as *peace wardens*.

Still another pertinent development was the twelfth-century appointment of *rangers* to enforce game laws created to "protect" from poachers, the likes of Robin Hood. Edward I in 1285 brought to London what Henry III had introduced to the tuns (towns) in 1252—a householder appointed as *constable* to ensure law and order. Edward III temporarily returned to the system combining police and judicial functions when in 1361 he issued the Justices of the Peace Act. This temporary return to an earlier tradition has proven of little consequence to contemporary English law enforcement.

The use of military force to put down mob violence prior to 1829 is probably of historical significance to English law enforcement. Following the rural to urban migration that accompanied the English Industrial Revolution of the mid 1700's poverty-precipitated mob violence led to the use of military force, which in turn doubtless influenced the passage of subsequent laws creating civil police.

The Metropolitan Police Act of 1829

Any consideration of law enforcement history must invariably include Sir Robert Peel. Sir Robert, as Home Secretary, was instrumental in persuading Parliament that police functions could best be served by each community forming its own police force. The historic milestone known as *The Metropolitan Police Act of 1829* [10] embraces this concept.

Sir Robert proved influential beyond the legislative machinery needed for developing what later was to become a police system envied by the world. The following recommendations proved to be not only legislative "guidelines," but organizational guidelines as well:

1. Stable, efficient, military type of police organizations.
2. Police under government.
3. Police "measured" by absence of crime.
4. Distribution of crime data.
5. Police deployment by both time and area.
6. Good police "image" for public respect.
7. Professional police demeanor.
8. Recruitment and training of good personnel.
9. Police officers "numbered" in the interest of public security.

10. Accessible police stations.
11. Police hired on a probationary basis.
12. Creation of official police records.

Following these recommendations, Colonel Charles Rowan and Richard Mayne headed a commission that organized the London Metropolitan Police. On September 29, 1829, 1000 policemen in six divisions began operations out of a headquarters at the *rear* of Four Whitehall Place that was entered via a yard once owned by Scot kings—hence, "Scotland Yard."

The Obligatory Act of 1856

Although English law enforcement during the "Peelian Era" involves many significant developments, the most relevant consideration to American law enforcement may be the *1856 Obligatory Act* [11]. This act eliminated the "hit-or-miss" adaptation of the Metropolitan Police Act of 1829, and required every county to create a police force. Although this ensured police protection for every community, it also amplified a police problem felt to far greater degree in America than England: The problem of standardized police practice.

England, in effect, has resolved most major problems relating to variations in police practice. American law enforcement, however, coping with major laws passed in fifty jurisdictions that are geographically dispersed over areas dwarfing England, continues to seek standardized practices wherever possible. But in spite of seeming differences between the two countries, such as British police failing to carry firearms, efforts to standardize the police practices of the two countries appears somewhat comparable (possibly due to such similarities as there appear to exist between the FBI and Scotland Yard).

DEVELOPMENT OF AMERICAN LAW ENFORCEMENT

Less than three years after the pilgrims' 1620 arrival in the Massachusetts area, a relatively large concern known as the Dutch West India Company set up operation in New Amsterdam (the present New York City). By 1629 the need for law enforcement had become sufficiently strong to motivate the Dutch West India Company to appoint a peace officer known as the "schout-fiscal." Two years later the City of Boston followed the example and appointed a peace officer and six assistants to station themselves on a hill overlooking the town each night at sunset [12]. Virtually every settlement in New England soon followed suit and the historical tradition of American police was underway, but under way along "British lines" of course.

Justices of the peace, empowered similarly to their English predecessors, were appointed in Massachusetts in the late 1600's [13]. At the turn of the century, Philadelphia established a system known as the "watch and ward" meaning both night and day law enforcement [14]. The members of the watch and ward were selected more or less the way juries are selected today [15]. At about the same time, New York changed the name of "rattle watch" that evolved out of the schout-fiscal and called this system "constable watch." Other names that were assigned to these functions were: Court guard, night watch, town watch, military watch, watchman, marshals-watch, ward, and town crier.

As noted earlier in the history of English law enforcement, assigning all able-bodied men the periodic responsibility of serving as "watchman" tended to develop the practice of paying a substitute to serve. Thus the "professional watchman" emerged in pre-Revolutionary America.

The growth of American cities was accompanied by considerable law enforcement difficulty. Night watches proved inadequate to cope with day problems and the size of a given ward that a watchman was responsible to protect often proved unrealistic. Low pay and lower prestige plagued the professional watchman.

In response to such problems, Boston divided the city into two police districts in 1807 [16]. Although Boston did not establish a day watch until 1838, the combination of wards into two districts .proved a step toward centralization of police functions. Centralization efforts were made both by New York and Philadelphia in the 1830's, but it was not until the "native-born versus immigrant" riots of 1844 that sufficient public concern was generated.

Actually, a series of riots reflecting economic unrest swept the country several years before the native-born versus immigrant riots. In 1837, Boston experienced a riot involving some 15,000 that started between fire companies and the Irish population. Philadelphia experienced Negro riots a few years later. Philadelphia also became victim of the weavers' riots that developed over pay standards of weavers. Many other American cities in this period also experienced civil disturbance prior to the native-born versus immigrant riots of 1844.

The native-born riots, once started, continued without interruption for some three months. The militia was finally called out and the ensuing public reaction motivated the 1844 law establishing day and night police in New York City. Watchmen were eliminated and 800 policemen were appointed to serve under a single chief. Other American cities were not long in following. It seems noteworthy that this New York law was passed only 15 years after the Metropolitan Police Act of London sponsored by Sir Robert Peel.

The development of law enforcement since 1844 regrettably has been blighted from time to time by corruption, brutality, and ineffectiveness [17]. Although history affords no single explanation of the police problems reflected in various literature, it seems reasonable to assume that the practice of appointing police on the basis of political considerations contributed to the difficulty.

By the 1850's, laws were passed in various parts of the country requiring the *election* of police administrators. Although this weakened the "political spoils" system of appointment, it complicated police efficiency by placing politicians in charge of police affairs. A definitive study of urban versus rural law enforcement might well reflect the presence of this very "problem" in the later twentieth century.

But whether a definitive study would reflect such a problem (or whether such a situation would necessarily be defined as a problem) appears relatively unimportant to the history of American law enforcement. Although Appendix B merely reflects historical "highlights," careful study of the events bears out the decentralized nature of police development. With some 18,000 American townships [18], it is not surprising that political variations would continue to prevail in law enforcement. Such variations would seem all the more likely in view of this country's simultaneous development of "Peelian" metropolitan police, rural constabulary, "frontier lawmen," and federal law enforcement.

A further consideration in the development of American law enforcement relates to the difference in the cultural backgrounds of the immigrants making up the population. What these various people sought in terms of law and order no doubt varied. Consider the now mythical western sheriff attempting to bring his "anti-cow-rustling" skills to bear on the violence of San Francisco's early Chinatown, or New York's 1844 immigration riots, or the federal government's concern with interstate prostitution. Appendix B should be interpreted in terms of such considerations.

SUMMARY

Following the discussion of the role of law enforcement and the scope of the American crime problem, this chapter undertook the presentation of both the philosophy and history of enforcing laws. The law enforcement philosophy expressed here is that individuals conforming to society's regulations are entitled to *personal safety.* This philosophy also entitled the conformer to *property security* but only to the degree that a given society permits the individual to acquire property rights. In this regard, it was noted that the task of enforcing law where the individual is permitted to acquire property rights becomes more complex.

The specific philosophy of American law enforcement includes providing personal safety and property security and yet makes a fundamental distinction between enforcing law by *apprehending* violators (police function), and enforcing laws by *punishing* violators (court function). Law and order philosophically became the product of the combined functions of American police and American courts while the society in general shares the broad and basic responsibility of preventing law violations.

Chapter Three presented the historical development of enforcing law beginning with prehistoric man and continuing to the present. The influences of the ancient Middle East, the Roman Empire, and the feudal era are the background for the impact on American law enforcement of British law in general and of the accomplishments of Sir Robert Peel in particular. Variations in political aspects of the development of American law enforcement are attributed to the simultaneous growth of urban, rural, frontier, and federal police functions, as well as the major background differences in the population of the 18,000 American townships.

ANNOTATED REFERENCES

Adams, T. (ed.), *Criminal Justice Readings,* Goodyear, Pacific Palisades, Ca., 1972. An excellent compilation of virtually all contemporary police problems related to the discussion of philosophy in this chapter.

Barnes, H. E., and N. K. Teeters, *New Horizons in Criminology,* 3rd ed., Prentice–Hall, Englewood Cliffs, N.J., 1959. Chapter 15 affords a particularly good commentary on police history and Chapter 18 gives a generally good background for discussing law enforcement.

Chapman, S. G., and T. E. St. Johnston, *The Police Heritage in England and America,* Mich. State Univ. Press, East Lansing, 1962. This booklet presents a timely collection of factors in British police background.

Germann, A. C., F. D. Day, and R. R. Gallati, *Introduction to Law Enforcement,* Thomas, Springfield, Ill., 1962. Chapter 2 elaborates a relationship between society and the individual.

More, H. (ed.), *Critical Issues in Law Enforcement,* Anderson, Cincinnati, 1972. Chapter 1 in particular affords an excellent context for this discussion of philosophy.

Sullivan, J. S., *Introduction to Police Science,* McGraw–Hill, New York, 1966. Chapters 6 and 7 provide perspective for the Chapman and St. Johnston reference above.

Tappan, P. W., *Crime, Justice and Correction,* McGraw–Hill, New York, 1960. Chapter 11 elaborates the traditional police role in detecting violations of law.

NOTES

1. T. A. Fleek, and T. S. Newman, "The Role of Police in Modern Society," *Police,* March–April 1969, p. 21.

2. A. C. Germann, F. D. Day, and R. R. Gallati, *Introduction to Law Enforcement,* Chapter 2.

3. J. S. Sullivan, *Introduction to Police Science,* p. 123.

4. Germann, Day, and Gallati, *op. cit.,* p. 37.

5. H. E. Barnes, and N. K. Teeters, *New Horizons in Criminology,* 3rd ed., p. 288.

6. P. W. Tappan, *Crime, Justice and Correction,* p. 586.

7. Germann, Day, and Gallati, *op. cit.,* p. 38.

8. S. G. Chapman, and T. E. St. Johnston, *The Police Heritage in England and America,* pp. 11–15.

9. *Ibid.*

10. *Ibid.,* pp. 13–14.

11. *Ibid.,* p. 15.

12. E. H. Savage, *Boston Watch and Police,* 2nd ed., Boston, 1865.

13. R. B. Fosdick, *American Police Systems,* Century, New York, 1920, p. 59.

14. *Ibid.*

15. H. O. Sprogle, *Philadelphia Police Past and Present,* Sprogle, Philadelphia, 1887, pp. 24–27.

16. J. L. Flinn, *History of Chicago Police,* Conkley, Chicago, 1887, p. 52.

17. Barnes and Teeters, *op. cit.,* pp. 211–26.

18. Chapman and St. Johnston, *op. cit.,* p. 32.

CHAPTER FOUR

Leadership in Law Enforcement

The field of law enforcement is very fortunate to have been greatly endowed with so many fine and outstanding men who have provided the vital and necessary leadership required in the administration of justice for the development of this professional field. It is with feelings of respect, admiration, and appreciation that we have chosen eight outstanding leaders in law enforcement and herein present brief biographical sketches on each: Sir Robert Peel, Allan Pinkerton, August Vollmer, Orlando Winfield Wilson, John Edgar Hoover, William H. Parker, Leonarde Keeler and Quinn Tamm.

SIR ROBERT PEEL

(1788–1850)

Sir Robert Peel was a famous British statesman who founded the London police force in 1829. The police have been called "Bobbies" after Peel's nickname ever since. Today, in the office of the Royal Commissioner of Police in Great Britain's New Scotland Yard, there hangs a majestic portrait of Sir Robert Peel.

Peel was born on February 5, 1788, in the town of Bury in Lancashire. He was the son of an ambitious businessman who built a large cotton-textile manufacturing industry, purchased a vast estate at Drayton, entered the House of Commons in 1790, and was made a Baronet in 1800. Robert Peel was the eldest son in the family and was educated at Harrow School and Christ Church, Oxford, where he was the first person to ever achieve a double first in classics and mathematics in the new degree examination.

While a member of the House of Commons, he made his brilliant first speech which led to his appointment as Undersecretary for War and the Colonies. In appearance, Peel was a tall, handsome, well-built man with reddish hair and blue eyes who was considered something of a dandy in his dress. He enjoyed participating in sports and was an excellent marksman. His solid exterior concealed a complex and self-conscious personality. Peel was a very proud and shy person with scrupulous integrity and a prickly sense of honor. These attributes accounted for much of his ambition and idealism in his pursuit of politics. His early training and experience accounted for his habitual caution and reserve. By nature he was very quick-tempered, stubborn, and courageous, and although sometimes obstinate, his mind never lost its flexibility and imagination. During most of his life, Peel was ill at ease with strangers, impatient with fools and bores, and he often gave an impression of aloofness and frigidity. Yet with intimate friends, he was considered lively and affectionate and to those in trouble, unusually generous and warmhearted. Peel was endowed with a first-class intellect, an exacting memory, and an immense

FIGURE 4.1. *Sir Robert Peel. Courtesy C. P. Cushing, New York, N.Y.*

capacity for work. This resulted in his outstanding success as an administrator, and as Prime Minister he supervised every aspect of departmental policy.

In the House of Commons, his practical knowledge, political sagacity, and persuasive debating skill made him the greatest parliamentarian of his time. Yet his stiff public manner and lack of aptitude for the lesser arts of management made it difficult for him to win the real loyalty of his followers. During his political career, Peel suffered the criticism that he lacked foresight and had chosen the affiliation of the wrong party. Many overlooked the fact that his public stand and outlook was formed in an older and more aristocratic period of politics. Though recognizing the need after the Reform Act for government to be based on organized parties, he still held that ministers of the Crown were servants of the state and not the mouthpieces of sectional interests. With those beliefs, he made a more important and permanent contribution to the structure of the Victorian state than any other statesman of the period. At the same time, by insisting on fundamental changes in the national interest, he did much to preserve the continuity of the aristocratic parliamentary rule in an age of social distress and class conflict.

In 1812, Peel accepted the difficult post of Chief Secretary for Ireland and, during his term of office, he made his reputation as an able and incorruptible administrator. In Ireland he was faced with the first serious Catholic agitation since Pitt's Act of Union in 1800. In 1814, he was largely responsible for the suppression of the Catholic Board, the semi-illegal central committee of the movement, and thus effectively checked the course of Irish agitation for another 9 years. Increasingly, however, he was impressed by the endemic anarchy of Irish society and the economic poverty and disorganization from which it derived. To deal with the problem of crime and disorder he carried through the Peace Preservation Act of 1814 which made possible the formation of a body of national police, later to become known as the Royal Irish Constabulary. They were popularly called "The Peelers."

Peel distinguished himself in every role he assumed and, in 1817, was elected to the coveted honor of membership of Parliament for Oxford University. In 1818, Peel left Ireland and although he remained a strong supporter of government he declined any appointments except for that of acting as chairman of an important currency committee in 1819 which brought about the return of the gold standard.

In 1820, Peel married Julia Floyd, the beautiful younger daughter of General Sir John Floyd, a veteran of the wars in India and second in command of the forces in Ireland when Peel first went there. Peel's marriage was highly successful and he enjoyed a serene family life. Following his marriage he built an elegant house in Whitehall Gardens and began the collection of paintings in the Dutch, Flemish, and contemporary English schools for which he became famous among art connoisseurs. In 1822, Peel accepted the post of Secretary of State for the Home Department and a seat in the cabinet of Parliament. His first task was to meet the long-standing demands in Parliament made by the Whig legal reformers calling for a radical change in the criminal law. He immediately set out to reform the laws and the police. Many of the problems of lawlessness and disorder in England stemmed directly from the conditions following the war in France. In addition to these adverse conditions, the Parish Constable System in London began to break down and as it did, it spread to all parts of the country. Thus, there were no real means of securing observance of the laws. In a series of five acts in 1823, Peel carried out most of the reforms that were suggested by the Mackintosh Committee in 1819. In addition, he attempted to establish a police force but was rebuffed by the Police Committee. Between 1825 and 1830, he effected a fundamental work of consolidation and reform covering three-fourths of all criminal offenses. All during this time Peel met with much opposition and he continuously failed to accurately gauge and understand his opposition. Many in Parliament felt that all that was necessary for solving the crime problem were more humane laws. This was, of course, based on the absurd assumption that laws were self-enforcing. Peel made a progressive reduction in the severity of punishment for many of the laws, but the main object of his work was to repeal obsolete legislation, to simplify judicial procedure, and to reduce the mass of old and confused penal laws to a small number of short, intelligible statutes. Since capital punishment was as controversial an issue then as it is now, Peel preferred to move very slowly, retaining a wide degree of administrative discretion while waiting to see the effect of his initial measures.

The rising statistics of crime convinced Peel that legal reform should be accompanied by improved methods of crime prevention and detection which he felt could best be carried out through the development and institution of an effective policing force. In 1829, after garnering support the previous year, Peel introduced into Parliament "An Act for Improving the Police in and Near the Metropolis" which became known as the Metropolitan Police Act of 1829.

Peel established the headquarters for the Metropolitan Police at Scotland Yard, where it exists today in the city of Westminster, a part of the greater London area. The nickname of "Bobby" for its members was a popular tribute to the founder of the force, and London police are frequently referred to as such today. It was Peel's philosophy that in the general administration of the country, the main task of the Home Office was to preserve order in periodic disturbances that arose from unemployment and agitation in the industrial districts. He was increasingly concerned over the activity of the trade unions following the removal of the restrictive Combination Acts in 1824 and 1825, but he observed a policy of nonintervention in industrial disputes and tried to induce both management and labor to conform with the law. He instituted local pressure to see that the cotton mills were properly inspected and called for severe changes in the child labor laws. As a direct result of Peel's creativeness and foresight for law enforcement of the future, there are now 127 separate police forces in England and Wales—52 county forces, 73 city and borough forces, the Metropolitan, and the city of London police. This contrasts greatly with more than 40,000 police jurisdictions in the United States today.

After his success in the formulation of the Metropolitan Police, Peel formed the Conservative Party in the House of Commons. Although the party was conservative in regard to the British Constitution, Peel labored to make the party concerned with the nation's welfare and as leader of the Conservative Party, he became Prime Minister of Great Britain in 1834. He held this office for one term, took a brief sojourn, and was reinstated again in 1841 and held the office an additional 5 years. After a brief illness in 1850, Peel died at the age of 62. His name is known throughout law enforcement, past and present, and he will always stand as an outstanding leader in the forefront of the history of law enforcement.

ALLAN PINKERTON

(1819–1884)

Allan Pinkerton, who came to the United States to avoid arrest in his native Scotland, became internationally famous as a private detective and is known in America today as "America's first private eye." Allan Pinkerton was born in Glasgow, Scotland, on August 25, 1819. The son of William Pinkerton, a Glasgow police sergeant, Allan experienced independence very early in life when his father was killed as a result of injuries received while trying to maintain order during a Chartist riot. Allan was but 10 years of age at the time of his father's death and he and his brother were forced to go to work to help support their mother. Their first jobs were running errands for a pattern maker. Although there was plenty to do in Scotland's largest city, Allan carried parcels to dockyards and factories on both sides of the Clyde river. He insisted that he wanted to learn a trade and in 1831 was indentured as a cooper's apprentice. For 7 years young Allan Pinkerton learned to make barrels and casks and became a master craftsman at his trade. During his early working years he became a member of a Chartist group in spite of what had happened to his father years earlier. He was sincerely convinced that the demands of the "People's Charter" for political reform were just.

Because of his commitment to his job and his deep involvement with the Chartist

FIGURE 4.2. *Allan Pinkerton. Courtesy Pinkerton, Inc., New York, N.Y.*

organization, Pinkerton became so engrossed with his activities that he was too busy to set a wedding date with his fiancée Joan Carfrae. One evening a whispered warning to him by a former associate of his father changed everything in the life of Allan Pinkerton. Within a few hours Allan Pinkerton and Joan Carfrae were husband and wife, and they immediately set sail on a voyage to Canada which was not just a honeymoon pleasure cruise. Pinkerton had been advised that if he remained in Scotland he would be arrested as an enemy of the Crown because he was considered a dangerous agitator as a result of his activities in the Chartist movement. This movement was a revolt of the working men of the British Isles against the political power of the wealthy landlords, and although they were content to petition Parliament and march in demonstrations, young Pinkerton belonged to a group within the organization that believed that they would gain greater recognition sooner by staging disruptive and riot type of activities.

During their voyage to Canada, they went through one of the worst storms of the year of 1842 and regrettably found themselves shipwrecked 200 miles off their course on the sandbar of Sable Island near the coast of Nova Scotia which is known to seamen around the world as the ''graveyard of the Atlantic.'' Pinkerton and his 18-year-old bride both survived the shipwreck and when they reached safety ashore they were met by a band of Indians who came out of the woods and surrounded them, demanding that the women hand over their jewelry. Since most of the immigrants were poor, they had just a very few trinkets that attracted the Indians. When the Indians spied Mrs. Pinkerton's wedding ring, they demanded it and after reluctantly surrendering it, she never again wore a wedding ring. After salvaging some of their personal possessions, the Pinkertons boarded another schooner and proceeded through the Great Lakes to Detroit. Why Pinkerton changed his mind about going to Canada is unknown.

Upon arrival in Detroit Pinkerton purchased a horse, a harness set, and a ramshackle wagon, and after stowing away some simple necessities, he and his wife set out for Chicago, Illinois. After a successful journey, Pinkerton sold the horse, wagon, and harness for food and lodging until he could find a job in the Chicago area. Jobs were scarce. Although 5 years had passed since the panic of 1837, the city still felt the pinch of hard times. He was greatly discouraged by not being able to find a position in the trade he had mastered. After a time he introduced himself to some fellow Scots who were well established in the Chicago area and asked them for help. He was soon hired to make barrels at Lil's Brewery. For working from early morning until 6:00 at night he received 50¢ a day. Pinkerton saved his money and told his wife that one day he would own his own shop. His wife, patient and loving, encouraged this ambition and was pleased at his announcement a short time later that they were moving to Dundee, a small farming town 38 miles northwest of Chicago. In a brief time the Pinkertons were settled in a one-story wooden house surrounded by a small garden on a hill just 300 yards from the Fox river. Pinkerton combined his cooperage shop with his living quarters. He worked long hours in the rear of the residence and proudly advertised himself as the ''only and original cooper of Dundee.''

In 1848, Pinkerton sold his cooperage shop to his foreman and moved with his wife and son William, who had been born in 1846, back to Chicago. This move was the result of much recognition that had been given to Pinkerton for his efforts in solving two counterfeiting cases near Dundee. The sheriff near Dundee had made young Pinkerton a deputy sheriff, enabling him to act officially. His duties were so well performed that the sheriff of Cook County, William Church, asked Allan Pinkerton to become a member of his staff. The time and the place could not have been more propitious for a man with an extravagant taste for self-righteousness and the sort of brawn developed by swinging a ten pound cooper's hammer. Mid-nineteenth century Chicago was beginning America's painful, often bloody, transition from frontier to urban society. Law enforcement was faltering between mere inefficiency and dedicated corruption. Into the power vacuum stepped the indefatigable, incorruptible Pinkerton who had become a self-made gang buster.

Shortly after returning to Chicago, Pinkerton's bravery and recognition of his ability led to his appointment as a special agent for the United States Post Office Department. In this capacity he investigated for the government cases of fraud, extortion, and blackmail involving the use of mail. Later, when the city of Chicago disbanded its inadequate Constable Corps and established a regular police department, Pinkerton was asked to join the Chicago Police Department, and in so doing became the city's first and only detective in 1849. A year later, in 1850, Pinkerton decided to resign from the police department as he was unable to live on the income that he received in this position. He became convinced that the best way for him to support his family was to enter the field of private investigation.

In 1850, Pinkerton and a business partner opened one of the first private detective agencies in the world and the only one in Chicago. A year later his partnership with E. H. Rucker, a Chicago attorney, was dissolved and he assumed full charge of the activities, personally supervising every detail of the operation of the Pinkerton National Detective Agency until the day of his death, July 1, 1884. When Pinkerton opened the agency he initiated a slogan and a trademark, both of which have remained with the company. In addition, he developed a code of ethics. The slogan, "we never sleep," and the trademark, the open eye, which has been nicknamed "the eye" both have remained a part of the company. In addition, the nickname "private eye" was derived from Pinkerton's trademark. His code of ethics reflected the honesty and integrity that he possessed. Among its main points were: A statement that the agency would accept no gifts—not even rewards that had been offered before a case was accepted; the policy of never representing a defendant without the permission of the prosecuting authorities; the notice that the agency would not compromise with those having stolen property or take divorce cases or knowingly work for one client against another; a promise that the number of operatives assigned to a case would not be increased without the client's consent; and an understanding that daily reports would be submitted with all expenses itemized and that charges would be estimated in advance because payment was based on a daily fee.

In the early days it cost $3 a day to hire an ordinary operative, $8 for a supervisor and $12 for Pinkerton. Much of the criminal investigation work that brought the Pinkerton Detective Agency international fame has been taken over by the FBI and other modern police organizations, but the agency still tracks down law-breakers in the colorful tradition of its founder, America's first private detective.

Today the agency is the only American member of the *Lique Internationale des*

Societés de Surveillance, a world-wide federation of security organizations with membership limited to one firm from each nation. The agency enjoys and is proud of its international reputation.

AUGUST VOLLMER

(1876–1955)

August Vollmer has been called "America's greatest cop." Others have called him "the father of the modern cop," but most authorities today throughout the world call him "the father of modern police science." All three of these titles have been well earned by August Vollmer for he was America's foremost pioneer in the use of modern police methods. It is unfortunate today that so few people have any conception of his outstanding contributions to modern law enforcement and his tremendous humanity.

August Vollmer was born March 7, 1876, in New Orleans, Louisiana, and died November 4, 1955, in Berkeley, California. He was the son of John and Phillippine Vollmer who were natives of Germany. Vollmer received his education at the New Orleans Academy, and after the death of his father, a grocer, in 1884, his mother took the family to San Francisco, California, in 1888. Two years later they moved to Berkeley, California, where Vollmer began and had a vital impact upon the field of law enforcement in this University community nestled in the foothills of Berkeley.

From 1889 to 1905, Vollmer assumed a number of positions in the San Francisco

FIGURE 4.3. *August Vollmer. Courtesy Police Department, Berkeley, Ca.*

Bay Area which included 5 years' service as a letter carrier for the United States Postal Service in Berkeley. Additionally, he spent 1 year in the United States Army Field Artillery serving in the Spanish American War. It was during this time that he participated in twenty-five battles and engagements on the gunboat *Laguna de Bay.*

Vollmer's law enforcement career began April 10, 1905, when he was elected to a 4 year term as Town Marshal for the city of Berkeley. Fourteen days later the Board of Town Trustees appointed six police officers at a salary of $70 per month. In 2 short years, Vollmer had increased the size of his force to twenty-six regular officers, one special officer, and had included a provision for the rank of detective. Additionally, he developed a full set of rules for the police department which were approved by the Board of Trustees who governed the city.

In 1909, Vollmer was appointed Chief of Police under a new charter form of city government in the state of California. A short time later he established the first police training school in America, teaching some of the classes himself but also using professors from the University of California School of Law and the Physical and Social Science Departments. In 1916, he initiated the first classes in police science at San Jose State College, now known as California State University at San Jose, California. Courses of various types were offered through the years and, in 1931, San Jose State College awarded its first Bachelor of Science degree in Police Science and Criminology. Also during the same period the University of California was conducting criminology courses under the leadership of Vollmer, but it was not until many years later that this University awarded its first degrees in this subject area. Thus, in California, the concept of the formally educated police officer was born in 1916.

In the fall of 1929, Vollmer was made a full professor of police administration at the University of California. He served in that capacity until 1938 when he resigned to devote more of his time and life to writing and editing a series of police science books written by some of the very men he had trained. Vollmer was a great one to encourage police officers and police students to write about what they had learned so that other law enforcement officers would not have to learn everything about their jobs through the painfully slow process of practical experience.

In addition to the field of training, Vollmer made many pioneering achievements and contributions to the field of law enforcement and police science. In the area of transportation, he had placed all of his police officers on bicycles by 1911. Subsequently, he transferred them to motorcycles, and in 1913 half of the patrol force was on motorcycles and the other half in automobiles which he equipped with radios. The first police radio car was a Model T Ford with a crystal set and headphones, and the first police messages were transmitted to the officers by an amateur radio operator friend. Because of the noise of the motorcycles, of the objections of the citizens, and of the many officers becoming injured from accidents, motorcycles were discontinued and, by 1917, the entire police department was completely motorized with automobiles, each officer furnishing his own vehicle and charging the city a rental fee. This resulted in a large fleet for the size of the force and provided great flexibility in police operations. This practice continued for many years until very recently when the City of Berkeley discontinued this procedure and replaced the vehicles with city-owned distinctively marked vehicles.

In addition to the crystal radio, Vollmer also instituted another communications technique which became known as the Red Light Signal Recall System. This system required that red lights be mounted strategically throughout the city where they could be observed by officers on beats. Each officer was given a signal, and when he observed the light flashing his signal, he would then go to a conveniently placed telephone and call his central control to receive the message. Thus, the first police telephone-call box was born.

Vollmer also established a police records system in 1906 at a time when few departments kept any records. It was not until 1915 that the city council provided for the appointment of a police superintendent of records. This appointment established a central office for the control of reports of all police activity, and many of the techniques developed therein have been instrumental in developing modern-day police record-keeping.

In the area of police identification, Vollmer established one of the first fingerprint bureaus in the United States, and in 1909, the Board of Town Trustees provided him with sufficient funds to purchase the Bertillion fingerprint equipment. Vollmer also adopted the *modus operandi* system after studying the British procedure for establishing the method of operation by which various criminals worked. He was responsible for the first handwriting identification in his area and through the Police Chiefs Association of California he worked for the establishment of a central identification bureau in Sacramento. This bureau later became known as the State Bureau of Criminal Identification and Investigation and is now known as the California State Bureau of Investigation. As early as 1916, Vollmer, realizing the importance of a central fingerprint bureau, urged the Congress of the United States to establish a national bureau of fingerprint records in the Bureau of Investigation of the U.S. Department of Justice. When Attorney General Stone appointed J. Edgar Hoover as the first Director of the FBI upon the recommendation of Vollmer, Hoover established the fingerprint-identification section in the bureau.

During the winter of 1914, Vollmer created the first police juvenile agency. Part of the program of this agency was to assign boys to traffic control duties, thereby releasing uniformed police officers for other more important policing functions. The establishment of this innovative and creative procedure became known as the Schoolboy Traffic Patrol which today is a nationwide institution.

In addition to developing the first American *modus operandi* file, Vollmer also utilized the physical and social sciences in the solving of crimes, and in 1916, he employed a scientist from the University of California School of Medicine as a full-time criminalist to operate the nation's first crime-detection laboratory.

Vollmer was a stern man, a man with much integrity, who would not settle for average performance and insisted on strict adherence to the rules of conduct that he established for his men. He, too, was a sympathetic and humane person who insisted that not all people who come in contact with law enforcement officers should be put in jail, but that his policemen should be arbitrators, neighborhood friends, and that juveniles should never be placed in confinement. Additionally, he would not tolerate any physical or mental abuse of people with whom his officers came in contact. Vollmer's instructions were not always followed because of the quality of some of the personnel coming into the police service. His solution to this problem was to recruit students from the University of California as police officers and he was the first to use psychological tests including the psychiatric interview in selecting potential officers. Thus in 1918, another first was achieved by Vollmer. His "college cops," as they became known, have contributed greatly to the further advancement of modern law enforcement. One of the best known of his college cops was O. W. Wilson, the subject of another biographical sketch elsewhere in this chapter.

Throughout Vollmer's lifetime, many honors and awards were presented to him. In 1921–1922 he served as President of the International Association of Chiefs of Police. In 1929 Vollmer received the Harmon Foundation Gold Medal as the one single individual who gave his community the most valuable service that year. During the same year, he was selected to be the speaker at the inauguration of President Robert Hutchins of the University of Chicago.

In 1923, Vollmer received a leave of absence from the Berkeley Police Department to reorganize the Los Angeles Police Department and served that agency for 1 year as an interim chief. The agency had been suffering severe internal problems and Vollmer's first reorganization move was to establish the nation's first police task force or mobile striking force and to deploy them on a flexible basis to meet the urgent policing needs of the day. In this operation, Vollmer applied many military tactics, including the extensive use of pin maps. While he was Chief of Police, he expanded the scope of the *modus operandi* system through the use of the Hollerith machine, the forerunner of modern computers. He also designed and supervised the construction of the first "prison without bars," the forerunner of prison farms and prison camps of today, and he was first to organize the nation's only juvenile crime prevention division. Also, for the first time anywhere, he used standardized intelligence tests to classify and assign police personnel. Vollmer made many other recommendations that were not put into effect because of political opposition, but when a study was made in 1949 (25 years later), all of Vollmer's recommendations had been adopted, doubtless contributing to that department's reputation as a leader in law enforcement.

Throughout his career Vollmer was called upon to reorganize many police departments in this country and abroad. During his life, he was a constant source of inspiration to other people and continually urged young men and women to go ahead with contributions that would make the police more efficient. At his suggestion, one of his college cops, John Larson, developed the first polygraph or "lie detector." Later as the result of the encouragement by Vollmer, Leonarde Keeler of Northwestern University refined the instrument and became the nation's foremost authority on the polygraph. Clarence Taylor, another of Vollmer's recruits, was inspired by Vollmer to further develop a traffic safety device that he had accidentally discovered. Taylor by accident one day noticed the reflection of a bottle cap that was imbedded into the asphalt pavement. He developed this observation into what is now known as traffic lane buttons, a safety device in use throughout the world.

Vollmer made many contributions in the area of law enforcement literature and was also instrumental in arranging for the publication of many of the early books in the police field. His personal contributions were *Crime and the State Police* in 1935, *Crime, Crooks and Cops* in 1937, *Police and Modern Society* in 1936, and in 1949 his last book was *The Criminal*. Although his philosophy never appeared in print, it nevertheless had a major impact upon the lives of many men in the field of law enforcement and continues today to guide many people. Vollmer's philosophy, taken from his speech on Police Ideals in 1932, is as follows:

The possessor of an ideal can never be content with inaction, but is impelled by an irresistible urge to act in accordance with his ideal.

Attached to the service ideal is the spirit of courage; not physical courage, for never in the history of police departments have policemen been charged with exhibiting physical cowardice. By the spirit of courage is meant the moral courage that makes it possible for policemen to depart from old traditions in the face of ridicule, and experiment with new ideas and new inventions.

An integral part of the ideal of service is the spirit of tolerance. No country, institution, or person has a monopoly on truth, and that knowledge should compel intelligent police officers to respect the other man's point of view. The policeman who in his own opinion is right all of the time is undoubtedly, and usually, the man who is most always wrong, by actual observation.

Inseparable from the ideal of service is the spirit of sacrifice, which in the last analysis must always remain a spiritual offering. Men who enter the police department should be informed in advance that there is no material wealth possible in their chosen profession.

Attached to the ideal of service is the spirit of humility. The right type of policeman is ever mindful of the dignity of the police service, and is fully aware at all times of the responsibility of service and all of its implications.

Of all the contributions that he made to law enforcement, those who knew "Gus" Vollmer will remember him best for his great humanity and his love of mankind. Even those in the criminal society liked and respected this man. It is interesting to note that the prisoners for whom he built the first "prison without bars" gave him a testimonial banquet prior to his death.

After retirement he remained in Berkeley where he was constantly available to boys and girls and visiting policemen, and he carried on a staggering correspondence with police authorities throughout the world and was available to many criminology students as their coach while they were attending the University under the guidance of O. W. Wilson. Even criminals, impressed by Vollmer's honesty, integrity and fairness, occasionally called on him at his residence to pay their respects. The methods, procedures, and philosophies that Vollmer set forth for the law enforcement profession have become widely adopted and today are being carried on by the work of his disciples and those who have been influenced by him. August Vollmer, without any doubt, is "the father of modern police science."

ORLANDO WINFIELD WILSON

(1900–1972)

Orlando Winfield Wilson, internationally known, is widely recognized as one of the greatest authorities in the history of police administration. In the United States only his mentor August Vollmer and J. Edgar Hoover equaled him in stature as an influence for good in American law enforcement. His outstanding and brilliant career achieved the highest success in several related but different fields of criminal justice.

Wilson was born May 15, 1900, in Veblen, South Dakota, and died at his retirement home in Poway, California, October 18, 1972, at the age of 72. He was one of the six children born to Ole Knute and Olava Stoutland Vraalson. His father, an American-born lawyer of Norwegian parentage changed the Norwegian family name Vraalson to Wilson when O. W. was a boy. In his youth he moved with his family to San Diego, California, where he attended local schools. Wilson credited his father with instilling in him respect for excellence in any undertaking and once recalled that his father would not tolerate any member of his family not being at the head of his class. If any of the children fell below that expectation, Ole Wilson personally supervised their homework until they measured up to the desired level.

Upon completion of his high school education, Wilson attended the University of California at Berkeley where he majored in criminology in the Department of Political Science. In 1924 he received his Bachelor of Arts degree. Concurrently with his studies at the University, he had his first experience in practical police work as a patrolman with the Berkeley Police Department from May 1921 to April

FIGURE 4.4. *Orlando Winfield Wilson. Courtesy Police Department, Chicago, Il.*

1925. While an officer with this agency, he became the protégé of the Berkeley chief of police, August Vollmer. Vollmer, also a professor of police science at the University, persuaded Wilson to consider criminology as a career. As a direct result of his academic qualifications and the practical experience he had received while a member of the Berkeley Police Department, Wilson at the age of 25 was appointed police chief of Fullerton, California in April 1925. He served in that capacity only until December 1925, at which time he assumed the position of chief investigator for the Pacific Finance Corporation.

In March 1928, Wilson was appointed, on Vollmer's recommendation, to head the police department of Wichita, Kansas. This agency at that time was suffering from many internal problems. Within 5 years Wilson attracted nationwide attention by his success in reorganizing this agency. He introduced such innovations as easily identified police cars, lie detectors, and mobile crime laboratories, and he hired college students as part-time policemen. In 1936, he took a leave of absence to serve as an instructor in the Bureau for Street Traffic Management at Harvard University. His position as Chief with the city of Wichita ended in May 1939, when a change of city managers took place. The change was politically motivated by persons who opposed Wilson's vigorous enforcement of vice laws.

Wilson returned to Berkeley in July 1939, and was appointed professor of police administration at the University of California at Berkeley, succeeding August Vollmer who had retired. Concurrently, Wilson served as a police consultant to various cities throughout the world. In the course of this work he was able to apply and refine the results of both his practical and academic background.

In January 1943, his academic career was interrupted when he entered the United States Army as a Lieutenant Colonel in the Military Police Corps, serving as the Chief Public Safety Officer in Italy and England. During this time he earned the Bronze Star Medal and the Legion of Merit. After his discharge with the rank of Colonel in November 1946, Wilson remained in Europe as a civilian employee of the United States War Department, serving the United States Group Control Commission and the Office of the Allied Military Government in Germany as Chief Public Safety Officer in charge of denazification activities in the United States zone. He relentlessly enforced regulations and was one of the few officials willing to adhere to an edict restricting former nazi party members to ordinary labor. During his service in Europe Wilson prepared a public safety manual for liberated territories and for Germany. He planned and played a major role in the rapid development of civilian policing in West Germany, a factor which undoubtedly has played a great part in the rebirth of that country. Working with the military suited Wilson's temperament and for a time he considered making the Army his career. His overriding interest, however, remained in civilian police work and his desire to continue contributing to that field prompted him to return to Berkeley in 1947 to resume his post as professor of police administration.

From July 1950 to February 1960, Wilson served as Dean of the School of Criminology at the University of California. More suited for action than for talk, Wilson was not a popular lecturer among the students at the University. His lack of a Ph.D. degree also made him something of an outsider among his fellow professors. For a time, the professional standing of the School of Criminology was threatened by members of the Academic Senate who sought to restrict it to junior college status. But as a result of Wilson's efforts, the school remained on a university level and became one of the leading institutions of its kind in the United States.

Only in recent years has the academic world bestowed upon Wilson the recognition and acclaim that has been due him. For example, in 1962, Carthage College awarded Wilson an honorary doctorate degree and in 1965 Northwestern University, at its commencement exercises conferred upon Wilson a doctor of laws degree. In addition, Wilson has received many commendations and awards from numerous major organizations and fraternities throughout the United States.

Throughout his entire career, Wilson was a much sought-after consultant in the area of police and criminal justice services. It was as a consultant that Wilson entered the Chicago scene in January 1960, after obtaining a leave of absence from the University of California. The police commissioner of the city of Chicago had resigned and Wilson was named chairman of a five man committee to choose a new police chief to replace the commissioner. After about a month of screening during which almost one hundred persons were considered, the other members of the committee recommended to Mayor Richard J. Daley that the post of police commissioner be offered to Wilson. Although Wilson was at first reluctant to accept the post, he finally agreed to do so after being promised a free hand in running the department, full support by the mayor, and complete separation of the police force from any political pressures. Wilson retired from active service within the academic world and was given the status of Professor Emeritus. On March 2, 1960, Wilson was installed formally as Acting Commissioner of the Chicago Police Department. As the nation's most publicized police chief Wilson was faced from the beginning by a number of challenges. On the day he took office the State Attorney for Cook County and Mayor Daley's chief political opponent challenged the appointment claiming that Wilson was ineligible because he had not been a resident of Chicago for 1 year. Wilson's position was ultimately upheld by the City Council, which upon recommendation of Mayor Daley, approved an ordinance establishing the office of Superintendent of Police in place of the previous Commissionership.

Shortly after taking office, Superintendent Wilson addressed the officers of the Chicago Police Department and laid down rigid rules of conduct for them. His approach evoked considerable opposition and for a time the Chicago Police Patrolmen's Association demanded his removal. Some of his opponents nicknamed him the "professor," and accused him of being too academic in his approach to existing problems. In addition, there were many sceptics who doubted whether a man with his professorial background and visionary ideals would last long in the environment which surrounded the department at the time of his appointment. To those of us who knew him, however, there was no question but that he would succeed and succeed he did. He turned the Chicago Police Department into one of the finest major city police departments in the world. In July 1966, Wilson drew fire for a statement in response to a press question regarding Richard Franklin Speck. He said: "I am absolutely positive that this man is the murderer." Speck was later convicted for the murder of eight student nurses at a residence maintained by the South Chicago Community Hospital. Some legal scholars felt that this statement by Wilson tended to convict Speck before he had a hearing and lessened his chances for a fair trial.

Throughout his career Wilson always insisted that the civil rights of a suspect should not be violated. He did, however, criticize court decisions that have freed criminal suspects on the basis of procedural technicalities. One such case resulted in the 1964 decision of the United States Supreme Court reversing the Chicago murder conviction of Danny Escobedo because a confession had been obtained from him before he had the chance to talk to a lawyer. Wilson always felt that police officers should be unhampered in their right to conduct reasonable investigations, and he attributed the laxity of the courts to an increasing tolerance for wrongdoers. Wilson felt that one of the problems police face is when sympathy for the unfortunate merges into favoritism for the criminal. It was his further view that tolerance for wrongdoers has turned into a fad in America. He felt that intolerance toward criminal behavior is what is needed.

Wilson has expounded his views in several books, articles, and pamphlets. His best-known book, *Police Administration* (published in 1950 with new editions in 1963 and 1972), has gained nationwide acceptance and has been translated into Spanish, Arabic, and Chinese. The book is typical of the man, spartan of style and relentless in organization. Wilson has also written other outstanding books which have contributed greatly to the law enforcement and criminal justice field. In 1942, he wrote *Police Records: Their Installation and Use* and in 1957, *Police Planning*. He also edited *Parker on Police* in 1966. This book presents the views of the late William H. Parker, Chief of Police of the City of Los Angeles.

Wilson had a great capacity for making methodical decisions appear to be sudden and decisive, but more important, his success was due to his tremendous ability to make important decisions with great conviction. Wilson was a man of tremendous energy and walked with great, bounding strides which conveyed a sense of movement and progress. His mind was like a steel trap and he had an uncanny ability to detect weaknesses in a plan or proposal. More than anything else, he combined an exhaustive knowledge of his profession with an overwhelming belief that what he was doing was right.

During his career he was not without his detractors and criticizers. But they were few. Many of his concepts were labeled controversial, but few remained unaccepted. Many of his innovations may have at one time seemed even radical, but today many of them are widely accepted in the profession of law enforcement. Although Wilson was a man of conviction, where his ideas did not meet wide acceptance, he learned the art of compromise, such as on the question of fire and police integration. He has been labeled by some to be a traditionalist, perhaps because he continued to support the concepts of August Vollmer as well as his own ideas. These concepts and ideas, although remarkably ahead of their time, have been well established in the law enforcement profession and have aided in providing the direction and status of the profession today.

Wilson was a member of many professional societies, most notably the American Society of Criminology which he served as President from 1941 to 1949. He was a life member of the International Association of Chiefs of Police, a member of the Military Government Association and a member of the Masonic Order. He was first married in 1923 to Vernis Haddon. By this marriage, which ended in divorce, he has a son, the Rev. Henry H. Wilson, who is an Episcopal priest in Germany, and a daughter, Sally Joe Wilson Genthner. In 1950, Wilson married Ruth Elinor

Evans, one of his former students, who is still active as a writer and lecturer. From this marriage another daughter, Patricia Anne Wilson, was added to his family.

Wilson was a thin, austere man who spoke in precise, academic phrases and measured every word. He retired from the Chicago police department in August of 1967, and lived in seclusion in his retirement home until he suffered the stroke which killed him. Wilson believed that the law enforcement profession has not yet achieved his vision of excellence for the police service, but we are nevertheless better off today because of his presence and influence and there is no question but that his ideals for the police profession will live on. To his professional contemporaries and personal friends he will always be remembered as "O. W."

JOHN EDGAR HOOVER

(1895–1972)

In the minds of the American public, the most famous American-born lawman and detective in history is J. Edgar Hoover, who directed the Federal Bureau of Investigation of the United States Department of Justice, for 48 years, serving eight presidents. Hoover died of natural causes on May 1, 1972, at his home in northwest Washington, D.C. President Richard M. Nixon said of him: "J. Edgar Hoover was one of the giants in the nation's history. Let us cherish his memory and be true to his legacy. Without peace officers we can never have peace. He was a peace officer without peer. He richly earned peace through all eternity."

Hoover was born in the capital city of the United States on New Year's Day, 1895. He was one of three children born to his parents, Dickerson N. and Annie Hoover, who were of Swiss descent. His older brother Dickerson, Jr. was born in 1880 and his sister Lillian was the last of the children to be added to the family. In later years, her son Fred G. Robinette became a special agent in the FBI under Hoover, and his son, Fred G. Robinette III, was personally sworn into the FBI by Hoover, his great uncle, in 1968.

The Hoover family was very tightly knit and were considered by their friends and neighbors to be very religious. They could be found worshipping together on Sunday in a local Presbyterian church with the remainder of the day being spent reading and studying the Bible. Hoover had an exceptional knowledge and understanding of the scriptures which may be attributed to his mother's tutoring and to the Sunday school he attended with the family. For a time it was thought by his parents that this young two-fisted, square-jawed man, who was an outstanding Sunday school teacher and loved by his pupils, was headed for the ministry, but such was not the case.

Little is known of Hoover's very early years in Washington, D.C., but history records that he attended Central High School where he was a serious student who earned high grades. He was greatly involved in debating and athletics, showing unusual leadership in both. Upon graduation from high school he was chosen to be the class valedictorian. Hoover had a desire for knowledge and was eager to continue his studies. He declined a scholarship at the University of Virginia and enrolled

FIGURE 4.5.   *J. Edgar Hoover. Courtesy Federal Bureau of Investigation, Washington, D.C.*

in George Washington University, attending night classes and working by day in the Library of Congress. It is believed that his library experience formed the basis for what was to develop later as the meticulous filing system of the FBI. In 1916, he received his LL.B. degree with honors, and a year later his Master of Laws degree. Although Hoover never entered the practice of law, he was, however, admitted to practice law before the bar of the District Court of the United States for the District of Columbia, the U.S. Court of Claims, and the United States Supreme Court. Later in life, Hoover received honorary degrees of every type from well-known universities throughout the United States.

Upon completing college, Hoover obtained a position with the Department of Justice. It was in this position during World War I that his capable handling of cases involving counterespionage came to the attention of the Attorney General who appointed him, at age 22, as a special assistant on July 26, 1917, to the enemy alien registration section; his responsibilities included prosecuting aliens deportable under the Sedition Act. One of his first major tasks was a study of subversive activities and it was his conclusion that the Communist Party then was engaged in a conspiracy to overthrow by force and violence all non-Communist governments in the world, including the United States. This conclusion dominated his thinking from that time on.

On May 10, 1924, Attorney General Harlan Stone selected Hoover to head the Bureau of Investigation in the Department of Justice. He thus became the federal government's top policeman at the age of 29. This assignment came at a time when the Bureau was under severe criticism but Stone believed that Hoover could restore public confidence.

During the turbulent years that followed, the agency became the FBI. Hoover and his agents gained nationwide praise as "G-Men" who helped rid the nation of such notorious gangsters as John Dillinger, Ma Barker, "Creepy" Alvin Karpis, and George "Machinegun" Kelly. Kelly is credited with labeling the hated government men G-Men.

As the nation's chief enforcement officer, Hoover wielded power among the mighty for nearly a half century, and he was highly popular with the public. Two presidents found the combination so unbeatable that they kept the bulldog-faced Hoover in office years past the mandatory retirement age of 70, with the result that he served longer than any other federal bureaucrat in modern times.

Hoover held a commission in the United States Army from May 1924 until April 24, 1942, at which time he resigned in view of the importance of the intelligence work of the FBI.

Hoover was unmarried and dominated the Bureau during his lifetime like no man in any other federal agency. It has been said that he lavished on the FBI the pride and possessiveness of a stern and watchful parent. He once stated that he never married "because of the competition the FBI would give my wife," and he once wrote in a magazine article that if he ever had a child he would "above all teach him to tell the truth . . . truth telling, I have found, is the key to responsible citizenship. The thousands of criminals I have seen in 40 years of law enforcement have had one thing in common: every single one was a liar."

When Hoover accepted his assignment from Stone, he did so upon two conditions. First, he must be assured of a free hand in personnel selection and policy, and second, he be responsible only to the Attorney General. With these guarantees accorded to him, he began a complete reorganization of the agency. As a result of the reorganization, many employees left the agency and "The Director," as he was later affectionately called, combed the country for competent, conscientious men who could be depended upon for hard work and efficient service. In his recruitment program he announced that the promotion system that he would utilize would be one where the employee would be judged only by performance. This was his way of putting into practice the teachings of fair play that he had learned in his early years in Sunday School. He also made his recruitment program clear, stating that neither race nor religion would influence his appointments. He stated, "How can I deny any man who measures up to our standards? I am not interested in whether a man is a Jew, a Catholic, a Protestant, a Negro or a white. What I am looking for is character and competence." Developing high-quality personnel was not an easy task for Hoover, but he accomplished it, and the same high standards are maintained to this day.

All during his career Hoover maintained that his men, from the highest to the lowest, were to serve as a team and for this reason FBI agents are rarely identified in Bureau press releases or case narratives for public reading. The entire team either shares the credit—or the blame.

A common misconception that is held by many is that Hoover built a national police force in the FBI and that it functioned as such. The agency does not function in this capacity nor has it ever done so during its history, for Hoover maintained that the same objectives could be achieved through cooperation of law enforcement agencies "without surrendering to the democratically repugnant concept of a centralized power police force." In 1969, Hoover stated, "Law enforcement represents this country's first line of defense in its efforts to control crime . . . this is where the war against crime must be won." Hoover always pointed out, even up until the time of his death, that the FBI did not decide what it would investigate. It is given responsibilities by Congress, by the President, and by the Attorney General. It is charged by law to carry out certain functions and, Hoover added, they *will* be carried out.

Even as Hoover became a legend and a household word in America, while he successfully built the FBI into an internationally recognized agency, he was but yet a man, living alone in his two-story house in pleasant northwest Washington. He enjoyed his home and could be seen gardening in his yard and caring for the roses of which he was very proud. He enjoyed football and baseball, but horse racing was his favorite spectator sport. Hoover preached respect for law and order and good citizenship was his goal. He was a fervently religious man and whether duty called him to Maine or to California he could be found on a Sunday morning inconspicuously sitting in a pew of a church, joining in praise of the Lord he loved and in thankful devotion. Hoover's favorite vacation area was La Jolla, California, and he often stated that if he were a field agent, that was the location he would like to be assigned to the most. His second choice was Butte, Montana, because he felt this locale had the best available hunting and fishing.

In the Bureau, "The Director" had many viewpoints regarding crime. With reference to crime prevention he often said, "Crime prevention should start in the high chair—not in the electric chair." And it was with this creed that he enthusiastically encouraged and supported the Boys Clubs of America as well as recreational facilities and character building programs. It was because of this strong feeling that Hoover served for over 30 years as a member of the Board of Directors of the Boys Clubs of America. Upon his death, this agency created the J. Edgar Hoover Freedom Award and announced that it would be made to the American who best typified those principles to which Mr. Hoover dedicated his life. Hoover was a member of several fraternities and he enjoyed his membership in Masonry. He was both a Royal Arch and Scottish Rite 33rd Degree Mason as well as a member of the Shrine. In addition, he was a member of many national and statewide law enforcement associations and participated actively as an honorary trustee of George Washington University, as a member of the National Court of Honor, and as a honorary member of the National Council of the Boy Scouts of America; he was a member of the National Advisory Council of the Girl Scouts of the United States of America and the International Supreme Council of the Order of DeMolay. He also was a member of the Columbia Country Club, Washington, D.C.

During his lifetime Hoover granted few interviews and authored only four books, the first of which was titled *Persons in Hiding,* 1938; second, *Masters of Deceit,* 1958; *A Study of Communism,* 1962; and his last publication, *J. Edgar Hoover on Communism,* 1969. Throughout Hoover's career he was warmly lauded for his performance as Director of the Federal Bureau of Investigation, and the inner corridor leading to his office was lined with plaques and citations from scores of organizations and with mementoes from notables that he had known during his lifetime.

Prior to his death, Hoover was asked what he felt his most important accomplishments as Director of FBI were, and, in the order of their importance as he saw them, they are listed:

1. Reorganization of the Bureau in 1924.
2. Consistent support received by the FBI over the years from a law-abiding and concerned public.
3. Nationwide centralization of criminal fingerprint records in the FBI Identification Division in 1924.
4. Establishment in 1932 of the FBI crime laboratory.
5. Establishment in 1935 of the FBI National Academy which provided a university level advanced training program for select law enforcement officers throughout the nation.
6. Capture and successful prosecution of numerous criminals including saboteurs, spies, kidnappers, and murderers.
7. Creation, development, and instrumentation of the national crime information center, which provides a comprehensive and swiftly efficient information exchange system to law enforcement throughout the country and Canada by a vast telecommunications network.

The Federal Bureau of Investigation has increased under Hoover's leadership and direction from 441 special agents in 1924 to 59 field offices located throughout the United States and Puerto Rico with 8000 special agents and 11,100 civilian employees. In addition to the major field offices, there are resident agencies as well as suboffices. It was Hoover's hope that the FBI's role in the future would be identical with its role in the past, that is, being a servant of the people. He believed that the success of the FBI was built on one vital base, which was the confidence of the people, and stated, "If we knock on a citizen's door, he does not have to talk to us or give our special agents information. This is a decision he must make. We can solve cases only if citizens furnish information." He further believed that for the FBI to be a responsible agency it was necessary to maintain the confidence and support of all the citizens in all areas of the country.

When Hoover died, President Richard Nixon ordered that his body lie in state in the rotunda under the capitol dome in Washington. Capitol police estimated that some 17,000 persons filed past Hoover's flag-draped bier. An additional 2000 persons attended the final rites at the National Presbyterian Church where Hoover was an ordained Elder and member. Prior to the funeral service, Dr. Edward Elson, Senate Chaplain and J. Edgar Hoover's pastor, eulogized Hoover for "his steadfast devotion to the nation, his elevated patriotism, his fidelity in a position of high trust, his commitment to justice and peace in the nation." As the funeral procession left the capitol and drove to the church by way of Pennsylvania Avenue, several hundred FBI agents, secretaries, clerks, and other personnel stood at attention in the rain outside the Justice Department in respect to The Director.

In his eulogy during the funeral service President Nixon said, "Today is a day of sadness for America, but it is also a day of pride. Once in a long while America is a land of giants. J. Edgar Hoover was one of the giants. He became a living legend as a young man. His death only heightens the respect and admiration accorded him in life. He had a great influence for good in our national life and the good that Hoover has done will not die. He made the FBI the finest law enforcement agency on this earth and in doing so became an institution in his own right."

WILLIAM H. PARKER

(1902–1966)

At the time the west was struggling to emerge from a frontier status, in the Black Hills area of South Dakota, run wild with scofflaws, one of the United States' foremost law enforcement officers, William H. Parker, was born in the town of Lead on June 21, 1902. Parker always had a life-long zeal toward improved law enforcement. This may have been fostered by the example of his grandfather, who was a frontier lawyer and a leader in driving the lawless out of the badlands of South Dakota.

FIGURE 4.6.   *William H. Parker. Courtesy Police Department, Los Angeles, Ca.*

William H. Parker's first job was that of a hotel detective and custodian which helped him to earn his way through high school in Deadwood, South Dakota, where he graduated with honors and was a leading debater. His flair for debate later made for his success and his outstanding recognition as a public speaker.

The Parker family moved to Los Angeles, California, during the roaring twenties. Deciding to put his debating skills to use, Parker enrolled at the Los Angeles College of Law in 1926, and, while attending law school, earned his living by driving a taxicab until he received his appointment to the Los Angeles Police Department on August 8, 1927. Three years later he had conferred on him the Bachelor of Laws degree and in the same year the State Bar of California admitted him to membership, which permitted him to practice law in the state of California. On April 26, 1956, he was admitted to the practice of law before the United States Supreme Court.

After completing his law school education and while a member of the Los Angeles Police Department, Parker married his fiancée Helen and they made their home in Los Angeles until his death. He served the city of Los Angeles for 39 years, 15 as Chief of Police, having been appointed to that position on August 9, 1950. His tenure as Chief was the longest tenure in the department's history. Today, Parker is recognized as one of the leading architects of that city's world-famous police organization. The comprehensive working knowledge of modern law enforcement acquired in a variety of assignments during his career has earned him the professional recognition and status in history as one of the foremost police administrators in the world. In recognition and memory of Parker, the city of Los Angeles has named the new, modern, multistoried police headquarters building *Parker Center.*

Shortly after becoming Chief of Police of an agency which became a model for police administrators throughout the world, Parker was personally commended by the Senate Committee investigating organized crime under the direction of Senator Estes Kefauver. The Committee took official notice of the effectiveness of the Los Angeles Police Department and similar notice was taken by state and other federal investigative agencies and by nationally known police and civilian authorities, with Los Angeles becoming known as the "white spot" in the nation's pattern of organized crime.

During World War II Parker entered the military service and served in the military government branch of the United States Army where he rose to the rank of Captain under the command of Colonel O. W. Wilson. His 26 month service in the European theater of operation put him in action in Africa, Italy, Sardinia, France, Austria, Germany, and Great Britain. He was directly responsible for the development of the police and prisons plan for the European invasion and later in prompting closer relationships between the police of both continents, Parker introduced democratic police systems into the cities of Munich and Frankfort. Those systems are still in operation today. Parker was wounded during the Normandy invasion and was awarded the Purple Heart Medal. Additionally, for his wartime contributions, he also received the European Campaign Medal with two stars, the American Campaign Medal, the Victory Medal and the Occupation Medal. From the Free French Government, he received the Croix de Guerre with a Silver Star. The Italian Government also awarded Parker the Star of Solidarity for his work in restoring civil government in Sardinia.

Upon his return to the police department in November of 1945, Parker served for a time in the traffic enforcement division and later was appointed director of the Bureau of Internal Affairs which he developed and organized. After his appointment as Chief of Police, he immediately reorganized the department to simplify and assure his control over its operations and to facilitate the attainment of police objectives. He also adopted the best of known police procedures and urged his exceptionally competent staff to develop even newer ones. The changes Parker instituted met with resistance in the department and in the community just as does any rapid change. What Parker did required more courage than is possessed by most men, but his courage was grounded on a great religious faith and he had a superb inherent quality that enabled him to carry his intentions into practice. Perhaps it was his faith that enabled him to weather the rough political siege that every police chief encounters during his career, and nowhere are the seas rougher than in a large American city. Like many other pioneers in the professionalization of law enforcement, Parker was confronted by endless obstacles and many scoffers. Parker's great qualities of leadership, developed as a result of his patience, diplomacy, sound judgment, unusual moral courage, and great physical and emotional strength, contributed to the success that he enjoyed throughout his entire career in law enforcement.

Chief Parker's accomplishments in working for improved law enforcement have received world-wide recognition. In 1952, he was appointed honorary chief of the National Police of the Republic of Korea and the nacreous-laid nameplate that adorned his desk while he was in office was a souvenir which he treasured from that nation. Additionally, he was the only representative of municipal law enforcement in the United States who was invited to participate in the 29th General Assembly of the International Police Organization (Interpol) in 1960 at Washington, D.C. In 1964, he was the first United States police administrator chosen by the Department of State to assist the Ministry of Home Affairs of the Government of India in redeveloping that nation's police procedures. This was an honor which he treasured, and when he was presented to the United States Supreme Court to be admitted to the practice of law before that court in 1956, he was presented by Warren Olney III, Assistant Attorney General of the United States. Many organizations throughout the world gave special recognition to Parker and his work. Among them were the Los Angeles Chamber of Commerce, B'nai B'rith, the American Freedom Club, the Greater Los Angeles Press Club, Town Hall, City of Hope, Sertoma Club, the Los Angeles County Bar Association, the Boy Scouts of America, the U.S. State Department, the Community Chest, Civil Defense, Veterans organizations, many legislative, educational, and religious bodies, and the American Legion. In addition, the St. George Medal was presented to him by the Cardinal Archbishop of Los Angeles.

During his entire career Parker always insisted in police professionalism and insisted that that professionalism be free of political control. Attesting to this is the fact that his continuing service took place under three mayors and twenty-three prominent citizens serving as police commissioners. Parker is recognized as one of the leading exponents of professionalism in police work. He was always an advocate of a close working relationship between the citizen and the police officer. He thus spent a great portion of his time addressing citizen, youth, community, and business groups.

It was not in Parker's nature to stop work even when he knew that unusual exertion might bring death. In the mid 1960s, Parker's health broke and he was forced to endure a dangerous operation for an aortal aneurysm and resection. Recovering from this surgery, Parker resumed his duties as Chief of Police. On July 16, 1966, he died after a heart attack struck him as he returned to his chair after accepting the last of many honors. He had been the honored guest at the United States Marine Corps' Second Marine Division Association banquet. The city of Los Angeles' rarely conferred accolade to its honored dead was bestowed on Chief Parker, whose body lay in state in the City Hall rotunda on July 19. Honor ceremonies were celebrated by the Catholic Archdiocese and burial was in the San Fernando Mission cemetery.

No better prototype for the peace officer exists today than that of the persistence to assure better law enforcement against unending obstruction that was exemplified in the life of William H. Parker.

LEONARDE KEELER

(1903–1949)

Leonarde Keeler was an outstanding criminalist who was born in Berkeley, California, on October 30, 1903, the son of an author and naturalist. Keeler had a normal childhood and progressed through the school system in Berkeley, whereupon he entered the University of California in 1923 and studied there for a short time. He later attended Stanford University where he graduated with an A.B. degree in 1931. By the time he had reached the age of 19 Keeler had begun the study of crime detection under August Vollmer, who was at that time Chief of Police of Berkeley, California. With the aid and assistance of Vollmer, in 1929, Keeler became a member of the staff of the Institute for Juvenile Research in Chicago, Illinois, and at the same time, again as a result of Vollmer's efforts on his behalf, he was appointed as a staff member of the criminologist's department for the state of Illinois. He served in this position for a period of 2 years during which time he examined some 500 prisoners on the polygraph at Joliet State Prison. Vollmer had trained Keeler in the fundamentals of the operation of this instrument and encouraged him later to refine and further develop this new and scientific instrument. In 1930, he became a psychologist and polygraph examiner at the Scientific Crime Detection Laboratory at the Northwestern University School of Law in Chicago, Illinois. The laboratory was established in 1929 and was the first of its type in the United States. The University made him an Assistant Professor of Law and Psychology and appointed him as Research Assistant in Psychology in 1933. In 1936, he became the head of the laboratory with the rank of Associate Professor.

Keeler established a private practice in Chicago in 1938, and in the following year he resigned from his laboratory responsibilities at the University to devote full

FIGURE 4.7.   *Leonarde Keeler. Courtesy Leonarde Keller, Inc., Chicago, Il.*

time to his work in private practice, which he continued until his death. His most notable contribution to the field of criminal justice was his personal refinement and further development of the Keeler polygraph, an instrument for the recording of bodily processes, popularly known today as the lie detector. The polygraph was used for evidence in a court for the first time in 1935 when it was submitted for consideration of a jury in the Circuit Court of Columbia County, Wisconsin.

Keeler developed a highly successful test procedure and technique for diagnosing deception from the physiological recordings which the instrument produced. This became known as the *detection of deception* technique. He made use of this technique, while a member of the Institute for Juvenile Research, on patients in mental hospitals, on inmates in prisons, and later in crime and personnel work. He taught his technique to a few selected students from time to time for a number of years and in 1948 initiated the Keeler Polygraph School in Chicago which he continued to operate until his death.

Keeler was frequently called upon as an expert witness in court cases and, in connection with his work, he traveled extensively in the United States and throughout the world. During World War II he handled many secret cases for the United States military forces and contributed vast amounts of technical advice, especially to the

Office of the Provost Marshal General. His work with the polygraph made him responsible for the screening of prisoners of war in 1945 and this work later took him to Germany. In 1947, he screened personnel in fission-materials departments of atomic manufacturing plants. He was an active member in many organizations and participated widely throughout the United States in many areas of law enforcement. From 1942 to 1949, he was a member of the Merit Council of the Illinois State Police and served on the Chicago Crime Commission. He was a member of the American Association for the Advancement of Science, the International Association for Identification, the International Association of Chiefs of Police, the International Association for the Detection of Deception, to name but a few organizations. In 1938, Keeler was honored by Lawrence College, who conferred upon him an honorary Doctor of Laws degree.

He was a man who was highly dedicated to his scientific endeavors, but he did enjoy periods of mountain climbing and travel which were his chief recreation. In 1930, Keeler married Katherine Applegate, the daughter of a businessman from Walla Walla, Washington. He suffered a short illness in September of 1949, which resulted in his death in Sturgeon Bay, Wisconsin.

The refinement, development, and contribution of the polygraph to the American system of justice by Keeler will go down in history as one of the most worthy of all instruments ever developed to aid in the detection of deception and the investigation of crime.

QUINN TAMM

(1910–   )

Quinn Tamm, the Executive Director of the International Association of Chiefs of Police, has provided American law enforcement with outstanding leadership throughout his career in the criminal justice system. His life began in Seattle, Washington, on August 10, 1910. In the early years of his youth his parents, Edward Allen and Lucille Katherine Tamm, moved to Butte, Montana, where he received his early education. Upon completion of high school he moved further east and entered the University of Virginia at Charlottesville, where he obtained a B.S. degree in 1934.

Mr. Tamm's interest in law enforcement became clear early in his career. At the age of 24, following graduation from the university, he applied for and received an appointment to the Federal Bureau of Investigation where he served from 1934 to his retirement in 1961. During an outstanding career with the Bureau he progressed through the ranks to Inspector and, in 1954, was appointed by J. Edgar Hoover as Assistant Director of the Bureau's Identification Division. It was not long until Hoover recognized his leadership ability and gave him, as Assistant Director, the responsibility for the Bureau's training and inspection division in 1956. Later, in 1959, he was named to head the laboratory division, the post he held until his retirement.

FIGURE 4.8. *Quinn Tamm. Courtesy International Association of Chiefs of Police, Gaithersburg, Md.*

During his career, Tamm had always been interested in the International Association of Chiefs of Police and the leadership and services that it was providing to the professionalized area of law enforcement. The organization, although 68 years old, only had a full-time professional staff of ten. In addition, the work of the Association was done by standing committees of the membership. Soon after assuming his position as Field Services Director in 1961, Tamm was named as Acting Executive Director and later confirmed to this position by the Board of Directors in October, 1962, during the sixty-ninth annual conference at St. Louis, Missouri.

From this point he began to build the Association into a strong and viable force for the professionalization of police services. Tamm has brought a presence and prestige to the position of IACP Executive Director. He has opened lines of communication between all groups of law enforcement at each government level.

Tamm surrounded himself with proven experts in the field of police administration. With the assistance of these experts and his foresight and administrative ability, he has been able to translate the mission of the Association into reality. As a tax exempt nonprofit private organization, the funding projects were a serious problem. However, the excellent support of his executive staff gained for the Association a Ford Foundation grant for the Professional Standards Division projects. The expertise of the Field Services Division management surveys has gained added prestige and the Association has come to be recognized as the official voice for professional law enforcement in the United States. Presidential commissions and congressional committees frequently call upon the office of the Executive Director to articulate the needs of law enforcement nationally, and the national media call upon the office to appear upon network television and to present articles in news publications to further the cause of professional police services. Mr. Tamm was recently called to testify in support of the Omnibus Crime Control and Safe Streets Act as well as numerous other bills affecting law enforcement at the federal level. He is frequently called upon by national and state government agencies, commissions, and committees as a special advisor and consultant. He is a very forceful speaker and has the fortitude to say publicly what he sees as the inefficiencies in American criminal justice proceedings.

Both the professional staff and requests for services of the IACP have mushroomed. Today the headquarters staffs more than 125 personnel, each with proven expertise in criminal justice administration and possessing a wide range of credentials extending through the doctorate degree. The Association owns and operates a brand new modern office building in the Washington suburb of Gaithersburg, Maryland.

On February 2, 1948, Quinn Tamm married Ora Belle Phillips who bore him two sons, Quinn Tamm, Jr. and Thomas Mark Tamm. Like many of his peers, Tamm has deep religious convictions; he is a Roman Catholic and an active member of the Knights of Columbus. He enjoys membership in the Rotary Club, the Associated Public Safety Communications Officers, the International Association of Chiefs of Police, the International Union of Local Authorities, the International Platform Association, the Advisory Board of the Institute of Criminal Justice and Criminology for the University of Maryland, and he serves actively and provides great leadership for the Board of Directors of the Police Foundation.

Quinn Tamm has received many honors and awards from around the world in recognition of his outstanding leadership and dedication to the professionalization of law enforcement. He will always be widely recognized and respected as a leading authority in law enforcement and criminal justice.

SUMMARY

Although there have been many in law enforcement who have contributed to the growth, development, and professionalization of this public service field, only eight have been presented, as a representative cross-section of men who have made major contributions to the field. Each has, in his own way, made a driving and effective impact upon this area of public service. With the continued effective and efficient leadership that is present today in the twentieth century, law enforcement public service will rise to new heights and will be supported by a favorable and strong public attitude.

ANNOTATED REFERENCES

Block, E. B., *Famous Detectives,* Doubleday, Garden City, N.Y., 1967. Thirteen true stories of the world's greatest detectives.

Current Biography, Wilson, New York, Yearly. Contains brief biographical outlines.

Lavine, S. A., *Allan Pinkerton: America's First Private Eye,* Dodd, Mead and Co., Cornwall Press, Cornwall, N.Y., 1963. The life and exploits of Allan Pinkerton and his family, including a description of the famous organization which bears his name.

Whitehead, D., *The F.B.I. Story,* Doubleday, Garden City, N.Y., 1963. A well written history of the Federal Bureau of Investigation.

Wilson, O. W., *Parker on Police,* Thomas, Springfield, Ill., 1957. An outstanding collection and presentation of Police Chief William H. Parker's thoughts and views on ten different police subjects including his personal philosophy.

CHAPTER FIVE

Theories of Crime and Delinquency

Most problems and most questions can be studied from more than one point of view. It is a misconception to assume that there is only one way of considering criminal behavior. Certainly one must consider not only the criminal act, but the criminal as well. Students of the problem must recognize all possible attitudes and points of view [1].

Criminal behavior is complex and has many different meanings in as many social contexts. To the judge and policeman, stealing, for example, is contrary to lawful behavior and the individual who steals is a criminal. To the psychologist, who is interested in the theory of learning, the individual learned to steal—a lesson that society as a whole wishes he had not learned. To the psychiatrist, stealing may be viewed as a way of resolving some emotional conflict or tensions which have arisen from the individual's inability to cope with life's situations. To the citizen whose property was stolen, the theft is a threat to the safety of property and should be punished. To the relatives, spouse, or parent of the thief, stealing may be viewed as the work of the devil, as a mental disorder, as an act of rebellion, as an attempt to ruin the family reputation, as a bad habit, or even as an act of carelessness about getting caught which should be avoided the next time he steals. To the law violator's friends, stealing may be an act in an exciting and dangerous drama, particularly in the youth culture, and the young thief may be judged by whether he lives up to their code, shares with them the bounty, or refuses to tell on those who have stolen with him [2]. From the educator's point of view, particularly when considering juvenile crime, delinquency is learned, and in looking for conditions that give rise to delinquency he finds many that are common to other kinds of poor learning development—broken home, poverty, emotional conflicts in family life, retarded mental development, poor neighborhood background, etc. It is necessary therefore to study these conditions which lead to crime and delinquency [3].

Many believe that crime and delinquency have definite causes. Some blame poverty, others slum conditions, and still others find the cause for criminal acts within the warped personalities of the offender. One reads that the home or the parents are to blame, that poverty, school, and teachers are at fault, or that the churches have in some way failed to meet the needs of modern youth. Modern urban society, with its increased facilities for communication, with better and faster means of transportation, with greater concentrations of population, quite different from the rural life of a generation or two ago, has to some writers had a great influence on the present problem of adult and juvenile crime. The causes given for crime are almost as numerous as those who write or talk about the subject [4].

No doubt some of these beliefs are more or less correct. The careful student, however, must try to determine whether any one, or indeed whether all, of the causes given may be symptoms of other causes. If he wants to understand the problem, the educator, the student of the law, the psychologist, the psychiatrist, the social worker must strive to dig deeper than many of the superficial reasons that are often given for producing criminals and delinquents.

In the same way that there are those who believe they know the cause of crime, there are those who think they know how to cure it. Some believe that more, better, or stricter laws will solve the problem. They often forget that laws are only as effective as the public concern for their enforcement and that adding more legal prohibitions will not deter individuals from becoming involved in criminal activities.

Just as there is no single cause for crime and delinquency, so it is doubtful that there is any single, simple solution to the problem. It is a misconception of the problem to believe there is a simple solution or that one can be found. Only when local communities become aroused, only when all agencies cooperate and coordinate their efforts, and only when the citizens of a given community work together, can they hope to successfully attack the problem.

MYTHS AND MISUNDERSTANDING

Throughout the ages, it has been quite popular for each generation to believe that they have discovered the true cure or causes for adult and juvenile crime. Contacts with various groups of people—experts and laymen alike—indicate that very strong opinions are held on this subject. And each holds to his own concept with unusual tenacity.

As with many social problems, nearly everyone forms a snap judgment, becomes a self-appointed expert, and is anxious to "do something about the rapid increase in crime." Individuals and groups often forget that "doing something about criminal and delinquent behavior" means that the public and the community at large must be willing to do something about itself.

Fortunately, community action is seldom guided by the popular misconceptions about crime and delinquency. Nevertheless, these misconceptions are myths and are sufficiently widespread to warrant critical examination. It will, therefore, be necessary to explore some of the ideas which are misleading or incorrect, but which still, like legends, persist in the folklore surrounding criminal behavior. That there is no denying there may be an element of truth in some of these misconceptions, however, does not change the premise that such misconceptions should be open to serious challenge as *absolute* or *categorical* statements concerning the nature and sources of criminal behavior. To place credence in half-truths which have been falsified through overgeneralization and indiscriminate application would result in a psychological "Berlin Wall." Subscription to such fallacies would prevent clear thinking and the conception of programs for the prevention and treatment of the criminal and youthful offender.

The problem of popular misunderstanding is vividly captured by Roucek and Warren [5], who state:

An adequate, scientific approach to problems of delinquency and crime is hindered by the popular misunderstandings remaining in the folklore and common sense approach to the problem. In the following paragraphs, the term "criminal" will be used to include "delinquent" merely for purposes of brevity.

The first misunderstanding is that criminals *are a separate type of people.* Popular thinking tends to lump together all criminals as being people who are different from other human beings and who, among themselves, are pretty much the same. Actually, the range of individual differences among criminals is as wide as that for the general population, and their behavior can be interpreted and understood according to the same principles which govern the behavior of law-abiding persons. Nevertheless, the misunderstanding persists, and it militates against the institution of programs which would deal with the criminals by recognizing the individual circumstances surrounding each case and seek their rehabilitation through an application of scientific principles of human behavior.

Another misunderstanding is the viewpoint *that criminals have no morals.* This involves the fallacious notion that criminals are not motivated by normal human desires and that they are lone wolves who do not seek or need the approval and affection of other people. Actually, most crime is a group phenomenon, involving cooperative association of several parties. In addition, criminals are found to subscribe to many of the *mores* to which law-abiding people give their loyalty, and in addition have strong group *mores,* such as that of loyalty to one's own group and the duty not to squeal, or inform legal authorities about one's fellow criminal.

Another important misconception is *that crime has a single cause.* Criminologists, through careful research over many decades, have found that crime is usually associated with a combination of factors, rather than any single one like feeble-mindedness, broken homes, etc.

A fourth important misconception is *that crime is prevented by strict penalties.* Many people advocate severe punishment as a deterrent to crime. However, no such relationship has been found to exist between the frequency of crime and the intensity of punishment. It is said that during the reign of Henry VIII pickpockets did their most extensive business among the crowds gathered to watch the public hanging of criminals, many of whom were being hanged for stealing.

Fallacies such as those cited by Roucek and Warren lead the expert into impractical, mirage-like plans and create hopes which could not possibly be successful, no matter how much time, effort, and money is put into them.

THEORETICAL APPROACHES TO CRIMINAL BEHAVIOR

Why does crime occur and why does it increase at such a rapid rate? The assumption often is made that a clear knowledge and understanding of the causes leading to criminal behavior can lead naturally to a clear understanding of how to control and prevent crime.

This type of reasoning is based on the frequent experience of successfully solving a problem after the causes have been determined. Some conquests of infectious diseases have followed this sequence of solution. The problems, so to speak, of infectious diseases, flood control, and highway construction have been solved in this manner—by understanding and forming a clear picture of the causes. It should be noted, however, that in such instances the causes are relatively simple and few. This is certainly not true of human behavior.

Knowledge of causes does not always result in the ability to control a problem when the causes are both extremely complex and numerous. For example, much is known about the causes of many cardiac diseases, such as those in the cardiovascular and metabolic areas, without a corresponding ability to control or prevent these illnesses. In some such instances the causes themselves are very complex and not subject to control. Causation of crime has more in common with this latter circumstance than it does with the more simple and hopeful relationship described for many infectious diseases and the threats of natural environmental forces.

It should be noted that, although control of problems may be aided by the knowledge of causes, it does not always depend completely on a full understanding of causation. Medicine has many instances of the development of successful treatments, and even of preventive methods, before the causes of some illnesses were known. Similarly, efforts to control or prevent criminal behavior need not and must not, in fact, await a comprehensive statement of causes.

A number of factors associated with crime have been identified in a fairly complete way. Many factors are part of broad social and economic problems which are, themselves, as difficult to control as is criminal activity. These statements are not made to indicate any attitude of defeatism, but only to indicate the complexity of the problems of criminality and the limitations of the advantages that can be expected from a delineation of the factors that relate to criminal behavior.

It is not illogical for the person engaged in prevention and treatment to be concerned with factors related to criminal behavior; he is better prepared to treat, prevent, or rehabilitate if he knows what causes such antisocial behavior. Yet it is astounding what a wide variety of answers will come—even from the experts—from a simple question like: What factors contribute to criminal behavior? The answers to this question are classified in three brief general groups of categories of factors relating to crime: sociological, psychological, and physiological.

Sociological Factors

From time to time, various factors have been found, or supposed, to be related to criminal behavior. Unless a specific theory is discussed, it is preferable to speak about related factors rather than causal factors, since causal factors imply a simple set of relations that do not exist. *Criminal behavior, like other forms of behavior, is responsive to social and economic conditions, and other dominant features of society.* Deviate behavior has occurred ever since there have been laws and moral codes. City life, popula-tion mobility, divergence in values, in life styles, and in opportunities for social and economic advancement, family instability, the lure of quick wealth and social success through activities on the fringe of conventional socie-ty—these characteristics of modern society, as well as the increased tendency to use the police and courts to settle minor disputes that generally have been considered private matters, are not in themselves necessarily the causes of crime, but they are contributory factors. Such characteristics provide the context within which patterns of antisocial behavior arise and are transmitted. They make more difficult the operation of informal social control, which has always been more important than formal legal controls in maintaining the moral order of society.

For effective control of crime, then, it becomes necessary to seek modes of compensating for our counteractions which either encourage or foster deviate behavior.

As we have seen, many studies of crime and delinquency suggest that the rates of deviate behavior are highest in the deteriorated areas of our larger cities. These are the areas in which the most recently arrived, low-in-come immigrants have settled. Also living in such areas are those who have drifted there because of failure to compete successfully for more desirable living space (because of lack of skills, disease, or other disability), and persons who have located in those districts because of a desire for freedom from conventional restraints. These neighborhoods are characterized not only by physical deterioration, but also by great heterogeneity of background and moral standards, lack of neighborhood solidarity, lack of opportunities for youth to participate, meaningfully, in the kinds of activities that are available to children in more favored neighborhoods, and by the presence of "success-ful" members of the underworld, who are regarded as heroes by the youths. These circumstances of life often are associated with unstable families and a high incidence of illegitimacy and desertion, leading to both marginal employment, with inadequate supervision for the needs of children, and the absence of a father figure with whom the child can identify and look to for supervision, guidance, and affection.

Antisocial behavior has been found to be particularly high among the minority groups and in homes that have been broken by deaths, desertion, or divorce. The importance of the family in the development of personalities is well known. Homes characterized by marital conflict, or by absences of an important member, understandably contribute more than their share to crime and delinquency. It is important, however, to recognize the fact that not all children from broken homes become criminals; therefore this can hardly be considered the sole factor.

In underprivileged environments, crime and delinquency may not be so much an expression of economic need as an individual maladjustment—a patent, behavioral expression of basic conflicts that confront the adult, child, and adolescent. It must be added that neither the basic conflict of values nor crime is confined by any means to the urban slums. They find their most favorable expression in such an atmosphere, but they also are found in the society at large.

Another aspect of the contemporary environment (strictly in the area of delinquency) that is significantly involved in the problem arises from the very high premium put on certain forms of success and the preoccupation of many parents with their own social and occupational success. When this is coupled with the freedom that adolescence can achieve from parental restriction, the family as a source of sound values and mechanism of social control is weakened further. There is evidence that middle-class youths emulate for "kicks" many of the behavioral patterns that have their origins in relatively deprived areas. These expressions of rebellion from parents are likely to appear where parental standards are inconsistent or too stringently applied to the adolescent and not wholly manifested in parental behavior.

There have been major fluctuations in the amounts of criminality that appear to be associated with major social and economic changes. At least in recent years, crime has increased in times of economic prosperity marked by hedonistic (life of pleasure) values in many circles—such as the 1920's, the 1950's, and the 1960's—and has fallen in times of depression. We do not yet know about the factors that mediate between these broad changes and criminal behavior. Detailed studies along these lines and other areas mentioned earlier should be most enlightening.

An extremely popular theory relating to crime and delinquency is offered by the late Edwin H. Sutherland [6] who developed a theory referred to as *differential association*. According to Sutherland, a person becomes a criminal because of an excess of definitions favorable to violation of law. When any person becomes criminal, he does so because of contacts with criminal patterns and also because of isolation from anticriminal patterns. Any person inevitably assimilates the surrounding culture unless other patterns are in conflict [7].

The hypothesis suggested here as a substitute for the conventional theories is that white-collar criminality, just as other systematic criminality, is learned; that it is learned in direct or indirect association with those who already practice the behavior; and that those who learn this criminal behavior are segregated from frequent and intimate contacts with law-abiding behavior. Whether a person becomes a criminal is determined largely by the comparative frequency and intimacy of his contacts with the two types of behavior. This may be called the process of differential association. It is a genetic explanation both of white-collar criminality and lower-class criminality.

Those who become white-collar criminals generally start their careers in good neighborhoods and good homes, graduate from colleges with some idealism, and, with little selection on their part, get into particular business situations in which criminality is practically a folkway and are inducted into a system of behavior just as into any other folkway.

The lower-class criminals generally start their careers in deteriorated neighborhoods, and families find criminals at hand from whom they acquire the attitudes toward, and techniques of, crime. The accessibility of such association with criminals and delinquents and in particular segregation from law-abiding people is a common condition of the slum.

The essentials are the same for the two classes of law violators. This is not entirely a process of assimilation, for inventions are frequently made, perhaps more frequently in white-collar crime than in lower-class crime. The inventive geniuses for lower-class criminals are generally professional criminals, whereas inventive geniuses for many kinds of white-collar crime are generally lawyers.

A second general process is social disorganization in the community. Differential association culminates in crime because the community is not organized solidly against that behavior which presses in one direction while fewer forces press in the opposite direction.

In business, the "rules of the game" conflict with legal rules. A businessman who wants to obey the law is driven by his competitors to adopt their methods. This is well illustrated by the persistence of commercial bribery in spite of the strenuous efforts of business organizations to eliminate it. Groups and people are individuated; they are more concerned with their specialized group or individual interests than with the larger welfare. Consequently, it is not possible for the community to present a solid front in opposition to crime.

The Better Business Bureaus and crime commissions, composed of business and professional men, attack burglary, robbery, and cheap swindles, but often overlook the crimes of their own members. The forces that infringe on the lower class are similarly in conflict. Social disorganization affects the two classes in similar ways.

The factor or process that is suggested here hypothetically as the explanation of both upper-class and lower-class crime is that the criminal behavior is learned in direct and indirect association with persons who had practiced the same behavior previously and in relative isolation from those who opposed such behavior. In both classes a person begins his career free from criminality, learns something about the legal code that prohibits certain kinds of behavior, and learns in various groups that other kinds of behavior that conflict with the general code may be practiced. Through contact with these variant cultures he learns techniques, rationalizations, and the specific drives and motives necessary for the successful accomplishment of crimes.

If he is reared in the lower socioeconomic class, he learns the techniques, rationalizations, and drives used in petty larceny, burglary, and robbery; if he is reared in the upper socioeconomic class and is engaged in an occupation characteristic of that class, he learns techniques, rationalizations, and drives used in frauds and false pretenses. The process of acquiring criminal behavior is identical in the two situations, although the contents of the patterns which are transmitted in communities differ [8].

Psychological Factors

Psychological factors relate primarily to an individual psychological pathology, some forms of which are predisposed to criminal behavior. *Psychological factors involve the inner tensions and emotions, unresolved conflicts and unsatisfied needs of the individual that underlie antisocial behavior.* It should be noted that many of the factors described as productive of criminal and delinquent behavior also contribute psychological pathology. Personality disturbances can occur in any section of society, whereas sociological factors such as deteriorated neighborhoods are confined to identifiable areas. Occurrence of criminal behavior by an individual residing in an area not conducive to antisocial behavior frequently reflects personality disorders rather than the existence of a widespread criminal or delinquency culture. It should also be noted that the conditions of family life in underprivileged areas operate to increase the probability of psychological disorder among children. The end results, therefore, are that in criminal and delinquent areas individuals with personality disorders tend to be numerous and there is a ready arena of deviate culture in which to react in a negative manner. In less criminally oriented areas, however, psychological disturbance on the part of a few individuals may still be expressed through criminal or delinquent behavior, and they may even be able to recruit other individuals who might otherwise not show this behavior. Such relationships further illustrate the extreme complexities of the factors related to crime and delinquency.

Many psychologists and psychiatrists consider the criminal and the delinquent to be products of personality maladjustments. The socialization process is regarded as producing either healthy or unhealthy personalities, and criminal behavior is considered a correlate of the latter.

Psychiatrists have, on the whole, amended an earlier convention that the criminal or delinquent is essentially a psychotic person. Other schools of criminology, however, have not yet entirely ruled out psychosis as a factor related to crime and delinquency. They have concentrated their focus largely on one psychosis, namely, schizophrenia, which appears to be directly related to criminology; they also have devoted a great deal of attention to the relationship between the "psychopathic personality" and crime. If schizophrenia is the most frequent psychosis found among prisoners or delinquents in institutional facilities, it is also the most frequent in society. The rates of schizophrenic symptoms are higher, however, in the deteriorated sectors where criminal and delinquent behavior operates at a maximum.

Psychological research has contributed chiefly facts concerning deprivations in human needs, desires, and individual deviations in personality. *Sheldon and the late Eleanor Glueck,* noted authors and lecturers, concerned themselves with the personalities of delinquents and how they differed from those of nondelinquents.

The Gluecks ascertained that delinquents are more extroverted, vivacious, impulsive, and less self-controlled than the nondelinquents. They are less fearful of failure or defeat than the nondelinquents. Furthermore, the Gluecks found that delinquents are less concerned about meeting conventional expectations and are more ambivalent toward, or far less submissive to, authority. They are, as a group, more socially assertive. To a greater extent than the control group, they express feelings of not being recognized or appreciated [9].

The psychoanalytical approach traces behavior deviations to the repression of basic drives. Such repression is occasioned by the mores or demands of civilized life and produces a conflict between the superego or conscience and the basic drives such as sex and hunger. Another conflict is between desire for success and limited life opportunities. The source of these mental conflicts is unknown to the victim. He seeks release from conflicts either by some mental substitute such as daydreaming and other flights from reality, or by overcompensatory behavior, which may be delinquent or criminal. Thus delinquent and criminal behavior is seen as an unconscious effort to solve an emotional problem.

Sigmund Freud, the founder of psychoanalysis, felt that the central core of this approach (theory) involves the notion of basic mental conflicts due to certain incompatible elements of the personality with the unacceptable portions repressed into the unconscious and kept there by the "censor," a term used to describe the capacity to force unity and harmony into obvious and conscious personality by repressing the undesirable elements into the subconscious.

But the repressed ideas, impulses, or complexes continue to exist, even though put out of the conscious mind, and a considerable portion of ordinary mental activity consists of the "roundabout" ways in which the repressed elements of personality seek to evade or outwit the censor and achieve some sort of indirect expression. *The three basic elements of the personality that must be brought into balance are the id, the ego, and the superego.* Delinquent and criminal behavior, under this general theoretical orientation, is to be understood, simply and directly, as a substitute response—some form of symbolic release of repressed complexes. The conflict in the unconscious mind gives rise to feelings of guilt and anxiety with a consequent desire for punishment to remove the guilt feelings and restore a proper balance of good against evil. The delinquent or criminal acts in order to be apprehended and punished [10].

Psychologically oriented students of delinquency, on the other hand, tend to emphasize the personality attributes that distinguish delinquent from nondelinquent behavior.

Research studies found, for instance, that the average delinquent boy is more psychopathic manic than the average nondelinquent boy. Psychologists think the source of personality deviation among delinquents is lack of acceptance and affection for a child by his parents. The aforementioned psychological explanation advocates that feelings of insecurity, inadequacy, withdrawal, frustration, and rebellion develop in the child.

Physiological Factors

If crime was due to a sole physical factor, and that factor was a wart on the end of the nose, then it would be a simple matter to collect all criminals and delinquents with warts on the ends of their noses and remove them by surgery—thereby eliminating crime. *As we well know, however, the physical factors in criminal behavior are more subtle and complex than any other factor. In fact, there may be many who would question any physiological basis for antisocial behavior.* Most investigators feel that health and disease play a rather minor role, but let us briefly examine what we call physiological factors and attempt to ascertain their importance in understanding criminal and delinquent behavior.

Factors such as body build, intelligence, sex, race, general appearance, and the presence or absence of congenital defects are some of the physiological factors that may or may not have a direct relationship to criminality. In the past the validity of such factors was given impetus by numerous studies, especially genetic studies of family groups such as the "Jukes" by Dugdale and the "Kallikak" by Goddard, which showed that long lines of members of the same families committed crimes of all sorts and were dangerous social misfits. Out of these studies came the idea that defective heredity played a major role in criminal behavior. This particular belief continued until 1930 when further studies revealed that the most mentally retarded do not become criminals or delinquents and those who do become involved in deviate behavior are gullible and easily led. Furthermore, although feeble-mindedness has long been associated with criminal and delinquent behavior, the validity of such studies is weakened by the fact that the extent of feeble-mindedness in the noncriminal and delinquent population is not precisely known and the fact that a larger proportion of the more intelligent criminals elude the law. Although it is true that physiological factors may play a minor role in the overall picture of crime, some factors require closer scrutiny. What is the significance of the high percentage of abnormal electroencephalograms among those involved in criminal acts? How much do we really know of the birth of the criminal and/or delinquent and that all-important first 15 minutes of life? The picture is confused and until answers are found to these questions, and many others, there can be little hope that the student of criminality will be enlightened in the near future.

Cesare Lombroso (an Italian Army physician), sometimes referred to as the "Father of Criminology," in his writing, affirmed the atavistic origin of the born criminal and suggested a close relationship between crime, epilepsy, insanity, and degeneracy, as a whole—in other words, a type of man more primitive and savage than his civilized counterpart. He studied a series of 383 skulls of criminals and recorded the percentage frequency of a considerable number of forehead and other cranial features. Comparison with savage and prehistoric skulls led Lombroso to theorize the born criminal as a physical type characterizing primitive man and even animals [11].

Ernest Hooton's (Harvard anthropologist) research on the physiological aspects of criminal behavior led him to contend that criminals are organically inferior. Hooton concluded that crime resulted from the impact of environment on the low-grade human organism, therefore, it followed that the elimination of crime can be effected only by elimination of the physically, mentally, and morally unfit, or by their complete segregation in a socially aseptic environment [12]. He further concluded that: (a) Criminals are inferior to noncriminals in nearly all their bodily measurements; (b) physical inferiority is significant principally because it is associated with mental inferiority; (c) the basic cause of the inferiority is due to heredity and to situation or circumstance; (d) dark eyes and blue eyes are deficient in criminals, and blue-gray and mixed are in excess; (e) tattooing is more common among criminals than noncriminals; and (f) long and sloping foreheads, long, thin necks, and sloping shoulders are also in excess among criminals in comparison with noncriminals.

William H. Sheldon developed the technique of applying body type to individual delinquents. His three basic body types are: (a) The *endomorph*—having a predominance of visceral and fatty tissue; (b) the *mesomorph*—having a predominance of muscle, bone, and connective tissue; and, (c) the *ectomorph*—predominance of skin and nervous tissue.

According to Sheldon, each body type is characterized by specific traits of temperament and personality such as: (a) Endomorph—fat and characterized as a slow-moving individual who is warm and affectionate; (b) mesomorph—the muscular boy who is characterized by loud speech, laughter, and excessive vigorous discharge of physical energy; and (c) ectomorph—tall and lean type who appears to be a "bundle of nerves," continually displaying short, quick, jerky movements, and strained speech.

MULTIPLE CAUSATION: AN ECLECTIC APPROACH

In many penal institutions doctors, lawyers, editors, engineers, and public officials swing into line with fellow convicts when the bell rings for meals or lock-up time. But still crime marches on. Murder, robbery, assault, kidnapping, and the like continue to flourish in all parts of the world.

Mistakenly, the uninformed public believes that it has the solution to the paramount problem of crime and delinquency. "Stop gambling" was one of the earliest suggestions, and laws accordingly were passed prohibiting gambling in almost every state. "Close houses of prostitution and get rid of dope peddlers" were additional remedies offered by well-intentioned but ill-informed persons.

Equally convincing was the contention years ago, and even today, that if every child were given a fair chance to obtain an education and recreational facilities his criminal tendencies would be restrained and crime could be greatly diminished. In responding to such beliefs, the educational system has been overhauled and in some communities, improved and playgrounds have been established in most of the towns and cities of America, but still crime and delinquency spread alarmingly.

For every situation arising in connection with crime and delinquency which captures the attention of the public for the moment, ignorant persons mistakenly believe that they have the one and only answer to the perplexing problem [13].

Many criminologists have stopped trying to find a single theory that will explain crime and delinquency.

SUMMARY

This chapter explores some of the ideas, regarding crime and delinquency, which are misleading or incorrect, but which still negligently persist in the folklore surrounding delinquency. Although there may be an element of truth in some of the misconceptions they are open to serious challenge as absolute or categorical statements concerning the nature and sources of criminal and delinquent behavior. The main concern, here, is that such fallacies would prevent clear thinking when innovative programs are designed for the prevention and treatment of the adult and youthful offender. Misunderstandings discussed in this chapter are: Criminals are a separate type of people, criminals have no morals, crime has a single cause, and crime is prevented by strict penalties.

The latter part of this chapter discusses theoretical approaches to criminal behavior and as such, for teaching purposes, theories are classified in three brief general groups of categories or factors leading to crime: Sociological, psychological, and physiological.

Sociological factors, such as urbanization, population morality, divergence in values in life styles and in opportunities for socioeconomic advancement, family instability, are not in themselves necessarily the causes of crime, but they are contributory factors. Such characteristics, as pointed out in this chapter, provide the context within which patterns of antisocial behavior arise and are transmitted. This chapter points out also that the rates of deviant behavior are highest in the deteriorated areas of our largest cities. These are the areas in which the most recently arrived immigrants have settled. Also living in such areas are those who have drifted there because of failure to compete successfully for more desirable living space (because of lack of skills, disease, or other disability) and those who have located in those districts because of the desire for freedom from conventional restraints. These circumstances of life often are associated with unstable families and a high incidence of illegitimacy and desertion, leading to both marginal employment, with inadequate supervision for the needs of children, and the absence of a father figure with whom the child can identify and look for supervision, guidance, and affection. Naturally, the effect of the social problems contribute more than their share to crime and delinquency.

Psychological factors are discussed in this chapter and relate primarily to an individual psychological pathology, some forms of which are predisposed to criminal behavior. Psychological factors involve the inner tensions and emotions, unresolved conflicts, and unsatisfied needs of the individual that underlies their social behavior. Personality disturbances can occur in any section of society, whereas *sociological factors* such as deteriorated neighborhoods are confined to identifiable areas. This chapter also points out that the conditions of family life in underprivileged areas operates to increase the probability of *psychological* disorders among children. This chapter further points out that the end results, therefore, are that in criminal and delinquent areas individuals with personality disorders tend to be numerous and there is the ready arena of a deviant culture in which to react in a negative manner.

The final section of this chapter discusses *physiological factors* and discusses the importance of such physiological factors as body build, intelligence, sex, race, general appearance, and the presence or absence of congenital defects—these are some of the physiological factors that may or may not have a direct relationship to crime and delinquency. The validity of such factors are discussed, particularly the genetic studies of family groups such as the "Jukes" by Dugdale and the "Kallikak" by Goddard, which showed that long lines of members of the same families committed crimes of all sorts and were dangerous social misfits. The picture regarding physiological factors is confused and until answers are found to many questions, there can be little hope that the student of criminology will be enlightened in the near future. The rest of the chapter examines the futility of the efforts made so far by scholars and noted social scientists to predict delinquent behavior.

ANNOTATED REFERENCES

Barnes, H. E., and N. K. Peters, *New Horizons in Criminology,* 3rd ed., Prentice–Hall, Englewood Cliffs, N.J., 1959, pp. 74–116. This book is a classic and is mandatory reading for all students of police science—particularly the pages mentioned in which Barnes and Peters cover theories of human behavior and point out succinctly that crime or delinquent activities occur only when a peculiar combination of personal and social factors comes together with an ordinately unique physical structure of human being to create this specific kind of situation. In other words, the authors delve quite deeply into psychological, sociological, and physiological factors that affect criminal behavior.

Kavaraceus, W. C., and W. B. Miller, *Delinquent Behavior: Culture and the Individual,* National Education Association of the United States, Washington, D.C., 1959. Kavaraceus and Miller discuss the question of broken homes and their relationship to juvenile delinquency and point out that a broken home has a different connotation in the lower-class cultural pattern as compared to the middle-class family.

Sutherland, E. H. and D. R. Cressey, *Principles of Criminology,* 5th ed., Lippincott, Philadelphia, 1955. For a brief discussion of the theory of ''differential social organization'' discussed in this chapter under Theoretical Approaches to Crime and Delinquency, the student should consider Sutherland and Cressey's volume.

Taft, D. R., *Criminology,* 3rd ed., Macmillan, New York, 1956. For an excellent discussion of the anthropological approach and an introduction to criminology, Taft's volume is a classic.

Vollmer, A., *The Criminal,* Foundation Press, New York, 1949. Although first published in 1949, Vollmer's book provides a lucid analysis of the causes of crime and contains information useful for the practitioner as well as the academician.

Yablonski, L., *The Violent Gang,* Macmillan, New York, 1962. The author describes a violent gang by means of sociopsychological theory. Furthermore, he discusses the influences, and pathological personalities, thus exploring the area in more detail than was possible in this chapter.

NOTES

1. E. H. Stullken, ''Misconceptions About Delinquency,'' *Jour. Crim. Law, Crim., Pol. Sci.,* Vol. 46, No. 6, March–April 1956, pp. 833–842.

2. *Ibid.*

3. *Ibid.*

4. *Ibid.*

5. J. S. Roucek, and R. L. Warren, *Sociology, an Introduction,* Littlefield, Adams & Co., Ames, Iowa, 1956, pp. 130–31.

6. E. H. Sutherland, and D. R. Cressey, *Principles of Criminology,* 5th ed., p. 159.

7. *Ibid.*

8. W. C. Reckless, *The Crime Problem,* 2nd ed., Appleton–Century–Crofts, New York, 1955, pp. 224–25.

9. S. Glueck, and E. Glueck, *Unraveling Juvenile Delinquency,* Commonwealth Fund, New York, 1950, p. 102.

10. *Ibid.,* p. 119.

11. D. R. Taft, *Criminology,* 3rd ed., p. 79.

12. G. B. Vold, *Theoretical Criminology,* Oxford Press, New York, 1958, p. 59.

13. A. Vollmer, *The Criminal,* p. 18.

CHAPTER SIX

Legal Aspects of Law Enforcement

Having considered in the preceding chapter some of the theoretical aspects of criminal behavior, consideration is now turned to violations of criminal laws. As will be noted shortly, the violation of criminal law is by definition the violation of a respective state's penal code—a written law passed by the state's legislators—and a common law which, although lacking in legislative "cement," is through precedent just as binding. Perhaps a brief clarification of what will later be discussed as "criminal law" might prove useful:

There are actually two major divisions in American law: the *Common Law,* derived first from the Germanic regions and then from England, and the *Civil Law,* derived first from Roman influences and then from France. The Common Law system is a process of developing law "continuously" by reference to precedence, whereas Civil Law is based on specific codes that are written and "legislated." Put another way, Common Law seeks to remain "common" by using court rulings from similar cases in the past as a guide for current dispositions. Civil Law, on the other hand, concerns itself with precise interpretation of an appropriate, but legislated statute. A further distinction might be made in the "accusatorial" nature of Common Law, and the "inquisitional" nature of Civil Law. But technical distinctions between Common Law and Civil Law are no longer crucial, since American courts have come to function under a combination of both systems. In this combination there is what some consider excessive dependence on precedent and constitutionally dictated due process which tends to relate more to Common Law than to Civil Law. Nevertheless, American jurisprudence, particularly the Common Law, combines both law forms [1].

115

Both of these law forms, then, constitute what will be discussed in this chapter as criminal law—the legal aspects of law enforcement.

The primary responsibility of law enforcement is not "technical legalities" but the provision of personal safety and property security for those members of the society who conform to "the law." Yet there is a rather general expectation that policemen also "understand" laws to which there is conformity. After all, these are the very laws that policemen enforce. Police agencies respond to this expectation by requiring officers to know enough law to *recognize* crime. But rare is the police officer who claims extensive knowledge of the complex variety of statutes clogging judicial court calendars.

Of course it can be argued that policemen have little need for the working attorney's legal knowledge in order to enforce laws that are concerned primarily with immediate safety and security. The entangled courtroom nuances of civil, probate, corporate, appeal, and even some criminal law, are thought by many to fall outside the sphere of a peace officer's concern. But even if this viewpoint is adopted, it remains apparent that most law enforcement careers include courtroom testimony experience and, in some instances, civil court experience as well. Examination therefore is needed of the legalities that directly and indirectly involve policemen in a court process—the philosophical distinction made in Chapter Three between police and the court functions notwithstanding.

Technical distinctions between common law and civil law are no longer crucial, however, since American courts have come to function under a combination of the two systems. There is what some consider an excessive dependence on precedence and the constitutionally dictated due process which tends to relate more to common law than to civil law. American jurisprudence nonetheless combines both law forms.

THE LEGAL SYSTEM

Criminal Law

Although American courts function under a combined system that is possibly "weighted" toward common law, American police find themselves necessarily more concerned with the civil law or the codified statutes. Some of the codified statutes, known as *substantive* criminal law, are of particular concern to police because it is through substantive law that society prohibits homicide, rape, assault, robbery, and similar crimes against personal safety or property security.

The two major categories of *substantive* law violations concerning police are known as *felony* and *misdemeanor.* Although agreement exists that felonies are serious crimes and misdemeanors are less serious, the various state laws differ widely as to where the line is drawn. More often than not, the penalty for the offense determines the classification—felonies punished by prison and misdemeanors punished by jail or fines.

As a matter of interest, the notion of using the punishment to determine whether the crime is a felony or a misdemeanor relates to the concept of criminal *liability.* This concept not only holds the offender criminally liable but also holds those who conspire with or abet the offender subject to judicial sanction. The phrase "accessory before or after the fact" stems from this concept.

But regardless of the manner in which felons or misdemeanants are distinguished, the apprehension of these offenders introduces police to the court process. In the case of misdemeanants (particularly traffic violators), the police introduction to court is often direct, whereas with felons, introduction is usually through the prosecution. In either event the court process becomes a frequent adjunct to police investigations and arrest responsibilities (Appendix A).

Criminal Court

Throughout the various state, county, and city jurisdictions, numerous methods are used to organize the court system. Gross confusion is the consequence of trying to explain *all* court organizations for *all* jurisdictions. The organization of the criminal court, however, can be readily explained since it is consistently divided into three parts: The *lower courts* (also known as police, magistrate, or inferior courts), the *trial courts* (also known as superior courts), and the *appellate courts* (also known as appeal courts) [2].

The lower courts set certain bails, hear preliminary cases, and deal with misdemeanors. These responsibilities will be discussed as the chapter progresses. Lower courts are presided over by judges, magistrates, justices of the peace, police justices, or even laymen. More often than not, the presiding judge performs the function of interrogator and advisor of both state and defense witnesses as well as the function of jury in determining the guilt or innocence of the accused. The lower court's function of hearing preliminary matters is of considerable importance as will be seen in the discussion of the criminal court process.

The trial courts frequently hold jurisdiction over both felony and misdemeanor offenses but in practice tend to deal primarily with felonies.

The appellate courts serve to review possible legal errors made by lower courts or trial courts. Court verdicts that are appealed through the appellate courts customarily involve extremely technical interpretations of legalities rather than appeals for clemency or mercy as such.

Criminal Court Process

Since most criminal court actions, whether felony or misdemeanor, begin with police arrests with warrants [3], the subject of *arrest* is particularly important and is reviewed in depth in Chapter Fifteen. Arrest, however, is merely one segment of a somewhat involved sequence that makes up the criminal court process.

The criminal court process is made up of various combinations of some or all of thirteen steps. These variously combined steps are:

1. Offense.
2. Report.
3. Investigation.
4. Warrant, usually via a written complaint.
5. Arrest.
6. Charge (booking and/or prosecution).
7. Indictment or information.
8. Arraignment and plea.
9. Bail.
10. Preliminary examination.
11. Trial, both prosecution and defense.
12. Verdict of either jury or judge.
13. Sentence or disposition.

Police involvement in the various parts of the criminal court process is direct in some instances, indirect in others, and unrelated in *verdict* and *sentence*. In most instances, the *offense* is reported to police who in turn *investigate* with or without a *warrant* (depending on circumstances) and make an *arrest*. The suspected offender is booked under a *charge* that may or may not be the charge for which he is prosecuted. Police provide the prosecutor with information reported or developed through the investigation but then are not involved in the ensuing *arraignment* and *plea* (except perhaps to provide prisoner security). Police also generally are removed from the process of *indictment* or information—indictments coming from secret grand jury hearings and information being sworn to a prosecutor [4]. "Sworn informa-tion" to the prosecutor is exactly what the term implies—information about an alleged crime that has been sworn to be true. The *grand jury* differs from the petit jury in both its secret proceedings and its function. *Petit juries* are composed of "ordinary veniremen" drawn from the community to serve as jurors in court cases. Grand juries usually are composed of "leading citizens" and they hear matters pertaining to virtually every segment of the community. The secrecy of the grand jury hearings tends to permit preparation of criminal prosecutions without "tipping the prosecutor's hand."

But whether indicted by secret grand jury hearing or brought to court on prosecutor information, the resulting criminal trial is for all intents and purposes the same as the trial following the police arrest without warrant.

Returning to the situation that is initiated by arrest without warrant, there is an additional step of the arraignment and plea (plea of either "guilty" or "not guilty"). This is the *preliminary examination* for alleged felonies and is actually optional to the accused. A jury trial is also optional in many states. That is, a person accused of a felony may choose to waive the preliminary examination and enter a plea in the lower arraigning court just as in the case of a misdemeanor. In some states the right to a jury trial may also be waived. But since the preliminary examination of alleged felonies is for the purpose of determining whether there is sufficient evidence to "bind the defendant over for trial" (i.e., a *prima facie* case), waiving this step of the criminal court process is as significant as waiving the trial by jury.

Although these steps do not customarily involve police, the ensuing steps in the criminal court process often become increasingly relevant to law enforcement. Indeed, many criminal trials, once undertaken, whether on the "booking charge" or a "reduced plea" to the prosecutor, frequently reach final disposition as a result of police testimony.

Courtroom Testimony

The very nature of law enforcement virtually assures the need for police to be called not only as witnesses, but in many instances as "star witnesses." For this reason, it becomes necessary for police to understand the nature of courtroom testimony.

Truth, as called for by the court, is the object of the trial. Attorneys are officers of the court and as such are charged with the responsibility of seeking the truth in much the same way that police are charged with keeping the peace. There are many complicated rules that govern evidence and testimony, but each rule exists for the purpose of developing truth as called for by the court. The use of these rules, however, frequently gives the impression that witnesses are being tripped up or forced to contradict themselves. But regardless of how the questions are phrased, the witness responding to cross-examination with the truth has little cause for anxiety. "Clever questions" pose relatively little threat—particularly in view of the judge's responsibility to protect the witness from the "have-you-stopped-beating-your-wife" variety of questions.

The truth, however, often incorporates far more than the question calls for—or for that matter far more than the court requires. This being the case, the witness is expected to define truth as being honest in specific answers to equally specific questions. The judge may allow a question to be asked because it does not call for answers that violates rules of evidence. The witness who gives an answer containing more information than called for may then prejudice a jury or even force the removal from evidence the acceptable segments of testimony. This is possible even when the total response including the "excessive" is all completely true. This embarrassment, like most courtroom embarrassments, occurs primarily when uncalled-for information is volunteered by witnesses forgetting that the judge and the attorneys are trying the case—not the witnesses.

Questions stress facts rather than opinions, and opinions will be acceptable only when the judge specifically allows. Chances are that the witnesses have been thoroughly "briefed" by the attorney in advance, thus making preparation possible.

Preparation for testimony is usually not difficult but it is always important. Fellow police officers are entitled to the good impression afforded law enforcement by the well-prepared and well-groomed police witness.

Once an officer is aware that he will appear in court, good preparations require a careful review of notes and records relating to the case on trial. The majority of facts to which police testify are in police reports or notes. Although reference to these sources is acceptable during testimony, a better impression is made when "first-hand" responses are forthcoming. Some police confer with the prosecutor immediately prior to the court date in order to ensure sharp, concise, and straightforward testimony that inspires the court's confidence.

The confident (not cocky) police witness is less likely to be subjected to prolonged or confusing cross-examination and is better able to deal with this eventuality if so subjected.

Personal appearance is another important part of preparation. Whether in uniform or civilian attire, clean, neat, and conservative clothing makes a favorable impression—as, of course, does well-trimmed hair and a clean-shaven face. Erect posture contributes further to the favorable impression.

Personal conduct and demeanor becomes even more important in the court than "on the job," if that is possible. There are clear implications for an officer of the law to come to a court of law carrying a newspaper to read while he waits to testify or causes disturbances or in any other manner reflects disrespect for the dignity of the court. Registering surprise and disbelief at the testimony of other witnesses along with "natural" but unprofessional mannerisms do little to assure the court that police are as objective as possible.

Preparation may even entail rehearsing anticipated responses to ensure concise testimony. Deliberate effort to appear poised and impartial helps to remove the feeling that police are anxious to seek convictions no matter what. A part of such poise is an unemotional but audibly clear voice delivering responsively concise answers. A few examples of responsively concise answers to an attorney's questions may prove helpful.

Attorney:	What was your conversation with the defendant after the fight?
Poor Response:	We all decided that the defendant started it and I still think he did no matter what he says.
Good Response:	I told the defendant that several witnesses stated that he started the fight.
Attorney:	What were your observations when you arrived at the scene of the disturbance?
Poor Response:	The defendant was so drunk he was acting mean but he's probably mean when he is sober.
Good Response:	I observed the defendant stagger and I detected alcohol on his breath. I also observed him attempting to strike the reporting party twice.
Attorney:	How was the victim dressed?
Poor Response:	She was practically naked.
Good Response:	She was attired in a half-slip, a bra, no outer garments, only one stocking and one shoe.
Attorney:	How were the victim and the defendant getting along when you arrived?
Poor Response:	They were having a lot of fun.
Good Response:	They were mutually embracing each other.

Attorney:	Was the victim resisting the defendant's advances?
Poor Response:	No, she was asking for it because she liked it.
Good Response:	The victim appeared to be cooperating in the mutual embracing.
Attorney:	What was your response to the situation?
Poor Response:	I told the victim she wasn't fooling anyone with such an obviously phony story.
Good Response:	I advised both the victim and the defendant that the report would require further investigation.
Attorney:	Who struck the first blow?
Poor Response:	It must have been the defendant.
Good Response:	Both witnesses I interviewed stated that it was the defendant.

"Loaded" Questions

Attorney:	Are you an expert policeman?
Poor Response:	I solved this case didn't I?
Good Response:	Police deal with people's behavior and I believe there cannot be expertise on anything as unpredictable as human behavior—but there are various degrees of ignorance to which my experience relates.
Attorney:	You seem to want the court to believe you have a perfect memory. What color socks do you have on?
Poor Response:	What's that got to do with the case?
Good Response:	(Inform attorney as to color of socks—do not become flippant and state "Which Foot?")

Fortunately, "loaded" questions are the exception rather than the rule. Notice, however, that the truth as called for by the questions continues to serve its function even when cross-examination takes this regrettable turn. In any event, the judge controls the cross-examinations sufficiently to permit the witness to retain dignity. "Loaded" questions based on hearsay (i.e., information not of the witnesses' own knowledge) might place the witness in the vulnerable position of being unable to rely on *truth*. But here, too, the witness is protected by the rules of evidence that preclude this unfair tactic by precluding the use of hearsay evidence.

There then is little, if any, reason for the police officer to lose his confidence or composure on the witness stand in criminal court if *adequate preparation has been made.*

Civil Liability

This chapter began with an assertion that police are required to have a thorough understanding of law in order to recognize crime when they see it. Crime in this context is the violation of statute and little more. There are, however, further legal implications of crime. Although these implications deal with the court process rather than law enforcement, they nevertheless relate to the police judgment on arrest.

The concept of *mens rea* is a fundamental principle of Anglo-American law. Simply stated, *mens rea* means that for an illegal *act* to be a crime, the actor must have *intent* to commit crime. Of course, criminal negligence laws also define an act as including a failure to perform a legally required duty. But the significant point is that intent theoretically is required to define an illegal act as a crime. Of course, the intent of the person is technically beyond the scope of police observing an illegal act. But it remains relative to police judgmental factors in "marginal arrests."

Proving the "intent segment" of *mens rea* is not as crucial in civil courts because, unlike criminal courts, the civil court deals with contracts, marriages, probate, and similar matters. Civil courts seek to return witnesses to *status quo ante,* or to remedy damages done. "The state" or "the people" are not involved in civil court cases. It is rather a matter of a *plaintiff* (suer) versus a civil defendant (sued). Punishing the responsible party then is not a goal of the civil court. Civil law, however, allows for punitive damages in some cases of civil *torts. A civil tort is a harm done to one's person, property, or reputation by another.* Suffering this harm entitles a suit or tort to recover "damages" from the offending party. But the concept of "punitive damages" permits the civil tort to serve much the same function as the criminal trial—at least insofar as the party losing such a suit is concerned.

The matter is complicated further by certain illegal acts becoming vulnerable to civil tort because a criminal court defined the act as being "intended"—intent being the necessary requisite to make an illegal act a crime. Put another way, being convicted of assault in the criminal court (which presumably combines the assaulting act with an assaulting intent) carries whatever criminal penalty is imposed. The conviction itself then may well be the basis for the "victim" to sue the convicted (even if in jail) for "damages." This suit is filed, of course, in an entirely different court (a *civil* court) but uses the criminal court process as its basis. And the same principal holds true for stolen or damaged property. Criminal conviction of the theft could serve as the basis for civil suit to recover losses or for "damages." In some jurisdictions, a "victim" can sign a criminal complaint seeking the arrest and the prosecution of someone and that same day file a suit against the same person for "damages" in precisely the same act.

Such matters occur frequently, but more important, they frequently involve police personnel. In seeking to persuade the civil court jury, attorneys for the *plaintiff* (suing) and occasionally for the civil *defendant* (the sued) subpoena arresting officers as witnesses. Although this is less true when an actual criminal conviction serves as evidence of "civil guilt," police nevertheless remain subject to almost constant civil court appearance in cases involving both courts. Police judgment in arrest becomes increasingly significant.

Arrest

The subject of *arrest* will be discussed in detail in Chapter Fifteen. But a few of the legal implications of arrest and "false arrest" might clarify the question of civil liability.

With certain variations in different states, arrest laws are more or less uniform. In essence, a police officer, or a private citizen for that matter, is empowered to make an arrest when a misdemeanor has been committed *in his presence.* Many feel that this power should be extended to include that of arresting persons the officer *had reason to believe* committed a *misdemeanor.* Crimes classified as *felonies* customarily justify arrest on the basis of *reasonable cause.*

The question of what or "how much" cause is reasonable as a basis for arrest is crucial to law enforcement. For arrest, especially wrongful arrest, with its terrible potential to require great force and even lethal force, is never to be considered "routine"—*never* because of the officer's safety, *never* because of the humane principles involved, and *never* for reasons of civil liability.

But the implications of "reasonable causes" for arrests go even beyond these considerations.

When the American Constitution was created, it was created by men embittered by the indiscriminate use of English colonial practices. These practices included using the "general warrant" that virtually permitted unrestricted arrest or "search and seizure" [5]. As a corrective method, the Constitution's architects sought to set forth a requirement that an arrest could only be made for "probable cause." This concept was designed to protect the citizen and also the police: "If the officer acts with probable cause he is protected even though it turns out that the citizen is innocent." (Supreme Court, *Henry v. United States,* 1959.)

But what if the officer did not act with "probable cause"? The very process of empowering arrest for crimes not committed in the officer's presence tends to complicate the issue of probable cause. With the vast variations from one jurisdiction to another, however, little can be done to afford a precise definition of all causes nor for that matter a definition of which causes are probable or reasonable.

The subject nevertheless remains valid for local law enforcement examination if for no other reason than becoming aware of the department's liabilities, or indeed the arresting officer's *personal* liability, in "false arrest" damage suits in the civil courts. The question of liability insurance that covers "false arrest" is customarily a departmental policy matter dictated mainly by the laws of the particular state. But personal or departmental liability should be clearly understood by all personnel empowered to make arrests without warrants.

POSTING BAIL AND BOND

The matter of bail or bond is a subject thought by many to be removed from police interest. To the extent that police ordinarily are not directly involved in the bail or bond segment of the criminal court process, there would appear to be some justification for this implied indifference. The fact is, however, that it is the policeman's judgment in "marginal court cases" that often determines the "booking charge." And it is this charge that usually determines the amount of the bail and indeed in some jurisdictions whether or not bail is possible. Further, the arresting officer frequently is called upon to provide answers regarding bail. The legal implications of a bail appear appropriate for brief discussion.

Bail in most jurisdictions is security for a "promise to appear" later. The bail process is posting an amount of money, or arranging for a bond for an amount of money, which is automatically forfeited if the promised appearance is not made. Bail can be granted for an accused person at any stage of the criminal court process after arrest through trial and even pending appeal of conviction in certain jurisdictions [6]. Most states exclude only capital offenses in the granting of bail.

Bail has been a controversial subject for some time. The March 19, 1948, issue of the *New York Times* carried a feature noting that the Kings County

Grand Jury had given six indictments on over ninety counts of abuses by bail bondsmen and their "runners" ("bondsmen" professionally "put up" a bond to "cover bail" for a fee paid by the accused). The abuses for which these bondsmen were indicted generally related to the excessive fees charged the accused. And the significance of bondsmen charging exorbitant fees tends to grow somewhat in view of the high percentage of accused persons requiring bondsmen because of their financial inability to otherwise raise bail money.

Critics of bail contend that bondsmen select only clients who have been charged with minor crimes and are unlikely to "flee" because more serious offenses create a greater risk of forfeiting the bond by "nonappearance." The critics further contend that the "bondable low risks" are the very persons who could be released "on their own recognizance" (i.e., a judicial discretionary alternative to bail) without financial surety of later appearance. Such an arrangement is claimed to afford financial savings not only for the accused but also to the state in not having to maintain custody pending bond arrangements.

The issues are far from resolved in most jurisdictions. But even without direct involvement, police continue to retain legitimate interest in the subject of bail.

SUMMARY

Against the background of the role of law enforcement, the scope of the crime problem and the philosophy of enforcement, this chapter presents the law as providing personal safety and property security to the community, in which police are not necessarily concerned with legal technicalities. Nevertheless, police generally are expected to understand enough law to *recognize* crime. For this reason, some understanding is needed of the legal system in general.

American law is actually a combination of *common law* and *civil law.* Common law is derived from England as an "accusatorial" system and remains "common" by using as guidelines the precedence of earlier court rulings. Civil law is derived from France as an "inquisitional" system and is concerned with strict interpretation of appropriate statutes.

Police necessarily find themselves more concerned with laws of a "civil nature" known as *substantive* criminal statute. This is true because it is the substantive law that forbids what have come to be known as *felonies* and *misdemeanors.*

Apprehending felons and misdemeanants brings police into contact with the criminal court, which is divided into *lower courts, trial courts,* and *appellate courts.* Because contact with the criminal court process is a necessary adjunct to police activity, the process itself is presented as significant. The criminal court process includes various combinations of some or all thirteen steps that depend on specific circumstances. The police involvement is direct in some instances, indirect in others, and nonexistent in still others.

Through indictment and information, alternatives to police initiative in bringing offenses to trial are created by the *grand jury* or *prosecutor.* .

Police testimony is important to the criminal court trial, and methods of attaining maximum effect of police testimony is worthy of police concern. Such methods include conscientious preparation for testimony, strict adherence to *truth* as called for in court, good appearance and demeanor, and confidence. Civil liability is also important to police because of the relationship of civil *torts* to arrest and criminal court conviction. "False arrest" is also a primary concern in terms of "probable or reasonable cause" to arrest without warrant. Of less direct concern but nonetheless important is the concept of *mens rea* which requires both an illegal *act* and an *intent* in order for crime to exist.

A final consideration in terms of legal aspects of law enforcement is the consideration of bail as a method assuring later appearance of accused persons who have been arrested. Bail as a concept is somewhat controversial in terms of allegedly being more readily available to those most unlikely to "flee" than to persons charged with graver offenses. Allegedly exorbitant fees are also related to the controversy concerning bail.

ANNOTATED REFERENCES

Cahn, E. (ed.), "Criminal Guilt," *Social Meaning of Legal Concepts,* Vol. 2, New York Univ. Press, New York, 1950. A clear statement regarding the isolated subject of legally defined guilt.

Eldefonso, E., A. Coffey, and J. Sullivan, *Police and The Criminal Law,* Goodyear, Pacific Palisades, Ca., 1972. Detailed elaboration of all significant legal variables in law enforcement.

Esselstyn, T. C., "The Social Role of a County Sheriff," *Jour. Crim. Law, Crim.,*

Pol. Sci., Vol. 44, July–Aug. 1953, pp. 177–85. A definitive commentary on social roles within legal contexts.

Hart, H., "The Aims of the Criminal Law," *Law and Contemporary Problems,* Vol. 23, Summer 1958, pp. 401–42. A good discussion of societal restrictions on behavior.

Tappan, P. W., *Crime, Justice and Correction,* McGraw–Hill, New York, 1960. Chapters 10–13 orient enforcement of law in the legally defined judicial process.

NOTES

1. E. Eldefonso, A. Coffey, and J. Sullivan, *Police and the Criminal Law,* p. 6.

2. P. W. Tappan, *Crime, Justice and Correction,* pp. 357–59.

3. *Ibid.,* p. 329.

4. Special Analysis, *Crime and Law Enforcement,* College Debate Series No. 16, The American Enterprise Institute for Public Policy Research, Oct. 6, 1965, p. 5.

5. Special Analysis, *op. cit.,* p. 95.

6. Tappan, *op. cit.,* p. 335.

PART TWO

Career Opportunities and Technical Aspects of Law Enforcement: Procedures and Problems

CHAPTER SEVEN

Careers in Law Enforcement

The impact of crime in America today is both reality and a state of mind, according to a prominent news media. The aforementioned source writes [1]:

... Few citizens actually die of fear, but its [crime's] chilling effects have become a grim part of daily life for millions in and around the nation's cities. While some statistics suggest that the crime itself may actually be leveling off, the fear of crime seems to be escalating into a fortress mentality that alters the way people see themselves and the way they live their lives. Its symptoms are terribly familiar: four locks on an apartment door, the evening bridge game abandoned (or played before sunset), all the cabs and buses that no longer make change, the armed guard inside a junior high school—and for nearly everyone, a perpetual feeling of vulnerability.

Although law enforcement agencies throughout the United States are concerned primarily with prevention of crime and the apprehension of criminals, their resources are dissipated among a large variety of functions, from enforcing traffic laws to handling dogbite complaints. Police agencies are called upon to deal with the petty offender, the juvenile offender, the destitute, and the mentally ill. The needs that compete for the services of police agencies are numerous and it is within this complex that the police forces confront

133

the problem of crime. As long as there are people with their concomitant problems, there will be a need for a *professional* police force.

Nothing is more challenging than being a policeman in a free society. For one thing, the police officer's immediate and singular duty requires him to keep the peace and insure the domestic tranquility. To accomplish this awesome task, his daily decisions deal with human life and liberty—decisions which by circumstance are often instantaneous.

The Constitution of the United States guarantees as much individual free-dom as human reason and the public safety will allow. To uphold that elusive ideal, the policeman is required to mediate family disputes that a trained psychologist would find inexplicable, dismantle bombs assembled for lethal destruction, cool the emotions of angry young students, and without fear or favor, judiciously enforce a multiplicity of laws. The job demands a person of uncommon skill; it requires a personality tempered by restraint, under-standing, and character—qualities which often elude the angry critics of law enforcement.

IS THERE A NEED FOR POLICE PERSONNEL?

There is currently, throughout the nation, a critical need for qualified young men and women in the various fields of law enforcement. This is especially true in the larger cities in the nation [2]:

> . . . Cities around the nation are increasing the effective size of their uniformed forces through hiring, scheduling changes and systematic introduction of civilian workers who free desk-bound cops for duty in the streets.

According to the President's Commission on Law Enforcement and Ad-ministration of Justice, approximately two-thirds of the police departments are below their authorized personnel strength. On a national average, the Commission's report states that cities are 10% below strength. This is not due principally to a shortage of police candidates but to a shortage of successful ones. Between 1966 and 1971 success rates on entry examina-tions decreased from 30 to 22% on a national average. The Los Angeles Police Department, which has set high standards and maintains them rig-orously, accepted a large number of applicants in 1971. A total of 12,330 police applicants were tested for those qualities during 1971: of that, less than 8% satisfied the mental, physical, and character requirements that determine eligibility for appointment as a Los Angeles police officer. Only 940 recruits entered the Police Academy, but after 5 months of strenuous training and a 1 year probationary period, the exacting process of selection had eliminated approximately 250 more men. At the same time that applicants' success rates are declining, retirement rates are threatening to rise. This is chiefly because the most rapid modern increase in the size of police departments occurred just after the end of the Second World War, and 20 years is the average—though by no means universal—period of service that a police department requires of its officers before they become eligible for pensions. To cite Los Angeles again, in 1971 no less than 41% of the force were eligible for retirement. Taking into account the 5.4% rate at which officers have left the service for all reasons (retirement, resignations, disability, dismissal, death) over the last 5 years, the present authorized strength of the nation's departments, and the fact that each year the authorized strength rises by 3%, it is calculated that bringing departments up to authorized strength in the 1970's will take 50,000 new policemen.

Several factors account for the difficulties encountered in recruiting candidates to fill the several thousand vacant positions in law enforcement agencies through the nation. Some of these factors are: Rapid population growth, higher police recruitment standards [3], increase in crime, and shorter term retirement systems for police work. There are no indications that recruitment problems will diminish in the near future—quite the contrary is expected; the problem of the recruitment of police personnel will continue to increase.

Emphasis on Education and Training

Crime, like a widely swinging pendulum, rampant and unrestrained, at long last is starting to feel the steadying grasp of orderly control (nonviolent crimes, according to FBI statistics, has shown a decrease in 1973). The blatant threat to communities has been reduced to a challenge. That challenge, however, is nonetheless intolerable. Police agencies continue to meet it with maximum effort and unswerving determination.

Yet according to crime statistics the ugly fact remains—the complexion of lawlessness has undergone a radical and chilling change. Violent crime (i.e. assaults, murder, robbery, forceable rape, to name the most serious) has, according to FBI statistics, shown a significant increase. For some, arson and bombing have become the means to an undefined end, especially for those who are contemptuous of society and bent upon a wanton and senseless destruction of "the Establishment."

FIGURE 7.1. *Police cadets, a rapidly expanding program throughout the country in modern and progressive police agencies, fulfill important duties and assignments and gain practical police experience in local enforcement agencies prior to entering the police profession on a full-time basis. The cadet shown above mans the communications console. Courtesy Police Department, San Diego, Ca.*

But as the face of crime assumes a new identity, so do the staggering burdens borne by the officer in the field. An endless pattern of unsought responsibilities dictated by caprice and circumstance has been thrust upon him for instantaneous solution. No longer is his high antagonist solely the known or suspected criminal. To his dismay, he is all too frequently confronted by the hostile citizen who openly vents his emotions with weapons or abusive language. In this turmoil of change, the man in uniform has become a double target.

A policeman's capacity to perform under these most trying conditions rests almost entirely upon the depth of professional training which he receives— training which 5 years ago would have been labeled irrelevant and unneces- sary. Today, this training is an absolute necessity if the police officer is to fulfill his sworn obligations to the community and the Department—to mention nothing of preserving his own life.

Law enforcement today is not the same as it was even a decade ago. The modern police profession emphasizes training and education. Many new police-science educational institutions and in-service training programs have been developed during the past few years. As of January 1972, the United States had more than 300 separate institutions that offered degree programs or basic training courses. California led the nation with 96 such institutions.

Even with the large number of education and training facilities available, the demand for qualified applicants still outpaces the supply. This is primarily because a large number of agencies now select only applicants who have had *some college training.* Numerous agencies require the applicant to possess at least an associate of arts degree as an employment requirement.

The need for persons of high intelligence and maturity who can develop the ability to apply the scientific and human-relations techniques now em- ployed in crime detection and prevention is unprecedented in the history of law enforcement. Since the police field now offers intellectual challenges on the level with other scientific and professional pursuits, one of the officer's most important weapons is knowledge about human relations and scientific methods of criminal detection. A recruit can no longer be hired and immedi- ately sent into the field without the proper training. With the national increase in college attendance and the upgrading of many levels of employment, the police service cannot afford to satisfy itself with youths who are below the average level of education. Public service makes strong demands upon one's values and self-discipline and these by-products of higher education are becoming imperative for a law enforcement officer's performance as a true professional.

Therefore the emphasis in law enforcement is on *training* and *education.* Studies have shown that the modern law enforcement officer is better trained and educated than at any other time in history. The field of law enforcement is now attempting to attract young persons of high caliber, many of them graduates of 2 and 4 year colleges. As a result of the upgrading in law enforcement personnel, members of the various agencies throughout the United States approach their work with professional attitudes. Education and training is imperative in order to deal properly with people and to handle the various kinds of police incidents. The range of modern police techniques is so broad that academic education is only one step in the right direction [4].

> . . . There is fancy new equipment . . . Denver, New York and Washington, D.C., among others, are experimenting with computers to analyze city crime patterns and predict where extra forces should be assigned. The Atlanta police have discovered that helicopters equipped with two million-watt searchlights can cut nighttime burglaries by 30 percent in a defined area. Washington, too, has been using copters . . .

Further in-service training is necessary because of specialization in the areas of narcotics, juvenile work, polygraph work, administration, and records.

No longer is higher education viewed by the general society as a means for succeeding; it has now become insurance against being on the bottom. Statistics today reveal that more than 45% of the 18- to 21-year-olds in the United States are studying toward formal degrees. If this trend continues, at least 60% of the youngsters in this age category will be enrolled in college-level classes by 1980. A former Secretary of Labor, W. W. Wirtz, recently stated, "The machines now do most jobs that a high school graduate can do, so machines will get the jobs because they work for less than a living wage. A person today needs 14 years of education just to compete with the machine."

The emphasis on education is also stressed by the International Association of Chiefs of Police [5]:

> The gradual implementation of the Model Police Standards Council Act will encourage police organizations to look to the community college for competent youths who can measure up to the demands of public service careers.
>
> This Act, forward looking and positive, has been developed after several lengthy and penetrating discussions by the IACP's Councils on Education and Training. These councils were created as advisory groups under IACP's Ford Foundation grant to police education and training. The final product has emerged to give law enforcement a strong thrust forward into the professional world. Basically, it describes, for any state wishing to avail itself of such guidance, a model standards council and its duties, responsibilities, and obligations. While each state is granted the opportunity to inaugurate its own provisions at some future date—perhaps five years hence—the Act nonetheless is very positive in calling for two years

of higher education achievement upon entrance into further police employment. Further higher education, with appropriate incentives, is called for beyond the two-year level to the point where law enforcement will ultimately demand a Bachelor's Degree of its applicants. Such action again makes it very clear the key role played by the community college and its importance to future police progress and advancement.

It is quite apparent, then, that the educational qualifications for employment as a peace officer are as rigid as the physical and emotional qualifications. Therefore it is incumbent upon those desiring to enter the field of law enforcement to personally contact local, county, state, and federal police agencies—specifically the personnel officer—in order to ascertain the qualifications required for a particular agency. Only after consultation with representatives of the aforementioned agencies and a careful review of available literature (brochures, "handouts," bulletins, job announcements, etc.), should the prospective peace officer apply for a position for which he *qualifies.*

SELECTION FOR APPOINTMENT AND MINIMUM STANDARDS

Selection and training of peace officers are closely related functions. They work together in getting the job done. The first requirement is the definition of standards; what attributes, levels of achievement, degrees of competence, and so forth are required in the police officer? For example, there are certain physical attributes that are indispensable. No one would hire a blind man as a recruit. Similarly, the recruit should measure up to certain standards with respect to intelligence and other factors. The standards to be met are determined in part by the nature of the job and in part by the decision of the hiring authority. If candidates hired possessed all the knowledge and skill required, no further training would be necessary. The better qualified the recruits are, the easier it is to get them ready to do the job. Naturally, with less-qualified applicants, more training is necessary.

In order to regulate standards and establish uniformity in recruiting, the State of California, by legislative action in 1959, created the Peace Officers' Standards and Training (POST) Commission. Effective October 23, 1960, the POST Commission, under Section 1002 of its Rules and Regulations, established the following minimum standards for employment as a peace officer in California:

1. Citizen of the United States.
2. Minimum age of 18 years.
3. Fingerprinting of applicant for purposes of a record clearance.
4. Shall not have been convicted by any state or by the federal government of a crime, the punishment for which could have been imprisonment in a federal penitentiary or a state prison.
5. Good moral background as determined by a thorough background investigation.
6. Graduation from high school or passing of the General Education Development test indicating high-school graduating level, or a score on a written test of mental ability approved by the Commission (POST), and equivalent to that attained by the average high-school student.
7. Examination by a licensed physician and surgeon. Only those applicants who are found to be free from physical, emotional, or mental conditions that might adversely affect performance of his duty as a peace officer shall be eligible for appointment.
8. An oral interview shall be held by the hiring authority or his representative, or representatives, to determine such traits as the recruit's appearance, background, and ability to communicate.

It is emphasized by POST that these are *minimum standards.* Higher standards are recommended whenever the availability of qualified applicants meets the demand.

The standards that police departments typically require police candidates to meet fall under several headings. Every department has detailed and rigidly enforced *physical standards* such as:

1. *Medical history.* Each applicant must supply to the examining physician a statement of the applicant's medical history of past and present diseases, injuries, or operations.
2. *Vision and hearing.* The applicant must possess normal hearing and normal color vision. He must possess normal visual functions and visual acuity with not less than 20/40 vision in each eye without correction and corrected to 20/20 in the better eye and not less than 20/25 in the weaker eye.
3. *Teeth.* Freedom from excessive decay and infection.
4. *Varicosities.* A serious medical problem with varicose veins will eliminate a prospective police officer.
5. *Flat feet.* A severe case of flat feet may cause disqualification.
6. *Height.* Requirements are from 5 feet, 8 inches minimum to 6 feet, 6 inches maximum. (For policewomen: 5 feet, 3 inches minimum.) There are no height requirements in many positions allied to regular police work. This requirement, however, is undergoing rapid change; and in some jurisdictions do not exist.
7. *Weight.* Must be in proper proportion to height. (For policewomen, at least 115 pounds.)
8. *Complete physical examination.* Includes a chest x ray; ear, nose, throat, and nervous system examination, blood analysis, and urinalysis.

Good Moral Character

Many departments insist on prior residence in the community for a given length of time. Every department demands *good moral character* and some jurisdictions (particularly in California) require a *personal-history investigation.* The purpose of the personal-history investigation is to find examples of any character traits in the applicant's life which might prevent his becoming a successful peace officer. The results of the investigation are usually evaluated by the department head and/or hiring authority to determine the applicant's suitability.

The first step in the personal-history investigation is the completion by the applicant of a detailed personal-history statement upon which the investigation will be based. The investigation is strictly confidential and the last step will be an interview with the present employer following permission by the applicant. If the applicant resides in a distant community, a letter requesting that the local law enforcement agency conduct an investigation will be necessary.

Examples of some of the questions hoped to be answered in the investigation are:

1. Does he ever display a violent temper?
2. Does he drink when things go wrong?
3. Does he "go to pieces" when confronted by danger or a crisis?
4. Is there any evidence or indication of emotional instability?
5. Is he well adjusted and will he make a good police officer?
6. Does he possess high ethics and morale?
7. Is he intolerant or prejudiced against other races or religions?

These and other similar characteristics may be revealed only through the personal-history investigation. Names of spouse and close relatives will be checked through appropriate files to determine whether they have criminal records, are in prison, or may be in any status or position that may adversely affect the applicant's obligations as a peace officer.

The investigation will include a check of as many of the following *sources* as possible:

1. Military records from the service of the United States or jurisdictions therein, if applicable.
2. Documents, including driver's license, high-school diplomas, or other suitable record of graduation.
3. Birth or naturalization record to determine age and citizenship.
4. All local police files.

5. Police files in all cities in which the applicant has lived or worked.
6. State criminal records.
7. FBI records.
8. State department granting driver's license.
9. All schools attended.
10. References and relatives.
11. Present and past neighbors and landlords.
12. Fraternal and social organizations.
13. Credit records.
14. Any sources that previous contacts show to be important.

Because of the exhaustive personal-background investigation, it is not unusual for prospective police officers (a requirement in most police schools) to prepare a complete resume (including copies of as many of the documents as possible) in a neat packet folder, catalog, or other system to have available when seeking employment.

Psychological Testing

Some departments give *psychological tests* and some do not. When such examinations are required, they are designed, hopefully, to disqualify those applicants who are emotionally unstable. Potential risks are rarely, if ever, hired. Most of these personality tests are of the "self-report" type. Instead of the actual observation (although some marginal cases may be followed through by a staff psychiatrist) of the behavior of the applicant, these tests require that the applicant answer questions about his behavior and his feelings. The behavior being observed in such tests, then, is indirect behavior; the person reports on what he has done, what he would like to do, how he feels, and how he "would" feel given a certain situation. The reliability of such tests generally is good. These tests appear to "tap" persisting attitudes of behavior. Psychologists continue, however, to have unsettled arguments about the validity and usefulness of such tests [6].

Physical-Agility Tests

Physical-agility tests are given to every police applicant. In order to qualify for a position, the applicant must meet certain physical requirements. These agility tests include a series of physical exercises that ascertain the physical ability and coordination of the applicant.

Included in the physical-agility examination is an obstacle course to test the coordination, stamina, agility, and physical strength of the participant. The obstacle course *may* include hurdles, chin-ups, climbing over ground or through obstacles, use of ropes to swing across an open pit, and running a specific distance within a "set" time.

In order to qualify, the applicant must be in good physical condition. A passing score must be recorded in *all* events. In every police agency in the United States, such physical-agility tests are mandatory. Needless to say, those individuals contemplating a career in law enforcement should keep themselves in good physical condition.

Oral Board

After successfully passing the screening process (i.e., physical psychiatric, and written examinations) the applicant is confronted with the most important phase of the entrance examination—*the oral board.*

The oral board attempts to conduct a critical examination of the applicant's qualifications by carefully questioning the applicant to ascertain *his aptitude for the job: His intelligence, his moral character, his emotional stability, his social attitudes.* The consequences of putting on the street officers who, however highly educated, are prejudiced, slow-witted, hot-tempered, timid, or dishonest are too obvious to require detailed discussion. For these reasons, the oral board thoroughly screens candidates; the President's Commission on Crime also recommends [7]:

> Until reliable tests are devised for identifying and measuring the personal charac-teristics that contribute to good police work, intelligence tests, thorough back-ground investigations and personal interviews should be used by all departments as absolute minimum techniques to determine the moral character and the intel-lectual and emotional fitness of police candidates.

Research [8] in the area of selection procedures—oral boards, specifical-ly—reveals the *assets* and *liabilities* of those who actually failed. Review of these comments on rating sheets of men who passed oral board examinations shows the following *assets* which were remarked upon, and are assumed to reflect the oral board's ideas of personal characteristics that are relevant to job performance in the field of law enforcement:

> Good appearance, able to speak up, forceful, able to fit into discipline, capable of being trained, sincere, flexible, uses good English, energetic, mature, sustained interest in personal advancement, genuine interest in becoming a peace officer,

stability, wholesome, conscientious, good past experience in police work (if any), good educational background, well-adjusted.

What are the liabilities that the oral board felt were so significant that they merit a decision by the Board to fail the candidate? Here are the liabilities described:

Immature, psychopathic personality, highly opinionated, lying, great uncertainty about himself, failure to understand law enforcement, overprotected, no drive or energy, dull thinking, appearance not conducive to respect, buckles and freezes under pressure, daydreamer, lacks understanding of human nature, history of delinquency, inability to satisfactorily explain rap sheets, too many traffic violations, false statement to Board regarding arrests, false statement on application, rigid and too authoritarian, unsophisticated, homosexual and effeminate appearing.

What, in essence, are the personal traits the oral board is "looking for"? To be consistent in this discussion, the question could be answered only by citing three questions *all* members of oral boards ask themselves on each applicant:

1. What traits in the applicant might ultimately affect the public?
2. What traits in the applicant might ultimately affect his relationship with fellow officers?
3. What traits might cause a medical problem in the future?

In discussing the selection process and standards for employment, the authors have attempted to focus on the *reasons* for selective screening of police recruits and, conjointly, to make the prospective peace officer cognizant of the factors leading to successful and unsuccessful results.

Probationary Period

Police administrators do not feel, rightfully so, that the recruiting process is *over* once the applicant has passed through the *selection process* and is hired. There is still an important phase—the process of properly orienting the recruit. Before he ever goes to work, the recruit should be oriented so he will know enough to "stay out of trouble" in the field until he is trained to be a policeman. At the same time, speaking generally, the orientation process is "selling" him at the outset on the organization which he has just joined.

The recruiting process is still not completed. Now comes the process

FIGURE 7.2. *Courtesy of Police Department, Los Angeles, Ca.*

referred to as the *probationary period*. The probationary period is designed
to be a part of the recruiting process and it customarily ranges from 6 months
to 2 years.

The President's Commission on Law Enforcement and Administration of
Justice recommends that:

> Entering officers should serve probation periods of, preferably, 18 months and
> certainly no less than one year. During this period, the recruit should be system-
> atically observed and rated. Chief administrators should have the sole authority
> of dismissal during the probation period and should willingly exercise it against
> unsatisfactory officers [9].

The probationary period gives the hiring agency an opportunity to determine
with some accuracy whether the recruit is adaptable to the job. During this
period the recruit is very carefully trained and closely supervised. Depending
on the length of the probationary period, a supervisor's report is required
every 30–90 days evaluating the recruit's progress on the force.

The probationary period is designed to be part of the recruiting process.
This period, furthermore, is designed to afford the organization an opportunity
after the examinations (screening process) to evaluate the recruit while he

TABLE 7.1

Career path	Requirements	Pay step rates[a]					Highest annual rate in rank
		1	2	3	4	5	
POLICEMAN I—Recruit	High school graduate or equivalent.	889	938	990	1,046[b]	1,105[b]	13,259
POLICEMAN II—Radio Car Officer, Footbeat, Communications, Desk	18 months as Policeman I		990	1,046	1,105	1,166	13,990
POLICEMAN III—Crime Task Force, Divisional Vice, Intelligence and Training Officer, Instructor, Dispatcher, Investigator Trainee	18 months as Policeman I or II plus successful completion of Policeman III written and oral evaluation.		1,046	1,105	1,166	1,230	14,762
POLICEMAN III + 1—Crime Task Force Squad Leader, Accident Investigation Follow-up Investigator, Vice Coord. Sr. Lead officer	Same as Policeman III plus selection by Division Commander and approval by Bureau Chief.		1,105	1,166	1,230	1,298	15,576
INVESTIGATOR I—Specialized Detectives, Geographic Detectives, Administrative Vice, Administrative Narcotics, Intelligence	3 1/2 years as a Policeman I, II, III, or III + 1 and successful completion of Civil Service written and oral exam. (Substitution of college or prior experience for up to 1 year of the required experience.)		1,166	1,230	1,298	1,371	16,453
SERGEANT I—Uniformed Field Supervisor—Patrol/Traffic	Same as Investigator I			1,298	1,371	1,448	17,372
INVESTIGATOR II—Sr. Investigator. Narcotics, Juvenile, Administrative Vice, Bunco/Forgery, Robbery/Homicide	One year as Investigator I or Sergeant I and successful completion of Investigator II evaluation.			1,298	1,371	1,448	17,372
SERGEANT II—Instructor—Training Academy, Assistant Patrol Watch Commander, Captain's Adjutant, Labor Relations Investigator	One year as Sergeant I and successful completion of evaluation process.			1,371	1,448	1,528	18,332
INVESTIGATOR III—Investigator Expert, Supervisory Investigator	One year as an Investigator II and successful completion of evaluation process.			1,448	1,528	1,613	19,356

[a] An example of possible salary increases after a 6-month training period and annually thereafter. This chart does not reflect pay rates for the nine positions of Lieutenant I and above. [b] Applies only to advance step hiring. Source: Police Department, Los Angeles, Ca.

is actively engaged in his tasks. If, with constructive supervision, he is unable to adapt to his duties during the probationary period, then he may be dismissed summarily (without delay or benefit of any hearing).

In *summary* then, in the *selection for appointment* process, there is a need to determine the qualifications first in the recruiting process, age, education, physical condition, and so on. A continuous program of recruitment presupposes those basic qualifications. In a recruitment program, the steps are: *Applications, written examinations, agility tests, fingerprinting, oral appraisal boards, an estimate or an opinion of emotional stability, medical examination, and an investigation of personal history.* Even then, there is one more step—*the orientation process and probationary period.* Rating the recruit is a very important responsibility of the probationary period.

Police Salaries

Although salaries in law enforcement vary throughout the United States, in small cities the median annual pay for a patrolman is $5600, in large cities it is $6300. Typically, the maximum salary for nearly all positions is less than $1000 over the starting salary. On the other hand, a special agent of the Federal Bureau of Investigation begins at more than $9000 a year and, if he serves long enough, can reach, without promotion to supervisory position, $18,000. Although that salary scale is out of the question at the present time in most cities, especially small ones, the trend in the United States is definitely toward higher salaries. Furthermore, those cities unable to increase starting minimum salaries for policemen are raising the maximum salaries substantially so that police careers will offer long-term financial inducements (see Table 7.1).

The salaries of male and female law enforcement officers are equal in most jurisdictions.

Salaries in police work are based on two types—*base salary* and *additional salary increment.* A peace officer's base salary is his established pay according to his rank, length of time in rank, and job seniority. Additional pay relates to all money paid to an officer in addition to his base salary. Such pay revolves around *fringe benefits* in the form of medical care, sick leave, insurance, military leave, housing, compensatory time off, and retirement programs (see table 7.2).

Fringe benefits in certain areas are:

1. *Hazardous duty* increment (i.e., motorcycle duty differential pay, in some jurisdictions, may add up to $71.00 per month to the base salary).

2. *Marksmanship bonus* for those who qualify.
3. Assistance in the *tuition payments* for those officers enrolled in police-science programs or courses related to law enforcement.
4. Besides tuition fees, assistance also may be provided for the *purchasing of textbooks* for courses in which the officer may be enrolled.
5. *Uniform allowances* on a yearly basis for "plainclothes" as well as uniformed officers.

TABLE 7.2. *Example of Fringe Benefits*

Salary Bonuses	
Marksmanship	$ 2/mo. to $ 16/mo.
Motorcycle officer	115/mo. to 132/mo.
Helicopter pilot	381/mo. to 447/mo.
2 Years of college[a]	49/mo.
4 Years of college[a]	101/mo.
Prior police experience[a]	up to 216/mo.
Benefits	
Retirement	
40% of salary @ 20 years	
55% of salary @ 25 years	
70% of salary @ 30 years	
Life insurance available	
Medical insurance available	
Credit union available	
Organized sports program	
All uniforms and equipment furnished	
Additional education	
City paid tuition	
Graduate scholarships	
Work schedules adjusted	
Other	
8 days off per month	
11 holidays	
14 days vacation per year	
21 days vacation @ 10 years	
12 days sick leave (can accumulate up to 100 days)	
Paid overtime at time and one half	

[a]Available only to Policeman 1.
Source: Police Department, Los Angeles, Ca.

There are many areas of salary differential payments which are beyond the scope of this chapter. Each jurisdiction attempts to devise a salary differential plan according to their own organizational structure and department resources.

In order to be successful in recruiting and keeping veteran officers, law enforcement agencies accord top priority to consideration of fringe benefits and salary differentials. A young man entering the police service realizes he cannot amass great wealth, but he and his family are entitled to a scale of living that will provide him with the moderate advantages of a home and an opportunity to afford for his children a proper degree of social, recreational, and educational opportunities.

Advantages and Disadvantages of Law Enforcement as a Career

As in every profession, there are advantages and disadvantages. Before preparing himself for entering the field of law enforcement as a career, the prospective peace officer should give consideration to both the *advantages* and *disadvantages* of such work.

Advantages

For anyone considering a career in law enforcement, the advantages are numerous.

The Challenge

Certainly, no one will disagree that police work is one of the most challenging professions for those who possess the attributes for the job—initiative and a desire for personal involvement in promoting the welfare of the community, state, and nation. The authors doubt that there is a comparable vocation that affords every officer (ranking or otherwise) an opportunity for personal satisfaction, personal contribution, and a stimulating (certainly not boring) involvement.

Promotion

The opportunity for advancement through the ranks is one of the best "selling points" in law enforcement. The person who qualifies wants his chance. An advancement for the ambitious officer means higher rank, increased increment, additional responsibility, and increased prestige. Competition from "outside" the department is very limited because promotions usually are made from within the organization. Police executives throughout the United States are fine examples of men who have "gone up through the ranks" [10].

The careers of the late O. W. Wilson, U. E. Baughman, T. Bailey, J. P.

TABLE 7.3. *An Example of Possible Range of Promotion*

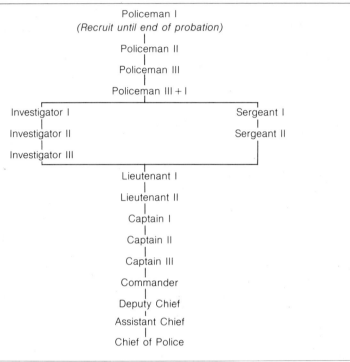

Source: Police Department, Los Angeles, Ca.

August, the late Chief William H. Parker, former Chief of the City of Los Angeles, and Stephen P. Kennedy, former Commissioner of Police of New York City, should prove one inescapable fact—those who are ambitious, resourceful, competitive, energetic, intelligent, and *motivated* can move up through the ranks in the police field (see Table 7.3).

Salaries

If salary is the only criterion by which a particular profession is evaluated, employment as a peace officer would not be considered. Nevertheless, starting salaries have shown a tremendous increase during the last 5 years. Police salaries, for the most part, compare with private industry; furthermore, police salaries compare quite favorably with those in many other vocations and professions which require more time and finances in preparing for the job. In some jurisdictions, salaries may top $800 per month; for instance, Palo Alto, California, Mountain View, California, and Oakland, California.

These communities are not considered large and the police agencies are rather small.

Employment in Local Communities

As previously discussed, the opportunities for employment with police agencies are extensive—qualified personnel are needed. More and more, the smaller communities are voicing their opinions in the area of improvements in police selectivity. Thus the result has been the energetic campaigning on the part of local law enforcement agencies to keep potential candidates in the community. Needless to say, those students enrolled in police-science programs in colleges throughout the nation can find excellent opportunities in a profession on the *local level*. The opportunities on the local level are unlimited for those young people who are just starting their professional training.

Pride

Personal pride gained from dedication to the service of justice is one of the greatest advantages of a law enforcement career. The entire space of this chapter would be necessary to sketch every case of skilled, courageous, and devoted police service like this one: Two officers in San Francisco recently courageously risked their lives and placed their "reputations on the line" by refusing to become involved in a gun fight with two obviously "hopped-up" drug addicts in a crowded pharmacy; they permitted themselves to be forced outside at gun point and the felons were apprehended by an alert detective team.

Such a close look at the job of a peace officer is often necessary to remind the careerist of an important fact: A man can be proud to wear the uniform of a police officer. Pride that has been earned is a healthy quality.

Disadvantages

Although the advantages for considering police work as a career outweigh the disadvantages, a close scrutiny of the negative side of police work must be presented.

Growing Disrespect for Police

Carrying out with proper efficiency and discretion the complicated law enforcement and community service tasks that the police are expected to perform is a formidable assignment under the best circumstances—that is, those in which the public sympathizes and cooperates with the police. These circumstances do exist to a considerable extent in most rural, small town, and suburban communities, and in many big city neighborhoods. The chief limitations on police work in those places are the talents and skills of police-men and police administrators, and the funds, equipment, and facilities avail-able to them. In city slums and ghettos, the very neighborhoods that need and want effective policing the most, the situation is quite different. There is much distrust of the police, especially in boys and young men, who are among the people the police deal with most often. It is common in those neighborhoods for citizens to fail to report crimes or refuse to cooperate on investigations. There is, in these communities, *apathy, hostility,* and *ignor-ance* on the part of the inhabitants. Often police are sneered at or insulted on the street. Sometimes they are violently assaulted. Indeed, everyday police encounters in such neighborhoods can set off riots, as many police depart-ments have learned.

This is the problem (Chapter Eighteen covers this special problem thor-oughly) that usually is referred to as "police-community relations." It is overwhelmingly a problem of the relations between the police and the minor-ity-group community, between the police and Negros, Puerto Ricans, and Mexican-Americans. It is as serious as any problem the police have today.

Anxiety and Tension

A policeman is subject to many strains. Hostility is bad enough, but it is often accompanied by overt aggression against the police. Every officer is aware that, so far as some people are concerned, he is disliked and perhaps even hated. He is feared by some and, as previously indicated, regarded with contempt by some. Worse still, he is considered fair game for physical attacks by a few. His job is often dangerous and, very frequently, thankless. The result is a state of anxiety and tension which naturally differs from one man to another and which rises and falls from time to time depending on the social climate. In peak periods fear is certainly not unknown. Fear is experienced by every intelligent officer.

Frustrations in Police Work

There are many frustrations in police work—at least things perceived as frustrating by the officers. "The juvenile court releases a boy caught by an officer after a dangerous high-speed chase." "An undeniably guilty criminal gets off scot-free because of some technicality in the law." "In civil disobedience cases, nonviolent lawbreakers must be picked up bodily and removed from the public streets." The aggravated apathy and lack of cooperation of the general public is a constant source of irritation. These and a thousand other frustrations combine to nag the officer every day.

The frustration is heightened for the police when the unenforceable law creates a new criminal problem that is more serious than the law was designed to solve—for example, broad segments of the population in the United States are undeterred by fear of prosecution and involvement in illegal betting is on an increase. Such unenforceable laws are covered thoroughly in the report by the President's Commission on Law Enforcement and Administration of Justice. Some excellent examples are cited.

Unpleasant Tasks

There is no disagreement that one of the most unpleasant aspects of law enforcement is that police work calls for continual direct contact with antisocial deviates and the suffering of human beings. The police officer must control himself and cannot permit his emotions to be expressed when he arrives at the scene of an auto accident and observes death, mutilation, and serious injury. There are many other horrors he must witness: The pitiful cry of parents when their child's body is recovered from a watery grave; the agonizing screams of a family burning to death in a holocaust; an incident of sexual assault on a 9-year-old girl; or the bruised face of a child severely beaten by his father. In carrying out the investigation of these cases, the first reaction on the part of the officer, naturally, is an emotional one. His profession and personal pride demand, however, that he maintain control of himself and of others, and that he respond with professional proficiency to assist the victim, ensure the safety of the citizen, and apprehend the guilty.

Employment Opportunities

Recent statistical information regarding employment opportunities in law enforcement indicates that it is one of the largest semiprofessional employment organizations in the United States. The law enforcement organizations in 1973 included 500,000 jobs in 40,000 separate jurisdictions on federal, state, and local levels of government (not including private agencies). *Some* of the *opportunities for employment* on the aforementioned levels are:

Federal

Bureau of Investigation	Internal Revenue Service
U.S. Marshals	(special agency)
Border Patrol	Bureau of Customs
Secret Service	Post Office Inspectors
Bureau of Narcotics	Coast Guard (Intelligence Division)
Department of Interior	Department of Defense

State

Highway Patrol
Bureau of Criminal
  Identification
  and Investigation
Narcotics Bureau
Alcoholic Beverage
  Control Bureau
Police

Private

Detective agencies
Security agencies providing
  services for:
Railroad (special agents)
Aerospace industries
Chain stores
Banks

Local

Sheriff
Coroner
District Attorney
Public Defender
Police

Private

Commercial airlines
Credit agencies
Hotels
Insurance companies
Manufacturing plants
Motion picture companies
Universities

At this time, law enforcement probably cannot claim to have reached professional status as an occupation. There is no denying, however, that it is fast approaching this ideal. During the last three decades, law enforcement achievements have been quite impressive. Such contributions by police agencies have generated new opportunities for service and an even greater need for higher standards and professional conduct [11].

The municipal police constitute by far the largest body of professional police in the United States. The urban area of the country, which includes places having over 25,000 population, embraces a total of about 70,000 people, who are protected by 135,000 policemen. Ninety thousand of these law enforcement officers work in cities over 250,000 population [12].

According to Gammage, author of *Your Future in Law Enforcement,* these large metropolitan areas have a ratio of approximately 2.5 police jobs per 1000 of population; furthermore, Gammage states that the ratio decreases in the smaller cities (25,000–250,000) to 1.67 jobs, and subsequently to a low of 1.5 jobs for every 1000 inhabitants.

Constables' offices, sheriffs' offices, prosecuting attorneys' offices, and county and parkway police employ about 66,000 police officers.

State police, state highway patrol, and state investigative agencies employ over 14,000. Today, state law enforcement agencies are among our best examples of progressive law enforcement. High standards of police administration are made possible by there being enough officers to handle the necessary tasks. Any of these state police, highway patrol, and investigative units maintained by state governments are worthy of consideration by persons seeking careers in law enforcement. In the number of jobs, California leads with over 3,500 in the department of the California Highway Patrol alone and an additional 1,000 or more in its state investigative and regulatory agencies. Pennsylvania, New York, and Michigan have state police forces of over 1,000.

Federal police consist of eight regular police agencies and a score of others with auxiliary police authority. Six of the regular police agencies—the Intelligence Unit, the Alcohol Tax Unit, the Division of Investigation and Patrol of the Bureau of Customs, the Secret Service, the Bureau of Narcotics, and the Inspection Service—are in the Treasury Department. The Federal Bureau of Investigation and the Immigration Border Patrol are in the Department of Justice. The entire federal police establishment totals over 25,000.

In particular, the Immigration and Naturalization Services, through the Border Patrol, offers splendid opportunities to intelligent and energetic young men who are interested in immigration law enforcement and who want to prepare themselves for positions of greater responsibility through on-the-job and Service-offered training. Recently, the Service has directed most of its recruiting efforts toward finding suitable college-trained personnel, and its three-month training program for recruits is one of the best in the federal service [13].

WOMEN IN POLICE WORK

Currently, there are more than 5000 women in the United States who are employed as policewomen. This is in addition to the more than 4500 women who are employed by the government in law enforcement and related fields such as: Correctional workers, social workers, immigration and customs inspectors.

Women have been utilized as police officers for many years—since 1905 to be exact, when Mrs. Lola Baldwin was appointed to do protective work with girls at the Lewis and Clark Centennial Exposition in Portland, Oregon.

Although the policewomen in most cases have completed their tasks satisfactorily, their assignments usually were exclusively in the jobs of matron,

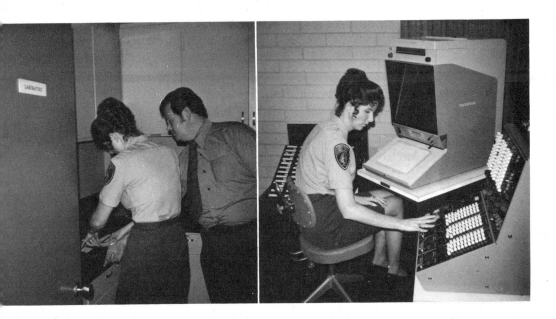

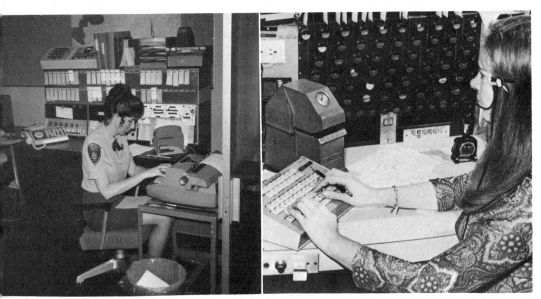

FIGURE 7.3. *Courtesy of Sgt. Frank Furtaw, Police Department, Campbell, Ca., and Police Department, Los Angeles, Ca.*

clerk, or social worker (employed by a police agency). During the last decade, however, the role and status of the policewoman has improved dramatically. They have been placed in positions commensurate with their training and education. Such improvement can only be attributed to the policewomen's hard work and careful attention to the quality of completed tasks. Increased emphasis on college training, perhaps, is the most significant factor in the policewoman's achievement of higher status in her profession.

The major contribution of the policewoman to law enforcement still remains, however, in "crime prevention" as a juvenile officer. In this capacity, police-women are active in cases in which women or children are involved either as victims or offenders. Primarily, policewomen deal with females, regardless of their age, and boys under the age of twelve. There are few cities in which policewomen attempt specific casework with the "predelinquent" child. Furthermore, they may have a definite duty to discover, evaluate, investigate, and rectify antisocial conditions and circumstances in individual cases. They are considered, however, to have an additional responsibility to encourage the schools, social agencies, and child-guidance clinics to undertake this responsibility where there is no adequate local program to promote its establishment.

The modern policewoman has the greatest potential value to law enforcement in preventing crime today. This is because she—even more than a policeman, no matter how well trained as a juvenile officer—has at hand the strong backing of the community groups which are essential if the problems involved in controlling or removing community "moral hazards" are to be met. Fortunately, earlier policewomen sold the value of this movement to all the greater national organizations of women well over 20 years ago.

Although it is recognized that women's value to law enforcement is primarily in the area of crime prevention (juvenile field), women as "undercover" agents have had a wide vogue in fiction and some small counterpart in reality. Their best future in the crime detection field of police work, however, may be largely as trained technicians in crime-detection laboratories. It is even possible that in the field of traffic control, which is essentially an engineering problem, women engineers can be of great help to the police. Most progressive police administrators also are finding that there is a great place for those women not specifically trained (colleges, universities, junior colleges, etc.) in the "functional" operations of a police department, that is, stenographic, clerical, records, communications, and radio, to mention a few.

As equal opportunity employers, police agencies could no more discriminate against an applicant on the basis of sex than it could on the basis of a person's racial, ethnic, or religious background. Therefore, employment opportunities in the police field for women will in all likelihood show a tremendous increase in the 1970's. Although not in great numbers as yet, it is not unusual to see women riding the streets in police cruisers, tagging speeders, arresting drunks, investigating burglaries in cities such as Peoria, Ann Arbor, Philadelphia, Miami, Dallas, Los Angeles, and San Francisco.

Chief Robert B. Murphy of the San Jose Police Department (450,000 population—police personnel numbering some 723), who recently won approval for a manpower increase, acknowledges that the expansion could well include female police officers. Chief Murphy stated in an interview:

> . . . If women apply for the jobs—and there are 40 positions to be filled—pass all the tests and meet all other requirements, we would have to accept them as the openings came up. Women would have to pass the same rigid physical examinations as men, however, and perform the same agility tests before they could put on a uniform, or be behind the wheel of a car.

According to Chief Murphy, during the first week of January 1973, his agency was allocated $3.5 million for *more police personnel,* part of the revenue sharing funds from the Federal government. *It is expected that other undermanned police agencies throughout the nation will be using revenue-sharing monies to bolster their staffs.*

The $3.5 million allocation to the San Jose Police Department will permit the department to initiate the testing procedures for hiring police officers. Chief Murphy further stated:

> . . . Of the 40 police officer positions to be filled, four of the positions have been authorized for women. . . . Should four women qualify they will be utilized in the juvenile, vice, and narcotics divisions.

A review of the San Jose Police Department's staff reveals that women already have indicated a desire to secure employment with the agency. Three women recently took the written examination and passed. In the agility tests, however, two of these entrants failed and the third entrant did not make an appearance. The aforementioned review of personnel also revealed that at that time (January 1973), the San Jose Police Department had two female police officers, each with 10 years of service; one serving as an investigator in the juvenile bureau, the other as liaison officer with the District Attorney's office. There are seventeen *assistant* policewomen, whose duties besides transportation and searching female prisoners, are mainly record-keeping, filing, and other office work. These assistant policewomen are authorized to carry firearms. With regard to the forthcoming examination (i.e., 40 additional officers to be hired), the Assistant Chief, Ross Donald, stated:

> If the top 10 on the eligibility list turned out to be women, they would be in position to be hired. I don't view the physical or agility tests as being insurmountable either.

Opportunities for capable women in the field of law enforcement have shown a tremendous increase during the last 15 years. Studies reveal that there are numerous vacancies on the staffs in many large cities. There is a current shortage for qualified women in law enforcement. Authorities believe that the current shortage will continue unless more qualified young women become interested in police work as a career. As previously stated, police work for women has achieved professional status, and as a consequence, standards for employment as well as salaries have shown an increase.

Qualifications

Generally, throughout the United States, the job qualifications are the same as those for a policeman. In a few jurisdictions, the educational qualifications may be higher. There is no general agreement as to the standards with regard to physical size, but higher standards of health and physical condition usually are required. The minimum (generally 21) and maximum age requirements are higher.

Selection Process

The same selection principles used in the hiring of a policeman prevail, except for modifications in the area of physical-agility tests. Furthermore, one female is usually included on the oral interview board. The probationary period with close supervision applies.

Training

Policewomen are involved in the same basic training as males; except, once again, with modifications in the hand-to-hand combat classes.

JOB OPPORTUNITIES WITH RELATED AGENCIES

For those students enrolled in police-science schools whose interest may be in *penology, probation,* or *parole* (some colleges—such as San Jose State

University in California—have programs for a degree in penology within the Police Science Division), there are many opportunities for employment. A degree in police science or penology would certainly qualify a student for a career in corrections, probation, or parole. There continues to be a growing need for qualified personnel in this closely related field. State parole and correctional departments as well as county probation and correctional facilities are requesting additional employees every year.

According to the National Survey of Corrections and the U.S. Department of Justice, Bureau of Prisons, there is a need in the *juvenile* field to increase the number of probation and parole officers from the present 7706 to approximately 13,800. Furthermore, the Commission's survey reveals that by 1975 it is estimated that 23,000 officers will be required to carry out the functions essential to community treatment of youngsters. For *adults,* according to the President's Commission, there is an immediate need for almost three times the number of probation and parole officers currently employed. Population projections point to a requirement of 23,000 officers by 1975.

Since the student being introduced to law enforcement will be confronted with many questions pertaining to *penology* (the study of the reformation and rehabilitation of criminals and the management of prisons), a brief discussion of the field of corrections is appropriate at this time.

Corrections Today

The Federal Bureau of Prisons survey on the field of corrections gives the first accurate picture of the number of offenders under correctional authority on an average day: 1.3 million. This total is so much larger than had ever before been estimated that it has startled even those familiar with the field. Moreover, if present trends in arrests and convictions continue, 10 years from now the system will be facing even more extreme pressures. The juvenile system, because of the rapid increase in the number of young people in the population, will be most hard pressed. Adult probation and parole treatment will suffer because of the trend toward probation or early parole rather than prolonged confinement.

Role of Probation-Parole Officers

During the course of one's career as a police officer, contact with probation and parole officers will not be uncommon. Therefore, a concise statement regarding the aforementioned fields appears to be appropriate prior to discussing the field in general.

Probation is a legal arrangement whereby a person convicted of a criminal offense is released by the court (under certain conditions) *without* commitment to an institution under supervision of a probation officer. *Parole* is the release of a convicted criminal from a correctional institution after he has served a minimum portion of his sentence. It is a "conditional release" contingent upon the parolee's conforming to specific rules and regulations while under the supervision of a parole officer. If the parolee is unable to conform to demands upon his behavior, his parole may be revoked by a board (a committee invested with such authority) and he is subsequently returned to prison to serve out his sentence. To avoid confusion, then, *probation* is granted by a judge in lieu of commitment to a correctional institution.

A probation officer, unlike a parole officer, is considered first as a *court officer* or "arm of the court" and second as a *social case worker*. As a court officer, the probation officer (like the peace officer) is responsible primarily to the court (community) and secondarily to the client—as long as the best interest of the client is compatible with that of the community.

Both the parole and probation officer accord consultation and guidance to both the client and his family, utilizing principles of casework in order to rehabilitate him, if possible.

The following is an excerpt from Chief Justice Burger's Report on the Federal Judiciary delivered to the American Bar Association at San Francisco on August 14, 1972:

In the federal system we have 640 probation officers. Some of these officers have caseloads from 150 to 300 cases as against a recommended figure of 35. By any rational measurement, we ought to have more than double the number of probation officers now available. In retrospect we acted far too timidly when we asked Congress for 348 additional officers this year. The House has approved 100 and the Senate has approved 236; the result awaits the compromise that will be reached in the conference committee. I repeat we should have asked for 650 more—I regret that we did not do so.

This is a crucial area of need. From discussions with many district judges, I have learned that in close cases on the question of probation, convicted persons are sometimes being sentenced to prison because the sentencing judge knows that the shortage of probation officers makes it impossible to give the close supervision required to those released. If we have learned anything about the correctional process, it is that many of the people sent to prisons would have had better prospects of being restored to useful life if they were placed on probation under close professional supervision, rather than confined. Laying aside all compassionate and humanitarian considerations, we see that a probationer can be given close supervision for less than one-tenth of what it costs to keep that same person in prison.

I urge the Association to give a very high priority to persuading Congress to provide adequate probation and parole personnel.

Qualifications. Almost all probation-parole officers (92% according to the latest survey by the Department of Health, Education, and Welfare) in cities 500,000 or more are college graduates. This proportion decreases consistently as the size of the community becomes smaller; so those areas with less than 50,000 people have the smallest portion of college-educated officers (50%). In California, the *minimum* educational qualification is a college degree, preferably in sociology, penology, police science, criminology, or psychology.

Except for the physical qualifications (physical qualifications are more demanding for police officers), entrance qualifications are similar to that of police officers.

Salary. Annual entrance (nonjourneyman positions) salaries in probation-parole vary widely by region, ranging from $7600 in the South to $9400 on the Pacific Coast.

Region	*Annual Median Salary*
Northeast	$6900
North Central	$7600
South	$6900
Mountain	$8500
Pacific	$9400

Opportunities for advancement are similar to those of a police officer with advancement to a higher classification dependent upon passing civil service promotional examinations. Salary increment, however, is possible without advancement to supervisory positions. This is possible because of seniority and change of classification pay raises (due to experience).

It is beyond the scope of this book to treat inclusively the organization, methods of operation, and employment standards of the various types of related agencies in the United States that represent a source of potential employment for the aspiring police candidate. However, the following section regarding career opportunities is a good starting point.

Employment Opportunities

Employment opportunities in correctional work indicate that it is one of the largest professional and semiprofessional employment organizations in the

United States [14]. According to the National Survey of Corrections and the U.S. Department of Justice, Bureau of Prisons, more than 121,000 people were employed in corrections in 1968. Only a small proportion of correctional staff had treatment and rehabilitation as their primary function; 24,000 or 20% of the staff, were probation and parole officers working in the community, and educators, social workers, psychologists, and psychiatrists, working in institutions. By contrast, 80% of correctional manpower had major responsibility for such functions as custody and maintenance.

Correctional agencies across the country face acute shortages of qualified manpower, especially in positions charged with responsibility for treatment and rehabilitation. Employment opportunities, therefore, for correctional workers are expected to be excellent through the 1970's. Problems of additional staff are required now to achieve minimum standards for effective treatment and control many more thousands will be needed in the next decade.

Glaser puts it this way [15]:

> The primary need, however, is in recruitment and training of line personnel who are committed to correctional careers and oriented to correctional change. . . . Historically, almost all changes in the mode of dealing with criminals not only have altered the training required for correctional personnel, but also have drastically increased the number of persons employed in correction. This pattern was obvious in the early part of the 19th Century, when confinement replaced hanging as the standard penalty for felonies and again in the 20th Century, when probation and parole became widespread. It is even more current today, when correctional change is occurring more rapidly than ever.

According to the President's Commission on Law Enforcement and Administration of Justice, in the *juvenile* field there is a need to increase the number of probation and parole officers from the present 7706 to approximately 13,800. Furthermore, the Commission's survey reveals that by 1975 it is estimated that 23,000 officers will be required to carry out the functions essential to community treatment of youngsters. For *adults,* according to the President's Commission, there is an *immediate* need for almost three times the number of probation and parole officers currently employed. Population projections point to a requirement of 23,000 officers by 1975 [16].

Manpower Requirements

There are primarily four major correctional functions which can be identified, each containing a number of different occupations, but generally homogenous from the standpoint of manpower development needs [17]. The first category consists of *group supervisors, guards, and other institutional personnel* concerned generally with the custody and care of offenders in group sentence. The second comprises *case managers,* responsible for assembling information about individual offenders, developing specific treatment programs, and supervising probationers and parolees in the community. The third category consists of the *specialists, academic, and vocational teachers, and therapists,* who work in correctional programs. The last category includes a diverse group of *technical and service personnel.*

Custodial Personnel and Group Supervisors: This category of employees comprises over half of the total correctional manpower. It includes those who are variously designed as prison guards or correctional officers in adult institutions and those who are called cottage parents or group supervisors in juvenile institutions. In adult institutions, these are the employees who man the walls, supervise living units, escort inmates to and from work, and supervise all group movement around an institution. In juvenile institutions, they provide the bulk of hour-by-hour supervision for youngsters.

Present shortages for adult State institutions would require the immediate hiring of 9500 custodial personnel. The greatest shortage in the area of custodial personnel is among those who work in jails and other local adult institutions.

Case Managers: Some offenders need intensive attention in small cases, others in larger cases, while still others require only normal contact with an officer. This principle applies equally to institutional and community-based staff.

Any efforts which seek to improve the quality of correctional services must immediately confront the need for more case managers. Simply to meet existing needs requires an increase from 17,400 to 55,000 case managers—more than tripling the present status.

Specialists: Staff members classified here as specialists possess essential professional skills needed in the rehabilitation of offenders. Included in this category are vocational and academic teachers, psychologists, and psychiatrists.

The clinical specialists represents somewhat different manpower problems, partly because of his change in role and partly because of extremely scarce supply. It is clearly *impossible* that corrections in the near future will obtain all the full-time therapists needed for work in correctional institutions.

Technicians and Service Personnel: Another manpower group to be considered consists of those who are responsible for the maintenance and operation of the correctional system as well as for providing various specialized services to offenders. This diverse group includes electricians, farm managers, foremen of industrial shops, researchers, and secretaries. The bulk of these employees work in institutions.

Detailed data are not available by the various types of personnel in this category. At present, about 34,000 persons are employed in technical and service tasks in corrections. By 1975, it is estimated about 81,000 technicians and service personnel will be needed [18].

Advantages and Disadvantages of Correction Work as a Career

There are *advantages* and *disadvantages* in every profession. Prior to preparing himself for entering the field of corrections as a career, the prospective correctional worker should give consideration to both the advantages and disadvantages of such work.

Advantages

As in police work, for anyone considering a career as a practitioner in corrections, there are many advantages.

The Challenge

Correctional work is one of the most challenging professions for those who possess the attributes for the job. The authors doubt that there is a comparable vocation (except, perhaps, for police work) that affords every practitioner (in any level of correctional work) an opportunity for personal satisfaction and stimulating involvement.

Security and Independence

Security and independence are usually mentioned together for maintaining morale and incentive. Under a properly administered merit system, both of these conditions exist. The practitioner in corrections who can feel that his employment is fairly safe as long as he performs satisfactorily also feels that he is independent of political influence. Both state and local correctional employment are the auspices of state or local merit system rules. Therefore the worker is afforded the security provided by the Department of Civil Service. This particular situation is likely to be conducive to freedom of thought about the job and the possibilities for improvement.

Salaries

Although the item of salaries is brought to the attention of the reader during the initial phase of this chapter, at the risk of being repetitive, the authors feel that it is an appropriate subject when discussing advantages of correctional work.

Security is closely related to salaries. Salaries in the field of corrections, when considered in the terms of personnel standards set up by various professional groups, are substandard. However, it should be pointed out that, although salaries are considered low, they have been improving quite significantly as compared to other professions (i.e., teachers, welfare workers, and hospital personnel). Salary increments granted at intervals—as specified by merit systems—are important incentives for staff development.

Starting salaries have shown a tremendous increase in the last 5 years. Correctional practitioners' salaries, for the most part, compare with private industry; furthermore, correctional practitioners' salaries compare quite favorably with those in many other vocations and professions which require more time and finances in preparing for the job.

Opportunity for Promotion

The opportunity for advancement through the ranks is one of the best "selling points" in correctional work. The individual who is motivated and qualifies would find that there is an opportunity for increased increment, additional responsibility, and increased prestige. This is noted by Frank who states [19]:

A desirable rearrangement of the correctional process in recent years has been projected a greater democratization within the institutional organization and an increased permeability of institutional boundaries. At one extreme is a serious consideration being given to the more direct involvement and participation of the inmates in therapy and resocialization by and for themselves, such as the demonstration and experimental projects in the California institutions. At the other extreme are the expanding use of the half-way house or pre-release centers, and the work-furlough programs of the Federal Bureau of Prisons. Of more immediate significance to the correctional officer are the new expectations and demands being made of him as the distinction between the custodial specialist and the treatment specialists becomes less sharp. Correctional officers are now being asked to serve as group counselors, as case aides to the professional worker, and active participants on treatment teams or sub-classification committees, and more competent sources of information on behavior patterns of individual inmates.

This change in the opportunity structure, which not only tolerates but expects such new roles for the correctional officer, may in time conceivably provide that indispensable link between occupational roles and organizational requirements which so frequently constitutes the basis for the change from an occupation to an emerging or marginal profession.

Although the above quotation refers primarily to the correctional officer, many other factions of correctional work are undergoing vast changes in the area of opportunity for advancement and salary increment. Therefore, correctional work does offer lifetime guarantee opportunities with reasonable promotional ranges and increasingly challenging opportunities.

Employment in Local Communities

As discussed throughout this chapter, the opportunities for employment with correctional agencies are extensive—qualified personnel *are* needed. More and more, the smaller communities are voicing their opinions in the area of improvements in correctional selectivity. Thus the result has been the energetic campaigning on the part of local correctional agencies to keep potential candidates in the community. Needless to say, those students enrolled in criminology programs in colleges throughout the nation can find excellent opportunities in the profession on the *local level.* The opportunities on the local level are unlimited to those young people who are just starting their professional training.

Pride

Personal pride gained from dedication to the service of justice and the well-being of society is one of the greatest advantages of a career in corrections. The correctional worker is interested in the welfare of the people. As such, he appreciates the "inherent worth of the individual" and respects the "inalienable rights of people." He believes in his profession and has, or develops, skills in working with people, in establishing a relationship, and entering into the perceptual life of his clients. Through these skills he develops basic trusts in many of his clients and then, through his relationship with them, effects more stable functioning and often change in their behavior. The mere fact that he is in a position to effect a change in the lives of people—change for the better—this is an important motivating factor and sufficient reward.

Disadvantages

Intensive Pressure

Pressure, frustration, never enough time. Pressure for leniency and for punishment as well make it necessary for the practitioner to have confidence in his own confidence to deal with probabilities. The correctional practitioner must have the patience to deal with aggressive and hostile attitudes of the offender who resists his efforts to help and the equanimity to use sanctions for the protection of the offender and the community. In probation-parole, it is not unusual to work with extremely high caseloads. This is an administrative problem that has probably plagued probation-parole officials for many years. Whenever probation-parole programs are subject to criticism, the

oversized caseload is usually identified as the obstacle to successful operation. Efforts to reduce caseloads have been the source of continuous trouble
between probation-parole administrators and local and state budget authorities. Although there has been some improvement in this particular area,
improvements have not been consistent or fast enough.

In regards to the *institutional staff,* the situation is quite similar. As indicated
in the section pertaining to employment opportunities in the correctional
institutions, the authors pointed out the need for increased staff in order
to meet the standards set by professional groups.

Anxiety, Tension, and Frustrations in Correction Work

A related program to intensive pressure are the negative side effects such
as anxiety, tension, and frustrations. The correctional worker is subject to
many strains. Hostility is bad enough, but it is often accompanied by overt
threats against the practitioner. There are occasions, when the correctional
practitioner is disliked and perhaps even hated. He is feared by some and,
as previously indicated, regarded with contempt by some. The job, very
frequently, is often thankless. The result is a state of anxiety and tension
which naturally differs from one man to another and which rises and falls
from time to time depending on the work load. There are many frustrations
in correctional work—at least things perceived as frustrating by the correctional worker. Extremely high caseloads, as previously mentioned, makes
it almost impossible to do an adequate job. The correctional worker finds
it necessary to "cut corners" in order to complete assigned tasks. Furthermore, the practitioner finds it almost impossible to do a thorough and complete
job in the area of casework services and court investigations. Therefore,
it is not unusual to find that a correctional worker (i.e., institutional workers,
parole officer, probation officer, etc.) on many occasions, develop "guilt
feelings" and subsequently such feelings leave a derogatory effect on his
performance. *He is frustrated and overworked.*

Lack of Public Support

The public continues to hold rather a negative attitude about correctional
services on the state and local levels. The image the public has of correctional
practices has, to a great degree, been created by movies, television shows,
and all the other paraphernalia of today's public communications. There is
no denying, however, that there is a new restiveness in the public about

correctional work and its effectiveness which suggests that the image of the correctional worker is very rapidly deteriorating. The public has, recently, been reluctant to support correctional programs, especially those that are to be implemented in the community. The Joint Commission on Correctional Manpower and Training and the President's Commission on Law Enforcement and Administration of Justice, and *Task Force Report: The Police,* reports that [20]:

The public not only does not have a great deal of information about corrections, but it also has an unfavorable attitude toward it. Negative orientations toward corrections are reflected in a number of ways. First, the public does not have a high degree of confidence in corrections in general. Most national surveys find, for example, that despite the many specific negative feelings expressed toward law enforcement, the vast majority of the prisoners interviewed—7 out of 10—have a high regard for the field. However, when persons are asked to indicate their confidence in corrections, this figure declines to 50 percent. Second, the public has even less confidence in correctional workers. The Joint Commission on Correctional Manpower and Training found that about 50 percent *or less* of those interviewed expressed confidence in probation officers, parole officers and prison guards, despite the general upgrading in quality of correctional personnel in recent years. Third, career opportunities are not only not visible to the public, but they are not even considered seriously. When a national sample of high school and college age youths were asked whether they had ever considered corrections as a career, only one percent replied that they had considered it "seriously," and only 15 percent had considered either "seriously" or "somewhat seriously."

Correctional administrators and educators are seeking and, in most instances, find new ways to rehabilitate law violators, to provide voluntary compliance with societies' restrictions, and to furnish competent, economical, and streamlined correctional services. Most of these administrators, a few years ago, were in exactly the same situation—attempting to decide on a career. Relevance of the future, in the field of correctional work, will come from young people who are just starting their professional training. *Look around, investigate, and evaluate; there is no denying the need for qualified persons.* Furthermore, career opportunities are unlimited and the person who selects correctional work as his chosen profession may be embarking on a lifetime career of satisfaction.

Finally, correctional work offers career opportunities to young people seeking employment in an active and interesting vocation. Those who are attracted to work with people and who find satisfaction in using their skills in helping others resolve problems of living, find correctional work worth exploring.

Many persons have been challenged and excited by the opportunities of work in the field of corrections. There is need for more persons of like purpose and good endowments.

SUMMARY

There is currently, throughout the United States, a critical need for qualified young men and women in the various fields of law enforcement. This is especially true in the larger cities in the nation. Studies reveal that there is a need for more than 50,000 policemen in the 1970's, just to fulfill positions already authorized due to revenue sharing. Studies further show that approximately two-thirds of the police departments are below their authorized personnel strength—about 10% below strength. This is not principally due to a shortage of police candidates, but to a shortage of successful ones.

Several factors account for the difficulties encountered in recruiting candidates to fill the several thousand vacant positions in law enforcement agencies throughout the United States. Some of these factors are: *Rapid population growth, higher police recruitment standards, increase in crime, and shorter-term retirement systems for police work.* There are no indications that recruitment problems will diminish in the near future—quite the contrary is noted; the problem of the recruitment of police personnel will continue to increase.

Law enforcement today is not the same as it was even a decade ago. The modern police force emphasizes training and education. Many new police science educational institutions and in-service training programs have been developed during the past few years.

Selection and training of peace officers are closely related functions. In order to regulate standards and establish uniformity in recruiting, the State of California, by legislative action in 1959, created the Peace Officers' Standards and Training (POST) Commission. POST, under Section 1002 in Rules and Standards, established minimum standards for employment as a peace officer in California.

In the selection process, most police departments give a prospective peace officer the following tests (not necessarily in the following order): physical-agility tests, written examinations, oral examinations, psychological examinations, exhaustive personal-history examinations, and a medical examination.

The members of the committee conducting the oral board examination (part of the selective process which eliminates many candidates) usually ask themselves three questions:

1. What traits in the applicant might ultimately affect the public?
2. What traits in the applicant might ultimately affect his relationship with fellow officers?
3. What traits might cause a medical problem in the future?

After the candidate has successfully completed the selection process and is hired as a peace officer, there is still one other important phase to over-come—probationary status. The probationary period is designed to be a part of the recruiting process and it may last 6 months to 2 years. This period will give the organization an opportunity to ascertain, with a certain degree of accuracy, the employability of a recruit. If the recruit is not adaptable, he may be summarily dismissed.

The major contribution of the *policewoman* to law enforcement is in the area of crime prevention as a juvenile officer. In this capacity, policewomen are involved in cases in which women or children are either offenders or victims. Policewomen normally deal with women, regardless of age, and boys under the age of twelve. As indicated in Chapter Seven, due to the equality status demanded by women and the nondiscriminatory mandates of modern police practices, we can expect a significant increase in women hired by police agencies.

The concluding part of Chapter Seven discusses the field of corrections, the potentiality for employment, and the qualifications of employment. As indicated, the field of corrections is rapidly expanding with opportunities for employment in many levels of correctional work, such as probation and parole officers, custodial staff, teachers in institutions, office workers and many others.

ANNOTATED REFERENCES

Blum, R. H. (ed.), *Police Selection,* Thomas, Springfield, Ill., 1961. Presents an intelligent discussion on the organizational and administrative aspects of police planning; also informative in matters pertaining to police selection.

Blum, R. H., W. L. Goggin, and E. Whitmore, "A Study of Deputy Sheriff Selection Procedures," *Police,* Dec. 1961. A good comprehensive research on selection procedures; oral boards, psychological tests, etc.

Challenge of Crime in a Free Society, A Report by the President's Commission on Law Enforcement and Administration of Justice, U.S. Government Printing Office, Washington, D.C., 1967. Police and correctional personnel are thoroughly covered in Chapters 4 and 6.

Gammage, A. Z., *Your Future in Law Enforcement,* Richard Rosen Press, New York, 1961. Description of job opportunities in law enforcement and related training.

Gammage, A. Z., *Police Training in the United States,* Thomas, Springfield, Ill., 1968. This book affords the prospective police officer the opportunity to survey the field of law-enforcement training and employment available in police work.

Institute for Training in Municipal Administration, *Municipal Police Administration,* The International City Manager's Association, Chicago, 1961. Particularly good in discussing philosophy and methods utilized in municipal police agencies. Good breakdown of law-enforcement agencies and their responsibilities.

Task Force Report: Corrections, A Report by the President's Commission on Law Enforcement and Administration of Justice, U.S. Government Printing Office, Washington, D.C., Chapter 9. Correctional personnel is covered thoroughly in this chapter.

United States Government Organization Manual, General Services Administration, U.S. Government Printing Office, Washington, D.C., 1973. Describes federal governmental agencies and their particular responsibilities.

Wilson, O. W., *Parker on Police,* Thomas, Springfield, Ill., 1957. A collection of lectures, speeches, and the personal philosophy of the late Chief Parker of Los Angeles is presented by a noted author in the police field.

NOTES

1. *Newsweek,* "Living With Crime, U.S.A.," December 18, 1972, p. 31.

2. *Ibid.,* p. 36.

3. As an ultimate goal, the President's Commission recommends that all police personnel with general enforcement powers have baccalaureate degrees. See *The Challenge of Crime in a Free Society,* President's Commission on Law Enforcement and Administration of Justice, U.S. Government Printing Office, Washington, D.C., 1967.

4. *Ibid.*

5. J. D. Stinchcomb, "The Community College and Its Impact," *Police Chief,* August, 1966, p. 6.

6. For a complete analysis on psychological testing for peace officers, interested readers are referred to: R. H. Blum, W. L. Goggin, and E. Whitmore, "A Study of Deputy Sheriff Selection Procedures," pp. 66–68.

7. *Op. cit.,* p. 110.

8. Blum, Goggin, and Whitmore, *op. cit.,* p. 7.

9. *Challenge of Crime in a Free Society, op. cit.,* p. 111.

10. A. Z. Gammage, *Your Future in Law Enforcement,* pp. 98–99.

11. Gammage, *op. cit.,* p. 11.

12. *Ibid.*

13. *Ibid.,* pp. 12–13.

14. For a detailed discussion of the field of corrections and employment opportunities, refer to: W. Hartinger, E. Eldefonso, and A. Coffey, *Corrections: A Component of the Criminal Justice System,* Goodyear, Pacific Palisades, Ca., 1973, pp. 119–146. Reprinted by permission of the publisher.

15. D. Glaser, "The New Correctional Era—Implications for Manpower and Training," *Crime and Delinquency,* Vol. 12, No. 3, July 1966, p. 210.

16. *Ibid.,* pp. 95–98.

17. *Ibid.*

18. All of the categories (Custodial Personnel and Group Supervisors, Case Managers, Specialists, and Technicians and Service Personnel) adopted from *Task Force Report: Corrections,* pp. 95–98.

19. P. G. Garabedian, "Challenge for Contemporary Corrections," *Federal Probation,* Vol. 33, No. 1, March 1969, p. 5.

20. *Task Force Report: Corrections, op. cit.,* p. 198.

CHAPTER EIGHT

Police Organization

Efficient organization is imperative if police services are to be carried out effectively. Organization of police tasks is especially crucial to law enforcement work because of the need for coordination. There must be coordination of speed, accuracy, care, and adherence to time schedules if proper law enforcement services are to be implemented and maintained.

Because of the importance of organization, it is incumbent upon each future police officer to comprehend the agency he will become part of, and, through such understanding, be able to draw a clearer prospective of his own future within the law enforcement structure.

In considering the organization of a police department, it is good to bear in mind the objective that a governmental jurisdiction has in creating a police agency. Police departments are created to provide a service. There is no need to go further in delineating the purpose of a police department—why community, county, state, and federal governments create police agencies—than to establish the fact that the agencies have a job to do, an objective. Establishment of this fact is necessary to understand that *organizing* a force facilitates the accomplishment of the police purpose—the protection of persons and property [1].

To assist in the accomplishment of a police force's purpose and facilitate the assignment of duties, officers are separated into units; each person in the organization thus comprehends precisely the extent of his duties. According to authorities on law enforcement organization [2], for purposes of assignment, police tasks must be grouped according to their purpose, their clientele, or their method of functioning. That is, the purpose of some tasks is to control traffic, investigate crime, or control vice or juvenile crime, and so on. The assigned duties, however, are also grouped or classified according to place, time, and the level of authority that is desired in the performance of a particular duty.

When police services have been organized according to their nature, place of performance, and the time they will be performed, the agency is itself divided into units charged with the performance of these tasks. These units represent the structure of the organization. Needless to say, the establishment of lines of control is imperative in order to assure that the units will work effectively together.

ANALYSIS OF ORGANIZATION

Perhaps the best analogy of an organization, according to a noted authority [3] in the field of police organization and administration, is to think of organization in terms of the human hand:

> Your hand is made up of fingers and the fingers may be considered the major divisions of an organization and the phalanges subdivisions. The hand has dexterity, it is able to do remarkable things. It can pick up small objects, thread a needle, and perform delicate feats of surgery. Without control, the hand would lack its dexterity. So also is it with a police organization.

LINES OF CONTROL AND COMMUNICATION

Taking the foregoing analogy into consideration, it is mandatory that lines of communication and control be established when creating organic units within the police organization. It is essential for the reader to be cognizant of the levels of authority within a police organization, since police agencies customarily are divided according to level of authority. Although there is flexibility, police organizations are directed and controlled through a vertical chain of command, that is, communication channels traveling via vertical combinations of superior officers—each rank forming a different level of authority.

Such control is necessary in order to give the organization life, because the organization itself lacks feeling, discretion, and the power to initiate action. Therefore, lines of control are necessary for authority to be delegated and information to flow freely in all directions. *Communication* is of paramount importance if all members are to understand their positions in the total organization and their job in relation to the tasks of others. In the organizational structure of police agencies, there is a definite vertical chain of command, for example, the *chief, assistant chief* (if the department is large enough), *inspector, captain, lieutenant, sergeant, patrolman,* and *matron* and *clerks.* The patrolman is not a ranking officer. Each rank may be divided into two or more grades, each grade usually carrying salary differentials. Although the grade usually is determined by seniority (years of service), the distinction often may be one of assignment. For example, the title of captain frequently is given to the supervisor of each functional division.

SMALL POLICE AGENCIES

Before becoming involved in a more detailed discussion of assignments and the organization that is created to facilitate their performance, we should

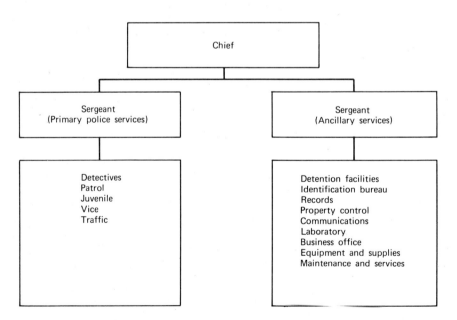

FIGURE 8.1. *Vertical command chain.*

consider the relatively small police departments. Where do they fit in? Is it justifiable to remark, "The organizational structure of the Los Angeles, San Francisco, or New York police departments does not apply to small law enforcement agencies." To answer this question and clarify the point, let us consider the biochemist (the branch of chemistry that deals with plants, animals, and their life processes) who utilizes the microscope to identify the component elements and gain some knowledge about the minute things with which he works. There is some advantage in analyzing police duties under a magnifying glass. In so doing, it is possible to see more clearly the details of the component elements and also to identify the principles that underlie their performance.

The job of law enforcement agencies is substantially the same in every jurisdiction. There is, then, fundamentally very little difference between the police job in Chicago and the police job in a community of 10,000. There is a difference in degree but not in character. And the performance of administrative and organizational tasks in a small department also is quite similar to that of the large police organization. As previously stated, there is a difference in degree. In a small community, instead of a force of twenty-five to fifty men performing some administrative task, this duty and many other such tasks will be the responsibility of the chief of police or perhaps a single member of his force.

Where the size of the police department warrants it, a ranking officer is

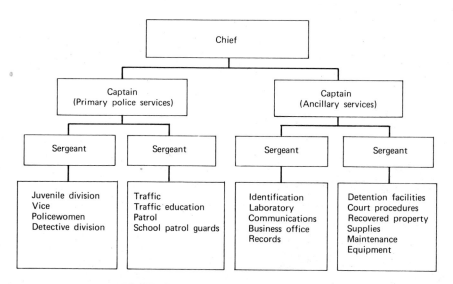

FIGURE 8.2. *Horizontal command chain.*

responsible for the supervision of operations. If the size of the police department does not merit a ranking officer in charge of operations, a sergeant may assume these duties. This type of organization could be organized very easily along two vertical lines as indicated in Figure 8.1.

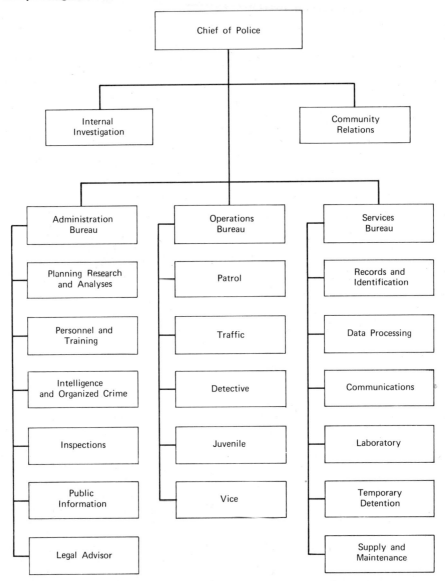

FIGURE 8.3. (a) *One form of a well-organized municipal police department for a growing city.*

The small departmental organization shown in Figure 8.2 will require closer supervision as the department expands, thereby making it necessary to place the supervisory responsibility on ranking officers. In other words, various police services that may require closer supervision may be moved out of the vertical chain of command and be reorganized on a horizontal level [4].

As indicated in Figure 8.2, because of the horizontal growth, there are now two units responsible for the line functions of a police agency and two units under ancillary services—both under the supervision of a ranking officer with the sergeants acting in the capacity of front-line supervisors.

It can readily be seen that the potential for growth and flexibility with law enforcement agencies is inherent in the structure. The flow of communication (both ways) is an important factor in the organization of police functions. As any agency expands its services, so must it provide for additional sections to cover such functions. Figure 8.3 conveys some understanding of the type of police services a growing community may demand.

An organization has both *physical* and *psychological* aspects. The physical organization by itself would be a totally inadequate device. Its components

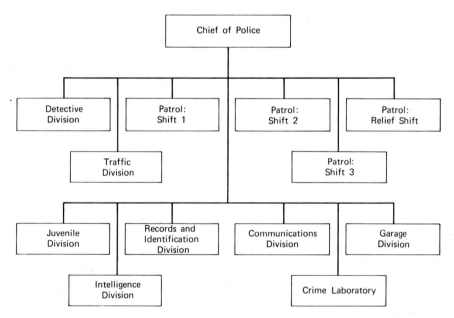

FIGURE 8.3. (b) *An example of a poorly organized municipal police department for a growing city. Source:* Task Force Report: The Police, *President's Commission on Law Enforcement and Administration of Justice, 1967, pp. 46–47.*

would operate without consideration of relationships with the other units. The psychological aspect of establishing communication and lines of control among the many units is a necessary feature of a workable organization. It is necessary, however, to maintain a reasonable span of control so that an individual has under his direct supervision no more immediate subordinates than he can manage.

CHARACTERISTICS OF AN ORGANIZATION

Now let us consider some of the characteristics of an organization. An organization has a unity of purpose because it is created to accomplish a certain objective. However, it must also have unity of action which is attained through direction and control. There must be coordination which is best described by the example of two men engaged in moving a piano that is too heavy for either to lift by himself. In order to move the piano, it is necessary for the men to work as a team; if each worked independently, the piano would not move. Their efforts, therefore, must be coordinated in order for them to work in unison. One of them must give some direction and this is leadership, which is essential to an organization if it is to work effectively.

Each person in the organization must know what his particular task is but his knowledge cannot be restricted to his own task. He must know what to expect of the other man, that there is a man who is prepared to assist him in accomplishing the task.

All members of a good organization are amenable to direction, that is, they are disciplined. They anticipate and are prepared to accept direction, coordination, and control. There must, therefore, be leadership. Someone must direct the members and coordinate their activities. There also must be control, the concomitant of direction, which has been called the consequence of command in action. There also must be intelligence because control depends on knowledge of conditions. Finally, there must be purposeful action which depends on planning.

In creating the physical structure of a police organization composed of units charged with the performance of similar or related tasks—that are similar or related in nature, in place, in time, or in level of authority—it is not necessary that every force should follow a model pattern. There may be justifiable differences. The test of the merit of an organization is the test of workability. If the organization enables the force to accomplish its purpose more effectively, then it is a good organization. If, on the contrary, it impedes the efforts of its members, the organization is faulty in some respects [5].

PRINCIPLES OF ORGANIZATION

According to the late O. W. Wilson, an authority in the field of police administration and organization, there are some fundamental practices in the organization of armed forces, of industry, and of public agencies which are applicable to law enforcement. These practices are [6]:

1. Tasks similar or related in purpose, process, method, or clientele are grouped
   together in one or more units under the control of a single person. In order
   to facilitate their assignment, these tasks are divided according to (a) the
   time, (b) the place of their performance, and (c) the level of authority needed
   in their accomplishment.
2. Lines of demarcation between the units are clearly drawn by precise definition
   of duties which are made known to all members so that responsibility may
   be placed exactly. Such definition avoids duplication in execution, and neglect
   resulting from an unassigned duty.
3. Channels are established through which information flows up and down and
   through which authority is delegated. These lines of control permit the delega-
   tion of authority, the placing of responsibility, the supervision of operations,
   and the coordination of effort; the individuals and groups are thus tied together
   into a unified force susceptible to direction and control. The lines of control
   must be clearly defined and well understood by all members so that each
   may know to whom he is responsible and who, in turn, is responsible to
   him.
4. Each individual, unit, and situation must be under the immediate control of
   one, and only one, person thus achieving the principle of unity and command
   and avoiding the friction that results from duplication of direction and supervision.
5. No more units or persons are placed under the direct control of one man
   than he is able to manage.
6. Each task is made the unmistakable duty of someone; responsibility for planning, execution, and control (implemented by inspection) is definitely placed
   on designated persons.
7. Supervision is provided for each person at the level of execution regardless
   of the hour or place.
8. Each assignment of responsibility carries with it commensurate authority to
   fulfill the responsibility.
9. Persons to whom authority is delegated are invariably held accountable for
   its use.

ANALYSIS OF POLICE SERVICES

Since the organization of police functions is created to facilitate the accomplishment of police tasks, it is wise to analyze the police tasks in order

to see the type of organic units there should be within the structure. Duties that are similar or related in some respects should be gathered closely together and thus form a recognizable unit for assignment to the organic divisions.

1. *Primary police services (line operations).* These are direct services to the public. Such services provided by a police agency to a citizen and to a community are a primary task; needless to say, it was for this purpose that the police department was originally formulated.
2. *Ancillary (auxiliary) services.* Although police departments were not created to provide ancillary services, such services are indispensable to the line officers in accomplishing their specific duties. The primary tasks are services to the community; the ancillary tasks are services to the policemen.
3. *Administrative services.* These services (thoroughly covered in Chapter Nine) are staff maintenance services and are the personal responsibility of the chief of police. Since the chief must delegate authority in the performance of his administrative duties, these tasks may be classified in terms of service to the chief.

Before discussing these categories, there is still another category that should be discussed briefly, an area that usually is displayed quite predominantly in the larger police organizations: *Specialization.*

SPECIALIZATION

Law enforcement agencies, recognizing the growing challenge of special problems in the enforcement of laws, have expanded their activities to meet this challenge and its effect on the welfare of the community and its citizens. Police departments have organized special units (i.e., juvenile units, human relations units, special patrol units, etc.) within the structure of the department, staffed with personnel having qualifications in the particular fields [7].

The decision to specialize is based on the theory that a specialist, because of his superior knowledge and more intimate acquaintance with a specific problem, can do a better job. In larger, more complex communities, the need for specialization is generally considered to be more pressing. Specialization in large police departments is probably both essential and inevitable. The question, therefore, is not whether to specialize, but what added duties should the specialists assume and what should they take away from other personnel. But before considering the positive and negative aspects of specialization, it is appropriate at this time to consider specialization in juvenile control.

There have been many opinions expressed as to the role of the police in programs designed to control and prevent juvenile delinquency. Modern police thinking accept the theory of rehabilitation as being a realistic approach in most cases, and police departments have adopted techniques and methods designed to further that purpose.

Special training units within the police department, participation in the community efforts, and official stress on prevention rather than on arrest and prosecution are some of the measures being devised and implemented throughout the country. It is generally agreed that these activities constitute a major police role in the prevention and control of juvenile delinquency [8].

Law enforcement agencies, recognizing the growing challenge of juvenile delinquency, have extended activities to meet the challenge and its effect upon the welfare of the community and its citizens. Police departments have organized special units within the structure of the department, staffed with personnel having qualifications in this particular field. Special training of the personnel has been inaugurated to stress the importance of rehabilitation of youthful offenders over punitive action.

The purpose of such a unit is concentration on the understanding, control, and suppression of juvenile delinquency; the elimination of detrimental influences; and the protection of delinquent, dependent, neglected, and mistreated minors. Generally speaking, these special units have the same objectives as the entire department. However, in view of the fact that the juvenile court laws are essentially protective and rehabilitative, it is frequently necessary to modify the law enforcement procedures established for the handling of adults when dealing with juveniles.

Specialized juvenile units in police departments are known by various names in the United States. They are called, for example, *crime prevention bureaus, youth aid bureaus, juvenile bureaus, juvenile divisions,* and *juvenile control bureaus.*

The following duties are considered appropriate for juvenile control units:

1. Processing into disposition juvenile cases investigating by other units, with a possible exception of traffic cases.
2. Special patrolling of known juvenile hangouts where conditions are harmful to the welfare of unknown or suspected children.
3. Maintenance of records on juvenile cases.
4. Planning and coordinating a delinquency prevention program.

The question of a juvenile officer's responsibility for the investigation of offenses is a significant one in those departments big enough to allow for a great deal of specialization. Some such departments hold investigation by juvenile officers to a minimum, assigning cases to be cleared to an appropriate squad without reference to the age of the person thought to have committed the offense. In others, the juvenile control routinely investigates certain offenses connected with juveniles. In this latter instance, a juvenile control unit might be given responsibility for investigating and processing to disposition such specific cases as:

1. Offenses concerning children and the family such as neglect, abuse, or abandonment.
2. Adults contributing to the delinquency of minors, employing minors in injurious, immoral, or improper vocations or practices, and admitting minors to improper places.
3. Processing, possession, or sale of obscene literature when children are involved.
4. Bicycle thefts.
5. Offenses committed on school property.
6. Offenses involving juveniles, except forcible rape.
7. Gang warfare among juveniles and other such cases.

It is particularly important for the juvenile control unit to have separate quarters in a police station. If possible, the outside entrance to these quarters should be located so that children and their parents can come and go without passing through other quarters in the building, but access to the other sections should be easy and convenient for the juvenile offenders.

Whether to assign officers to specialized duty in connection with juvenile cases, the extent and degree of that specialization, and the duties and responsibilities of the specialists are important questions for police administrators. The decision to specialize is based on a theory that a specialist because of superior knowledge and more intimate acquaintance with the problems can do a better job. In large, complex communities, the need for specialization in the correspondingly large police departments is probably both essential and inevitable. Therefore, the question is not whether to specialize, but just what added duties should the specialist assume and which ones should be drawn from other personnel.

Problems in Specialization

Movement toward specialization in work with juveniles has, of course, produced its problems. Police executives have had to experiment and evolve policies largely by trial and error. There are some special situations to be considered:

1. Danger exists in that there may be a tendency for nonspecialized personnel to ignore matters which they really should handle.
2. Overemphasis on specialization may produce inhibition to effective communication, and may also generate morale problems. Remarks by a patrolman, such as "Forget it—that's a job for Diaper Dicks" are not entirely fictitious.
3. Another potentially dangerous situation is the overdependence of the executive policymaker on the naturally biased viewpoint of the specialist to whom he turns for guidance. Such policy decisions are likely to perpetuate difficulties by subordinating general objectives to those of the specialist.
4. Certain administrative problems are concomitant with the decision to specialize. The *first* of these is how and on what basis to select a specialist. Other problems concern the training, the duties, and the pay of such people. These questions, like the others, have no simple and universally applicable answers. What is good and proper in one community could be quite out of line in another.
5. The source of personnel for special assignments and promotions is ultimately the *patrol division.* The very nature of police organization makes this inevitable. We have here what is at once a paradox and a dilemma. The patrol division is generally considered to be the backbone of the police organization. As such, it should be strong and dynamic. Police officials should seek ways to make the patrol more efficient and effective. Cutting off the cream of the personnel to handle specialists' duties defeats this aim to a degree. The dilemma results from the fact that the best people possible for specialized assignments (including assignments to the juvenile control unit) are usually selected, but in so doing police agencies run the risk of leaving the patrol force to the least qualified men. This process can have an unfortunate psychological effect in that the patrol division comes to be regarded as the part of the organization in which to begin and from which to get out of as quickly as possible. It is looked upon as only a stepping stone to better things, the least desirable of police assignments since the so-called "best men" do not stay there.

Despite the potential "dangerous problems," some specialization is necessary. One reason is that the formula for handling juvenile cases arising from provisions of the law and juvenile court procedures would, in many instances, take officers away from their regular duties too frequently and too long, whereas this follow-up work can be performed economically by specialists. Even if every officer could be trained to do the job well, it would be administratively unsound to have every man try to handle to completion all details of every child. Then too, without some specialization, there would be some desirable programs that would never get off the ground. Only someone with a special interest and the necessary background can take the initiative to "spark" such programs.

In summary, then, it can be said that the decision to establish a separate functional unit which is responsible for matters related to juveniles must be based on demonstrated need for more effective utilization of departmental manpower. Need may be evaluated in a number of ways, such as:

1. Inability of regular investigators to clear cases involving juveniles.
2. Juvenile-case processing removing patrolmen from their beats for an extended period of time.
3. Community insistence on police involvement in nonpolice-youth programs.
4. Desirability of assigning a juvenile court officer to present cases.
5. The extent to which the department is required to provide social background data to the juvenile court.

As previously indicated, juvenile officers must be selected from the group of experienced line officers. This selection should be open and competitive to assure that the best-suited men are chosen from all of those available. Juvenile officers should be assigned rather than appointed. Preservice training should be required to assure adequacy of knowledge and skills required in the new position.

Consideration must be accorded to both the *advantages* and *disadvantages* before resolving each question of specialization. It is impossible to give a categorical answer in reference to specialization. It is not good sense to state categorically that specialization is or is not a negative aspect of police work; this is a decision that depends on the circumstances of the particular situation.

Let us briefly review the advantages and disadvantages of specialization.

Advantages

Specialization facilitates placing responsibility. Fixing responsibility is essential to effective operation. Then, too, without specialization, some desirable programs might never be initiated. Only someone with a special interest and the necessary background can take the initiative to "spark plug" such programs. Specialization, furthermore, facilitates the training and development of experts, because it narrows the areas of focus. More intensive training can be given a relatively small group of specialists than can be given to the entire department. And, as previously indicated, the narrowed field of interest and activity of specialists enables them to develop skills within their

FIGURE 8.4. *Officer serving the Court (Bailiff) is a necessary auxiliary service to the Court. Courtesy of the Office of the District Attorney, Santa Clara, Ca.*

field that could not be developed by the rank and file of the organization. Because of the aforementioned points, an *esprit de corps* also is promoted and special police interest is stimulated and public interest is aroused; the latter two are desirable within certain limitations.

Disadvantages

There are some dangers in specialization in that nonspecialized personnel may tend to ignore matters which they really should handle. Overemphasis on specialization may produce inhibitions to effective communication, and may also generate morale problems. For example, remarks by a patrolman referring to the juvenile unit, such as "Forget it—that's a problem for the Diaper Dicks," are not entirely fictitious. Another potentially dangerous situation is the overdependence of the executive policymaker on the naturally biased viewpoint of the specialist to whom he turns for guidance. Such policy decisions are likely to perpetrate difficulties by subordinating general objectives to those of the specialty. Tasks of command are made more difficult because of the complicated interrelationships that spring up as more and more specialized units are created. Finally, territorial coverage may be diminished by specialization; for example, two patrolmen engaged in general patrol, each on his own beat, provide twice as much coverage than when the tasks are divided between them so that each engages in a specialized patrol covering the area of both beats.

Regardless of the danger of specialization, in large police organizations, the need for special skill and ability may establish the necessity for certain units to specialize in one specific police service. The amount of work to be done, regardless of the quality of the personnel, the need for special skill or ability, or the importance of the job, may justify specialization. For example, in checking time-limit parking, where an amount of work in a limited area and time occupies the full-time attention of one man, there may be justification for assigning one man to the job [9].

Interference with usual duties, the size of the force, and the area of jurisdiction also may justify specialization in a small force. Usually, however, there is neither the need nor possibility of specialization that exists in a large force. Also, although a force of 500 men policing a city will have a high degree of specialization, a state police force of similar size engaged in policing its widespread areas could not have such complete specialization. Each state policeman must perform all police tasks regardless of their nature [10].

So here we have the three categories: *Primary police services* (line operations), *ancillary services,* and *administrative services,* along with, at times, *specialized services.*

PRIMARY POLICE SERVICES

The primary tasks are performed in many police departments by five units that, for convenience, we will refer to as divisions: A *patrol* division, a *traffic* division, a *detective* division, a *vice* division, and a *juvenile* division. These are the units created in a police department of suitable size to provide service directly to the public. These functions are direct field operations, to which ordinarily about two-thirds of a large urban police force is assigned. It was for the performance of these tasks that the police department was created.

Organizational problems are found within each of the five functional units, but a discussion of these problem areas is beyond the scope of this chapter.

ANCILLARY SERVICES

As previously indicated, ancillary tasks are those services provided to the policemen who are engaged in serving the public so that these men may be able to serve the public most effectively. Services within this field include *records and communications* (dispatchers), *service and maintenance, laboratory, detention facilities* (jail), *bailiffs,* and *fingerprinting technicians.*

The need for a special unit providing each of the ancillary services does

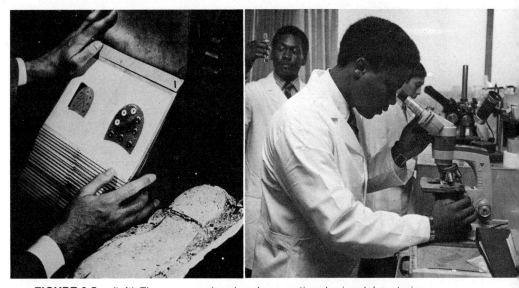

FIGURE 8.5. (left) *The many regional and one national crime laboratories provide varied and highly technical services to municipal and county police agencies. Here, an examiner in the FBI laboratory compares a cast of a shoe print against the reference collection of rubber heels in order to make an identification. Courtesy Federal Bureau of Investigation, Washington, D.C. (right) Analysis of criminal evidence is an extremely critical auxiliary police service. Courtesy Police Department, Los Angeles, Ca.*

FIGURE 8.6. *The communications center of the police department is a vital element in the successful operation and organization of the police agency. Courtesy of Metropolitan Police Department, St. Louis, Mo.*

not exist in every department. It is important, therefore, that the prospective police official recognize, regardless of the size of the organization, that there are tasks to be performed which are related to records, communications, maintenance, criminalistics (the analysis of physical evidence), custody of prisoners, and control of property. Whether a separate unit is created for the performance of each of these categories depends largely on the size of the organization. These tasks must be examined by the chief in determining whether to provide performance units in a number adequate to meet the needs of the agency.

From the point of view of developing an organization that will assist the force members in accomplishing their purpose, none of the ancillary tasks is as important as *records* and *communications,* which are essential to effective control. Incidents must be recorded, and departments vary in their methods of recording incidents that they are called upon to investigate.

Administrative ingenuity is necessary in ancillary services in order to assign fill-in tasks to persons who must be at a *post* to deal with important but infrequent tasks. Such persons should be occupied at all times because a busy policeman is a contented policeman who gains satisfaction in his job whereas idleness breeds discontent. Ingenuity should be used in providing fill-in tasks, therefore, not only for economy but also for morale.

ADMINISTRATIVE SERVICES

Since this particular area is fully covered in Chapter Nine, our discussion here will merely sketch the highlights of administrative services as they pertain to organization.

The head of any organization must plan, organize, staff, direct, coordinate, control, report, and budget.

The tasks of the administrator may be divided into two broad categories. *First,* there are those that relate to business *management* of the organization—the administrative tasks found in a law enforcement agency are substantially identical to those found in any other organization. *Second,* in contrast to these, there are administrative tasks relating to the operation of an organization such as a police department.

Of all the administrative tasks, personnel administration is the most important. Personnel administration includes *recruitment, selection for appointment and promotion, training, rating discipline, and welfare*—areas covered in other chapters of this textbook.

Other administrative tasks relate to budget planning and execution, accounting, purchasing, payrolls, and various management operations that may be found in any kind of organization. And finally, police administration includes public and official information and relations; the relationship of the police to the public; the relationship of the members of the police force to the official family, especially to those at higher levels of authority; and the information that must be provided to each force member.

Let us consider next the administrative tasks of operations. The chief of police must control his force and operations. He is concerned with the consequences of direction to control his force effectively. The chief, needless to say, must have intelligence (be kept abreast of the organization by subordinates) to control his force and must use his intelligence effectively. The importance of intelligence is reflected in the chief's knowing what conditions are and maintaining suitable controls. The good administrator must be cognizant of the conditions within his own organization and the "climate" within the community. On the basis of the intelligence gained via investigation, inspection, observation, and research, the administrator is able to plan effective operations with the assistance of his ranking officers.

RANK OF SUPERVISORS AND DESCRIPTION OF ORGANIZATION UNITS

In analyzing the complexity of present-day police services, the late O. W. Wilson [11] observed that there are problems in the areas of uniformity relating to the identification of *functional, time,* and *place units* in law enforcement agencies. The following terms, however, according to the aforementioned author, represent common practice.

POST: Specific station—whether it be an office or a desk at headquarters is not significant—to which a police officer is assigned to accomplish his task. A patrolman directing traffic at a particular intersection or crosswalk, "guard duty" at an athletic event, and the taking into custody of an individual wanted by a police agency (all points bulletin) are examples of a post.

ROUTE: Since a route is a length of a street or several streets, traffic patrolmen usually are assigned to a route for patrol purposes. On some occasions, if a particular route does not cover a lengthy street, foot patrolmen may be assigned to the route.

BEAT: Habitual area assigned for motorized and foot patrol. Frequently, the assignment of motorized traffic officers may take the place of a route.

SECTOR: Supervised by a sergeant, a squad of patrolmen may be assigned to a sector which may include two or more beats, routes, or posts.

DISTRICT: Most cities are divided into territories geographically or politically for specific reasons—for example, school districts. Each district has its own police station responsible for normal police operations. This district force is referred to as a company and is supervised by a district captain.

DIVISION: In departments lacking district stations, divisions are supervised by captains. Division commanders decentralized among district stations usually have the rank of major, inspector, assistant chief, or captain. Functional units such as traffic, patrol, detective, records and communication, juvenile, vice, and maintenance, are called divisions. Each division has jurisdiction-wide responsibilities and coverage.

PLATOON: Officers of a division (i.e., vice, traffic) are assigned to one shift or watch (Figure 8.7)—this is referred to as a platoon. A platoon is usually commanded by a lieutenant and its responsibility is to the entire city or district (if the city is divided into districts). Furthermore, as in a military structure, a platoon may be composed of several squads. Each squad is assigned to sectors of the city or district. In order to facilitate the ever-present problem of making assignments, divisions that find it necessary to be on duty for more than one shift may divide officers into platoons. This would be accomplished on the basis of the hours of the day they are on duty, without regard to the number on duty or the rank of the officer responsible for supervision.

BUREAU and SECTION: If tasks within a division make additional specialization necessary, classification of personnel according to their duties is appropriate. As a result of such classification, functional units developed within a division are referred to as bureaus. When a group is regularly assigned to a specific locale, the aforementioned designation serves a useful purpose—they are easily identifiable. If the bureau finds it necessary to specialize further, its personnel frequently are separated into sections. However, extensive subdivisions are found only in very large departments. The rank of a bureau chief is usually a lieutenant. On occasions, however, rank may be determined by the size and responsibilities of the office. According to the late O. W. Wilson:

The principal reason for creating a bureau may be to designate a post or location in order to facilitate assignment and to direct persons most readily to the location. If this is the sole reason, the bureau may not have a head, although it may be a functional unit. An information bureau is an example.

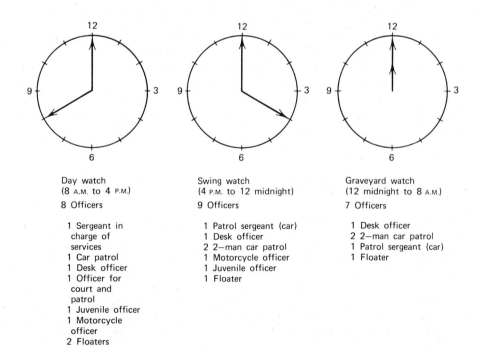

Day watch
(8 A.M. to 4 P.M.)

8 Officers

  1 Sergeant in
    charge of
    services
  1 Car patrol
  1 Desk officer
  1 Officer for
    court and
    patrol
  1 Juvenile officer
  1 Motorcycle
    officer
  2 Floaters

Swing watch
(4 P.M. to 12 midnight)

9 Officers

  1 Patrol sergeant (car)
  1 Desk officer
  2 2–man car patrol
  1 Motorcycle officer
  1 Juvenile officer
  1 Floater

Graveyard watch
(12 midnight to 8 A.M.)

7 Officers

  1 Desk officer
  2 2–man car patrol
  1 Patrol sergeant (car)
  1 Floater

FIGURE 8.7.   *Twenty-four hour police coverage.*

SUMMARY

Efficient organization is necessary if police services are to be carried out effectively. Organization of police tasks is especially crucial to law enforcement work because of the necessity for coordination of accuracy, speed, care, and compliance with time schedules.

The purpose of organizing a police force is to facilitate the accomplishment of the police purpose. In organizing a force to assist in the accomplishment of its purpose and facilitate the assignment of duties, officers are separated into units; each person in the organization thus comprehends precisely the extent of his duties. For purposes of assignment, police tasks must be grouped according to purpose, clientele, or function.

It is imperative that lines of communication and control be established when creating organic units within the police organization. Such control is necessary (as long as it remains flexible) in order to give the organization life because the organization itself lacks feeling, discretion, and, as a consequence, the power to initiate action. Therefore, lines of control are necessary for authority to be delegated properly and communication to flow freely in all directions. In the organizational structure of police agencies, there is a definite vertical chain of command, such as *chief, assistant chief, inspector, captain, lieutenant, sergeant, patrolman, matron,* and *clerk.*

The job of law enforcement is substantially the same in every jurisdiction regardless of its size. There is a difference in degree but not in character. And the performance of administrative and organizational tasks in a small department is quite similar to that of the large police organization.

There are, generally, two types of organizational structure: Vertical and horizontal lines of organization. Usually, police services that require closer supervision may be moved out of the vertical chain of command and reorganized on a horizontal level.

As previously indicated, an organization has a unity of purpose because it is created to accomplish the police purpose. However, it must also have unity of action which is attained through direction and control. Leadership is essential in an organization if it is to work effectively.

The principles of organization as advocated by O. W. Wilson are:

1. Tasks similar or related in purpose, process, method, or clientele are grouped together in one or more units under the control of a single person.
2. Lines of demarcation between the units are clearly drawn by a precise definition of duties which are made known to all members so that responsibility may be placed exactly.

3. Channels are established through which information flows up and down and through which authority is delegated.
4. Each individual, unit, and situation must be under the immediate control of one, and only one, person, thus achieving the principle of unity and command and avoiding friction.
5. No more units or persons are to be placed under the direct control of one man than he is able to manage.
6. Each task is made the unmistakable duty of someone—responsibility must be designated.
7. Supervision is provided for each person at the level of execution.
8. Each assignment of responsibility carries with it commensurate authority to fulfill that responsibility.
9. Persons to whom authority is delegated are invariably held accountable for its use.

Law enforcement services may be divided into three broad categories: (a) Primary services, (b) ancillary services, and (c) administrative services. *Specialization* is another area which may or may not be desirable. There are advantages and disadvantages to specialization. The decision to specialize is based on the theory that a specialist, because of his superior knowledge and more intimate acquaintance with the problems, can do a better job.

ANNOTATED REFERENCES

Bristow, A. P., and E. C. Gabard, *Decision-Making in Police Administration,* Thomas, Springfield, Ill., 1971. An administrative overview of policy decisions in law enforcement.

Institute for Training in Municipal Administration, *Municipal Police Administration,* The International City Managers' Association, Chicago, 1961. Covers aspects of police administration and lines of communication as well as other areas of administrative control.

Leonard, V. A., *Police Organization and Management,* Foundation Press, New York, 1964. Thoroughly covers the organizational and administrative aspects of police agencies.

Smith, B., *Police Systems in the United States,* Harper & Row, New York, 1949. Police organizations throughout the United States are analyzed and discussed.

Wilson, O. W., *Police Planning,* Thomas, Springfield, Ill., 1952. A classic in the area of organization, communication, and principles of police planning.

Wilson, O. W., *Police Administration,* McGraw–Hill, New York, 1963. A classic discussion of administrative function in law enforcement.

NOTES

1. O. W. Wilson, *Police Planning,* p. 3.

2. O. W. Wilson, *Police Administration;* V. A. Leonard, *Police Organization and Management;* A. P. Bristow, and E. C. Gabard, *Decision-Making in Police Administration.*

3. The late O. W. Wilson, noted author of many books and articles; retired Superintendent of Police, Chicago.

4. J. L. Sullivan, *Introduction to Police Science,* McGraw–Hill, New York, 1966, p. 168.

5. Wilson, *Police Administration,* pp. 8–9.

6. *Ibid.,* p. 10.

7. For additional reading in the area of specialization refer to: E. Eldefonso, *Youth Problems and Law Enforcement,* Prentice–Hall, Englewood Cliffs, N.J. Essentials of Law Enforcement Series, Chapter 5, 1971; and E. Eldefonso, *Law Enforcement and the Youthful Offender,* 2nd ed., Wiley, New York, 1973, Chapter 11.

8. J. E. Winters, "The Role of Police in Prevention and Control of Delinquency," *Federal Probation,* Vol. 21, No. 2, June 1957, p. 3.

9. *Ibid.,* p. 32.

10. *Ibid.,* p. 35.

11. *Ibid.,* p. 12. See also, B. Smith, *Police Systems in the United States;* and O. W. Wilson, "Progress in Police Administration," *Jour. Crim. Law,* Vol. 42, 1951.

CHAPTER NINE

Police Administration

Having considered police organization in the preceding chapter, attention is now directed to the *administration* of the police organization—to police management. Before proceeding with this discussion, however, it might be useful to relate police administration to the management of other criminal justice organizations such as probation, prison, or parole. Perhaps this relationship is seen in the following [1]:

Suspected or reported crime
Police investigation
Arrest
Preliminary court functions
Detention/release (bail or own recognizance)
Trial/prosecution/defense
Pre-sentence probation
Sentence
Probation/court/prison/parole

Imagine a ''connection'' between each of the criminal justice functions depicted, and consider the following against the background formed by these connections [2]:

. . . Criminal justice can function systematically only to the degree that each segment of the system takes into account all other segments. . . . The system

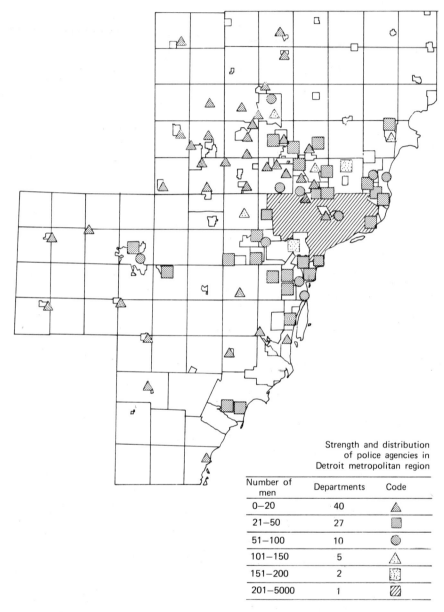

Strength and distribution of police agencies in Detroit metropolitan region

Number of men	Departments	Code
0–20	40	△
21–50	27	▦
51–100	10	◉
101–150	5	△
151–200	2	▦
201–5000	1	▨

FIGURE 9.1. *Fragmentation of Urban Police. Source:* The Challenge of Crime in a Free Society, *President's Commission on Law Enforcement and Administration of Justice, 1967, p. 121.*

is no more systematic than police relationship to prosecution, court relationship to police, prosecution relationship to corrections, corrections to law. . . .

In the absence of such connections, the fragmentation discussed in Chapter One multiplies and grows. Indeed, the fragmentation may grow to the point that the criminal justice system is a nonsystem [3]. It is within this understanding, the broad context of criminal justice, that police administration functions or fails to function. And with such an understanding, consider the following comment on administering any tax-supported organization [4]:

> If it were possible for the head of an organization to perform all of the work himself without the help of any additional personnel, it is conceivable that he would have to use only a small part of the administrative process. Once he had organized his work, his administrative functions would be limited to a bit of planning and nothing else. However, for the most part, an organization run by one man is not readily conceivable because even the most hearty of men have their limitations as far as physical and mental capacity are concerned. However, the one-man operation would need little administration because that one individual would be in complete control of the situation. The need for the administrative function increases with the growth of an organization because the larger the organization the more the administrator will be out of actual touch with work situations. . . .

Of course, in a single chapter of a book that spans virtually all of the principles of law enforcement, the emerging technology of police administra-

FIGURE 9.2. *Police Chief Edward M. Davis, reviews annual report prior to its presentation. Courtesy Police Department, Los Angeles, Ca.*

FIGURE 9.3. *Police Chief David Michel discusses high crime rate with division commanders. Courtesy Police Department, Anaheim, Ca.*

tion cannot be dealt with in depth. Nevertheless, the complexities inferred in the above cited quotation provide a background against which police administration will not be considered.

If all applicants for starting positions in law enforcement were asked to discuss their motives for seeking the job, at least a few would probably mention the desire to become *chief* one day. And whether or not applicants generally desire the responsibility of being chief, most would probably express an interest in promotional advancement through departmental organizations such as those discussed in the preceding chapter. Like most occupations, law enforcement jobs not only allow, but also encourage "getting ahead."

It might then be said that, from the start, the typical law enforcement career has a goal to achieve one or more "levels" of departmental leadership. This chapter deals mainly with the "top level" or the administrative level of departmental leadership, those positions bearing the titles of inspector, captain, division commander, chief, commissioner.

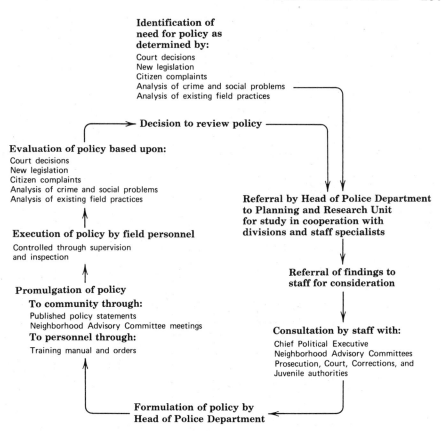

Identification of
need for policy as
determined by:

Court decisions
New legislation
Citizen complaints
Analysis of crime and social problems
Analysis of existing field practices

➤ **Decision to review policy**

Evaluation of policy based upon:
Court decisions
New legislation
Citizen complaints
Analysis of crime and social problems
Analysis of existing field practices

Referral by Head of Police Department
to Planning and Research Unit
for study in cooperation with
divisions and staff specialists

Execution of policy by field personnel
Controlled through supervision
and inspection

Referral of findings to
staff for consideration

Promulgation of policy
  To community through:
  Published policy statements
  Neighborhood Advisory Committee meetings
  To personnel through:
  Training manual and orders

Consultation by staff with:
Chief Political Executive
Neighborhood Advisory Committees
Prosecution, Court, Corrections, and
Juvenile authorities

Formulation of policy by
Head of Police Department

FIGURE 9.4. *Example of formulating and executing police policy. Source:*
Police Department, Los Angeles, Ca.

Although various levels of "rank" exist, departmental leadership in general consists of two parts. These two parts in turn relate to the "line and staff" organization discussed in the preceding chapter. The first part of a department's leadership is the direct supervision given the line officers who perform the actual duties required by the community. This type of leadership is provided by sergeants, supervisors, and, in some departments, lieutenants. Direct leadership of this nature generally is accomplished by interpreting *regulations* and by following procedures called departmental *policies*.

Although many descriptions are available, law enforcement policy can best be understood in terms of how it differs from *regulations*. Policies in a sense are merely "guidelines," whereas regulations, like the law itself, allow for very few "exceptions." Regulations govern the actual performance of departmental personnel and provide for sanctions and punishment [5]. On the other

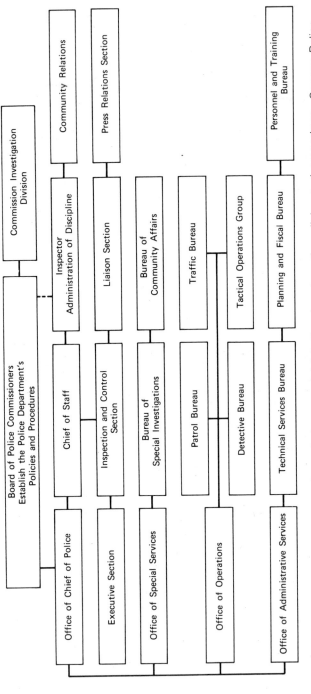

FIGURE 9.5. *Board of Police Commissioners establish the department's policies and procedures. Source: Police Department, Los Angeles, Ca.*

hand, policies offer flexibility and are less stringent than the more rigid regulations.

Both policies and regulations are determined by the second part, the "staff" part, of departmental leadership which frequently is referred to as the "administration." Members of the administration frequently bear the title of inspector, captain, division commander, chief, assistant chief, commissioner, and so on. Setting up policy and regulation is only one responsibility in the line and staff organization. Whether it be patrol activities, detective functions, or traffic matters, determining policy and regulation is merely an effort to gain consistency in achieving departmental goals through leadership—leadership much the same as any line and staff business organization having a "middle management" (i.e., supervisors like sergeants) and a "management" (i.e., executives or presidents, like captains and chiefs) [6]. Although management (i.e., administration) determines both regulation and policy, the setting of policy is the function with which administrative leadership is most often identified.

ADMINISTRATIVE LEADERSHIP

Setting Policy

As already indicated, departmental regulations customarily demand strict conformity. For this reason, all personnel are expected to know, understand, and conform to departmental regulations. But since administrative policies in many instances can be thought of as guidelines, they also are in a sense comparable to strong recommendations. Put another way, regulations outline procedures, methods, or activities that *will* be followed, whereas policies reflect what *should* be followed. Of course, the policy is set with the expectation that every effort will be made to avoid exceptions, but also with the understanding that exceptions are possible.

Setting policy, as opposed to setting regulation, might further be clarified by noting that policies at times determine how regulations are used. As an example, a department regulation may require job applicants to have 2 years of college along with certain physical and mental qualifications. This same department might well establish a *policy* of considering only those applicants who have completed 4 years of college *unless,* of course, only those with 2 years of college happen to apply thereby creating exceptions.

Administrative policy can be set for virtually every activity or function of

FIGURE 9.6. *Police Chief David Michal receives intelligence reports and discusses them with division administration. Courtesy Police Department, Anaheim, Ca.*

the department, whether or not regulations previously existed. Departments usually adopt policies on personnel, recruiting, hiring, training, discipline, equipment, purchasing, arrest procedure, and conduct, to name only a few areas.

Unlike department regulations which are consistently in written form, policies may or may not be written and may be called, for example, department philosophy. But whether presented to line personnel verbally or in written form, policies serve the same guideline purpose.

Department policies or guidelines are influenced by numerous considerations such as unique community problems, public opinion, fiscal budget, political considerations, and law. For instance, the policy on the size of a department (i.e., number of personnel, amount of equipment, building, etc.) obviously depends on the size of the fiscal budget which in turn may depend on political matters. And the size of the department, at least the ratio of police officers to citizens, clearly affects the department's policies on all operational functions.

There are many managerial functions that also affect the departments policies and operational functions. Perhaps a cursory view of some of the functions, along with a brief managerial explanation of the philosophies involved, might be useful.

FIGURE 9.7. *First-line supervisor discusses beat problem with patrol officer. Courtesy Police Department, Anaheim, Ca.*

Managerial Philosophies and Functions

Broadly stated, administration of *any* organization can be placed in one (or more) of three general categories: (*a*) COMMAND MANAGEMENT, (*b*) MANAGEMENT THROUGH PERSONAL RELATIONS, and (*c*) MANAGING BY RESULTS.

These three broad categories of management occur in one of three "systems": (*a*) FUNCTIONAL SYSTEM meaning *more* administrative concern for *what* gets done than *who* does it or *how*, (*b*) DYSFUNCTIONAL SYSTEM in which *more* administrative concern is given *who* does it and *how*, than *what* gets done, and (*c*) IN-BETWEEN SYSTEM in which administrative concern vacillates back and forth between FUNCTION and DYSFUNCTIONAL.

Administratively, the COMMAND MANAGEMENT approach is one of *continuous orders.* A fairly good case can be made for seeing this approach as more effective in dysfunctional systems than functional systems [7].

MANAGEMENT BY RESULTS, on the other hand, emphasizes clearly defined roles and functions with personnel strongly accountable for both. A good case for this approach can be made in *either* a functional *or* a dysfunctional system [8].

Beyond these considerations, police administration influences the impact of policy in the relative concern for "production" as opposed to "morale" as will be discussed shortly. Within this sphere of influence, a very wide range of managerial concern focuses on the emerging *science* of administration—for example, the budget process.

Fiscal Budget Policy

Administrative policy, it can be said, is a matter of interpreting and reacting to many influences or, in some cases, reacting to overt pressures. Many of these influences are somewhat detrimental to the department's efficiency, but by far the greatest threat to efficiency are those influences that weaken or reduce the size of the department budget. For this reason, interpreting and reacting to influences that are detrimental to the budget becomes a high-priority responsibility of administrative leadership. Interpretation and reaction to such influences must produce, among other things, policies that seek to gain maximum efficiency for every tax dollar spent. The importance of gaining the most police efficiency for the available tax dollars cannot be overemphasized since it goes without saying that there are never sufficient funds to ensure "ideal" police services needed by the community. It is crucial therefore that administrative leaders in law enforcement acquire considerable skill in the art of persuasion when dealing with legislative bodies responsible for dispersing tax funds.

The administrative leadership has the yearly responsibility to use such things as crime and safety statistics to prepare a department budget. The budget is actually a plea for sufficient funds to maintain or expand a department capable of meeting existing and expected crime and safety problems. The salaries of new officers and new leaders are frequently more significant than even expensive equipment such as automobiles or electronic computers. Buildings of course are the greatest budget item, but these confront the administration less frequently.

Customary procedure in the preparation of a department budget includes the accumulation of detailed records [9]. The records should include a complete analysis of the time and the manpower used to accomplish all services. Cost of equipment is obviously a valid item to record along with any other expenses accumulated by the department. Various fines and other money transactions that routinely involve law enforcement of course relate to the budget.

Still another and far more distressing aspect of the budget are the political considerations relating to enforcing laws affecting groups directly contributing major tax support or otherwise wielding power with those who pass judgment on the size of a law enforcement budget.

Selective Enforcement Policy

The understaffed department cannot enforce all laws or enforce all laws equally at all times. This regrettable comment on the consequence of under-staffing remains true in spite of the obvious ideal of uniform law enforcement. "Selective" enforcement policies then become necessary.

Selective enforcement policies are influenced by administrative interpretation of public support which in turn often is related to a department's relationship with the press. Policy dealing with the types of laws to be enforced is particularly sensitive to public opinion as well as to political influence and, of course, to the severity of manpower shortages [10]. The unique problems of the community, which often include the availability of taxes, frequently create still further influences on the setting of selective enforcement policies. Often that which influences administrative leaders in setting policies on budgets is precisely the same as or are at least related to that which influences setting policies on selective enforcement.

Public Opinion

Unhappy is the department that functions in a community in which typical citizens expect law enforcement to *completely* eliminate crime and safety problems. Another extreme of equal detriment is a community expecting absolutely nothing from law enforcement insofar as crime and safety is concerned [11]. Fortunately, *public opinion* usually falls somewhere between these two extremes. Of course public support is a universal goal of law enforcement.

One of the more difficult tasks of administrative leadership is to judge public opinion accurately enough to set department policies that retain public support for the line officer while enforcing the law as consistently and efficiently as possible. Policies that guide officers toward public support are particularly difficult to conceive in a changing society.

Evidence of changes confronting both line and staff personnel can be found in tragedies such as the one occurring in the Queens section of New York City in March of 1965. A 28-year-old woman named Catherine Genovese was attacked on three separate occasions over a span of 40 minutes by a knife-wielding assailant. During that time, no fewer than thirty-eight persons heard the woman scream for help or actually witnessed the attacks. Yet not one of them telephoned the police let alone went to the aid of the victim. Finally, after nearly 40 minutes, a 70-year-old woman in the neighborhood called the police. A squad car was at the scene 2 minutes later but by that time the woman was dead. Public apathy of this nature must in all too many instances become a major influence on administrative leaders setting department policies with the goal of gaining public support. In this particular regard, the administrative leadership often must set policy with the knowledge that changing the public's attitude toward police often depends on personal contacts which tend to be of less impact than the image of law enforcement generated in the press.

Judging public opinion sometimes requires administrative leaders to question whether the press *reflects* opinion or *causes* opinion. This question often arises when the local press consistently "headlines" crime to the point of stimulating what may seem to administrators to be greater citizen discussion of police activities than occurs in other communities with even higher crime rates but where the press is less inclined to sensationalize crime. The press of course argues that the public is entitled to all possible information on crime and any other social problems. And administrators customarily agree but only so long as public pressure as reflected or caused by the press does not totally divert police energies away from less sensational yet necessary activity.

Of course, the administrator's task of setting policies must take into account the types of problems that concern the public as well as other needs which must be met at the same time. For example, a series of assaults that become headlined are likely to result in public pressure through the community's political leaders in the direction of greater police activities to prevent assault. Yet the wise administrator is aware of the long-range consequences of removing line officers from "nearly jelled" stakeouts, from patrols in "recently quieted" areas, from "barely adequate" traffic programs, and so on. The policy of a department under such stress would probably be to avoid stripping *all* services to satisfy a single and possibly temporary need. And yet a policy decision would be necessary because the opinion of the public being served cannot be ignored by those serving it—at least not consistently ignored.

The difficulty here soon becomes a matter of emphasis—how much emphasis in each area. From the line officer's point of view, emphasis should focus on problems as they *exist*. From the public's point of view, emphasis should focus on problems as they are *perceived*. From the point of view of law enforcement administration, emphasis must focus in such a way that the line officer's morale and the public's support combine for maximum department efficiency. Of course this policy holds as a primary goal the reduction of the public's prejudices and resentment toward law enforcement [12].

From the point of view of both public and line officer, greater acceptance is possible when policies are announced well in advance.

Pressure Groups

Implicit in the discussion of efforts to gain public acceptance of policies is the acknowledgement of pressure groups. While detailed elaboration of this subject is not possible in a general text on principles of enforcing law, the outstanding book *Police Organization and Management* provides a pertinent context [13]:

> It is a basic principle of democratic government that administration must be responsive to public control. This is especially true of police administration because of the unique powers with which it is entrusted. Basic, also, is the fact that such control must find expression through formal channels of governmental structure, descending vertically from the people by way of the ballot box through the legislative body to the appointing officer, and through him to the police chief executive. It is likewise essential that responsibility flow vertically upward from the police to the appointing authority, and then from him to the legislature and finally to the people. These controls should be out in the open where they are exposed to observation and appraisal.
>
> Violation of this fundamental principle of organization is undoubtedly responsible for many of the ills and growing pains that have affected local government in general and police administration in particular. Violation takes the form of pressures and controls generated by special interest groups; they are usually brought to bear upon the weakest point or points in the organizational structure. The point of vulnerability may be the patrolman on the beat, the "gold braid" of the department, the police chief executive, the Mayor, the City Council, or a combination of two or more of these officials.

With this background in mind, attention is now shifted to administrative concern with police morale.

Morale

The morale of law enforcement personnel has been pictured as an inspiring attitude that lends itself to enthusiasm, initiative, and courage [14]. This view is elaborated as the primary source of success in police endeavor and can be maintained by leadership as well as by careful selection and training of personnel. The detailed description of personal traits associated with this definition of department morale of course probably resembles the detailed description of the personal traits of a good soldier. From the point of view of administrative leadership, however, department morale is considerably more complex.

It might seem that few if any morale problems would exist if administrative leaders were able to say to line officers:

> Our job is to enforce the law without exceptions and our department has enough personnel to do this job. We have an exact regulation that covers every situation and so your leaders will merely check your performance by regulation and this will prevent confusing contradictions of judgment. These exact regulations will also prevent "hindsight" reaction and further prevent pressures when the public or press examine a line officer's split-second emergency decisions. The public is aware of your sacrifices and is therefore most loyal.

The law enforcement administrator could not say these things even if he desired. If able to comment at all, the administrative leader would more likely say:

> Our job is to enforce the laws but we do not have enough personnel and resources to do so effectively. And we are expected to enforce laws in a way that we maintain the support of a community that is not always sympathetic with our problems. Because people having difficulties with the law have such varied causes and explanations, there is no way to give you the comfort of having an exact answer for every situation—and more often than not your leaders will evaluate your performance on your judgment rather than on your ability to follow precise regulations. Many of your judgments will be subjected to close scrutiny after the emergency moment has passed. The public you protect may well turn on you through misunderstanding of the nature and difficulties of your hazardous responsibilities.

So the complexities of the departmental morale are such that the administrative leaders face the task of fostering morale in a situation that *seemingly* discourages morale. But the peculiar thing about morale is that it is usually (but not always) high during stress and adversity. Perhaps this is best illustrated by the descriptive commendation regarding marine exploits on Iwo

Jima during the Second World War: "Uncommon valor was a common virtue." The feeling of camaraderie or brotherhood that frequently prevails among peace officers when under stress or in physical danger further illustrates this concept. The administrator who is aware of this is prepared to create a "common purpose" spirit through the use of the very adversities that seemingly threaten department morale.

Since policies frequently reflect a department's reaction to influences that are stressful to department personnel, the manner in which policies are transmitted to line officers becomes crucial in the administrative process of maintaining high morale.

Any indication that administrative leaders are aware of job stresses is well received by line officers experiencing the direct influence of Supreme Court decisions, public apathy, civil disobedience, and many similar considerations reviewed elsewhere in this book. Indeed, line officers consistently exhibit great tolerance of stress where department policy is seen as the administrators' conscientious effort to consider morale regardless of what other influences may dictate. Of course, this entails an administrative effort to make line officers aware not only of morale considerations, but also of the nature and importance of other major influences.

The line officer's confidence that administrative leaders are really in the "same boat" tends to create the common purpose spirit which in turn frequently produces high morale. This approach to morale, however, demands complete and continuing honesty between the "cop on the beat" and "the brass." The mutual understanding that accrues to this honesty not only encourages morale but is valuable in the solution of problems related to personnel problems such as assignment and scheduling. A still further advantage of honesty that bears directly on morale is the reduction of disciplinary methods in the department.

Discipline

Few if any discipline problems exist for administrative leaders who find themselves in the fortunate position of setting policies that satisfy both the community and departmental personnel—except perhaps in situations involving an officer's method or technique or certain kinds of personal behavior. If the community remains satisfied with (and confident in) the department's performance, there is less "need" to set policies that tend to place line officers in situations requiring controversial decisions. The selection and training of personnel in this regard is obviously important. For, indeed, the satisfaction of a community with the law enforcement agency clearly relates to the competence of police personnel. In other words, a community's confidence or satisfaction probably reflects adequate and uncorrupted police service—"all other things equal" with the press. When public pressures seek increased activity requiring possibly controversial decisions, however, discipline usually becomes correspondingly more likely through the increased possibility of unfavorable evaluation of an officer's judgment. The officer's methods and techniques obviously relate to his performance whether guided by regulation or judgment, but discipline is seldom necessary when the officer is able to follow departmental regulation or policy rather than his own judgment.

As an extreme example, an officer in pursuit of a traffic speeder is unlikely to create a situation requiring disciplinary action if his administrative leadership has set a policy that such pursuits should not be terminated without apprehension of the speeder. In such a situation, the officer could speed by what appeared to be a gas station holdup or purse snatching or any number of offenses without violating his departmental policies. If no clear-cut departmental policy exists, the officer must exercise his own judgment. But, of course, the community demands greater attention be paid to a felony (holdup) than a misdemeanor (speeding), so the officer must make a decision. He has to consider the speeder "might be" in a stolen car which may constitute a felony and the apparent holdup "might be" merely a customer-proprietor price dispute. Hopefully, bad judgment is examined in the appropriate context if disciplinary action is considered. For even when discipline is called for, fair consideration of extenuating circumstances almost invariably leads to greater acceptance of the need for discipline by the officer receiving discipline. And to the morale-conscious administrator, the image of being firm but fair is indispensable. Discipline that is firm but fair is by no means easy to provide within the confines of personnel codes that may not always fit other considerations in administrative decisions—particularly when discipline can take so many forms.

The types of discipline vary widely and range from verbal admonishment to suspension from duty. The varieties of discipline governed by personnel codes may or may not influence the administrative decision to use discipline. Far more important to the department's morale than the discipline itself is the belief that discipline *is* fair, rather than merely part of a code.

Administrative Control

As indicated in the preceding chapter, administrative officers have "command" responsibility in a law enforcement organization where line and staff is utilized. And since the overwhelming majority of law enforcement agencies are organized along the line and staff system, administrative officers can be assumed to be in command. Command, however, varies greatly from department to department. Most county sheriffs are elected and thus occupy a substantially different executive position than the appointed director of an agency that is merely one segment of a larger federal department. Both types of executives in turn exercise administrative control that has little in common with controls exercised by the police chief appointed solely on the basis of civil service examination, or the chief appointed by a mayor or city council. The influence of federal policy may bear little resemblance to the influence exerted by police commissions or city councils.

The administrator's wishes regarding the size of his department (personnel, buildings, and equipment) may or may not have great impact on the final decisions affecting the size of his department. But the influence of law enforcement administrators varies to an even greater degree concerning salaries, benefits of personnel, and in some cases the actual selection of personnel. It should not be surprising then that such influence varies greatly when it comes to police review boards or similar matters of department concern which are discussed elsewhere throughout this book.

In spite of the great variations in administrative control, however, the majority of law enforcement administrators share a common goal: Maximum public service through maximum efficiency through maximum morale through complete integrity.

Efficiency Versus Effectiveness

As noted at the outset of this chapter, however, law enforcement administrators function (or fail to function) within the broad context of criminal justice—police, courts, prosecution-defense, and corrections. Maximum public service through maximum efficiency and maximum morale through complete integrity, then, must relate to the *effectiveness* of overall criminal justice.

Just as an efficient automobile is not effective when merely spinning its wheels "efficiently" in the snow, so also is police *efficiency* of little administrative value unless overall criminal justice is *effective*. Effectiveness then is the goal of *all* criminal justice administration. There is a wide range of technology necessary to bring about such effectiveness; for example, MIS (Management Information Systems), MFRI (Managerial Function Role Interfaces), CBA (Cost Benefit Analysis), DTP (Decision Tree Planning), AMI (Accountability Measurement Index), PERT (Program Evaluation Review Technique), and a host of complex managerial procedures. Yet underlying the most sophisticated managerial development program is police concern for *effectiveness* rather than mere efficiency.

SUMMARY

Overall criminal justice was the context in which this chapter was introduced. It was stated that promotional advancement is usually a goal in law enforcement careers. It was further stated that "getting ahead" not only is allowed in police organizations but usually is encouraged.

The *levels* of rank to which law enforcement careers aspire are divided into two general parts. These two parts correspond respectively to the *line* activities and the *staff* activities presented in the preceding chapter. The staff level includes the department's administrative leaders who customarily are entitled inspector, captain, commander, chief, commissioner.

There is a distinction between *regulation* and *policy*—regulation being defined as allowing for few exceptions whereas policy serves in a guideline capacity. Policy is also distinguished from regulation in that policy in some instances determines *when* and *how* regulations are used. The task of determining a department's policies is one of the responsibilities of administrative leaders.

The various influences on setting departmental policies include law, availability of manpower, press, public opinion, political considerations, and, of course, the morale and efficiency of the department. Administrative leaders are expected to deal with these influences, along with the unique problems of the community, in a manner that affords maximum law enforcement service.

Maximum law enforcement service frequently requires an effort to gain tax dollars in order to buy new equipment and hire new personnel. The policies dealing with fiscal budget then become primary to administrative leaders.

Maximum efficiency, at least in understaffed departments, frequently requires selection of areas of emphasis. Policies in this regard are particularly difficult since the administrators frequently must respond to public opinion or political pressures that seek to use available manpower only in publicized areas of enforcement. These influences must be reconciled in turn with the morale of line officers charged with the responsibility of accomplishing policy goals.

Maximum efficiency requires high morale which sometimes can be fostered *because of* stress rather than *in spite of* it. Policies relating to discipline of course affect morale, but honesty between administrative leaders and line officers tends to resolve morale problems associated with discipline.

The chapter concludes with the observation that administrative leaders vary greatly in the degree of control they exercise over the department, although there remains a common goal of maximum departmental service to the community served.

It was also stressed that criminal justice *effectiveness* rather than police *efficiency* is the administrative goal.

ANNOTATED REFERENCES

Coffey, A., *Criminal Justice Administration: A Management Systems Approach,* Prentice–Hall, Englewood Cliffs, N.J., 3rd. ed., 1974. Presents a comprehensive systems approach to management in all segments of criminal justice: police, courts, prosecution, and corrections.

Columbus, E. G., "Management By System," *Police Chief,* July 1970; Pert, L. E., "Motivation: An Operational Staff Presentation," *Law and Order,* Aug. 1971; and Lynch, C. G., "The Forgotten Responsibility," *Law and Order,* January 1970.

Davies, D., "Police, Law and the Individual," *Annals of the American Academy of Political and Social Science,* Vol. 291, 1954, p. 145. Another well-done consideration of overall police relationship to community affairs.

Germann, A. C., *Police Executive Development,* Thomas, Springfield, Ill., 1962. A good overview of managerial staff development in the police organization.

Griffin, J. I., *Statistics Essential for Police Efficiency,* Thomas, Springfield, Ill., 1958. An excellent presentation of departmental essentials in police statistical data.

Institute on Police Management for Supervisory and Administrative Personnel, *Police Management for Supervisory and Administrative Personnel,* Thomas, Springfield, Ill., 1963. A discussion of the title subject within an administrative framework.

Larsen, G., *An Introduction to Police Personnel Management,* Northwestern Univ. Traffic Institute, Chicago, 1959. A good presentation of administrative problems relating to personnel matters.

Leonard, V., and H. More, *Police Organization and Management,* 3rd ed., Foundation Press, Mineola, New York, 1971. An outstanding coverage of the title subject area, particularly Chapters 2, 3, 4, and 5.

Wilson, O. W., *Police Administration,* McGraw–Hill, New York, 1972. A classic discussion of administrative function in law enforcement.

NOTES

1. Coffey, Allan, *Criminal Justice Administration: A Management Systems Approach,* Figure 1, p. 5.

2. *Ibid.*

3. Howlett, Frederich, and H. Hurst, "A Systems Approach to Comprehensive Criminal Justice Planning," *Crime and Delinquency,* Vol. 17, No. 4, Oct. 1971, pp. 345–54.

4. ————, *Principles of Civil Service Administration and Management,* Davis, Santa Cruz, Ca., 1972, p. 1.

5. M. Banton, *The Policeman in the Community,* Basic Books, New York, 1964, p. 216.

6. W. Pomeroy, "The Administrative Setting," *in* R. H. Blum (ed.), *Police Selection,* Thomas, Springfield, Ill., 1964, p. 20.

7. Coffey, *op. cit.,* Chapters 2–4.

8. *Ibid.*

9. J. I. Griffin, *Statistics Essential for Police Efficiency,* p. 3.

10. P. A. Devlin, "The Police in a Changing Society," *Jour. Crim. Law, Crim., Pol. Sci.,* Vol. 57, No. 2, June 1966, p. 123.

11. H. Ibele, "Law Enforcement and the Permissive Society," *Police,* Sept.–Oct. 1965, p. 15.

12. O. W. Wilson, "Police Authority in a Free Society," *Jour. Crim. Law, Crim., Pol. Sci.,* Vol. 54, No. 2, June 1963, p. 175.

13. V. Leonard and H. More, *Police Organization and Management,* 3rd ed., p. 22.

14. J. L. Sullivan, *Introduction to Police Science,* McGraw–Hill, New York, 1966, p. 197.

CHAPTER TEN

Police Patrol

In every law enforcement agency, no matter how large or small, the patrol division is the only division that can never be eliminated. If necessary, the patrol division can function by itself, but of course it will be most effective if supported by staff and auxiliary divisions such as custody, transportation, maintenance, detective, communications, records, juvenile, and the crime laboratory.

Since the typical law enforcement agency is small in size, the patrol officer must be able to carry out all functions of law enforcement. Today in the United States there are about 420,000 peace officers in 36,700 city police departments and 3050 sheriff's departments. A large majority of these agencies is composed of one to five men, rendering what is known as resident deputy type police services. In many cases, the local chief of police or sheriff is required to assume some patrol duties as well as attend to his administrative responsibilities.

When the officer in the small local agency is unable to perform his function because of inexperience, lack of skill or knowledge, etc., he then must obtain outside assistance from specialized and supporting county, state, and federal agencies who stand ready and willing to assist at any time.

In police agencies that are of a size and nature to adequately support staff and auxiliary divisions, and even in the small local police department, the patrol division, the backbone of every police agency, is the only police division that provides complete 24 hour service each day of the year to the people it serves and protects.

EVOLUTION OF PATROL

Police patrol is not new to the twentieth century. It had its beginnings in early civilization when man felt a need to protect himself from evil spirits and wild beasts that roamed the forest. As men became more civilized and banded together into groups or communities, they protected themselves and their food supply from raids by neighboring bands of men. Gradually, this protection became a more sophisticated operation, and the protection became a community concern. They began to protect themselves through a very crude form of patrol in their living areas. Eventually, this patrol duty was given over to a special group within the community to provide adequate and necessary protection for the community.

In Biblical days fighting and bloodshed were part of the times. Soldiers could be found in most communities to carry out the tasks of warfare and to protect the citizenry. Their policing duties, however, were somewhat simplified since most towns and cities of that era were completely encircled by high walls and the gates were locked at night.

The ancient Greeks maintained no police. In order to keep the peace in their cities, the law-enforcing duties fell on the shoulders of the several bodies of magistrates, the most important of whom were the *Astynomi,* or street supervisors. These men, small in number, were charged by law with the responsibility of keeping the streets swept, supervising construction of new buildings, and maintaining decency and morality on the streets of the city. In addition, they were charged with the responsibility of carrying out their necessary judicial functions of deciding all lawsuits that involved questions coming within their jurisdiction. There were other police duties that were tended by *Aqueduct, Market,* and *Corn* magistrates. Each of these divisions consisted of ten male member magistrates and they were charged with the policing duties as indicated by their respective titles of office.

In contrast to the Greeks' method of keeping peace and order, the Roman policing system was quite similar to today's system of law enforcement. A large body of about 7000 men, known as *constables,* was organized and detailed into precincts and divisions throughout Rome. Their primary function was to preserve order and to keep the peace. These Roman officers were probably the very first public safety officers as we know them today, for in addition to their policing duties they were the local firemen.

The basic concepts inherent in modern municipal law enforcement and especially in police patrol were derived from England. In 1252, the Watch and Ward Act laws were passed to provide police patrol protection for the citizens of that country. They were, however, grossly inadequate. From that time until Sir Robert Peel's police reform took place in 1829, the various attempts to provide systems of police patrol service to the citizens of England were often steps in the right direction, but insufficient to quell the rising tide of lawlessness. Criminal suspects were chased from one jurisdiction into another rather than arrested. In the minds of the local governing officials, this was more economical since it would not necessitate clothing, housing, and feeding them. In many areas there were no facilities available for such care and custody, and the prisoner would have to have been "farmed out" to one of the reputable citizens in the community. Citizens' fees for such services to the community were usually very large. As a result of this practice, recidivism was high and the people in the community protected themselves at night by staying within their homes and heavily barring doors and windows, just as the cavemen protected themselves by barricading their cave home entrances.

When Peel established the Metropolitan Police in 1829, it was thought that they would be well received. But they were not; they were referred to as "Peel's Bloody Gang" and other bigoted labels. It is possible that the strict policing that came about as a result of Peel's reforms was too much for the citizenry to accept all at once. Most of the new officers were Irishmen who had served in the English Army and, since a poor relationship existed between England and Ireland, the Irish policeman was not looked on with favor. These officers provided tough and strict patrol service to which the English were not accustomed.

Since the United States was, in the beginning, colonies of England, it is only natural that the first police patrol in America displayed a great likeness to that of the eighteenth and early nineteenth centuries in England. The first American villages were small and usually patrolled by a single, paid night watchman. His duty as a patrolman was to ring a bell at specified intervals, give the weather condition, and notify the constable in case of fire or disorder in the town. A single *parish constable* was the police officer in the community. About the middle of the nineteenth century, most American cities organized their police forces in a manner similar to that of London in order to cope with greater problems of keeping the peace as the society became more complex. Thus the *first* American police patrol force was established in Boston, Massachusetts, in 1838, when six men were selected and placed on daytime duty to supplement the existing *night watch*. The two units were combined 12 years later and today have grown into a fine metropolitan police agency.

Modern police patrol service has made vast changes in operation during the twentieth century. The primary factors affecting this change have been the adaptation of technological and scientific methods and instruments to the discovery of crime, better mobility through new modes of transportation, data processing and improved records systems, ultramodern communications facilities, judicial proof, and superior training.

IMPORTANCE OF POLICE PATROL

The patrol division in every police department is the largest and most important single unit providing the community with the service it expects. It operates on the central theme of the total police purpose, which is to prevent crime, and it acts as the eyes and ears of the chief police administrator. How the administrator solves the many and varied police problems depends heavily on the information furnished to him by the patrol force. Also through the patrol service, many of the elements contributing to emergency calls for service can be eliminated or changed by the routine operations of this division. Above all, the central theme of preventing crime is paramount.

For a crime to take place, three factors must exist simultaneously: (a) The *desire* of the person to commit the crime, (b) the *will* of the person to commit the crime, and (c) the *opportunity* to commit the crime. Should any one of these factors be removed by the work of the patrol division, the crime will not be successfully committed. No other division in the police profession can provide such a favorable influence over the potential perpetrator of a crime. The assignments and services carried out by the patrol officer have far-reaching importance and his competence reflects upon the entire police department. He is serving in the only branch of police service that is without limit in its responsibility and that is the only indispensable unit in the police agency.

OBJECTIVES OF THE PATROL FORCE

"To protect and to serve," the motto of the patrol force, best describes their objectives as they serve, police, and protect the community every hour of every day. Listed below are the principal objectives of every police patrol force in order of their importance:

1. *Prevention of Crime.* The well-trained patrol officer operating in a plainly marked patrol vehicle or on foot is unquestionably a deterrent force that aids in the prevention of a crime. Areas, situations, and conditions that are conducive to lawlessness are observed by the patrol officer and, through proper inquiry and investigation, he deters criminal activity.
2. *Protection of the lives and property* of the public from the criminal suspect, and protection against hazards and conditions adverse to the public safety. The general public looks to and depends on the police officer for its individual and collective safety. Citizens' property must be protected from crimes in times of disaster, their city must be voided of elements producing and harboring criminals and illegal activity, and their safety must be ensured through the uniform regulation of traffic laws and ordinances.
3. *Enforcement of the laws and ordinances* the patrol officer is sworn to safeguard and uphold with equal treatment and enforcement toward all. He must know without question his responsibility to the law. He must also possess expertise in the law and its various ramifications. In most cases an officer will not be afforded the time or the opportunity to obtain assistance when he is required to make on-the-spot investigations or decisions and take the necessary enforcement action.
4. *Preservation of the public peace* and tranquillity in the community. This objective requires a large portion of the patrol officer's time as he is required to handle persons who are disorderly, intoxicated, or under the influence of drugs, who are vagrants or trespassers, and those persons involved in crimes of violence as well as other related offenses.
5. *Detection and apprehension of criminal violators.* When the patrol officer makes an arrest on the spot and without warning, he must be right. There is no room for error. He, as well as the agency he represents, has much to lose if error occurs. In making the arrest, the officer must know and use the various techniques of arrest while also protecting himself, his brother officers, and the general public.
6. *Performance, in a courteous and helpful manner, of miscellaneous services* to the community at large—furnishing information upon request, giving directions, and providing general assistance. This final objective of the patrol force also applies to the staff and auxiliary units and divisions of any law enforcement agency.

The objectives of the patrol force are wide in scope but their achievement is marked by an even greater variety and range.

TYPES OF PATROL

Police agencies throughout the world today use many types of patrol, and in some areas a combination of these types is employed. The type of patrol used is determined by three fundamental but highly important factors: (*a*)

FIGURE 10.1. (left) *Today's foot patrol officer is more effective and in a position to provide many services with the aid of modern radio communications. Courtesy Police Department, Oakland, Ca.* (right) *Police officers daily make contact with children alone in the cities. Their duty: Find the parents and restore the children to them. Courtesy Police Department, Seattle, Wa.*

The kind of area to be patrolled and its topography, (*b*) the type of criminal violations and illicit activity that occurs in the beat district, and (*c*) the prevalence of crime within the district. Patrol areas in most jurisdictions are called *beats,* and each beat is patrolled during a specified time period. These time periods have many different designations such as *shifts, watches, tours of duty,* and *work shifts.* Each of these time periods covers a working span of 8 hours and in most cities there are three and sometimes four shifts of duty (providing for overlapping) provided every 24 hours to the community. The exact number of shifts fluctuates up or down depending on the amount of services called for by the community and the number of police patrol personnel available to provide the requested services.

Foot Patrol

Foot patrol is the oldest and most common type of uniform police patrol known and is employed extensively throughout the world, especially in Europe and Asia. Its development may be traced back to the time of the *Bow Street Runners and Patrols* of 1763 in England, when Henry Fielding created this force to prevent the criminal activity and general disorder which was rampant at the time. Today, foot patrol is still one of the most important and effective types of patrol service. Its use, however, is kept to a minimum by most police agencies because it has proved to be the most costly of the various types of patrol. The foot patrol officer is used most frequently in areas of dense population in the larger metropolitan centers where there is a concentration of police hazards. These areas or districts usually are confined to the downtown business districts and the slum and tenement districts of a city. In addition to performing the routine patrol services, the officer is responsible for traffic control and congestion on his beat. In many large cities such as Los Angeles, San Francisco, Chicago, and New York, the foot patrol officer may be observed directing traffic at street intersections or making himself generally available to the public as he patrols his beat. In the large suburban shopping centers that are mushrooming all over our country, he will be seen patrolling through the mall and nearby areas. Many agencies vary the foot patrol officer's time by having him spend a part of the time patrolling on foot during peak pedestrian and vehicular traffic hours and then as a second officer in a patrol car when his particular services are not so likely to be called for. Although foot patrol is costly to the taxpayer, it has many advantages and its frequent appearance in our cities should be re-established. Perhaps many cities now without police foot patrol will in the future follow the recommendations of the report of The President's Commission on Law Enforcement and Administration of Justice regarding this area of police service.

In his book *Patrol Procedures,* Payton lists six important advantages to foot patrol. Listed in part, these advantages are [1]:

1. The foot patrolman can provide immediate traffic control when it is needed. Being within a close proximity he will know when his assistance is needed due to the increase in traffic. He does not have the problem of parking his police vehicle, nor finding a place to park it without causing further traffic problems.
2. More person-to-person contact can be made with the public. This provides greater chances to promote good public relations. . . . The foot patrol officer makes more personal contacts and is seen more by the public than any other type of patrol and therefore becomes an important link between the department and public. Extreme care should be used in selecting an officer for this duty.
3. The officer can actually get to know the physical layout of his beat better. There are many things that an officer misses by patrolling his beat in a police car because of the speed he is traveling and because of the size of the beat,
4. He can get to know the people on his beat better. . . . This advantage enables the officer to meet and develop contacts which are of vital importance to all law enforcement.
5. A foot officer can sneak up on a situation, where a patrol car is easily noticed when it approaches.

6. By use of the new transistorized walkie-talkies, the officer can maintain communications with the department and mobile units. The lack of communications used to be a disadvantage. He can now be directed to trouble situations just as patrol cars are, and can immediately report trouble to headquarters.

Of all the advantages of routine police foot patrol, the person-to-person contact is the most valuable to any local law enforcement agency.

Horse Patrol

Next to foot patrol, the mounted or horse patrol is one of the oldest types of police patrol used. It is seldom seen in the United States, but is still being used most effectively in such large cities as San Francisco and New York. Many sheriff departments throughout the United States, however, still include mounted patrol in the organizational structure of their departments, but this is usually in the form of a reserve or auxiliary unit. The general absence of this type of patrol results from the high cost of operation and maintenance of the horses and their stable facilities, as well as the infrequent use made of such patrol except for mountainous or rough terrain and then generally only in emergency situations.

Mounted police horse patrol today is utilized in four specific ways, and in some jurisdictions it is used only at certain times of the year or on specific occasions. These uses are: (a) *Crowd control,* at which they are most effective; (b) *park patrol,* for providing maximum safety for people using the park, its trails, its roadways, and the multitude of paths and recreation facilities; (c) *beach patrol,* for which horses are more adaptable than motor vehicles; and (d) *posse and searching assignments,* to which horses are particularly valuable for the rough and mountainous areas. Many times the mounted patrol will be used to track down escaping felons and wanted persons. In addition, they are of great assistance in searching for and retrieving lost and injured persons in remote areas.

Until recent years, the mounted horse patrol force shared a handicap with the foot patrolman. He lacked communication with his headquarters and other emergency service agencies such as fire, ambulance, air and sea rescue agencies, to name but a few. But today the mounted officer is equipped with mobile transistorized two-way radios enabling him to communicate with his headquarters and other officers in the field to send and receive messages, information, and instructions. Although horse patrol would appear to be a thing of the past, it has a definite place in our modern-day police patrol system.

FIGURE 10.2. *Mounted patrol in park and recreation areas is still in operation in many areas in the United States. Here officers examine abandoned vehicle in Golden Gate Park, San Francisco. Courtesy Police Department, San Francisco, Ca.*

Bicycle Patrol

This form of patrol transportation was used quite frequently prior to the introduction of the automobile to police patrol service. It is still used in many areas of the United States and more predominantly in many foreign countries. A bicycle is quiet and of course may be ridden into areas where no automobile can travel. It is of great aid when the element of surprise is important and is valuable in conducting patrol of high crime-rate areas, in many cases making possible the apprehension of suspects in the act of committing a crime.

The police officer operating a bicycle and equipped with a transistorized radio is afforded the opportunity of covering a larger area in a shorter period of time with less physical fatigue than his brother officer on foot, yet his opportunity for observation and eye contact with the public is only slightly less than that of the foot patrolman walking his beat.

In more recent years, those cities using horses in parks and recreation areas have adopted the bicycle in their place, but have retained enough of the animals to take care of beach patrol, parade and crowd control as well as posse and search assignments.

Automobile Patrol

With the advent of the automobile, law enforcement agencies readily implemented this mode of transportation in their daily operations. It rapidly became the primary method of transportation for the police officer and today it continues to be recognized as standard operating equipment in police departments throughout the world.

The automobile has come to be the most economical type of police patrol and, to a large extent, has eliminated all other forms of mobility in law enforcement. However, many agencies with peculiar problems, needs, and topography continue to utilize other types of transportation on a limited basis.

It is irrefutable that the automobile is more advantageous for the general police patrol purpose under, of course, ordinary conditions. It has been found that the patrolman operating an automobile is more efficient and is able to cover more area with less fatigue, reach a scene of action of emergency faster and in better condition mentally, emotionally, and physically than an officer using some other method of transportation. In addition, an automobile may be operated in any type of climate and generally under all road conditions as well as providing protection against any number of factors that might affect the officer's performance.

Automobile patrol is one of the best means of preventive law enforcement. Its appearance throughout a city creates the impression of *omnipresence* in the mind of the potential offender as well as creating a favorable attitude toward the police on the part of the general public. The police automobile also allows important equipment to be taken to the scene of action, such as first-aid equipment, extra clothing, blankets, flares, investigative and fingerprint equipment, fire extinguishers, and other materials necessary to the health and safety of the public. Additionally, it provides for the transportation of prisoners and extra officers. In a sense, it is a mobile police station serving the public.

Patrol with Scooters and Motorcycles

Utilization of this type of vehicle by police departments is fairly common, but its use creates many problems. Taking everything into consideration, the operating cost and maintenance of the two-wheeled motorcycle exceeds that of a police automobile. Consequently, the motorcycle has slowly been replaced in many police departments with the automobile. In poor weather, officers do not operate this equipment because of the high probability of accident. For this reason, a police agency may operate an automobile at a slightly lower cost. Nevertheless, a need still exists for this equipment in the control and flow of traffic, especially in areas in which congestion is high. This factor, in the main, will ensure its continued use by law enforcement.

The three-wheeled motorcycle usually may be operated, like the automobile, under all road conditions, but it has the advantage of greater maneuverability in heavy traffic. The operation of the three-wheeled motorcycle requires less skill and it is not as dangerous as the two-wheeled cycle. The reason for this is that this type of equipment is limited by lower and safer speeds and is less tiring on the officer. This type of vehicle will be found performing traffic functions in heavily congested areas, enforcing parking regulations, providing escort services, patrol in parks, and so on.

Serious thought has been given in recent years to the abandonment of the three-wheeled motorcycle in favor of the small compact cars. These small cars would protect the patrol officer and his equipment from adverse weather conditions and offer greater personal safety to the officer. In addition, it would be available for use when needed to transport additional officers, prisoners, and/or health and safety equipment.

The small motorized scooter popular a number of years ago has reappeared on the market, not only in the United States but also in many foreign countries. Very slowly, different types and styles of the scooter classifications are being adopted by law enforcement agencies throughout America to replace bicycles, horses, and the three-wheeled motorcycle.

Police Canine Patrol

Since early civilization, the dog has been used as a means of providing protection for man and his family. Law enforcement history records the first use of dogs as an aid to officers in Europe as far back as 1608 in London. As time passed, the military adopted the use of these animals to aid in providing security and protection of various important and critical installations. In addition, they have been used in combat zones for a number of purposes and many of these animals distinguish themselves. Subsequent to the Korean War, dogs serving in law enforcement have become very popular and have become standard operating equipment in agencies of every level of government.

Police dog patrol is used most commonly in areas with high crime rates where foot patrol is essential but dangerous. They are especially effective in crowd control, civil rights disturbances, and in search for explosives and

FIGURE 10.3. (top) *Law enforcement utilizes police dogs to track, search, and aid the apprehension of criminal suspects as well as the seizure of contraband and explosive materials. Courtesy Police Department, San Jose, Ca.* (bottom) *A beat officer and his dog have successfully apprehended the criminal suspects. The trained dog guards the suspects, leaving the officer to perform important duties, communicate with his headquarters, and know that he is safe from attack by suspects while he is in the process of completing the arrest, transportation, and booking. Courtesy Metropolitan Police Department, St. Louis, Mo.*

drugs. Dogs that have been properly trained have established outstanding records for locating drugs and explosives. One dog, the famous "Ginger," owned by Robert Buesing, has even been declared an expert in the courts. Some proven advantages of police canine patrol (the best-suited dog is the German shepherd) are:

1. Their excellent sense of hearing and smell will detect a subject or material that might not be discovered by the police officer.
2. They are good protection for an officer and will prevent as well as repel attacks that might be made upon the officer.
3. The dog is an agile animal and can run fast and leap high, thus overtaking a fleeing felon faster than a patrolman.
4. They can stand guard on or hold a suspect, leaving the officer free to move about and search.
5. They are experts in locating lost persons and in tracing persons escaping or attempting to allude police officers.
6. They are invaluable in searching for many and various types of materials.
7. They are able to accompany an officer into areas where vehicles cannot go.

Dogs especially selected and highly trained for patrol work are relatively expensive and pose a certain maintenance problem, but these disadvantages should never justify the discontinuance of their use.

Dogs are used by law enforcement throughout the world. A leader in the development of proper and effective training of dogs for all levels of government and their respective agencies is Robert E. Buesing, President of Continental K-Nine, Inc., located at Norwalk, California.

It is unfortunate that in some parts of America in recent years, dogs were improperly utilized in civil rights demonstrations. This misuse of a very valuable law enforcement tool has thus resulted in numerous civil actions to outlaw the use of any animal by law enforcement agencies. When the public is led to see, through an effective program of communication, the philosophy of the police use of dogs as a defensive weapon for the officer and citizen alike, such efforts to outlaw the use of dogs in law enforcement will hopefully cease.

Aircraft Patrol

Police patrol from the air is considered a new method of patrol which has proven its worth and importance to law enforcement. It is, however, very expensive to operate and maintain.

The very first use of aircraft dates back to 1929 when New York City initiated the use of amphibian airplanes to patrol their harbors. In 1948, New

York City supplemented their amphibian aircraft with a helicopter. Noting an improvement in their patrol operation, the number of helicopters in service was increased by three and all other types were soon eliminated from the aircraft patrol service. As a result of this pioneering venture, many large law enforcement agencies have instituted the use of the helicopter to meet many needs experienced by the larger enforcement agencies.

In 1956, the Los Angeles Police Department started a helicopter patrol division. In the beginning they were used to patrol the vast freeway system in the city and assist the ground patrol units as necessary. Today, this agency has one of the largest police air forces in the world and the equipment and personnel are utilized on a 24 hour basis performing and assisting in every type of police, health, and safety service to the public.

Subsequently, San Francisco, Kansas City, Denver, Chicago, and numerous

FIGURE 10.4.   *Helicopter police patrol plays a vital part in the total police function. Here a law enforcement helicopter has assisted in the arrest of a criminal suspect by patrol officers using a conventional vehicle. The helicopter stands by to provide surveillance and cover from the air for officers on the ground. The officers personal safety and security are always of prime importance. Courtesy Sheriff's Department, Los Angeles, County, Ca.*

other cities have used aircraft patrol and, as a result of their performance and effectiveness, it is now a regular part of the service rendered to the public by the policing agencies.

The use of helicopters in police work by no means is restricted to municipal police agencies. Helicopters are also used a great deal by county sheriff departments, especially in counties that are very large in area or have unusual topography, such as Los Angeles County. In recent years federal law enforcement agencies have also adopted aircraft as an effective tool in combating crime and providing for national security.

Traffic control was once the largest part of any city helicopter program. But helicopters and fixed-wing aircraft are used today for land and sea rescue, civil defense emergencies, damage assessment, radiological monitoring, photographic surveys, surveillance, searches, capture of suspects and escaped prisoners, protection of airports, escorts, discovery of fires, the direction of ground parties in fire fighting or law enforcement, delivery and posting of court orders in inaccessible areas, investigation of low-flying aircraft, reseeding of grass and forest ranges, and atmospheric measurement of air pollution.

The Los Angeles County Sheriff's Department has instituted the use of fixed-wing aircraft to supplement the department's complement of helicopters. This progressive step in police patrol service will serve as a guide to law enforcement agencies throughout the nation which are establishing aerial patrol or expanding their current aerial capabilities. The philosophy of the use of the fixed-wing aircraft is that it will perform more effectively and economically as compared to the helicopter, and it is believed that the crime suppression capability will be greatly expanded by having a diversified aerial observation unit. The advantages of the fixed-wing aircraft include a prolonged air time, the ability to carry increased amounts of cargo of sophisticated crime detection equipment, and the capacity to fly at very slow airspeeds while remaining stable or to immediately accelerate to airspeeds of 160 miles per hour in response to an emergency situation. Additionally, they are capable of take-offs and landings in a distance of 100 feet or less. In aircraft patrol it is extremely important that progressive low-cost, high-serviceability programs be constantly implemented by law enforcement in order to provide the citizens of the country with the most effective and efficient use of the available revenue.

Marine Patrol

It is not recorded when boats were first used in law enforcement, but they have been used for such purposes for hundreds of years. In the United

States, police boats were first used in Boston Harbor starting in 1853. The New York City Harbor Police adopted the use of boats and pursued river and harbor thieves by rowing their boats in and around the various vessels in the harbor. A great amount of piracy upon vessels in port was thus aborted. This service was continued until 1916 when power boats were introduced into policing operations.

Cities such as Seattle, Los Angeles, New York, Cleveland, Chicago, and New Orleans, with close proximity to bodies of water, require boat patrol service.

American people are presently making greater use of the available various recreational areas, especially those that provide water sports. The boat, once a status symbol, is now commonplace in our society.

As the water recreational areas become more crowded, law enforcement has an ever-increasing requirement to provide police patrol-boat and scuba-diving services to these locations. The general duties and services provided are the following: (a) Retrieving drowned persons, (b) recovering evidence disposed of by violators and criminal suspects, (c) performing rescue work, (d) providing safety for swimmers, (e) protecting boats that are moored, and (f) enforcing speed and traffic regulations according to the harbor and navigation code and aiding in relieving water traffic congestion.

In seaport cities, police boat patrols usually are called *harbor police* or *harbor patrol*. In addition to providing the foregoing services to the public, the harbor patrol is responsible for policing the many nearby piers and warehouses; providing fire-fighting equipment and service for putting out fires observed while they are on their routine 24 hour a day patrol; preventing thefts and burglaries on boats, piers, and warehouses; apprehending criminals attempting to escape from the law and justice via the waterways; and apprehending smugglers trying to evade tariff regulations.

The responsibility of boat patrols to society is primarily prevention and service.

SPECIAL TYPES OF PATROL

In most of our large American cities, there is a growing need for police agencies to establish highly and specially trained patrol forces within the patrol division. These special forces serve as equalizers in the fight against crime. The unit is a highly mobile and flexible one, well-trained to cope with a variety of situations. The personnel composing the unit are usually hand-picked and are among the finest in the division. The idea of a special unit is not a new one. For many years New York, Chicago, Los Angeles, San Francisco, and other cities have organized, trained, and maintained such units. However, the widespread adoption that is beginning to take place in other local, county, and state agencies is rather recent.

The types of incidents that require this special unit, with the exception of catastrophe and public disorders, arise from the extraordinary needs created either from traffic or crime. These special units meet the problem head-on and work to restore peace and tranquillity to society.

Saturation Patrol

The principal purpose of saturation patrol, which involves an increase of the number of police personnel, is to reduce the crime rate and the clearance of crime through arrest or through creating the impression of *omnipresence,* thus discouraging criminal activity. This type of special patrol is used mainly in areas having an excessively high amount of street crime, a type of crime effectively deterred by saturation patrol. In most cases, this special force, although working as a patrol unit, wears civilian clothing and operates in unmarked police radio cars.

There are other situations, as previously mentioned, in which special units or patrol forces are needed. These particular units are difficult to justify, or prove a need for, at any one time because the incidents may not occur frequently. O. W. Wilson states:

Other situations that require above-normal police efforts, however, are unpredictable in time, place and character. Sudden surges of criminal activity, labor disturbances, riots, unusual community events, earthquakes, fires, explosions and war are examples [2].

In highly populated areas the unexpected problems that can arise are numerous. Provision must be made for these unpredictable situations which demand highly trained and skilled men. Creation of these units cannot and should not drain the regular police patrol force.

The Los Angeles County Sheriff's Department has solved this problem by creating and permanently establishing a *Special Enforcement Bureau.* Prior to the birth of this unit, the Sheriff was forced to draw upon district station personnel to form a manpower pool when an incident occurred that could not be handled by a district station. In the case of a large fire, for example, deputy sheriffs were assigned to extended shifts at the stations which were depleted of their normal complement [3].

The Special Enforcement Bureau trains at least 8 hours monthly as a unit on such special subjects as weapons practice, first aid, rescue, crowd control, riot psychology, racial problems, labor relations and strike control, and advanced baton techniques. The SEB is available to each of the district stations, and is centrally located to expedite assistance. Their assistance to the Los Angeles Police Department during the Watts riots of 1965 was invaluable in stopping rioting, arson, and looting. The late William H. Parker, then Chief of Police of the City of Los Angeles, gave them special praise and commendation for their demeanor during this crisis.

The special equipment utilized by SEB includes a mobile command bus and a mobile kitchen capable of feeding 200–300 persons at a time.

Team Patrol

In many ways, team patrol, or team policing as it is sometimes called, is similar to saturation patrol. They are alike in that both approaches try to place the greater amount of personnel where the largest amount of criminal activity is taking place. The crux of team patrol is flexibility. The majority of the area is observed by a skeletal force, while the bulk of the agency is ready to move at any time to the area of greatest need.

The English police are principally responsible for the development of this procedure. Their procedures are called the *Aberdeen Plan* and the *Salford Plan,* and both call for a constable team which varies according to the size of the area. A police sergeant commands each team. The individual constables are driven by patrol cars to their beat, thus giving the team mobility. All constables in England are capable of and are authorized to follow up on cases as far as possible without sending for specialized help. The *Aberdeen Plan* has resulted in the following: (*a*) Increased number of arrests, (*b*) large savings in manpower, and (*c*) upsurge of personnel morale.

The *Salford Plan* requires more flexibility because of the fluctuation of patrol districts. The districts vary in size with each shift. For example, if the crime index on street crimes indicates a high percentage in a concentrated area on the swing shift, then the patrol district is decreased and the area saturated with a police team. In this plan, a police team consists of nine constables with a sergeant in charge. The police vehicle is the working point of the team and is used by them as a mobile station. The work assignments are varied so that the patrolman does not become bored, get into a routine, and thus become careless.

The element of surprise is used extensively. Traditionally, the British constable has had a certain, definite beat and he has been held responsible for all crime occurring on that beat. Under these plans, he is still responsible, but beats are changed from time to time as the need arises to meet the modern and more pressing problems. The opportunity to map out the rounds of the beat officer therefore is no longer possible under these plans. The results of the *Salford Plan* have been: (*a*) The proportion of indictable offenses cleared by arrest has risen, (*b*) patrols make nearly twice as many arrests, (*c*) the number of incidents reported has increased, and (*d*) morale of the personnel has increased.

In more recent years the British police have been utilizing a new patrol system called *Unit-Beat Policing.* This system incorporates all the best features of traditional police patrol. The resident constables, foot and cycle officers, motor officers, and at least one detective form a team and cover a community of from 50,000 to 80,000 population. Additionally, the system includes a "collator" who functions as the crime analyst. The UBP system seeks to maximize contact with the public without sacrificing any mobility or communication. Most all of the English constables today have some form of transportation and are equipped with mobile communication.

Plainclothes Patrol

As our cities increase in size and population, techniques and procedures are developed to augment police personnel. One of these important techniques is plainclothes patrol. These are specialized patrol units created to relieve the foot and car patrol officers from so many called-for services so that they might pursue their primary duties of patrol.

The operation of this type of police patrol is not a true specialty, but rather a broadening of regular patrol service, with the same objectives and procedures as those of the uniformed patrol officer.

Plainclothes patrol is different in the respect that it has certain advantages in the accomplishment of its endeavors. Civilian dress and undercover police cars are only two of them. Plainclothes patrolmen can effectively carry out assignments that are impossible for a uniformed officer to even attempt. They conduct further investigation of a case or a suspect when it is needed before the case can be turned over to the detective division. They are a reserve for major crime problems and conduct preliminary investigations that are too time-consuming for the uniformed patrol officer. Where and when these plainclothes officers will be assigned is the responsibility of patrol commander or chief of police. Their assignment is usually determined by an evaluation of the area, the crime problems, and the ability of the regular patrol officer to handle those problems.

The actual duties of the plainclothes patrol officer cover many areas of police work. Their performance should not conflict with, or take on the appearance of, the responsibilities of the police detective. Patrol is never a supplement to the detective division. It is just the opposite. The principal of unity of command should always prevail.

Patrol Through Electronics

The world we live in is more and more influenced by science and electronics. This is not any less true for law enforcement. In the area of police patrol there have been many outstanding contributions because of developments in electronics. Probably one of the most important innovations has been the application of television to the patrol function. It was first used on a practical basis in West Germany for the control of vehicular traffic and now is found in every major police agency throughout Europe. The system design is a television panel providing for thirty receivers located at a control board and manned by one or more police officers. At various key points throughout the area, television cameras equipped with zoom lenses are housed in completely weatherproof facilities. The officers operate the cameras by remote control and can adjust each of the cameras individually to a panoramic view of 270 degrees. As the operator observes various situations in the field that need police attention, he directs the patrol officer to the exact location of the situation.

This sound and economical operation is best suited to larger cities or those general areas that contain a large concentration of people or vehicular traffic such as regional shopping centers and popular recreational areas. The first use of this type of patrol system met with generally good results in the control of prisoners in our jails and correction institutions, but is yet to be well received by the general population.

As time passes, there will be additional electronic devices used by police patrol divisions. In the near future, the patrol officer will have a small portable television receiver in his automobile and, upon his request from the field, he can see photos of suspects, observe printed criminal records, or receive a sharp and detailed photo of a complete set of fingerprints, to name just a few of the advantages. In time, he also will be able to transmit a television picture to his headquarters. Computers are an invaluable time saver to the patrol officer in the area of records searching.

PRIVATE POLICE AND SECURITY SERVICES

As the crime rate continues to increase in the United States and in many other countries of the world, citizens are becoming more alarmed and are feeling a need for increased protection in their businesses and their homes. Thus many business firms are employing, either as a part of their regular personnel or through private security companies, the services of private patrolmen to protect all phases of the total business operation. Many groups of private citizens have joined together and are using the services of private patrol agencies to provide additional protection to their property and holdings over and above that provided by their local police agency.

The development of private police agencies and industrial security firms has a long history, having evolved from the frontier days of our country when law enforcement was weak or nonexistent. At that time, bodies of citizens called *vigilantes* were organized to maintain law and order. In this manner the Pinkerton Detective Agency was born and is still in operation today.

This area of specialized service to the public by private industry has been growing at the rate of 10–15% annually. This growth is likely to continue at a rapid rate as long as the public feels insecure and as long as law enforcement is overburdened and unable to cope with the volume of criminal activity.

Public police and private security services generally are complementary, often supplementary, and occasionally competitive. Where both types of agencies are capable of providing the same services, it is generally agreed that three criteria should be applied in deciding which one to use: (a) The cost of quality public service and private service, (b) the nature of security and investigative services available to various population groups, and (c) the degree to which the delegated police power is to be exercised in an acceptable manner by the public or private police forces.

There are certain principles which define the roles and relations between law enforcement and private investigation and security. Governmental law enforcement agencies have as their primary responsibility the maintenance of law and order, the prevention of crime, the investigation of crime, and the apprehension of law violators. That which is public is policed by public law enforcement agencies. The policing of private property is the sole responsibility of the owner who may provide his own services or purchase them from specialized private companies.

As a general rule, private security services are concerned with private interests and their primary function is two-fold, the prevention of crime and the protection of their client. They also gather information for private and civil purposes. When they are invited or called, the municipal or county police will enter private property to restore order and enforce the law. Even when they are not called they may enter private property to prevent a crime or make an arrest. In addition, depending on crime patterns, they may frequently patrol private property which is accessible to the public, such as large shopping centers.

Women are playing an increasingly important role in the area of private police and security services. There are many situations in which a female security officer is more effective than the male.

The private investigator is also playing a more important role in the administration of criminal justice. Frequently the courts have found that a defense attorney has not used the services of a private investigator when he should have. It is poor policy for an attorney to measure distances, take pictures, interview witnesses, sketch crime scenes, etc. When private services are utilized, the attorney may interrogate the private investigator on the witness stand, thus providing a better defense of his client. More and more, the judiciary is taking the position that the private investigator is completely necessary in the functioning of our court system.

ACTIVITIES AND RESPONSIBILITIES OF PATROL

Routine Calls and Services

Routine calls and services account for the largest part of the work performed by any police patrol division. Each time a call is answered or service is rendered, the officer is establishing better public relations with the community for the benefit of his agency and the community. Routine duties consist in part of answering calls to receive, inspect, and then dispose of complaints, conducting inspectional services and reporting the findings, controlling public gatherings, observing, responding to every conceivable type of emergency, settling complaints that are of a noncriminal nature or that involve minor infractions of law, arresting offenders, collecting and preserving physical evidence, preparing reports, and testifying in court.

Crime Prevention

Crime prevention is a vital element in the successful operation of our law enforcement agencies. This function is relatively new as a responsibility of

FIGURE 10.5. *The protection and security of private property from the criminal society is a most important function of the police patrol officer. Courtesy Police Department, Oakland, Ca.*

our policing agencies. It is becoming clear that the best approach to our crime problem is to go directly to its roots which, in today's society, means investigating the many and varied factors in our communities which create criminal tendencies and subsequently lead persons to antisocial behavior.

Modern police officers are recognizing this need to aid in the prevention of criminality. Probably the greatest emphasis by the police and the individual patrol officer on the correction of such conditions is that of helping to establish sound community programs and rehabilitation programs for the delinquent person, focusing mainly on the younger generation. O. W. Wilson states:

Knowledge of the causes of criminality would facilitate its prevention, but there is no agreement among authorities in the field of criminal behavior about exact causes or their relative potency [4].

A sound program for effective crime prevention is that of creating the impression of the omnipresence of the police through efficient operation of the police patrol division. It has been proven through statistical analysis that wherever this impression has been created there has been a reduction in the number of offenses that have occurred.

The antisocial or criminally oriented person, it is known, will stay away from those areas where his illicit activities might be observed as a result of heavy patrol activity by the beat officers. Noted police administrators have stated that the presence of good police patrol substantially diminishes many crimes that are committed on impulse.

The cost of crime prevention is minimal when compared with property stolen, damaged, and destroyed; persons injured, maimed, and killed; and the cost and effect of the total program in the administration of criminal justice.

Public Disorders and Disasters

These phenomena are quite dissimilar, but some comparison can be made regarding the duties performed by the police officer assigned to patrol duties.

A public disorder always starts with the congregation of a crowd. The demeanor of the first law enforcement officer on the scene of the crowd often can prevent the situation from getting out of hand. The police officer on hand must always display a professional attitude and remain impartial regardless of the action of the crowd. It takes only a slight spark to transfer a quiet crowd into a fighting, screaming mob of humanity. Another method of prevention may result from reports by the officer on the beat to his superiors. Suitable and prompt action should then be implemented to ease any tensions that may exist.

Riot action is not always preventable. It may occur in spite of everything that is done to avert it. When this occurs control must be established. There are two principal methods for the patrol officer to employ. The first method involves the officer's knowledge of crowd psychology, together with the individual makeup and the general type of the crowd, in his use of the tactic known as persuasion. He must prevail upon such a group to remain in an orderly fashion and to obey the laws of the state. The end result in the use of this tactic can be satisfactory, but a great deal, of course, depends on the officer.

The second method involves the use of force and should be employed only after careful consideration has been given to all factors involved and only when there is sufficient personnel to carry out the tactical operations involved.

On any occasion when an officer is assigned to crowd control, he must remember that he is a servant of the people and that these people are human beings, the same as he, and that they are entitled to the same rights and privileges as any other citizen. It is incumbent upon the officer to treat people in the community as he would like to be treated. Loss of temper, use of insulting terms, and violations of a person's rights will create a greater problem in handling an unruly crowd, and his assignment to maintain or establish peace and order will not be possible. Of necessity, the patrol officer must always use common courtesy in these situations.

The Communist Party throughout the world, including the United States, is a master of deliberate exploitation and manipulation of mob violence, hysteria, and physical pressure. Their tactical strategy and operations are numerous and all of them are performed under cover. The Communists' plan is clever and well organized, and they see to it that any mob led by them, in the exploiting of unfavorable economic conditions or the production of bloodshed, excitement, and violence, is armed with weapons of a non-military nature such as sticks, clubs, stones, and homemade bombs.

The police patrol officer's function in public disorders and crowd control is as complex as it is important. To perform his duties in the properly pre-scribed manner, he must have special knowledge of crowd control and what transforms crowds into mobs. In addition, he must understand his role and responsibilities to himself and the people he protects. If an officer can grasp these important points, he can do what the people expect of him when he is called upon to assist in riot and crowd control.

Turning from riot control, let us examine briefly the role of the patrol officer in disaster situations. It is because the police accept the duties of other governmental agencies in emergency and disaster situations that their role under these conditions must be one of providing an extension of their normal functions. Only if this is done can other agencies of government move into a disaster area and function effectively.

In time of disaster, the beat patrol officer as well as his agency must be prepared to take control of the affected area in order to provide the required services, treatment, and protection that is vital at such a time. His primary duties involve him in many activities for which he is responsible and held accountable. Foremost, of course, is his responsibility to offer protection of life, property, and preservation of order. In addition he must apprehend all law violators; conduct searches for missing persons; perform rescue service; stand guard at critical points; prevent looting; conduct initial criminal investigations; transmit, enforce, and assist in carrying out evacuation orders; provide control and regulation of vehicular and pedestrian traffic to minimize delays, congestion, and conflicts which would prevent orderly and efficient movement of all regular and emergency flow of traffic. Although these are the principal functions of the patrol officer, he often is required to perform many special services to the public which are not normally required of him.

Traffic Law Enforcement

Traffic law enforcement has become a standard and accepted operation in municipal and county police agencies in the United States. Additionally, specialized state agencies have been established throughout the country whose sole function is to enforce all traffic laws and investigate traffic accidents. The traffic enforcement unit of any agency is the unit of police service that 90% of the citizens of the country will come into contact with. The traffic enforcement officer has more day-to-day contact with the general public than probably any other classification of police officer or division of police service. It is because of this fact that they are the agency's greatest public relations men. It is unfortunate that the officers' contact with the public must generally begin on a negative note, for it is when the officer stops the citizen to issue a citation that the initial contact is made. Traffic law enforcement is the one force that seeks to influence human behavior directly, individually, and constantly.

The primary objective of traffic law enforcement is to deter violators and potential violators of traffic laws and regulations. Probably the most important deterrent is psychological—the fear of the violator that he or she will be fined, jailed, lose the privilege of driving, suffer loss of prestige, embarrassment, etc., due to the pressures of the society.

The large policing agencies with a traffic enforcement responsibility most generally have special traffic enforcement divisions and some even have special accident investigation divisions to handle nothing but traffic accident investigation. However, as has been previously mentioned in this chapter, the majority of the policing agencies in the United States are small and have only the regular police patrol division to provide traffic control services and enforcement. Due to the tremendous number of vehicles operating in our country, along with the high traffic accident rate in every area of the nation, traffic control remains basically a patrol function.

Patrol officers are schooled in traffic law enforcement and accident investigation because many of their personal contacts with the citizens occur during the performance of these duties, and it is vital that, when the contact is made, it be as efficient, effective, and pleasant as possible under the prevailing conditions.

Much of the work performed by patrol officers in traffic control is centered around the theme of prevention. It is through this effort, by issuing warning notices, citations, and conducting traffic enforcement education, that violations and accidents are prevented. A number of varied other duties performed in traffic control include applying first aid to victims; summoning medical assistance; arranging for and providing the transportation of injured persons; extinguishing fires; preventing looting or loss of property at accident scenes; maintaining control of bystanders; making sure roadways at an accident scene are left in good order; interviewing witnesses; noting and preserving physical evidence; examining or testing drivers, vehicles, and pedestrians; making sketches and diagrams; taking photographs and measurements; writing reports; answering inquiries from citizens; and providing direction of traffic when necessary. In its broadest meaning, traffic enforcement is the activity connected with patrolling the streets and highways of our communities, prevention being the most important function of all.

Traffic control and patrol has had a long and colorful history. Before officers were equipped with the motorcycle in 1909, they utilized bicycles and the very early forms of motorized vehicles. After World War I, motorization of the police increased at a rapid rate. With the growth and development of the nation have come many new and badly needed tools for the traffic law enforcement officer. Today the traffic enforcement function of the police service is a science which is completely equipped to perform at maximum capability in order to be of service to those to whom they are dedicated to protect and to serve.

SUMMARY

The foundation of police patrol was laid when men first banded together and found it necessary to protect themselves and their families from adverse elements around them. Patrol progressed through the years, by trial and error, until today it has evolved into the largest and most important division in law enforcement. It may be stated that the foundation of successful police patrol operations is an adequate and smooth-functioning patrol division. Since the patrol officer is observed by the public more often than any other person representing the local government, he becomes a symbol of the police agency and the entire local administration. His honesty, integrity, and conduct in the fulfillment of his duties will greatly determine whether the citizens of the community have any confidence in him or their police agency. Whatever type of public relations exists, that program rests entirely upon the contacts and relationships established by the patrol officer in his contact with the people of the community. A mistake made by one officer will reflect poorly on the whole agency he serves.

The type of police patrol service runs the gamut from foot patrol to the implementation of scientific electronic devices by which the patrol function may be accomplished for the safety and well-being of the people.

The activities and responsibilities of the modern police patrol officer encompass a multitude of assignments and duties in routine patrol service, crime prevention, riots and disasters, and traffic enforcement and control. Small wonder that the police patrol division is indeed the backbone of law enforcement.

ANNOTATED REFERENCES

Applegate, R., *Crowd and Riot Control,* Stackpole, Harrisburg, Pa., 1964. A good discussion of the proper methods and procedures to be used by law-enforcement officers in crowds and riots.

Gourley, G. D., and A. P. Bristow, *Patrol Administration,* Thomas, Springfield, Ill., 1961. An excellent presentation of the operation, administration, and control of police patrol divisions. Well described and illustrated.

International Association of City Managers, *Municipal Police Administration,* Chicago, 1969. This reference is widely recognized as one of the two best presentations on modern police administration. No student, teacher, or law-enforcement officer should be without it.

Payton, G. T., *Patrol Procedures,* 2nd ed., Rev., Legal Book Store, Los Angeles, 1971. This reference is the only one of its kind. A good presentation of proper patrol procedures. It has been widely acclaimed and adopted as a basic text in police-science courses dealing with police patrol.

Whisenand, P., and J. L. Cline, *Patrol Operations,* Prentice–Hall, Englewood Cliffs,

N.J., 1971. A carefully and logically written discussion of the many operations of the police patrol function.

Wilson, O. W., *Police Administration,* 3rd ed., McGraw–Hill, New York, 1972. Highly acclaimed and considered the best, most up-to-date treatment of modern police administration; has been adopted as a basic reference by law-enforcement administrators throughout the world.

NOTES

1. G. T. Payton, *Patrol Procedures,* rev. 4th ed., p. 70.
2. O. W. Wilson, *Police Planning,* Thomas, Springfield, Ill., 1952, p. 273.
3. G. D. Gourley and A. P. Bristow, *Patrol Administration,* pp. 23–24.
4. O. W. Wilson, *Police Administration,* 3rd ed., p. 418.

CHAPTER ELEVEN

Investigation

In order to cope with the many facets of crime, the investigator in today's modern police agency must be skilfully and scientifically trained in the art of investigation. In addition, the man or woman selected for the work of criminal investigation must possess high personal integrity, superior intelligence, patience, and unswerving perseverance.

In every segment of our population, about five crimes are committed every minute of the day. With the crime rate rising faster than the population is increasing, it can easily be seen that the problem is becoming more acute, and the skills of the criminal investigator necessarily must be developed to the highest possible degree.

The specialized work of criminal investigation has two primary purposes: (a) The gathering of facts and other information for examination to determine whether a criminal violation has been perpetrated and, if there is a violation, to determine the identity of the violator; and (b) the collection, preservation, and preparation of evidence that will be admissible and effective before a court or jury to convict the defendant. In fulfilling these two purposes the investigator must adhere to, and be guided by, constitutional law. His evidence in a criminal case must be admissible in a court of law and must not be evidence secured against a defendant in violation of his constitutional rights.

The criminal investigator must be searching constantly for new and more refined methods of investigation, just as the crime community is never idle in devising new patterns of crime. Although it is almost always true that the courts are slow in accepting new methods of solution, especially in the use of scientific instruments, the search for more thorough methods should not be precluded.

Basically, investigation is an art. Since this is so, the difficult methods of surveillance and interrogation must be learned, not from a book, but from extended apprenticeship of practice and analysis.

The obvious direction of investigation must proceed from the scene of the crime to the apprehension and conviction of the guilty. Along the way, the investigator must logically proceed, step by step, to the correct solution. This is done by basic investigative techniques, which may be categorized loosely as follows: (*a*) Collection and preservation of physical evidence for presentation to the courts; (*b*) interrogation of suspects and witnesses; (*c*) surveillance of suspected persons, use of informants, stakeouts, and so forth; and (*d*) record and file checks at the Department of Motor Vehicles, utility companies, U.S. Post Office mail covers, etc., which could lead to the discovery of suspects as well as evidence.

The investigator's use of these techniques must be coupled with reasoning; he must weigh one piece of evidence with another and select only that evidence that will be admissible in a court of law. In the area of admissible evidence, the investigator should work closely with the prosecuting attorney. A skilled investigator must be a man of many talents, a man sensitive to the obvious, so that he can weed out evidence gained by false premise, unreliable witnesses, and other faulty sources.

THE INVESTIGATIVE PROCESS

Crimes do not occur on a fixed schedule or at a specific location. There is no way, of course, to accurately predict these factors, but with additional scientific advances in the years ahead, prediction may be a future possibility. The best that can be done today is to immediately begin an investigation, once a crime has been reported or comes to the attention of the police.

The police patrol division is usually the first representative from law enforcement to arrive at a crime scene; thus the patrol officer plays a vital role, at least in the preliminary work, in the investigative process. Often the final outcome or success of an investigation depends heavily on the action of the patrol officer who responds to the call. The crime scene thus can be protected, witnesses reached, medical attention arranged for the victim if necessary, and the perpetrator arrested if still at the scene or nearby.

The final objective of any criminal investigation is, of course, the conviction of the guilty through the court system. To this end, the investigator must prove with his legally obtained evidence that a particular crime has been committed and that the arrestee (or defendant) is the person who, in fact, did of his own volition commit the crime. To accomplish this in a court of law, the officer must first, through investigation, obtain answers to the traditional questions of *who, what, when, where, why,* and *how.* The identity and arrest of the criminal then becomes paramount in order that the investigative officer may bring his physical evidence and witnesses into court to substantiate the charges filed against the defendant.

When a crime is known or reported and the assignment to investigate has been made, the investigator must take immediate action to begin the investigative process. The first important factor he must evaluate is the information he has received. He may be able to solve the criminal investigation assigned to him from information he already possesses. There are times, however, when the investigator will be required to seek out and obtain information from other sources.

The officer's ability to make use of his own personal knowledge depends upon his past preparation. This entails a good knowledge and understanding of the law, court decisions, the rules of evidence, and court procedures. In addition, this ability depends further on certain intangible attitudes and mental habits that any good investigator develops.

There are a number of these attitudes and habits, the most important of which are *observation, suspicion, curiosity,* and *memory.* It is vital that the habits of *memory* and *observation* be developed as soon as possible after entering the police service, for it is on these two habits that much of the work and success of the officer will depend.

While emphasizing the importance of developing these attitudes and habits, it would be good to mention that a police officer must never become insensitive to the obvious. He must remain flexible.

There is a constant stream of criticism about the investigator's use of *informers.* As it stands today, however, this is one of the best methods of obtaining *information,* a primary tool of the investigator's trade. An informer is one who gives information to a police officer. It is impossible to state how many cases are solved by officers through the use of informers, but it is a known fact that informers provide tremendous shortcuts during investi-

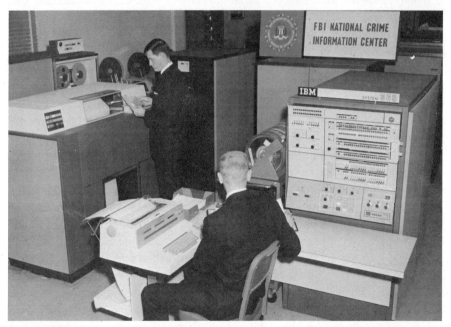

FIGURE 11.1. (top) *The FBI National Crime Information Center, located at FBI Headquarters, Washington, D.C. A vital area of N.C.I.C. are magnetic tape units shown in background. FBI technician is shown operating the Card Read and Punch Instrument. (bottom) FBI N.C.I.C. technicians at work with the magnetic tape units and the 1100 lives which are vital to the system. Courtesy Federal Bureau of Investigation, Washington, D.C.*

gations. Any investigator is only as good as his information, and an informer is often able to circulate and gain information in areas that would be closed to the police officer.

Police criminal records systems are a valuable information source for the police officer attempting to obtain additional information regarding a suspect, apprehended violators, witnesses, personal identification, and other data. The record division of any policing agency is its information center and the success achieved in dealing with the many phases of a complicated criminal investigation assignment often depends on the coordination of all records operations into a single records unit [1].

The exchange of information among all police officers, investigators, prosecutors, and other enforcement agencies makes possible the open channels of personal information and communication, so important in any investigation and in the overall fight against crime.

To aid and better meet the ever-increasing need for rapid communication and exchange of information, law enforcement has implemented the use of modern electronics. The National Police Teletypewriter Network provides interstate communication. The computer and data-processing machines have found a niche and are streamlining the many varied sources of information that are necessary to the effective and efficient operation of law enforcement agencies. The PIN system *(Police Information Network)* set up in California several years ago is considered one of the forerunners of present and future systems. The PIN system is a statewide, computerized data-processing record system consisting of four basic actions: Input, retrieval, updating, and deletion. Centrally located computers are fed information, from cities and counties representing ninety-three agencies, regarding wanted persons, stolen vehicles, outstanding warrants, and other valuable data. This information is available on a moment's notice to all agencies connected to the system; the system also allows participating agencies to communicate directly with each other through inquiry terminals, bypassing the main information center and saving time in the receipt of information from other sources. The Criminal Justice Information Control covers a wide area of information and includes subsystems dealing with wanted persons, stolen articles, and guns. This system of record-keeping is particularly important to the investigator as it ties together information about the overall progress of a criminal case. Thus it has the unique characteristic of eliminating the need for followup information sought by investigating officers. The system follows the arrested person in his route through all various agencies involved in the criminal justice system.

In 1965, the FBI embarked on the development of a national electronic information system and placed the system into operation on January 27, 1967. This system, known as NCIC *(National Crime Information Center)* [2] headquartered in Washington, D.C., has been put into operation to complement the development of electronic information systems—metropolitan and statewide—and to coordinate the setting of standards that will enable all systems to readily exchange information. The ultimate goal is for the system to encompass the entire nation and provide each law enforcement agency, in a matter of seconds, with desired information from files that are national in scope.

With these various systems at the federal, state, and local levels, the mobility factor of today's criminal element will no longer be to their advantage, as information from these systems will be readily available to any participating agency in the system concerning any one criminal or criminal act regardless of geographic boundaries. The systems will enable officers from coast to coast and from border to border to exchange and provide information, thus closing ranks around the fugitive of justice.

The sources of information available to law enforcement officers are many and varied. It is impossible for any one person to know everything; however, it is possible for a person to know where to obtain knowledge or information on practically all subjects. The more sources of information possessed by a police officer, investigator, or detective, the less complex his work will be and the more valuable he will be to the agency and citizens he serves. The most frequently used sources, in addition to those previously discussed, are information, records, and other data available from *city halls, county court houses, financial institutions, public utilities, transportation and delivery companies, local directories, state and federal agencies, commercial sources, schools and colleges, hospitals, newspapers, journals, magazines, churches, doctors, attorneys and accountants, special agencies and committees of the federal government and the Congress, real estate agencies, Better Business Bureaus, and Chambers of Commerce.*

INVESTIGATIVE TECHNIQUES

Communication is the key to knowledge. In order for the police investigator to solve a criminal offense or take effective action, he must first gather facts. This is accomplished for the most part by talking to people who have some knowledge of the particular situation in question. When this communication is performed orally, it is classed either as an *interview* or an *interrogation.*

It is an absolute necessity for every investigator, regardless of specialty, to be able to communicate effectively with people. Without such effective communication, the successful investigation and conclusion of criminal cases is made difficult, if not impossible.

INTERVIEWS AND INTERROGATIONS

In the course of their assignments investigators will expend a large amount of their time conducting interviews and interrogations of *citizens, complainants, informers, victims, witnesses,* and *criminal suspects.* There is a basic difference between the art and science of interviewing and that of interrogation. Therefore it is important to define them and explain the differences among them.

Interviewing may be defined as a formal or informal conversation between an official person and a subject for the express purpose of obtaining certain information pertaining to the subject's knowledge, information, background, character, or testimony. It may be readily concluded that the process of interviewing as defined covers a large area and could include that of speaking with suspicious persons on the streets, talking with witnesses to gain information and clearer understanding regarding a particular offense or investigation, or obtaining information with reference to the background of police applicants, criminal suspects, informants, or any number of persons. Through this process known as *interviewing,* the police officer and investigator will learn a great deal of information and facts which are of extreme importance to them if they are to fulfill assignments in a forthright manner.

In contrast, an *interrogation* may be defined as the questioning of a person who is suspected of, has confessed to, or in fact has committed a crime or public offense. *Interrogation is an art,* and competent interrogators are rare in the police profession. Much skill, experience, and training are necessary before a person is considered a master at interrogation.

The one factor that distinguishes the interrogation from the interview is the *atmosphere* in which each is conducted. The atmosphere of the interview is usually more relaxed and the person is more likely to "open up" and supply the desired information. In most cases it is simply a matter of the officer asking the right question in the right way that ensures the success of this technique. On the other hand, an interrogation usually is conducted with a person who is reluctant, for any number of reasons, to converse with a law enforcement officer. The atmosphere and tenor of the conversation is not as relaxed as in the interview, and the success or failure of the interrogation depends in large part, as stated before, on the skill and ability of the interrogator to discover the hidden knowledge or information possessed by the person being interrogated.

Interrogations are an important part of investigation, and in years past a vast amount of the solutions to crimes depended on the interrogation of a criminal suspect. Today, however, the many recent U.S. Supreme Court decisions have placed much tighter controls on the use of interviewing and interrogation and also on persons who perform such tasks while carrying out their assignments.

Recent Supreme Court rulings make it necessary for law enforcement officers to know whether statements, admissions, and confessions are admissible in court. For example, a confession of a murder suspect has little value if, by some legal error—no matter how small—on the part of the investigator, it becomes inadmissible evidence. Court rulings in reference to extrajudicial statements by the defendant are changing at an alarming rate in favor of the accused.

The greatest problem concerns the statements made by a person arrested for a criminal offense. These statements, admissions, and confessions fall under the severest scrutiny of the courts. The many rules in reference to these statements are continually being changed, interpreted, and revised, and often are so complicated, contradictory, and confusing that even trial judges, let alone the police officer, have difficulty in understanding and comprehending the many various rulings.

The police officer must be aware of the present emphasis of the courts on statements and confessions. Formerly, the pertinent question was: "Is the confession true?" But today the emphasis seems to be whether the statement, admission, or confession is free, voluntary, without coercion of any kind, and is made in the full and complete awareness and understanding of all the defendant's constitutional rights. This emphasis by the courts in interpreting the *fourth, fifth,* and *fourteenth* amendments to the *U.S. Constitution* places very severe restrictions on the investigator. Many previously tried and proven techniques of investigators are no longer of any value or use. Today's police investigator must develop and use new techniques which are acceptable to the courts. For more insight into the problems of interrogation, the student is referred to the case decision reached in *Miranda* v. *Arizona,* U.S., June 13, 1966, wherein the court stated:

The prosecution may not use statements, whether exculpatory or inculpatory, stemming from custodial interrogations of the defendant unless it demonstrates procedural safeguards effective to secure the privilege against self incrimination.

The decision reached in *Massiah* v. *United States,* 377 U.S. 201, stated that incriminating statements may not be obtained from a defendant in custody by subterfuge, such as the placing of an undercover officer in the same interrogation room or jail cell to obtain incriminating statements.

Custodial interrogation means questioning initiated by law enforcement officers after a person has been arrested and taken into custody or otherwise deprived of his freedom of action in any significant way. Prior to any questioning the peace officer must advise a defendant of his constitutional rights as follows: (*a*) He has the right to remain silent; (*b*) any statement he makes may be used as evidence against him in subsequent criminal court proceedings; (*c*) he has a right to the presence of legal counsel during any questioning and at all stages of the proceedings; and (*d*) if he cannot afford the cost of private legal counsel, a lawyer will be appointed immediately to represent and advise him during any questioning and at all stages of any subsequent criminal proceedings. The question then must be asked of the defendant, "Do you understand your constitutional rights?" He is not required to answer.

A language problem exists in some areas of our country, and some states are requiring that the foregoing admonition about constitutional rights be printed and given to the suspect in his language prior to any interrogation. He is then requested to sign a statement that he has read the admonition and understands it.

If the defendant indicates in any manner that he wishes to remain silent, the interrogation must cease. If he desires the services of an attorney at any point in the interrogation, the interrogation must cease until the attorney is appointed and present.

Statements obtained by the investigator from persons who are not under restraint and control are admissible before a court. There is at present no requirement of first advising such a person of his rights before questioning him about his knowledge or information concerning a crime. Thus, general questioning of citizens in a fact-finding process at a crime scene is not affected by the *Miranda* decision.

Once a criminal suspect is advised of all his rights and he then intelligently and specifically waives all of these rights, the interrogator or investigating officer may then proceed with questioning conducted in a proper manner. If, however, after waiving his rights, a suspect decides to withdraw his waiver, he may do so at any stage and the interrogation must cease.

One should not be dismayed by these recent developments. Many more are likely to come. Instead, law enforcement officers and their agencies will have to develop new ideas and work harder and more independently to do the same job and perform their sworn duty. The art of interrogation can never be replaced and will always be a useful tool to the investigator.

UNDERCOVER WORK

The use of undercover work is not confined to law enforcement agencies alone. Since it is one of the oldest investigative procedures, it is employed as necessary when desirable by business, industry, and government.

This investigative technique requires that the person performing the work discard his real identity and assume a role and identity that is in keeping with the goals and objectives of the particular investigation to which the undercover agent is assigned. The purpose of this technique is three-fold: (a) To conduct surveillance, (b) to obtain information, and (c) to obtain evidence that will be admissible in a court of law.

The success of such an investigation depends on how well the officer can penetrate a group or organization, obtain the desired information, and prevent himself from being identified. The officer who is most convincing in his role thus will be able to associate freely and gain the confidence of the suspects.

Undercover agents should be distinguished from informers as follows: Undercover agents are law enforcement officers, highly trusted employees, or average law-abiding citizens who are selected for this work on the basis of their honesty, integrity, reliability, special skills, mental alertness, and competence to obtain information by various methods from persons or groups involved in illegal or subversive activities.

Many crimes involve organization, and it is in this that undercover investigation is most useful. For example, in crimes involving illegal sales, smuggling, narcotics, prostitution, abortions, alcohol, blackmail, fraud, gambling, stolen property, subversive activity, and others, the use of undercover investigators is indispensable.

In every city there are citizens who are willing to do undercover work for compensation, out of respect for law and order, or because of loyalty and love of country. But not everyone (including police officers), even with high motives and in good faith, is the right kind of person to perform undercover investigation successfully. The best and most desirable type of individuals for undercover investigations are those who do have the foregoing qualities and who also possess good mental agility, complete self-confidence and control, and actor type personalities. With these attributes, such a person is better able to react to unexpected situations and emergencies without hesitation. In addition, but not always necessary, an undercover agent must be able to consume alcoholic beverages and yet remain mentally alert. A person with all of these qualities makes the most desirable agent, but unfortunately such an individual is not always available.

The possibility of success in undercover work is bright provided that the right type of persons are selected for each case. It is important to remember, of course, to treat each case individually. What may be true or successful in one case may not be so in another. No undercover assignment should ever be undertaken without first making adequate plans and preparations to carry out the plans; obtaining as much knowledge about the subject, group, or organization as is possible; and selecting the proper agent and providing for his cover and safety.

SURVEILLANCE

There comes a time in most police investigations when the investigator must go into the field to study and observe persons, places, or objects. This investigative process is known as *surveillance,* and it accounts for the wide and varied use of many techniques, abilities, and types of equipment. A common misconception is that the officer just has to walk or drive his car behind a suspected person to find out what he wants to know. There is much more to it than this. Like interrogation, *surveillance is an art* which is developed out of many years of experiments and the numerous collective experiences of trained investigators. Each individual case presents different conditions and requirements which must be met for the surveillance to be successful.

A surveillance is a secret observation dependent on sight and hearing, its principal characteristic being anonymity, which continues until the purpose of surveillance has been fulfilled.

There are two principal types of surveillance: *Moving* and *fixed.* When the *moving surveillance* technique is employed, the subject is actually followed on foot, by vehicle, or any other means to obtain the desired goal. In contrast, the *fixed surveillance* of a person, place, or object is maintained from one or more stationary points. The investigator conducting a surveillance must clearly understand his objective; evaluate activities, specific actions, and facts from his observations; draw correct conclusions; and conduct himself in accordance with all of the particular legal requirements related to the specific situation.

There are many diverse purposes for conducting surveillance. It may be used to prevent crime; to locate witnesses; to locate and arrest wanted criminals and suspects; to obtain information and evidence sufficient to make an arrest or obtain probable cause for the issuance of a search warrant; to locate areas and particular places frequented by suspects and criminal law violators; to record illegal activity taking place in a specific location or area; to make identification of suspects and of relationships maintained by known criminals; to verify information as well as facts; to protect persons, places, and objects; to locate missing persons; to establish timetables and movements of persons under investigation; to determine the best method and approach for making arrests, raids, and rescues; and to secure information to be used as a basis for an interrogation.

A police officer must be ready and able on a moment's notice to begin a surveillance program. But, if there is time, a great deal of planning should be done in advance in order to cope with any contingency. The successful surveillance program will be marked with sound reconnaissance and strategy.

METHODS OF IDENTIFICATION

The identification of persons is an extremely important part of the total law enforcement function and a vital element to every investigation. There are innumerable methods by which a person may be identified, and many of these are used daily throughout the world by law enforcement and governmental agencies as well as business and industries.

Of the many methods used, those most frequently employed by law enforcement are: *Portrait parle, photography, the artist's sketch and identi-kit, modus operandi, the eyewitness, fingerprints, voiceprint, and reports from the crime laboratory.*

The investigative process can be carried out to a point, but, beyond this, identification of persons, places, and things becomes absolutely necessary if the investigation is to be concluded successfully. To aid all law enforcement officers, police agencies the world over maintain extensive files and records on all types of people, places, and objects. When any investigation is initiated, the investigator consults not only local and county record bureaus, but also bureaus operated and maintained by the various state and federal agencies. On occasion, it has even been necessary to consult with record bureaus of foreign governments.

The *portrait parle,* simply defined, is a *verbal picture* or description of a human body. It was devised in 1882 by Alphonse Bertillon, a young clerk in the Paris police, and it is still today the most elementary, the most used, and the oldest means of making a physical description.

As often is the case, the police investigator must make identification by other means. *Photography* plays an important role in this respect. Often witnesses and even officers experience difficulty in accurately describing a person, place, or thing, but, when shown a photograph, they are able to make a positive identification of a person or confirm or deny the content of the photograph as it depicts a place or thing.

Often, even with the aid of photography, identification cannot be established, and it then is necessary to couple the technique of the verbal description with that of the *artist's sketch*. This technique for making identifications has developed and been greatly expanded over the past 20 years. The artist draws, colors, and shades as a verbal description is given to him. In recent years, some of the particular sizes, shapes, angles, and other features of the human head have been standardized to the point that, with a description and the manipulation of various plastic overlays of the *identi-kit,* an accurate picture of a person can be made in black and white in a period of a few minutes. Such a picture then may be transmitted by teletype to other agencies, and subsequently printed in newspapers and otherwise made public if necessary. This process has truly been an achievement and advancement in the field of identification.

In many investigations, no description of a person suspected of criminal activity is available. Thus the investigator will attempt to make an identification by analyzing the methods and techniques employed by the suspect, known as his *modus operandi* (method of operation), in the perpetration of his crimes.

A further avenue available is the confrontation of a suspect in custody with an *eyewitness.* This is accomplished most generally through a process called a *lineup* whereby the witness or victim observes and hears the suspect talk, but the suspect does not see the witness.

A criminal suspect generally will leave something of himself at a crime scene, thereby providing an investigator with avenues, recognizable only to him, of identifying the parties involved in the commission of the offense. *Fingerprints,* which establish identification beyond any doubt, and items of *physical evidence* removed from the crime scene when processed and analyzed by the *crime laboratory,* often provide the investigator with the information he must have to establish identification of the perpetrators when there are no witnesses or other avenues open to him.

Identification, by whatever means used to establish it beyond any doubt, is a most important and vital function of the investigator in any investigation he may conduct.

SCIENTIFIC FIELD AIDS

Many practical, technical, and electronic instruments have been developed for the use of law enforcement as well as business, industry, and the armed forces. But every tool possessed and used by law enforcement in its collective

FIGURE 11.2. (top) *A latent fingerprint expert is shown comparing latent and inked fingerprints in preparation for testimony in court. Courtesy Federal Bureau of Investigation, Washington, D.C.* (bottom) *Evidence at a homicide scene is carefully protected until criminalistic technicians arrive at the crime scene. Courtesy Metropolitan Police Department, St. Louis, Mo.*

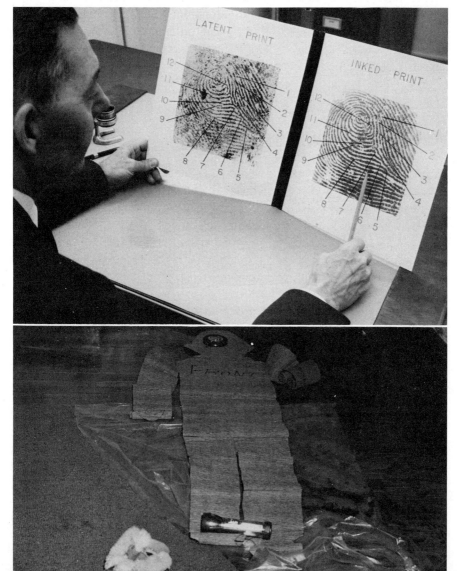

fight against crime is also utilized by our criminal society to fight against and sidetrack law enforcement for the furtherance of its own goals against society.

Such implements as microphones; recorders; cameras; binoculars; telescopes; chemicals; ultraviolet lights; fluorescent powders, pastes, and chemicals; inks; infrared lights; x ray; Geiger counters; weapons; radio, television; and electronic alarm systems are considered common in their everyday use by law enforcement investigators. Although each is common, strict rules, policies, and laws regulate their legal use. Any misuse of these items and others not mentioned could set a criminal free and cost an investigator or peace officer his job. But the criminal society is not concerned with such matters; their only interest is to use the equipment for their own benefit.

Scientific field aids are important to law enforcement. Without them the investigator's tasks in today's modern society would be insurmountable and citizens would be in peril of the criminal element.

PHYSICAL EVIDENCE

Each piece of physical evidence at a crime scene is important to the solution of that particular crime. For the investigator, it tells a story of who was present, what happened, when, where, and sometimes why the crime occurred, and ultimately how it occurred. Therefore, police officers, realizing the importance of such scenes, may appear to be overzealous in the protection of evidence until the police investigator and criminalist or his technician arrive and start their precise process of photographing, marking, collecting, and preserving the items of evidence.

There are many methods and procedures in which an investigator must be trained prior to performing the necessary steps in the preservation and collection of evidence. This is a lesser problem in large agencies than in small ones, for the large agencies usually have good crime laboratory facilities and can afford to employ experienced and trained experts to perform these important duties. The small agency is not so fortunate and often must rely solely on a regional crime laboratory for assistance when it is necessary.

Many more procedures and techniques than those briefly outlined in the preceding pages are used and often considered routine by police officers and investigators alike. The discussion here has only scratched the surface of the field of investigation but is presented to provide the preservice student with some understanding and comprehension of this vital area in the law enforcement profession.

SUMMARY

This chapter has attempted to present to the reader a brief overview of the art of investigation. The successful investigator must begin the job with a good knowledge of self, society, and people. He can learn the basic techniques of investigation from a book, but he must ultimately learn such arts as surveillance, undercover work, interview, identification, and interrogation mainly through patient practice and self-criticism. He should acquaint himself with the sources of information and with new inventions being constantly put to use in the area of law enforcement. The investigator should do his best to keep up with the times, to continue his education, and to acquaint himself with the most recently developed services available in the areas of data processing, identification, records, and communication systems.

The field of criminal investigation appears to be a glamorous occupation to the average citizen, but the truth is far different. Surveillance of a suspect, for instance, may be a time-consuming and tedious task, and the search of a crime scene unpleasant, exhausting, and tedious labor.

The present shortage of experienced investigators in every police department necessitates the increase in training of the patrol officer, who often is made responsible for the collection and preservation of evidence at the crime scene and does at least the preliminary investigation. The patrolman must sharpen his wits and develop the attitudes and habits of *observation, suspicion, curiosity,* and *memory.*

The ultimate goal of the criminal investigator is the successful presentation of his legally obtained evidence in court in order to obtain the conviction of the guilty.

ANNOTATED REFERENCES

Dienstein, W., *Technics for the Crime Investigator,* Thomas, Springfield, Ill., 1956. An easy-to-understand reference in crime investigation. Good reading for the novice or student desiring basic knowledge.

Fitzgerald, M. J., *Handbook of Criminal Investigation,* Arco, New York, 1960. A basic guide for the criminal investigator. Easy reading.

Fricke, C. W., and L. M. Kolbreck, *Criminal Investigation,* Legal Book Store, Los Angeles, 1962. Good introductory textbook for police-science students. Does not go into great detail and depth.

Inbau, F. E., and J. E. Reid, *Criminal Interrogation and Confessions,* Williams and Wilkins, Baltimore, 1962. One of the most widely recognized references on the subject of interrogation.

O'Hara, C. E., *Fundamentals of Criminal Investigation,* Thomas, Springfield, Ill., 1966. The student, police instructor, and criminal investigator will find this presentation to be one of the best references and most valuable as a basic guide to criminal investigation. Well illustrated.

O'Hara, C. E., and J. W. Osterburg, *An Introduction to Criminalistics,* Macmillan, New York, 1949. An excellent presentation of the basic elements, procedures, and fundamental techniques of criminalistics as they apply to police science and investigation.

Soderman, H., and J. J. O'Connell, *Modern Criminal Investigation,* Funk and Wagnalls, New York, 1962. This well-written text discusses basic, advanced, and technical elements of criminal investigation. Widely accepted and adopted by the law-enforcement profession as a basic reference. Used as a basic textbook in law-enforcement education and training programs throughout the world. Well researched, documented, and illustrated. Should be in every police, law, and student library.

Weston, P. B., and K. M. Wells, *Elements of Criminal Investigation,* Prentice–Hall, Englewood Cliffs, N.J., 1970.

NOTES

1. O. W. Wilson, *Police Records, Their Installation and Use,* Public Administration Service, Chicago, 1951, p. 9.

2. Federal Bureau of Investigation, "A National Crime Information Center," *FBI Law Enforcement Bulletin,* Vol. 35, No. 5, May 1966, pp. 2–6.

CHAPTER TWELVE

Criminalistics

The world of science has afforded us a life span unthought of in earlier years. It also has given rise to methods of exploring the heavens and the deep seas. The application of science to crime is known as *criminalistics*. The use of science to solve crimes has been employed for many years; however, the greatest strides have been made since 1930. Despite the advances that have been made, the area of criminalistics is still far behind business, industry, and other areas of government in taking advantage of the scientific and technological revolution.

The common conception of the criminalist is that of a chemist confined to the laboratory; however, the criminalist must be a scientist skilled in all phases of the physical sciences and who is a detective in every sense of the word. He must have a broad understanding of the appropriate processes to be used as well as an extremely intimate knowledge of each individual procedure involved. "The work of criminalistics is characterized by the great variety of relatively elementary subjects which must be mastered [1]. Too great a specialization in any one phase of the science at the expense of others can severely hamper the criminalist's effectiveness.

Prior to the latter part of the nineteenth century, physical evidence played no part in the detection, apprehension, or conviction of law violators.

The English rule of evidence sternly and quite properly rejected what it believed to be hurtful influences in its investigation of facts, and attempted to follow as the only safe guide, ''reasonable inference based on the teaching of experience, from facts testified to by persons whose credibility is secured by powerful safeguards and by documents, the authenticity of which is seditiously guaranteed [2].

This attitude was fine as far as it went, that is, in forming a high regard for oral and documentary evidence. Its fault lay in the fact that it completely disregarded scientific tests by which the other evidence could be verified. It was unthinkable at that time to use even the most basic forms of scientific tests.

HISTORY OF CRIMINALISTICS

First Uses

While investigative techniques were slow in coming, the confession was gradually being augmented by rudimentary evidence such as footprints and other obvious physical objects at the crime scene. In a case in Scotland in 1786, plaster casts were made of footprints, an act unheard of before.

Pioneers in the Field

The first organized detective force in the modern world was the famous *Bow Street Runners* of London [3]. Although the best interests of the people may not always have been served by the *Runners,* they did have some very good detectives, namely Townsend, Vickers, and Sayer. Each had his specialty: Townsend kept a record of the criminals caught, Vickers was a master at disguises, and Sayer was an expert on forgeries. The list of forerunners to today's criminalists is extensive, some of the notable ones being Alphonse Bertillon in individual identification and Colonel Calvin H. Goddard in ballistics. J. Edgar Hoover, although not a scientist himself, furthered the cause of science by establishing the FBI laboratory in 1932.

NEED FOR CRIMINALISTICS

Today the crime rate is rising, especially in the more populated areas. The reasons for this can be argued indefinitely. The ultimate aim of the criminalist is to analyze the evidence collected and submitted to him to prove either innocence or guilt. From the point of view of the police officer, solving the crime with the aid of criminalistics and bringing the perpetrator swiftly to justice is a great deterrent to would-be criminals.

The high cost of crime is another reason why criminalistics is valuable to law enforcement and the public. It is difficult to determine accurately the cost of crime to the taxpayer in the United States, but it is conservatively estimated to be in excess of $20 billion per year [4]. With this fact in mind, it is not possible to overemphasize the necessity of bringing all the resources of science into play in the fight to bring this high cost down.

It must not be forgotten that the same facilities available to law enforcement for the detection of criminals are also available to the criminal. It is a mistake to think that these facilities will not be used—using them may require a brilliant mind, but the underworld has the capability and will not hesitate to avail itself of criminalistics. One need only look at how modern communications have extended the realm of organized crime to see the problem.

The most challenging crimes to the investigator are, of course, the violent crimes such as murder. Besides the immediate interest these crimes create, they also are of interest to the investigator because of the latitude in investigation. However, approximately 57,000 motor vehicle deaths occur annually [5], and this is perhaps a more pressing problem than solving a murder. The criminalist may have an interest in the number of the deaths from routine motor vehicle accidents, but when the drinking driver and the number of deaths and injuries he causes is added in, the vastness of the problem can be seen. "Actually the enforcement of the law as it bears upon the problem of the drinking driver would be, in and of itself, a sufficient justification for the establishment of a criminalistics operation" [6].

PURPOSE OF CRIMINALISTICS

The purpose of criminalistics is to furnish recognition, identification, individualization, and evaluation of physical evidence by application of the natural sciences to law science matters. From the standpoint of the prosecution, criminalistics is slanted toward apprehending the violator and proving him guilty. From the standpoint of the criminalist, criminalistics focuses on analyzing the evidence and freeing the innocent as well as indicting the guilty. Most good police departments are attempting to elevate their standards through professionalization, but there is still the fear that some investigative and enforcement agencies are interested strictly in obtaining a successful

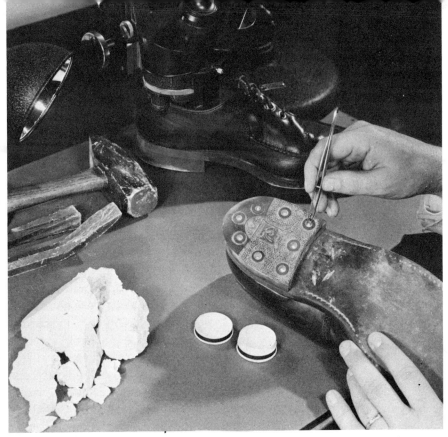

FIGURE 12.1. *The criminalistic technician performs many unusual assignments. Here, a technician removes safe insulation from the shoes of an arrested burglary suspect for examination in the laboratory. Courtesy Federal Bureau of Investigation, Washington, D.C.*

prosecution at all costs. Criminalistics has risen above this and is devoted to the administration of justice; its facilities will be used on behalf of the defendant as well as against him.

CRIME LABORATORY

The need for a crime laboratory depends largely on the size and type of community it is to serve. Some areas may have a higher incidence of crime and a correspondingly greater need for its services. In general, a concentrated population of 100,000 needs the services of a laboratory and at least one trained criminalist. Additional trained persons can be added at the rate of one for each 100,000–150,000 people [7]. The autonomous laboratory does not exist in the United States, but much may be said in its favor. In England the laboratory is under no law enforcement agency. Consequently, the freedom from fighting for its fair share of the budget and absence of the attendant political frays with other departments within the agency allows for a higher degree of service and a greater scope of scientific endeavor.

LOCAL LABORATORY

The local laboratory serves the immediate area in close proximity to the agencies that are served. The personnel staffing the laboratory, as in all cases, must be of high quality and capable of immediate action because most crimes are solved by the people who deal with them immediately and directly. The equipment of such a laboratory of necessity is limited and simple.

REGIONAL LABORATORY

Cases requiring more complicated services should be handled by a regional laboratory. In this situation the more expensive equipment can be in one central place where the more intricate examinations that are not critical as to time element can be handled. The regional laboratory may have to serve large rural areas and, in addition to the more elaborate equipment, must have at least a minimum amount of basic equipment. If rural areas are served by a regional laboratory, it must be remembered that the time lag can reduce the effectiveness of the analyses.

Although certain requirements for the physical layout of a laboratory are desirable, it is probably best to leave this planning to the person who is to operate it.

LABORATORY PERSONNEL

The director of the crime laboratory must have sufficient background in organization so as to be the nucleus around which an effective unit can be formed. Throughout the United States there is no specific occupational requirement, although it is thought by many that the director should be either a *chemist* or a *physicist*. There are, however, effective units that are led by lawyers and even policemen. As a part of the broad background, the director must have an acute awareness of the value of science in establishing fact. His personality must be compatible both with his subordinates and his supervisors. He must also have a keen insight into the relations of the laboratory work and the law.

Staffing of the laboratory will depend largely on its size and scope. In general, all criminalists must have a baccalaureate degree, preferably in science, accompanied by on-the-job training and further study. The possible exception to the baccalaureate degree requirement would be the recruitment of personnel from the police department who have a particular trait or specialty desired by the director. Because science has so many facets, care must be taken to cover the various fields with the best qualified persons.

The collection of evidence is by far the most important aspect in the criminal investigation. Yet, in many cases, this function is left to an individual who has had little training. Ideally the evidence should be collected by the criminalist; however, in most cases, one is not available. The solution, therefore, is to have a close working relationship with the agencies availing themselves of the laboratory services. If the laboratory makes known their requirements, much greater results will be secured. A possible solution is training classes for personnel of the various agencies. If all patrol personnel cannot be trained, at least those most likely to do the collecting should be trained. Liaison between the prosecuting attorneys and the laboratory also must be maintained so as to make the services available to them known.

AREAS OF INVESTIGATION AND ANALYSIS

The science of criminalistics has grown large in the field of law enforcement in the last 35 years, but this progress has been one largely of lateral expansion of processes known to science much longer. Only in the last 15 years has there been a real development of new processes and methods.

What have been some of the areas of investigation and analysis? Much could be written on this question, but for purposes of introducing the new student to the area of criminalistics, we will briefly examine only a few.

Firearms Examination

As the name implies, firearms examination directs itself to answering questions propounded by the employment of missile-projecting weapons used in the commission of criminal acts. These examinations range from the basic firearms identification technique of identifying the weapon from which a questioned projectile was discharged, through the operational and functional tests of guns, the determination by shot and gunpowder pattern tests of the distance from which a projectile was fired, to the final discovery of the kind of gun employed in firing a questioned projectile or cartridge case.

The technicians who conduct these analyses usually are considered to be experts in the field of toolmark identification. This involves the same principles used in firearms identification and results in the absolute identification of every kind of tool used by criminals and left at the crime scene.

Fingerprint Examination

The science of dactyloscopy predates the Christian era by many centuries and has been evidenced in varying degrees by successive civilizations. Fingerprint analysis has become particularly useful in criminal identification and this area of the science has made the most progress in recent decades.

Positive identification is made on the basis of the inked impression of the fingers on a fingerprint record card. The *Henry System* of classification and identification in fingerprint analysis is an alphabetical and numerical formula derived by the technician from the ten inked finger impressions on the card. From this, the identity of a person may be established positively.

Latent prints are made by persons every time anything is touched. The impressions left on objects can be lifted by several processes. The technician compares such latent impressions with the fingerprints on file on the inked cards. If a sufficient number of points of similarity are observed between the latent and known prints, with no inexplicable dissimilarities present, an identification has been effected by the technician.

Spectrographic Examination

Laboratory technicians operating the spectrograph are able to examine minute pieces of evidence that usually are too small to be analyzed or examined successfully by any other means. Specimens of any substance may be analyzed and compared by the spectrograph and spectrophotometer, both of which are infrared as well as ultraviolet. Two other instruments used to analyze evidence are the *x-ray diffraction spectrophotometer* and the *electron microscope.*

Each of these instruments performs a specific function in the determination of the metallic composition of materials under investigation, the examination

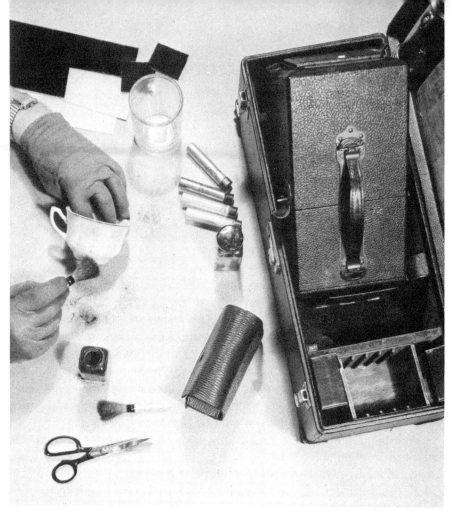

FIGURE 12.2. *An FBI expert dusts a cup for possible latent single fingerprint. Many police agencies throughout the country depend upon State and Federal auxiliary services to aid them in their fight against crime. Courtesy Federal Bureau of Investigation, Washington, D.C.*

and study of color and coloring agents, the analysis of many organic compounds, and the analysis of crystalline substances, as well as many others too numerous to be discussed here.

Of all the instruments, the *electron microscope* is the largest and most delicate of any of the instruments found in a laboratory spectrographic section. This microscope, for example, will allow magnification up to 100,000 diameters in contrast with 2000 diameter limit on the pre-electron instruments.

Each of the instruments is valuable in its own way as a tool of law enforcement. After examination of a piece of questioned material a technician will

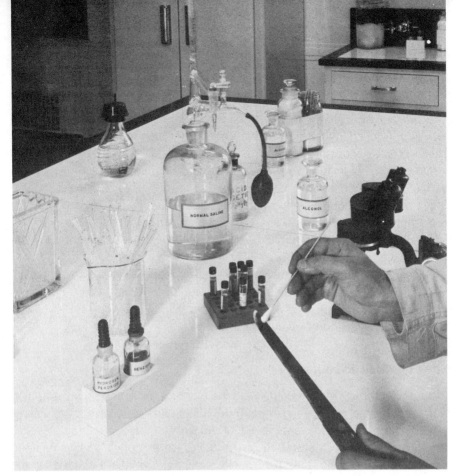

FIGURE 12.3. *Crime laboratory serological technician is shown conduct-ing a test on a knife to determine the presence of blood. Courtesy Federal Bureau of Investigation, Washington, D.C.*

be able to answer two questions for the investigators: (a) What is it? (b) What is its composition? As a result, it is often possible, for example, to ascertain the year and make of a suspected hit-and-run motor vehicle.

Serological Examination

The serologist in the crime laboratory is concerned primarily with evidence involving blood, but he also examines other body fluids as they may pertain to a crime under investigation. Suspects in hit-and-run, rape, and murder cases often have been brought before the courts through the identification of blood on clothes, weapons, and vehicles. Many suspects blame stains on other factors, but the serologist can prove or disprove any claims. Thus, he may clear the innocent person or help to convict the guilty.

General Chemical and Toxicological Examination

The primary function of this type of examination is to investigate deaths resulting from chemical substances and crimes committed with the aid of chemical substances. The vital organs, for example, of a suspected poison victim can be examined and tests conducted to prove or disprove poison as the cause of death.

It is important in criminal investigation to determine the identity and quantity of an unknown substance. Many beneficial and therapeutic substances are vital to humanity when controlled, but they can become as fatal as cyanide when abused.

General chemical examinations usually are conducted when any chemical material such as gasoline is used by a rioter or arsonist, when explosives are used to open safes, and when other unknown substances are employed to aid criminals in the perpetration of crimes.

Fiber and Hair Examination

Fiber and hair examination usually aid the officer conducting an investigation even though the analyses generally do not result in positive conclusions. Usually there are insufficient individualized and microscopic characteristics to positively identify the source of the collected evidence of hair or fiber. However, the analysis does help an investigator to place a suspect at the scene of a crime, with the victim, or in contact with stolen property. It is possible for the technician to establish beyond doubt whether the hairs or fibers submitted for examination match known samples collected, whether the material is human or animal, and in some instances it is possible to determine the sex, age, and race of the person from whom they originated. Other helpful facts that can be ascertained are whether the hair (or fiber) fell out or was pulled out, and whether it was crushed, broken, cut, burned, shattered, bleached, dyed, or artificially waved. Hairs and fibers are constantly intermingling with the objects they come in contact with, and their importance is never discounted by an investigator or crime lab technician.

Metallurgical and Petrographic Examination

Both of these specialized areas of science daily play an important role in the investigation of crime and apprehension of law violators. Each provides valuable information to assist in the linking of a particular suspect to a crime scene.

In metallurgical examinations, the technician determines whether two separate pieces of metal submitted to examination have a common origin. It is also possible to determine the manufacturer of a particular metal object. The types of cases in which the metallurgical examinations have proven to be of great value to the investigator are hit-and-run traffic cases, restoration of markings on guns which have been destroyed or left at crime scenes, and the identification of ownership in cases of stolen property.

While the metal is being examined the petrographic examiner can analyze any soil removed from the metal and ascertain its origin. Examination of mineral evidence is the primary function of petrography and much information can be learned from concrete, plaster, insulation materials, mortar, brick, stone, glass, sand, ore, dust, and similar substances.

Neutron-Activation Analysis

This is one of the newest and most promising techniques to be adopted in the criminalistics laboratory. It is considered to be the most sensitive method known for the detection of a majority of the elements in the *periodic system.* The system is precise, accurate, and ultrasensitive.

Historically, neutron-activation analysis may be traced to the discovery of artificial radioactivity in 1933 by Frederic and Irene Curie-Joliot. Almost immediately this analysis was recognized to be a valuable research tool.

FIGURE 12.4. (left) *Many technicians employed in crime laboratories are trained women criminologists. Here, a female technician compares a piece of cloth from a crime scene with a torn area in the trousers of a suspect.* (right) *Tool mark examiners usually can identify every conceivable tool used by criminals in committing crimes. Here, an FBI expert examines small pieces of tree wood. Courtesy Federal Bureau of Investigation, Washington, D.C.*

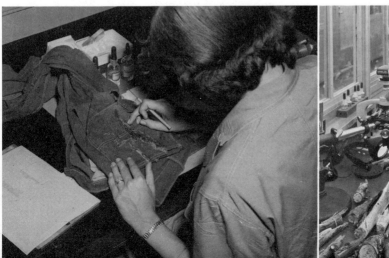

Since the 1930's, sensitivity has been increased through improved instrumental technique, and a greater abundance of higher neutron fluxes.

Neutron-activation analysis is used for the detection and measurement of trace qualities of almost all material submitted for examination which, by size or nature, is too small to be detected by the usual chemical analyses. Dr. Paul L. Kirk, the famed California criminalist stated before his death that "This technique promises to revolutionize the identification of criminal evidence." Virtually no sample of material is too small to be analyzed in this manner. For instance, a fleck of paint no larger than the period at the end of this sentence may be analyzed and classified. The uses of this analysis are limitless; it can help to identify and trace burglars, hit-and-run drivers, counterfeiters, and other criminals because almost everyone leaves some small proof of himself at the crime scene or carries a part of it away with him.

This analysis is almost always nondestructive, so that evidence may be preserved for presentation in court or saved to be analyzed by another method.

Radiological Examination

X-ray analysis has many investigative uses; x rays can be projected on a fluorescent screen or exposed on photographic film. The technique is a valuable aid in establishing, through dental records, the identity of unknown persons and mutilated or decomposed corpses. It is also valuable for use in the examination of baggage and suspicious packages; the location of defects or causes of failures in metal, wood, glass, and other substances; the detection of invisible writing or contraband concealed on the human body; the examination of the composition of bombs to aid in deactivating them; and in the comparison of similar-appearing specimens of cloth, paper, leather, biological samples, and other substances.

Uses of Photography

The use of photography in the police field was first employed in 1854 in Switzerland with the photographing of criminals. Since its early days, photography has grown into a complex art and is a most essential tool in law enforcement.

In the crime laboratory, the camera and its accessory equipment are considered to be of primary importance. The criminalist, in order to accomplish his purpose as a scientific technician in law enforcement, must be accomplished in the techniques of photography.

O'Hara and Osterburg state in their book that

. . . the four major functions of photography in the laboratory are to provide: (1) a record of the initial appearance of evidence; (2) a record of the scene of a crime or some aspect of a crime which cannot be preserved in its present state; (3) a means of illustrating points of evidence in court; (4) a method of making visible various aspects or details of evidence that cannot be seen by the human eye [8].

The laboratory photo technician must be proficient in such processes as photomicrography, which is the photographing of objects that are magnified from 2 or 3 diameters to 500 or more. These photos portray visually what the criminalist is able to observe through the microscope.

Three other well-known techniques are stereoscopic, infrared, and x-ray photography. Stereoscopic photography is employed to show important perforations, indentions, ridges, and other irregular features of a piece of evidence. The infrared photographic method, used most frequently in cases involving important documents, paintings, and other objects, brings out pen and ink writings and color separations. The x-ray photograph has been discussed already.

Questioned Documents

The examination and analysis of documents is believed to be one of the oldest sciences used by law enforcement in its fight against crime. An examination of such evidence involves the comparison, side by side, of handwriting that has been questioned with that of already identified handwriting. It is done to establish an identification of the person who executed the writing. Document examination, however, is not limited to handwriting analysis. It also encompasses printing of all kinds, forgeries, typewriting, checkwriter and protector impressions, inks, paper, writing that has been removed or destroyed, burned paper, rubber stamps, and a host of others related to this science.

No two people write exactly the same and this has been proved by an untold number of experts in this field. Identical training in penmanship may result in handwriting appearing to be identical; however, the process of executing the handwritten character is very complex, and individual characteristics in writing will always dominate those of some other similarly trained person. When a detailed examination is made of such script, the hidden or disguised peculiarities will be recognized.

The document examiner utilizes a great deal of costly equipment, and he must maintain a large amount of information in the form of collections, samples, and reference files. The most common equipment found in the document examination laboratory are the optical instruments such as various kinds of microscopes, special measuring devices, special photographic facilities and equipment, and ultraviolet and infrared equipment.

Polygraphic Examination

The polygraph, commonly called the *lie detector,* is a valuable investigative tool used extensively by law enforcement throughout the world. The key to its efficiency is the person operating it and his skill in the art of interrogation. Rightfully, operation of the polygraph and analysis of the charts produced from an examination are not a function of the criminalistic laboratory, but belong in the detective or investigative division of a law enforcement agency. Many agencies, however, consider this operation as part of the crime laboratory, and this is why it is often found there.

The *lie detector* is used not only by law enforcement agencies throughout the world, but also by numerous private organizations and business concerns, medical science, and the armed services.

The polygraph is composed of three major scientific components and a recording device. These components are the *pneumograph,* which measures respiratory patterns, the *galvanometer,* which measures changes in skin resistance to electricity, and the *cardiosphygmograph,* which measures pulse rate and blood pressure.

In 1895, *Cesare Lombroso* made the very first attempt with a scientific instrument of this nature, which he called a *hydrosphygmograph.* Further development was effected by such pioneers as Vittorio Benussi, William Marston, and John Larson. The late esteemed *August Vollmer,* in 1921, while Chief of Police of Berkeley, California, used Larson's instrument to aid him in personnel selection for his agency. *Leonarde Keeler,* who is recognized as the true developer of the modern lie detector, built a more satisfactory instrument than Larson's in 1926. Since that time and until his death in 1949, he continued to perfect the "Keeler Polygraph" as it is known today. Thus, Leonarde Keeler is considered to be the "father" of the polygraph.

The judiciary throughout the United States is most reluctant to admit the results of the polygraph examination into evidence in the courtroom except

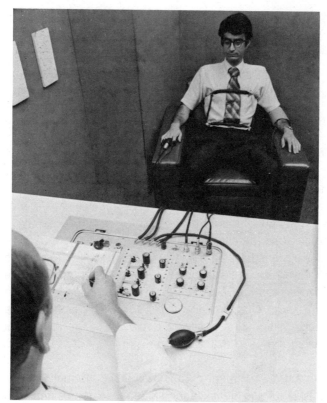

FIGURE 12.5. *The polygraph, commonly called the lie detector, is a valuable investigative tool. Here a qualified examiner conducts a test to aid in further investigation and interrogation of a possible suspect. Courtesy Police Department, Los Angeles, Ca.*

when there is an agreement and stipulation between the opposing parties to have such an examination performed and the findings considered by the court. There have been a few isolated cases in which polygraph results have been admissible as evidence, but these cases have been rare. At all times, the use of any results from a polygraph examination remain at the discretion of the court.

Regardless of its lack of acceptance in the courtroom, however, law enforcement finds it a valuable investigative, interrogative, and pre-employment selection aid. The operator of the instrument must be highly trained in its use and in the analysis of the charts produced. With expert and discriminate use, it is hoped that there will be a greater acceptance of this instrument's results in the courtroom.

In recent years, legislation has been passed prohibiting the use of the instrument in any area of employment except for the examination of police officers and applicants for law enforcement positions.

Voiceprint Identification

The search for truth in law enforcement involves answering the all-important question: "Is this the man?" Several processes have been used to aid officers in answering this question. The *Bertillon System* of the science of singlement and later the *Henry System* of fingerprints have contributed to answering the question. In the twentieth century a new process of identification—the *voiceprint*—is coming to be recognized. *Lawrence G. Kersta,* a physicist and former Bell Telephone Laboratory expert in speech research, has invented and introduced this new identification system. The foundation of this new identification system dates back to 1867 when Melville Bell devised a phonetic alphabet known then as *visual speech.* This system of handwritten symbols, which conveyed to the eye the detail of speech sounds, was later used by his son, Alexander Graham Bell, in his efforts to teach the deaf to speak. Although this system partially filled a gap in the search for a readable voice representation, the need existed for mechanically producing pictorial voice patterns.

Even with the development of much valuable information in this area, the means of efficient voice identification eluded researchers until the persistence of Kersta led to the present development and refinement of the technique and the adaptation of sound spectrograph equipment. It is a visible representation of a sound, caused by an electronic impulse inspired by the frequency, time, and loudness of that sound. The *spectrograph* makes the visible representation possible.

The major contribution of this new identification technique is, of course, in the field of investigation and scientific analysis. Voiceprint was first instrumental in the arrest of two Stamford, Connecticut, men in June of 1964, for telephone bomb scares to a large manufacturing company located in that city. It was next used in the case of an apostate policeman. This case, involving perjury, was conducted in New York state on April 12, 1966, and was the first time voiceprint testimony had ever been received as evidence in any New York court.

Voiceprints have been extremely valuable in reconstructing unintelligible messages. For example, the last message sent out before the crash of a Pacific Air Lines plane in flight between Las Vegas and San Francisco was deciphered, revealing that the copilot said he and the pilot had been shot.

A gun was later found in the wreckage and a bullet hole was located in the pilot's seat. The weapon was traced to a passenger who had lost a good deal of money in Las Vegas and who had purchased a large flight insurance policy.

Numerous other agencies have used the voiceprint in such cases as obscene telephone calls and a riot arsonist in the Watts riots in 1965 in Los Angeles.

In 1973, the California District Court of Appeals ruled that voiceprints may now be used as evidence in California criminal cases. The court in making the ruling stated "this identification technique has reached the level of scientific reliability and since 1968 scientific research in this field has continued. The technique has received recognition and acceptance in other jurisdictions, namely the U.S. Military Court of Appeals, the U.S. District Court, the Supreme Court of the State of Michigan, the Florida District Court, as well as numerous others in such states as New York, New Jersey and Connecticut."

No case as yet has been brought before the United States Supreme Court. The final acceptance of the voiceprint lies ultimately in their hands. Should they deny it as a legal identification procedure, it will still be useful to law enforcement in other areas.

FUTURE OF CRIMINALISTICS

Despite the increased use of technical inventions of the twentieth century, law enforcement still lags far behind industry in taking advantage of the scientific and technological revolution. It is felt that this, in part, is due to the reluctance of the courts to accept as tools to provide legal evidence in the courtroom those scientific and technical inventions made available to the American community at large.

Even small businesses employ modern technological devices and systems, but the Nation's courts are almost as close to the quill pen era as they are to the age of electronic data processing [9].

The crime laboratory has been the oldest and strongest link between science and technology and criminal justice. The best laboratories, such as the FBI's, are well advanced. There are also some excellent laboratories in key locations around the country. However, the great majority of police department laboratories have only minimal equipment and lack highly skilled personnel able to use the modern equipment now being developed and produced by the instrumentation industry. Techniques such as neutron-activation analysis and mass spectrometry permit the identification of ever smaller pieces of material evidence. Voiceprints and photographic developments will expand the ability to detect and apprehend criminals. To bring these advances more directly into police operations, improvement in crime laboratories must proceed in two directions:

(1) Establishment of laboratories to serve the combined needs of police departments in metropolitan areas.

(2) Expansion of research activities in major existing and in new laboratories.

The need for the regional laboratories follows naturally from the increasing expense of facilities and the increasing demand for individuals of superior technical competence. The research is needed to speed the application of new instrumentation possibilities [10].

SUMMARY

Criminalistics is, generally speaking, the scientific examination of physical evidence and the evaluation of findings in light of the law. The talents of the criminalist are used in equal measure to protect the innocent and indict the guilty.

The early use of investigative techniques in the laboratory may be traced back to the 1700's, and with the aid of talented men in the field such as Bertillon, Goddard, Henry, Keller, Hoover, Kirk, and Kersta, investigative techniques have progressed to a highly specialized field. Much improvement is desirable in the area of utilizing the latest discoveries of technology to bring the criminalistics up to the high standards of scientific implementation enjoyed by other areas of the American society.

Examinations in the criminalistics laboratory range from the uncomplicated measurement of blood alcohol levels to the sophisticated techniques of spectroanalysis and the increased use of neutron-activation analyses and voiceprinting.

To compete in any measure with the yearly increase in crime in the United States, it will be necessary to rely more and more upon the laboratory. At the same time it must be determined which devices are necessary in relation to the price we are willing to pay in dollars, invasion of privacy, and other social costs.

ANNOTATED REFERENCES

Jones, L. V., *Scientific Investigation and Physical Evidence,* Thomas, Springfield, Ill., 1959. An introduction to proper methods of investigation, and the collection, care, and preservation of evidence.

Kirk, P. L., *Crime Investigation,* edited by J. I. Thornton, Wiley Interscience, New

York, 1974. A detailed reference and guide for the criminalistics student, laboratory technician, and criminal investigator.

Kirk, P. L., and L. W. Bradford, *The Crime Laboratory,* Thomas, Springfield, Ill., 1965. A good discussion in considerable depth of the organization and operation of the crime laboratory.

O'Hara, C. E., *Fundamentals of Criminal Investigation,* Thomas, Springfield, Ill., 1966. Any student or peace officer will find this reference most valuable in obtaining a basic knowledge of criminal investigation and the elements of crimes.

O'Hara, C. E., and J. W. Osterburg, *An Introduction to Criminalistics,* Macmillan, New York, 1949. A most useful, concise, and easy-to-understand reference for every student in criminal investigation. Explains and details easy-to-follow procedures.

Turner, W. W., *Criminalistics,* Aqueduct Books, San Francisco, 1965. An excellent reference for the many facets involved in criminalistics. Well researched and written. Especially helpful to police officers and lawyers.

NOTES

1. C. E. O'Hara and J. W. Osterburg, *An Introduction to Criminalistics,* p. xiv.

2. H. M. Robinson, *Science Catches the Criminal,* Blue Ribbon Books, New York, 1935.

3. *Ibid.,* pp. 22–23.

4. P. L. Kirk and L. W. Bradford, *The Crime Laboratory,* p. 10.

5. National Safety Council, 1973.

6. Kirk and Bradford, *op. cit.,* p. 12.

7. *Ibid.,* p. 11.

8. O'Hara and Osterburg, *op. cit.,* p. 141.

9. *The Challenge of Crime in a Free Society,* A Report by the President's Commission on Law Enforcement and Administration of Justice, U.S. Government Printing Office, Washington, D.C. 1967, p. 245.

10. *Ibid.,* pp. 255, 256.

PART THREE

Crime in America and Police-Community Relations

CHAPTER THIRTEEN

Organized Crime

Organized crime [1], because of its inherent nature and structure, and because of the scope and complexity of its criminal operations, presents a special challenge to all levels of law enforcement. It is a society that seeks to operate outside the control of the American people and their governments. Its actions are not impulsive but rather the result of intricate conspiracies, carried on over many years and aimed at gaining control over whole fields of activity in order to amass huge profits.

"None of the varieties of organized crime is against the law. Further, in most democratic nations it is not illegal for a person or group of people rationally to plan, establish, develop, or administer an organization designed for the perpetration of crime—any more than it is illegal for detective story writers and university students to sit around trying to invent 'the perfect crime.' Neither is it against the law for a person to occupy a position in the division of labor or an organization designed for the perpetration of crime" [2]. The nefarious activities carried out by these organizations are, of course, against the law, and it is only along these avenues that organized crime may be pursued by law enforcement.

HISTORICAL BACKGROUND

Organized crime is a reality in the twentieth century regardless of the name it may be known by or referred to. Whether it is called the *Cosa Nostra,*

Mafia, or the *Syndicate,* its chief purpose is to gain power, control, and prestige in every level of society and government.

The name *Mafia* (Mah-fee-ah) comes from the Arabic word *maehfil* meaning union. It is the name of a secret Sicilian terrorist society. The Mafia began in the 1600's as an organization to combat corruption and tyranny in the Kingdom of the Two Sicilies. As time passed, criminal elements gained control. They waged bloody vendettas, robbed, murdered, and committed other illegal acts for their own purpose and benefit. This organization, as will be explained later, is powerful, not only in the United States, but also throughout the world. General recognition of the existence of the Mafia in the United States came toward the close of the nineteenth century. Prior to 1920, the activities of the various organized crime syndicates were beginning to build but it was the bootlegging business of the prohibition era of the 1920's which really produced recognition and intensive investigation by the United States Treasury Department. One such investigation resulted in the conviction of Chicago racket leader Al Capone. In the 1930's, with total emphasis on attempting to control organized criminal activity, the special racket group of Thomas E. Dewey in New York City secured the conviction of several prominent racketeers including the late Lucky Luciano, the one syndicate leader whose organizational genius made him the father of today's confederation of organized crime families. Attempts to control continued to increase and, in the early 1940's, an investigation by the FBI into a million-dollar extortion plot in the motion picture industry resulted in the conviction of several racket leaders, including the Chicago family boss who was then a member of organized crime's national council.

After World War II, there was relatively little national interest in the problem of organized crime. In 1950, the U.S. Attorney General convened a national conference on organized crime. A short time later, the historical hearings of the Senate Special Committee under the leadership of Senator Estes Kefauver began. This committee heard testimony from over 800 witnesses from nearly every state. These hearings only temporarily aroused the concern of the American public and there was little followthrough. The exception was the state of California which later conducted hearings regarding the level of organized crime that was ingrained throughout the state and who was providing its leadership. The Senate Special Committee exposed the problem to the government and the public but they failed to develop the investigative and prosecutive agencies that are necessary to root out the activities of the criminal cartels.

In 1957, the discovery of the meeting in Apalachia, New York, of at least seventy-five criminal cartel leaders from every section of the United States aroused national interest. Interest was further stimulated by disclosures to a Senate Select Committee investigating the infiltration of organized crime into labor and business. As a direct result of these disclosures came a concerted federal enforcement response, and special, institutionalized efforts on the local level have been steadily growing [3].

ORGANIZATION AND MEMBERSHIP

The nucleus of syndicated and organized crime in the United States is made up of two dozen groups operating as criminal cartels in the metropolitan areas of the nation. Membership in the nucleus is composed primarily of men of Italian descent. They are in frequent communication with one another and their smooth and unruffled functioning is ensured by a national body of overseers. [4] The organization as a whole was once commonly referred to as the *Mafia* and still carries this tag of identification to some degree. However, in more recent years it has been popularly known as *La Cosa Nostra*. J. Edgar Hoover stated to the Congress of the United States:

La Cosa Nostra is the largest organization of the criminal underworld in this country, very closely organized and strictly disciplined. They have committed almost every crime under the sun.

La Cosa Nostra is a criminal fraternity whose membership is Italian either by birth or national origin and it has been found to control major racket activities in many of our larger metropolitan areas, often working in concert with criminals representing other ethnic backgrounds. It operates on a nationwide basis, with international implications, and until recent years it carried on its activities with almost complete secrecy. It functions as a criminal cartel, adhering to its own body of "law" and "justice" and, in so doing, thwarts and usurps the authority of legally constituted judicial bodies [5].

In various cities across the land, the local core group may be known by any of various labels. These core groups work with and control other organized racket groups whose leaders for the most part are of various ethnic derivations. Additionally, the thousands of employees who carry out the day-to-day operations of organized crime represent a cross-section of the nation's population groups.

The current coalition of groups previously developed have grown since

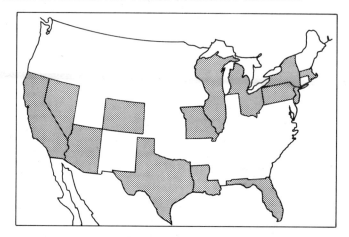

FIGURE 13.1. *States in which organized crime core group members both reside and operate. Source:* Task Force Report: Organized Crime, *President's Commission on Law Enforcement and Administration of Justice, 1967.*

the era of prohibition. It was during this era that the German, Irish, Jewish, and Italian groups competed with each other in the various racket operations. Since prohibition the Italian groups have been successful in switching their enterprises from prostitution and bootlegging to gambling, extortion, and other illegal activities. Many feel that they consolidated their power through murder and violence [6].

The members of the primary core groups live and are active in the states shown in Figure 13.1. The scope and effect of their criminal operations and penetration of legitimate businesses varies from area to area. Some of the groups in the nucleus are wealthier or more influential than others and it has generally been found these members operate primarily in New York, New Jersey, Illinois, Florida, Louisiana, Nevada, Michigan, and Rhode Island. By no means do the clear areas on the map mean that the areas are free of organized crime. On the contrary, for example, a variety of illegal activities in New England are controlled from Rhode Island [7].

It has been the concern of many that the identification of the Mafia's ethnic character has reflected poorly on Italian-Americans generally. This false implication has been eloquently refuted by one of the nation's outstanding experts on organized crime, Ralph Salerno, formerly of the New York City Police Department, and now retired. When an Italian-American racketeer complained to him, "Why does it have to be one of your own kind that hurts you?" Mr. Salerno replied:

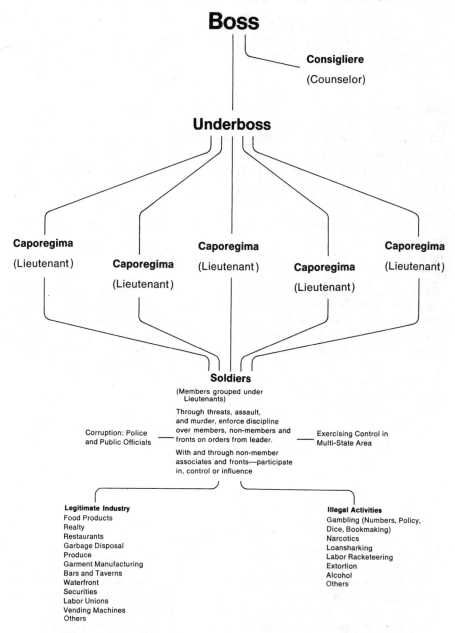

Boss

Consigliere
(Counselor)

Underboss

Caporegima
(Lieutenant)

Caporegima
(Lieutenant)

Caporegima
(Lieutenant)

Caporegima
(Lieutenant)

Caporegima
(Lieutenant)

Soldiers
(Members grouped under Lieutenants)

Corruption: Police
and Public Officials

Through threats, assault, and murder, enforce discipline over members, non-members and fronts on orders from leader.

With and through non-member associates and fronts—participate in, control or influence

Exercising Control in
Multi-State Area

Legitimate Industry
Food Products
Realty
Restaurants
Garbage Disposal
Produce
Garment Manufacturing
Bars and Taverns
Waterfront
Securities
Labor Unions
Vending Machines
Others

Illegal Activities
Gambling (Numbers, Policy, Dice, Bookmaking)
Narcotics
Loansharking
Labor Racketeering
Extortion
Alcohol
Others

FIGURE 13.2. *An organized crime family. Source:* Task Force Report: Organized Crime, *President's Commission on Law Enforcement and Administration of Justice, 1967.*

I'm not your kind and you're not my kind. My manners, morals, and mores are not yours. The only thing we have in common is that we both spring from an Italian heritage and culture—and you are the traitor to that heritage and culture which I am proud to be part of [8].

Internal Structure

The internal structure [9] of the organized crime nucleus establishes for them their permanency of form, their strength of organization, and their ability to control allied racket enterprises. In the nucleus of twenty-four groups or families resides the power that organized crime has in the United States today.

It is interesting as well as important to look carefully and understand fully this structure that provides so few a number with so great a power and effect upon a whole nation of people (Figure 13.2).

Each of the 24 groups is known as a "family," with membership varying from as many as 700 men to as few as 20. Most cities with organized crime have only one family; New York City has five. Each family can participate in the full range of activities in which organized crime generally is known to engage. Family organization is rationally designed with an integrated set of positions geared to maximize profits. Like any large corporation, the organization functions regardless of personnel changes, and no individual—not even the leader—is indispensable. If he dies or goes to jail, business goes on.

Each family is headed by one man, the *boss,* whose primary function is maintaining order and maximizing profits. Subject only to the possibility of being overruled by the national advisory group, his authority in all matters relating to his family is absolute.

Beneath each boss is an *underboss,* the vice president of the family. He collects information for the boss, relays messages to him and passes his instructions down to his own underlings. In the absence of the boss, the underboss acts for him.

On the same level as the underboss, but operating in a staff capacity, is the *consigliere,* who is a counselor, or advisor. Often an elder member of the family who has partially retired from a career in crime, he gives advice to family members, including the boss and underboss, and thereby enjoys considerable influence and power.

Below the level of the underboss are the *caporegime,* some of whom serve as buffers between the top members of the family and the lower-echelon personnel. To maintain their insulation from the police, the leaders of the hierarchy avoid direct communication with the workers. All commands, information, complaints, and money flow back and forth through a trusted *caporegima.* However, unlike the underboss, he does not make decisions or assume any of the authority of his boss.

Other *caporegime* serve as chiefs of operating units. The number of men supervised in each unit varies with the size and activities of particular families. Often the caporegima has one or two associates who work closely with him, carrying orders, information, and money to the men who belong to his unit. From a business standpoint, the caporegima is analogous to plant supervisor or sales manager.

The lowest level members of a family are the *soldati*, the soldiers or button men who report to the *caporegime*. A soldier may operate a particular illicit enterprise, *e.g.*, a loan-sharking operation, a dice game, a lottery, a bookmaking operation, a smuggling operation, on a commission basis, or he may "own" the enterprise and pay a portion of its profit to the organization, in return for the right to operate. Partnerships are common between two or more soldiers and between soldiers and men higher up in the hierarchy. Some soldiers and most upper-echelon family members have interests in more than one business.

Beneath the soldiers in the hierarchy are large numbers of employees and

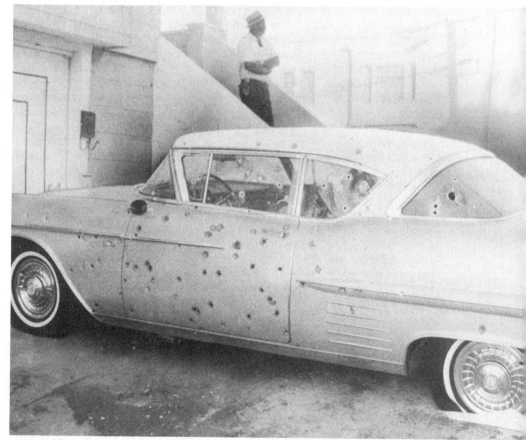

FIGURE 13.3. *A recalcitrant member of an organized crime family was slain in this vehicle by the family enforcer. Courtesy Police Department, New York, N.Y.*

commission agents who are not members of the family and are not necessarily of Italian descent. These are the people who do most of the actual work in the various enterprises. They have no buffers or other insulation from law enforcement. They take bets, drive trucks, sell narcotics, tend the stills, work in the legitimate businesses.

The structure and activities of a typical family are shown in the chart on the following page.

Organized crime groups are believed to contain one or more fixed positions for "enforcers," whose duty it is to maintain organizational integrity by arranging for the maiming and killing of recalcitrant members. And there is a position for a "corrupter," whose function is to establish relationships with those public officials and other influential persons whose assistance is necessary to achieve the organization's goals. By including these positions within its organization, each criminal cartel, or "family," becomes a government as well as a business.

The highest ruling body of the 24 families is the "commission." This body serves as a combination legislature, supreme court, board of directors, and arbitration board. Its principal functions are judicial. Family members look to the commission as the ultimate authority on organizational and jurisdictional disputes. It is composed of the bosses of the nation's most powerful families but has authority over all 24. The composition of the commission varies from nine to twelve men.

Members of this council do not regard each other as equals. Those with long tenure on the commission and those who head large families, or possess unusual wealth, exercise greater authority and receive utmost respect. The balance of power on this nationwide council rests with the leaders of New York's five families. They have always served on the commission and consider New York as at least the unofficial headquarters of the entire organization.

As the bosses realize that they cannot handle the complicated problems of business and finance alone, their authority will be delegated. Decision-making will be decentralized, and individual freedom of action will tend to increase. New problems of discipline and authority may occur if greater emphasis on expertise within the ranks denies unskilled members of the families an opportunity to rise to positions of leadership. Primarily because of fear of infiltration by law enforcement, many of the families have not admitted new members for several years.

The leaders of organized crime families acquire their positions of power and maintain them with the assistance of a code of conduct that is similar to the Sicilian Mafia's code—and just as effective. The code stipulates that underlings should not interfere with the leader's interests and should not seek protection from the police. They should be "standup guys" who go to prison in order that the bosses may amass fortunes. Loyalty, honor, respect, absolute obedience—these are inculcated in family members through ritualistic initiation and customs within the organization, through material rewards and through violence. Though underlings are forbidden to "inform" to the outside world, the family boss learns of deviance within the organization through an elaborate system of internal informants. Despite prescribed mechanisms for peaceful settlement of disputes between family members, the boss himself may order the execution of any family member for any reason.

The code not only preserves leadership authority but also makes it extremely difficult for law enforcement to cultivate informants and maintain them with the organization [10].

PURPOSES OF ORGANIZED CRIME

Organized crime is primarily concerned with achieving power and money. Many in our society feel that these goals are only normal, and perhaps they are. What, then, makes the difference between the goals of law-abiding organizations and the goals of organized crime? It is this: The laws and regulations these criminals adhere to, the procedures they use, and the unethical and immoral standards they observe, all are devised for themselves—their own lawless code of conduct—which they change when expe-

FIGURE 13.4. *Joseph Colombo, Sr., right, reputed underworld chieftain and his son, Joseph, Jr., April 1971, leaving the Criminal Division of the Supreme Court in New York where he was granted a reprieve from going to jail on a perjury conviction. Courtesy Wide World Photos, New York, N.Y. N.Y.*

dient and administer summarily and invisibly. They will commit any act known to man to achieve their purposes.

It is obvious that any citizen purchasing illicit goods and services from the underworld directly contributes to an underground culture of corruption, fraud, murder, and violence. However, criminal organizations dealing only in illicit goods and services are not the greatest threat to our nation. The real danger of organized crime is that profits received from the sale of illicit goods and services are then funneled into licit enterprises.

Organized crime is extensively involved in legitimate business and labor unions. In these areas it employs illegitimate methods like monopolization, terrorism, extortion, tax evasion, etc., to drive out or control lawful ownership and leadership and to exact illegal profits from the public. To carry on its many activities secure from governmental interference, organized crime corrupts public officials, which will be discussed in more detail later in the chapter [11].

Implications

Organized crime affects the lives of millions of Americans every day and unfortunately most Americans are not aware of how they are affected or even when they are affected. For example, the price of a can of tuna or a loaf of bread may go up 1 or 2¢ as the result of an organized crime conspiracy, but the consumer has no real way of knowing why he is paying more. Senator Kefauver stated in regard to this situation, "There can be little doubt that the public suffers from gangster penetration into legitimate business. It suffers because higher prices must be paid for articles and services which it must buy. . . . The public suffers because it may have to put up with shoddy and inferior merchandise in fields where gangsters have been able to obtain a monopoly" [12].

In 1965, Sheldon S. Cohen, the United States Commissioner of Internal Revenue, stated that between 1961 and 1965 more than $219 million in taxes and penalties had been recommended for assessment against subjects of the Federal organized crime drive.

A real impact of organized crime on the society is the vast sums of funds that the general society helps organized crime to accumulate from the innumerable petty transactions taking place every day, 24 hours a day. What are these "petty" transactions? Very simple, they consist of the 50¢ bets, the football pool, the quarters, dimes, nickels and even pennies that are dropped into racketeer-owned vending machines of every type, shape, and description.

Frequently, the activities of organized crime do not directly affect all individuals. Cigarettes that are smuggled and passed on to consumers through vending machines cost no more than tax-paid cigarettes but these smuggled cigarettes enrich the leaders of organized crime. Sometimes this type of activity actually reduces prices for a short period of time as can happen when organized crime, in an attempt to take over industry, starts a price war against legitimate businessmen. Even when organized crime engages in large transactions, individuals may not be directly affected. For example, a large sum of money may be diverted from a union pension fund to finance some type of business venture without any immediate and direct effect upon the individual members of the union or other type of organization. It is believed that such bootlegging type of activities cost, for example, the city and state of New York about $40 million a year in lost tax revenues [13].

It should be clearly understood that it is organized crime's accumulation of money that has such a great and threatening impact on America. A quarter in a vending machine or juke box means nothing and in reality results in nothing, but millions of quarters in thousands of vending machines and juke boxes can provide both a strong motive for murder and the means to commit murder with impunity. Therefore, organized crime exists by virtue of the power it purchases with its money. The millions of dollars it can invest in narcotics or use for lay-off money in union strikes give it power over the lives of thousands of people and over the quality of life in whole neighborhoods. The millions of dollars that it can throw into the legitimate economic system of our country give it power to manipulate the price of shares on the stock market, to raise or lower the price of retail merchandise, to determine whether entire industries are union or nonunion and to make it easier or harder for businessmen to continue in business [14].

To extort money from businessmen; to conduct businesses in such fields as liquor, meat, or drugs without regard to administrative regulations; to avoid payment of income taxes or to secure public works contracts without competitive bidding; the purpose of organized crime is not competition with visible, legal government, but nullification of it. There is no doubt that when organized crime places an official in public office, it nullifies the political process, and when it bribes a police official, it nullifies law enforcement [15].

To see the subtle way in which organized crime has had an impact on American life, we might examine the way of life of a well-known syndicate leader Frank Costello. In New York where he lived, his reputation was common knowledge, yet he moved around New York conspicuously and unashamedly. Perhaps ostracized by some people, but more often accepted, greeted by journalists, mingling socially with New York's society, and lunching with judges and prominent businessmen, he was accorded all the freedoms of a prosperous and successful person. On a society that treats such a man in such a manner, organized crime has had considerable impact, and yet the public has remained apathetic [16].

Few Americans seem to comprehend how organized crime affects their lives. They do not see how gambling with bookmakers or borrowing money from loan sharks forwards the interests of criminal cartels. Businessmen looking for labor harmony or nonunion status through irregular channels rationalize away any suspicions that organized crime is thereby spreading its influence. When an ambitious political candidate accepts substantial cash contributions from unknown sources, he may well suspect, but he frequently dismisses the fact, that organized crime will dictate some of his actions when he assumes office [17].

TYPES OF ILLEGAL ACTIVITY

There are perhaps three major types of activity in which organized criminal groups participate on a regular basis which offer them a maximum amount of profit at minimum risk of law enforcement interference. They offer goods and services that millions of Americans desire even though they are declared illegal by their legislatures. The three most prominent that will be mentioned here are *gambling, loan-sharking,* and *narcotics.*

Of the three, *gambling* is the greatest source of revenue for organized crime. It ranges from lotteries such as "numbers," or "bolita," to off-track horse betting, bets on sports events, large dice games, and illegal casinos. In areas where gambling operators are independent of a large organization and yet where organized criminal groups exist, the independent operation is likely to receive a visit from an organization representative who will convince the independent operator through fear or promise of greater profit to share his revenue with the organization. It is a well-established fact that most large city gambling is established or controlled by organized crime members through very elaborate hierarchies.

Number gambling follows the general pattern of organization of all large scale vice and crime. This consists of four basic elements: (1) An elaborate hierarchical organization of personnel, (2) a spacial organization in which a wide territory is controlled from a central metropolitan area, (3) the "fix," in which public funds, principally police and politicians, are drawn into and made a part of the organization, and (4) legal aid in which members of the legal profession become the advisors and consultants of the organization [18].

In addition, the profits that accrue to organization leaders move through channels that are so complex that even persons who work in the betting operation do not know or cannot prove the identity of the leader. Also, there has been an increased use of the telephone for lottery purposes and sports betting. The telephone has facilitated the bookmaker who may not know the identity of a second echelon person to whom he calls in the day's bets. Organization, as we understand the term, not only creates greater efficiency and enlarges the criminal market, but it also provides a systematized method of corrupting the law enforcement process by centralizing procedures for the payment of graft. Recently in one eastern area of the United States, a number of police agencies consolidated their entire operation into one county police department. The syndicate was particularly happy with the consolidation as they felt that protection was easier to arrange through one agency than through many. Additionally, the syndicate benefited from this consolidation to an even greater degree as the independents who were operating in the area were essentially stampeded into the arms of the syndicate for protection and the syndicate could pick and choose those operators whom they wished to admit to their operation.

It is impossible to accurately state what organized crime's gross revenue from gambling is today in the United States. It is estimated, however, that the annual intake varies from $7 to $50 billion annually. Legal betting at race tracks throughout the nation reaches a gross annual figure of almost $5 billion and most enforcement officials believe that illegal wagering on horse races, lotteries, and sporting events totals at least $20 billion each year. An analysis of the organized criminal betting operations clearly indicates that the profit is as high as one-third of gross revenue—or $6–7 billion each year. These figures are most conservative, yet it may be easily seen that there is substantial capital obtained from gambling and placed into the hands of organized crime leaders each year. Senator Kefauver stated, ''Gambling profits are the principal support of big time racketeering and gangsterism. These profits provide financial resources whereby ordinary criminals are converted into big time racketeers, political bosses, pseudo businessmen, and alleged philanthropists'' [19].

Loan-sharking, the lending of money at higher rates than the legally prescribed limit, is the second largest source of revenue for organized crime, and it is the gambling profits which provide the initial capital for loan-shark operation. Once an individual enters into a loan-shark relationship, it is very difficult for that individual to ever fully recover. Gamblers borrow money to pay gambling losses, narcotic users borrow to purchase heroin, sometimes small businessmen borrow when legitimate credit channels are closed to them; frequently, the same men who take bets from employees in a large industrial area also serve at times as loan-sharks. This money thus enables the employees to pay off their gambling debts or to meet household needs. The principal reason for nonrecovery is due to the fantastic interest rates that are charged to the consumer by the loan shark. Rates will vary from 1 to 150% per week. The amount of the percentage is determined by the relationship between the lender and the borrower, the intended use of the money, the size of the loan, and the repayment potential. Oftentimes, the loan-sharks will require that payments be made or come due by a certain hour on a certain day and even a few minutes default may result in a rise in interest rates. The lender is more interested in perpetuating the interest payment than collecting the principal and frequently force or threats of force of the most brutal kind are used to effect interest collection, to eliminate protest when interest rates are raised, and to prevent the beleaguered borrower from reporting the activity to law enforcement officials [20]. It is impossible to even estimate the gross revenue from organized loan-sharking, but profit margins are higher than for gambling operations, and many law enforcement officials and those well-informed on organized crime classify the business in the multi-billion-dollar range each year [21].

Narcotics, its sale and distribution, is organized like a legitimate importing wholesale-retail business. Within the last decade the United States has become a drug-oriented society. Heroin, once known only to a small number of people within the society, has become widely known in the United States and has made the United States the number one nation in the world for heroin addiction. The distribution of heroin, for example, requires movement of this drug through four or five levels between the importer and the street peddler. It is generally felt that the severe federal penalties for drug law violations have caused many in organized narcotic and dangerous drug activity to restrict their activities to importing and wholesale distribution. Organized crime does not become involved in the small-scale wholesale transactions or the retail level. Transactions with addicts are handled by independent narcotic pushers using the drugs that are imported by organized crime. The extremely large amounts of cash and the international connections that are necessary for large long-term heroin and drug relationships can be provided only by organized crime with careful syndicate planned operations. Conservative estimates of the number of addicts in the United States and the average daily expenditure for heroin indicate that the gross heroin trade is approximately $450 million annually, of which $50 million are probably profits to the importer and distributor. It should be realized that by the time these drugs reach the addict on the street, the cost has gone into the billions. Most of the drug profits go into the organized criminal activity in those cities in which almost all of the heroin consumption occurs [22].

Other goods and services are certainly a part of organized criminal activity in the United States. Prostitution and bootlegging were for a number of years a very major part of syndicate operations. However, today, they are playing a smaller role and this type of activity is declining in organized crime operations. Gambling has supplanted prostitution and bootlegging as their chief source of revenue. Before World War I, the major profits of organized crime were obtained from prostitution, but the passage of the Mann White Slave Act, the changing sexual mores, and public opinion have combined to make commercialized prostitution a less profitable and more hazardous enterprise. In addition, prostitution is difficult to organize and discipline is hard to maintain. Several important convictions of organized crime figures in prostitution cases in the 1930's and 1940's caused the criminal executives of the hierarchy of syndicate operation to be wary of further participation in this type of activity.

The production of illegal alcohol is also a risky business in this modern day of technology. The destruction of stills and supplies by law enforcement officers during the initial stages of production means the loss of heavy initial investment capital [23].

CORRUPTION OF PUBLIC OFFICIALS

In the prohibition era, corruption was evident everywhere and openly blatant [24]. Today's corruption is less visible and more subtle. Thus it is difficult to detect and assess the corruption that is taking place in the 1970's. Organized crime prospers wherever it has corrupted public officials, and as its scope and variety of activities have expanded, it has increased its need to involve public officials at every level of government. As government regulation expands into more and more areas of private and public business enterprise, the power to corrupt likewise affords the corruptor more control over matters affecting the everyday life of each citizen.

Throughout the years in a multitude of places, organized crime has corrupted those whose legitimate exercise of duties would block organized crime activity and whose illegal exercise of duties, responsibility, and authority, aids and assists it. It has been discovered in recent years that some local governments have been greatly influenced and dominated by criminal groups.

The neutralization of local law enforcement is central to organized crime operations and every effort is being made to corrupt its leadership at every level. The corrupt political executive who ties the hands of police officials who want to act against organized crime in a positive way is even more effective for organized crime's purposes. The American Bar Association has stated that the largest single factor in the breakdown of law enforcement agencies in dealing with organized crime is the corruption and connivance of many public officials. To secure necessary political power, much use of bribes or political contributions is used to corrupt the nonoffice holding, but politically influential, citizen to whom the public official may be responsive. It is difficult to accurately determine how extensive corruption is in officialdom. More vigilance and better ways to communicate information about corruption to law enforcement investigative personnel is needed.

CONTROL OF ORGANIZED CRIME

As previously discussed, organized crime *per se* is not illegal.

Our system of justice deliberately sacrifices much in efficiency and even in effectiveness in order to preserve local autonomy and to protect the individual. Sometimes it may seem to sacrifice too much. For example, the American system was not designed with Cosa Nostra-type criminal organizations in mind, and it has been notably unsuccessful to date in preventing such organizations from preying on society [25].

The bosses, lieutenants, and higher echelon of these organizations have ensured their freedom from arrest by making sure that they commit no crimes except conspiracy, which of course is extremely difficult to prove. The felonies committed by the Cosa Nostra are carried out by the lower echelon in the organization and, by necessity, these are the only people the police can arrest for these crimes. This leaves the big bosses open only to conspiracy and possible income tax evasion. And, interestingly enough, the latter category is the principal one for which Cosa Nostra bosses have been sent to prison within the past 30 years.

The efforts of government to control the cancer of organized crime has included every approach, from total apathy to swift and sure enforcement of the law. At the federal level of government, following the Kefauver hearings in 1951, the U.S. Department of Justice commenced a driving and stinging crusade against the leading figures identified in the hearings as the racket bosses. As a result of this crusade, federal prosecutors throughout the nation initiated investigations and prosecutions which resulted in the convictions of a number of high-level organized crime participants on federal law violations. Of those racketeers whom federal prosecutors were unable to convict, many were successfully deported under the authority of the Immigration statutes of the Department of Justice. In 1954, the United States Department of Justice formed an organized crime and racketeering division which would encourage the continuation of the investigative and prosecutive efforts against organized

FIGURE 13.5. *Mobster Joseph Valachi revealing the workings of orga-nized crime. Notice the family charts in background to show the evolution of gang control in New York since 1930. In testimony before the Senate Investigation Subcommittee, Valachi discussed how chart outlines the gangland wars between the various families and lists the succession in command as the top bosses are eliminated. Courtesy Wide World Photos, New York, N.Y.*

crime. In 1958, after the Appalachia meeting, the Attorney General created a special group on organized crime to gather intelligence information and hold grand jury proceedings on the conferees at the Appalachia meeting. As a result, a number were indicted but after trial and reversal of the convictions of twenty of these conferees for conspiring to obstruct justice, this special division was dissolved and its functions were assumed by the organized crime division of the Department of Justice [26].

In 1960, the FBI began to supply information to the organized crime division. The division was extremely understaffed and unfortunately could not adequately fulfill its functions, which included coordinating all federal law enforcement activity against organized crime. A year later, the division expanded its program to unprecedented proportions and in the next 3 years the intelligence reports that were received brought about an increase in the number of attorneys and thus the number of convictions increased. The cooperative effort that was established by twenty-six separate federal agencies against organized crime resulted in the convictions of over 60% of those brought to trial between 1961 and July, 1965. Most of the convictions resulted from tax investigations conducted by the Internal Revenue Service, and several high-level members of organized crime families in New York City were convicted through the efforts of the federal government agency controlling narcotic drugs. The FBI was responsible for conviction of numerous organized crime figures in New York City, Chicago, and elsewhere. As a result of the efforts of J. Edgar Hoover, statutes were enacted by the Congress which gave the FBI jurisdiction in interstate gambling cases. This authority aided the FBI in disrupting, through investigation and prosecution, major interstate gambling operations [27].

In 1965, a number of factors slowed the momentum of the drive against organized crime. It was felt by some that the government was taking unfair advantage of its powers in attacking organized crime through tax enforcement. Little by little, the activities of the organized crime and racketeering division dwindled.

As a direct result of the Omnibus Crime Bill of 1968, sometimes known as the Safe Streets Act, a new effort on the part of the federal government and allied agencies has been made in a most severe attack upon syndicate operations throughout the United States. These attacks have resulted in grand jury investigations and indictments which are actualizing convictions. There has also been a greater willingness upon some organized crime figures to provide information to federal agencies regarding the activities that various individuals are involved in. This combination of activity between organized crime and the United States Department of Justice is having definite impact upon the extent of organized crime operations in the United States.

In spite of all of the efforts that the United States government utilizes to control organized crime, the American public sets the limits in which the activities that are prominently engaged in by organized crime will be tolerated. The efforts by the various states and local units of government in their fight against syndicated operations of an illegal nature have, for the most part, met with negative results. This has been due largely to the apathetic attitude of the public as well as of state and local government toward the operations of organized crime. It has been the attitude and feeling of many in the society that the federal government has the responsibility for maintaining effective and efficient control of this cancerous problem. Many cities throughout the country wherein organized crime prominently exists do not even acknowledge through their governmental agencies or through their law enforcement agencies that organized crime is actively operating in their areas. At present, well-developed organized crime investigation units and effective intelligence programs exist within very few police prosecutive agencies.

There is, however, some evidence that local law enforcement and state prosecutors are acknowledging the threat of organized crime and are taking positive steps in their jurisdictions to set up effective and combative units against organized crime operations. Although not a great deal of organized crime activity takes place in the state of California, it was in this state in 1956 that the law enforcement intelligence unit was established. This was one of the first steps by a state toward the development of a network for the exchange of data concerning people active in organized crime. This agency has since expanded to numerous members throughout the United States. Its sole function is to gather and maintain information on organized crime activity and make it available to the various law enforcement intelligence units throughout the United States. The effectiveness of this program and local efforts is difficult to assess. Only New York and California have continuing state programs that have produced a series of convictions against major figures in organized crime. Additionally, coordinated police activity has substantially aided the process. On the local level, Chicago and New York City, where the organized crime problem is the most severe, appear to be the only cities in which large, firmly established police intelligence units continue to develop major cases against members of the criminal cartel [28].

Through the years, a most effective vehicle for providing and gathering information on organized crime has been the crime investigative commissions which have existed in a number of states. When these commissions have been established without having to rely on continuing government financial support and the resultant potential political pressures, the private crime commission has frequently rendered major service in exposing syndicate operations and corruption as well as arousing public interest. For example, the Chicago Crime Commission and the Metropolitan Crime Commission of New Orleans have in the past played major roles in informing the citizens within their areas of the menace of organized crime. These commissions have fulfilled substantial educational, investigative, and legislative functions as well. As the years have passed, other states wherein organized crime has been in operation have created such commissions which have been invaluable in the administration of justice in the control of illegal syndicated operations [29].

It is unfortunate, but there are in fact limitations on the efforts to control organized crime. Many of these limitations, which were extensive in the past, are beginning to subside, and law enforcement and the criminal justice system of the United States are beginning to have a most positive effect. One limitation is the difficulty in obtaining proof. And certainly proof must be beyond a reasonable doubt for conviction. Additionally, there have been a lack of resources and a lack of coordination. However, these weak points are diminishing as more funds are being made available to provide local and state law enforcement with the effective tools needed to carry out their functions in the control of organized crime. Coordination has greatly improved as a result of a greater understanding of the roles that each agency will play. Strategic intelligence, once very difficult to obtain, is now being used more extensively. It is believed by many that the failure to use available sanctions against organized crime, such as penalties and fines, are continuing to be a severe limitation on the control of this activity. Also, a lack of public and political commitment has been a severe limitation on its control as well. Without sustained public pressure, political office seekers and office holders have little incentive to address themselves to combating this problem, although they may give lip service to it. A strong drive against organized crime usually uncovers political corruption and this means that a crusading mayor or district attorney makes many political enemies. The vicious cycle perpetuates itself. Politicians will not act unless the public so demands, but much of the urban public wants the services provided by organized crime and does not wish to disrupt the system that provides those services. And much of the public does not see or understand the effects of organized crime in our society.

The national strategy for fighting this problem has in the past been primitive compared to the syndicate's method of operation. Because of the Safe Streets

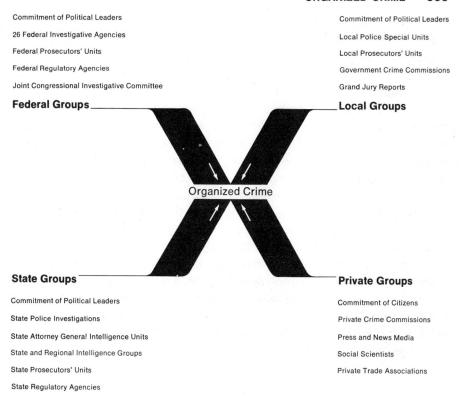

Commitment of Political Leaders

26 Federal Investigative Agencies

Federal Prosecutors' Units

Federal Regulatory Agencies

Joint Congressional Investigative Committee

Federal Groups

Commitment of Political Leaders

Local Police Special Units

Local Prosecutors' Units

Government Crime Commissions

Grand Jury Reports

Local Groups

Organized Crime

State Groups

Commitment of Political Leaders

State Police Investigations

State Attorney General Intelligence Units

State and Regional Intelligence Groups

State Prosecutors' Units

State Regulatory Agencies

Government Crime Commissions

Private Groups

Commitment of Citizens

Private Crime Commissions

Press and News Media

Social Scientists

Private Trade Associations

FIGURE 13.6. *Coordinated effort against organized crime. Source:* Task Force Report: Organized Crime, *President's Commission on Law Enforcement and Administration of Justice, 1967.*

Act of 1968, law enforcement has developed and is using methods today that are at least as efficient and sometimes superior to those of organized crime. The public and law enforcement must continue to make a full-scale commitment to destroy the power of organized crime. The President's Commission on Crime and the Administration of Justice, in its *Task Force Report on Organized Crime,* has suggested a national strategy in a strong coordinated effort against the organized crime groups and the activities which they participate in. This strategy would be a four point invasion composed of (*a*) Federal groups, (*b*) State groups, (*c*) local groups, and (*d*) private groups. Figure 13.6 indicates the principal functions of each of the four major groups of the society which has a responsibility to contribute in the effort to control organized crime operations. Since 1968 at the federal level, regulatory agencies, congressional investigative committees, and federal prosecutor units in the U.S. Attorney's offices across the country have been waging a strong and effective attack on organized crime. These attacks have been aided by state and local groups through state investigations, the development of criminal intelligence units, special regulatory agencies being established and crime commissions gathering information and evidence so as to greatly enhance the possibility of prosecution and conviction of organized crime leaders. Private groups in the society have been the slowest to involve themselves and make effective contributions. This has been primarily due to a lack of resources available to private groups as they are outlined in the chart. This integrated approach of combined action by the American people and its governments and its businesses is the best effective tool available to fight organized crime, but it succeeds only insofar as the nation permits it to succeed. Because the problem is so great, the various branches of government cannot act with success individually. It is a necessary component part of the national strategy that each help the other. It is the Commission's opinion that firm and positive action must replace words and that knowledge must replace fascination. Only when the American people and their governments develop the will can law enforcement and other agencies find the way to stop organized crime.

SUMMARY

The highly sophisticated structure of organized crime today is far different from what it was many years ago and its power for evil is infinitely greater. In the beginning, organized crime used to be an individual gang, consisting of a number of hoodlums whose activities were primarily predatory in character. Today, their activities are highly sophisticated, these activities having emerged during the prohibition era. The huge profits that were earned in the period of prohibition, together with the development of the twentieth-century transportation and communication facilities, has made possible larger and more powerful groups covering much greater territory.

In the last 30 years, organized crime has taken on many new characteristics. The most dangerous gangs today are not specialists in one type of crime, but are engaged in many and varied forms of criminality. Each family group today is multipurpose in character engaging in any racket wherever there is money to be made. Moreover, they do not rely on such crimes as robbery, burglary, or larceny as a primary source of income, but instead draw most of their revenue from the various forms of gambling, the sale and distribution of narcotics, prostitution, the various forms of business and labor racketeering, black market practices, and bootlegging into dry areas. The success that organized crime has enjoyed has developed as a result of gaining a monopoly of illicit enterprises or illegal operations which has provided them with huge financial profits. The success has also been aided by incorporating into their operation some of the same organizational methods that are found in modern business. As organized crime expanded its activities into many different fields and into many different geographic areas—wherever profits could be made —the men who have controlled such operations have become rich and powerful. The needy have been encouraged to gamble to solve financial problems, those who have been troubled with physical and psychological problems have been lured to destroy themselves with drugs, and the hard-working businessman has been extorted and those who have opposed them have been maimed or murdered and those sworn to destroy them have been bribed. Organized crime is the most sinister kind of crime in the United States, for it preys not upon a few but upon thousands. In a very real sense, it is dedicated to subverting not only American institutions, but the very decency and integrity that are the most cherished attributes of a free society. The leaders of organized crime pursue their conspiracy and preach their sermon that the government is for sale, lawlessness is the road to wealth, honesty is a pitfall, and morality a trap for suckers. The extraordinary thing is that the people have tolerated it for so long.

ANNOTATED REFERENCES

Challenge of Crime in a Free Society, President's Commission on Law Enforcement and Administration of Justice, U.S. Government Printing Office, Washington, D.C., 1967. A presentation of findings regarding the nature, impact, and effect of crime upon America.

Cressey, D. R., *Theft of the Nation,* Harper & Row, New York, 1969. A complete discussion and presentation of organized crime in America by one of the nation's leading authorities on the subject.

Cressey, D. R., *Criminal Organization,* Harper & Row, New York, 1972. A good discussion of the criminal organization.

Kefauver Committee, Special Committee to Investigate Crime in Interstate Commerce, *Third Interim Report, U.S. Senate Report No. 307,* 82nd Congress, 1st Session, 1951. A detailed presentation of the testimony offered to this committee regarding organized crime.

Salerno, R. F., and J. S. Tompkins, *The Crime Confederation: Cosa Nostra and*

Allied Operations in Organized Crime, Doubleday, Garden City, N.Y., 1969. This book is excellent in every respect as the story of organized crime is unfolded by the nation's leading experts in this field.

Task Force Report: Organized Crime, President's Commission on Law Enforcement and Administration of Justice, U.S. Government Printing Office, Washington, D.C., 1967. A good presentation in brief on the subject of organized crime. Much of the foregoing chapter on the subject was adapted from this public document.

NOTES

1. Much of the material and information in this chapter was obtained from the United States Department of Justice and the *Task Force Report: Organized Crime,* pp. 1–14.

2. D. R. Cressey, *Criminal Organization,* p. 81.

3. *Task Force Report: Organized Crime,* The President's Commission on Law Enforcement and Administration of Justice, pp. 10–11.

4. *Ibid.,* p. 6.

5. J. E. Hoover, 89th Congress, 2nd Session, 1966.

6. *Task Force Report, op. cit.,* p. 7.

7. *Ibid.,* p. 7.

8. *New York Times,* January 21, 1967, p. 65, col. 3.

9. *Task Force Report, op. cit.,* pp. 7–8.

10. *Task Force Report, op. cit.,* pp. 9–10.

11. *Ibid.,* p. 1.

12. Kefauver Committee, *Third Interim Report,* pp. 170–171.

13. *New York Times,* February 2, 1967, page 21.

14. *Task Force Report, op. cit.,* p. 2.

15. *Ibid.*

16. *Ibid.*

17. *Ibid.*

18. Carlson, *Numbers Gambling, a Study of a Culture Complex,* 68, Unpublished Ph.D. Dissertation, University of Michigan Department of Sociology, 1940.

19. Kefauver Committee, *op. cit.,* p. 2.

20. *Task Force Report, op. cit.,* p. 3.

21. *Ibid.,* p. 3.

22. *Ibid.,* pp. 3–4.

23. *Ibid.,* p. 4.

24. *Ibid.,* p. 6.

25. U.S. President's Commission on Law Enforcement and Administration of Justice, *The Challenge of Crime in a Free Society,* Washington, U.S. Government Printing Office, 1967, p. 7.

26. *Ibid.,* p. 11.

27. *Ibid.,* p. 11.

28. *Ibid.,* p. 13.

29. *Ibid.,* p. 14.

CHAPTER FOURTEEN

"Victimless" Crime?

As mounting permissiveness has crept into twentieth-century society, much attention has been focused upon the totally mythical concept referred to as "victimless crime." Those to whom the phrase is of philosophical importance are the same persons and groups in the society that cry for the release of society from the bonds of "ancient and medieval morality." As a result, many insist that laws prohibiting "victimless" crime should be repealed, not enforced, and they decry the very existence of such laws. The sum total of the advocates' total opposition and argument is: "How can one have a crime without a complaining victim?"

The concept of "victimless" crime is a misnomer. It is a sham. Victims do exist. Thousands. Who can look at the picture on the opposite page and say there is no victim? Unless family, friends, or the public at large complain, only the participants know the existence of the crime. There is a prime victim and it is society. The family, friends, relations, etc., are all "innocent bystanders" yet they become the aggrieved victims.

Since the turn of the century, we have gotten into a habit of coining catch phrases which have, perhaps innocently enough, eventually had quite an impact on the society. But many phrases are coined and deliberately designed to deceive. Such is the case with the term "victimless crime" and those supporting the concept wish to give respectability to the public offenses of gambling, drugs (including alcohol), prostitution, sex perversion, and pornography.

The laws which society lives by are the result of its needs. They are created by the law-makers to whom society has given full authority and power. Although the victims of "victimless" crime may not cry out, they are still victims because they are aggrieved in the most insidious manner. Many believe that "victimless" crime includes every conceivable form of criminality, most notably the organized variety. Any relaxation of enforcement and control of the "victimless" crimes will stimulate, further develop, and expand, as well as encourage, the growth of organized crime in any society.

Law enforcement in the United States has been caught in the middle of the problem and has suffered much undue pressure, criticism, and hardship over the issue of "victimless" crime. Many vocal, pressing, and influential persons and groups in society want law enforcement to relax or totally surrender enforcement of the prohibitory laws which they, as "responsible citizens" have had a part in helping to create and legislate. In addition, they view such relaxation and nonenforcement as the total answer to society's social ills. They are mistaken. This kind of action is not a solution. The solution is the strict enforcement of every law, thus providing every person and community a safe and stable area in which to live and enjoy life and be free from fear.

Efficient, effective, and impartial law enforcement will ensure this climate. If law enforcement were to abandon its responsibility, it would, in a sense, be turning over the society it is dedicated to protect and serve to the forces of corruption and utter chaos. If crime in the community, the nation, and the world is to be controlled, then the laws prohibiting antisocial and "victimless" crimes must be strictly enforced with due diligence.

HISTORY

The history of "victimless" crime extends back to the time of the ancient Middle East, the Roman Empire, and beyond, but it has only been since World War II that individuals and groups in the society have expressed deep concern over those categories of crime they consider should be reclassified and redefined. Prostitution, for example, they say, has been labeled the oldest profession known to man; the use and abuse of drugs and narcotics has plagued man for centuries and has been traced back to at least the fifth century, B.C.; men have gambled with and about every conceivable thing including the robe of Jesus Christ after he was crucified on the cross; and every society has experienced homosexual problems, with some cultures even today in other parts of the world still developing and grooming a homosexual in each family because it is a custom of that society or culture. Additionally, there has never been a time when alcohol was not a problem in the world. Today, alcohol ranks as the number one medical and social problem in the world with drug abuse classed a close second in order of rank and concerned recognition.

Since the landing of the Pilgrims in 1620, the United States has experienced varying degrees of magnitude in the area of "victimless" crime. Early Americans suffered as the society suffers today from the social cancers that plague man in his pursuit of pleasure, satisfaction, and escape.

SCOPE OF VICTIMLESS CRIME

"Victimless" crime is the mainstay of organized crime and provides for it a pathway to continuously engage in the full spectrum of criminal activity. The victimization and human suffering that are taking place today throughout the world is making a mockery of the libertarian cry for the elimination of all controls on prostitution, gambling, narcotics, alcohol, homosexuality, etc.

Gambling is the number one business of organized crime. Without it and the control they maintain over it, they would flounder like a fish out of water. With in excess of $20 billion in gambling receipts and $10 billion in loan-sharking receipts each year, organized crime is powerful enough to overshadow the largest corporations in the United States.

The "victimless" crime advocates propose that the most effective way to remove gambling from the control of organized crime is to legalize the forms of gambling that are now illegal. Observations made in the United States as well as other countries clearly establish that the legalizing of gambling does not necessarily hurt organized crime. Additionally, schemes such as state lotteries and off-track betting cannot even begin to compete with illegal gambling for a number of reasons. Also, licensed casino gambling is often controlled by organized crime. There is concrete evidence that organized crime is increasing its illegal gambling income through the medium of legalized gambling.

The number of public offenses taking place involving sex and perversion throughout the nation is shocking. Millions of dollars are reaped each year from each source, for the benefit of organized criminal operations and syndicates. It is reasonable that with prostitution revenues producing in excess of $250 million each year, organized crime views it as an important and worthwhile business operation and maintains national, regional and local control over it. Added to the prostitution problems are the estimated 3–15 million homosexuals in the nation, many of whom are active in the pornography industry, and it is not difficult to see the many reasons for the high number of public offenses taking place and for the decline in morality throughout the nation.

Pornography offenses number in the thousands. The gross receipts derived annually by the pornography industry which likewise is heavily controlled by organized criminal syndicate operations is well over $200 million [1]. The large-scale production, distribution, and sale of various forms of hardcore obscenity on a nationwide basis is staggering to the imagination. The distribution of such materials throughout the United States is controlled by men with Mafia connections.

The scope of the "victimless" crime problem as it relates to *narcotics* and drugs is alarming when it is remembered that this "victimless" crime ranks second in stature by the American Medical Association's appraisal of "victimless" crime. The total average number of direct drug-related deaths occurring each year in the United States is 13,000. New York City and Los Angeles average 1000 drug-induced deaths each year; 90% of all such deaths involves heroin, and 80% occur as a direct result of hard-drug overdoses such as heroin. This high price in human life is far greater than any dollar amount that could be attached to this "victimless" crime. As a result of the drug problem, more than $1.5 billion worth of property is stolen by addicts every year to pay for the necessary drugs to satisfy their addiction.

Alcoholism is one of the greatest social problems in the United States and a most serious medical problem. Yet many crimes committed while under the influence of alcohol are called victimless crimes. Who then is the victim of the social drinker or alcoholic when he or she drives an automobile into a crowded street intersection filled with people, or when he steps from the curb into the path of an oncoming car or attempts to fly an airplane and crashes on take-off with none of the passengers surviving? Alcohol does claim its victims, in one way or another. Research studies into the alcohol problem reveal that 70% of all Americans over 21 years of age use alcohol in one form or another and further that there are a little over 6 million alcoholics in the United States.

Alcoholism is involved in 50% of all fatal auto accidents and each year there are approximately 55,000 lives lost on our highways and over 2 million serious injuries. The estimated annual cost of traffic accidents is $10 billion, and the estimated 1.7 million alcoholics in industry represent a loss of $2.5 billion per year. In addition, alcoholism presents a serious problem to law enforcement. They arrest in excess of 2 million people each year for public offenses directly involving alcohol. The great volume of these arrests places an extremely heavy load on the operation of the American criminal justice system and the taxpayer. The $18 billion alcohol industry in America was once looked upon in disfavor and enjoyed no respect. Today, many average Americans look to this industry to satisfy needs and desires for pleasure, happiness, and escape as well as a supplier of a food supplement. It is interesting to note that expenditures for alcoholic beverages by the American people each year nearly equal the total that is spent on private education and research, and on religious and welfare activities.

Thus, it is easily seen that the scope of the total "victimless" crime problem in the United States is monumental not only in total numbers of persons involved but also in the cost of human life and injury, the cost to the American taxpayer in supporting the criminal justice system and the public monies that are spent on the problem which could, in the name of humanity, be better and more effectively expended for mankind.

TYPES OF VICTIMLESS CRIME

Gambling

It is an undisputed fact that illegal gambling provides the major source of revenue for organized crime in the United States. There are many forms of gambling which include horse and sports bookmaking, lotteries, numbers schemes, illegal casinos, and commercial dice and card games. Individual criminal organizations in cities throughout the nation may exhibit varying degrees of independence from any centralized control of their gambling operations by national bosses, but the foundation of almost all of these criminal enterprises on illegal gambling serves to provide organized crime with a certain degree of cohesiveness.

All gambling operations have an absolute need for free services in order to remain viable: (a) The "line," giving odds and point spreads; (b) fast results from the race track or sporting event, and (c) the ability to "lay off" excessively heavy wagers. These services are under the complete control

FIGURE 14.1. (top) *Roulette game in operation in a large gambling casino. Courtesy United Press International, New York, N.Y.* (bottom) *Large crowds line up in front of off-track betting corporation windows at Grand Central Station, New York City. Courtesy Wide World Photos, New York, N.Y.*

of the major criminal organizations, which give them control over client organizations and individuals [2]. The gambling-based confederation of criminals is held together by the glue of force. As Ploscowe noted in his paper titled "New Approaches to the Control of Organized Crime" in 1963: "The muscle and murder continue to be the ultimate weapons on which organized crime rest." The gambling industry in the United States is widespread and produces in excess of $20 billion in illegal wagers each year. Of this sum, approximately $7 billion accrues to organized crime as profit. Rufus King has given the following breakdown of gross profits by the type of gambling: Card games, $1 billion; dice games and roulette, $3.6 billion; coin-operated devices, $500 million (net); lotteries, policy and numbers, $5 billion; and bookmaking and pool selling, $10 billion [3].

The majority of the dollars derived from gambling flows into the coffers of organized crime to be used to finance other illegal activities such as their participation in the illicit narcotic traffic, prostitution, bootleg liquor and various forms of racketeering enterprises such as extortion, shakedowns, and usury. It is an established fact that gambling profits are also used in financing legitimate businesses both as a front for criminal rackets and as a genuine investment for the illegally obtained funds which are of course not reported on tax returns. The accumulated wealth is also used to corrupt law enforcement and other public officials in order to secure their cooperation [4].

Grand juries throughout the nation, after making investigations into gambling crimes, have stated that such crimes are behind some of the most obnoxious criminal enterprises known to man and that many killings which take place every day throughout the nation are involved in some way with gambling ventures. A Brooklyn, New York, grand jury probing organized gambling recently stated its belief that some 300 unsolved gangland murders which had occurred in New York City during the past decade were in some way related to organized crime.

Directly connected with the gambling industry is a vicious criminal activity known as loan-sharking. It is conservatively estimated that the annual gross receipts from loan-sharking to organized crime is about $10 billion, most of which is net profit. This immense income is produced from a working capital of about $5 billion. Such a profit rate is not surprising in view of the fact that the criminals involved charge their victims from 250 to 1000% annual interest. The legitimate question of where loan-sharks could possibly find customers for loans with such exorbitant interest rates is frequently asked. "Inveterate gamblers who patronize establishments frequently become hopelessly in debt and desperately in need of money. Loan-sharks affiliated with gambling house proprietors loan money at exorbitant rates of interest" [5].

The United States Chamber of Commerce states that a gambler does not really need to go to a gambling establishment to gamble or place a bet as there is a bookmaker in three out of every four companies employing fifty or more people [6]. In this connection, the President's Commission on Law Enforcement and Administration of Justice states, "The same men who take bets from employees in mass employment industries also serve at times as loan-sharks, whose money enables the employees to pay off their gambling debts—payments may be due by a certain hour on a certain day, and even a few minutes' default may result in a rise of interest rate. The lender is more interested in perpetuating interest payments than collecting the principal; and force or threats of force of the most brutal kind are used to effect interest collection, eliminate protest when the interest rates are raised, and prevent the beleaguered borrower from reporting the activity to enforcement officials" [7]. It is not uncommon for a loan-shark victim subjected to this type of pressure to embezzle or steal from the company employing him in order to meet the organized criminal's demands. The final irony of this "victimless crime" is that gambling profits provide the initial capital for loan-shark operations.

There are many evils connected with illegal gambling. One of the most severe is that of corruption—corruption on a massive scale—corruption that is essential to the very existence of successful and lucrative gambling operations. The organized criminal, in particular, possesses no scruples. He has one thought in mind and that is to protect his source of ill-gotten income. With some $6–7 billion in financial resources, it is therefore not surprising that the gambling czars who make murder the way of life do not hesitate to engage in wholesale bribery and coercion of government and law enforcement. Such corruption has in recent years captured whole cities and turned the functioning of politicians and police alike to the criminal purposes of underworld bosses [8]. In this climate the only people who are not victims are the controlling criminals. There are many in society who strongly support the legalization of gambling and extol it as a great revenue-producing activity whether operated governmentally or privately. This is largely a myth. Revenues which are so produced are generally very small [9]. Revenues that are obtained by this method are considered the most regressive form of taxation imaginable.

Gambling contributes nothing to the welfare of society. It produces no goods, no services. It does, however, produce corruption, violence, murder, and a multitude of other criminal activities on a grand scale. Gambling, whether it be by bookmaking or through lotteries, illegal dice games or card games, produces victims in our society by the thousands.

Narcotics and Dangerous Drugs

A resolution passed by the American Civil Liberties Union, at its bi-annual conference in June of 1970, shocked every right thinking man. It was resolved that an individual has a right to use his own body as he wishes and that this right includes the use and possession of narcotics. They further declared that the use and possession of drugs is not a crime *per se* and therefore criminal penalties should not be invoked against the user or possessor and further that compulsory treatment or incarceration of drug users is a violation of civil liberties. Immediately, responsible citizens in every realm of society labeled this action absurd and irresponsible. One can only thus assume that it is the philosophy and belief of the ACLU that dangerous drug and narcotic possession and abuse is a "victimless" crime and that such activity concerns only the drug user. The cost of drug abuse to the nation and to society as a whole is overwhelming not only in dollars but in the needless loss of life. It is estimated that approximately 14,000 citizens in our society relinquish their life to the self-induced use of drugs annually.

The opiate group, including *heroin* and *morphine,* is not only extremely physiologically and psychologically addictive but use of opiates frequently results in debilitation, disease, and death. Death usually overtakes the opiate addict as a result of overdose but it can also come as a result of withdrawal.

Barbiturates are as effective killers as the opiates. They have a high addiction potential, are very frequently used for suicide, often lead to accidental death by overdose, and are especially dangerous in combination with alcohol. There is ample evidence that barbiturates are a significant causal element in many traffic fatalities. Additionally, many barbiturate addicts die during withdrawal. Addicts who have undergone barbiturate withdrawal state that the experience is worse than heroin withdrawal.

The abuse of *amphetamines* can result in dependency and quite frequently psychosis. Often a syndrome resembling paranoid schizophrenia may occur with the use of any of the amphetamines. It is most common in addicts or patients taking large doses of the drug, but it may occur after single doses of one or two tablets. There is strong evidence that prolonged amphetamine abuse may also lead to irreversible brain damage and possibly to a fatal liver and kidney disease known as "necrotizing angitis." Additionally, it is not surprising that amphetamine abuse is a predisposing factor toward involvement in traffic accidents.

Cocaine use is becoming increasingly popular. It is medically considered very injurious both physiologically and psychologically, leading to a dependence or a habituation. The manifestations of cocaine use are euphoria, exhilaration, appetite loss, digestive disturbance, sleeplessness, hallucinations, and many develop a paranoid type of psychosis. Those who use large doses often enter an irreversible state of convulsion with death as the final occurrence. There has always been strong evidence that the use of cocaine by unstable people causes increased aggressiveness and paranoid delusions which lead to crimes of violence against other persons.

The nonmedical use of the *hallucinogenic drugs,* of which LSD (D-lysurgic acid diethylamide) is by far the most powerful of the known hallucinogenic drugs, has been associated with a number of very serious problems. There is undeniable and well-documented evidence that LSD is responsible for long-term recurring psychosis in users, and medical science has revealed that continuing use of this drug leads to brain and chromosome damage. The drug has also been a precipitating factor in numerous suicides. If other hallucinogenic materials are taken in sufficient quantity, it is the belief of the medical profession that the same effects will occur. For example, the ingestation of morning glory seeds (whose active principle is lysurgic acid amide) has resulted in both psychosis and suicide. Hollister in his book, *Clinical Psychosis,* states, "A personality deterioration has followed the repeated use of psychotomimetics (hallucinogenics) by habituates. Presumably tired of the 'game' of life, they decide to play the 'no-game game,' becoming socially unproductive after a previously promising start in life. Antisocial behavior often follows and a disregard of ordinary social conventions often brings them in conflict with the law, or often creates an attitude which does not draw the line at illegal behavior" [10].

Cannabis sativa, more commonly known as marijuana, whether consumed orally, through injection, or by smoking has a very deteriorating effect both physiologically and psychologically upon the user. The intoxicating material causing these effects is known as delta-L-tetrahydrocannabinol, a reddish-colored resin more commonly known as *THC.* Of the various forms of marijuana found, *hashish* is considered the most potent as it contains approximately 40% THC, making it fifty-seven times more active than the strongest conventional smoking marijuana. It is therefore not surprising that the chemically active substance in marijuana provokes an organic brain syndrome, the severity of which depends on individual vulnerability, dose of drug, psychological state, and frequency of use [11].

The National Institute of Mental Health has developed substantial evidence that marijuana use may indeed cause brain damage; whether such damage is irreversible is still a question, and it is not necessary that the user indulge in *charas, hashish,* or some other potent form of marijuana. The ordinary leafy substance will do the job [12].

Much has been written and discussed concerning the controversy of the possible relationship between marijuana use and the user's eventual progression to heroin addiction and/or the abuse of other hard drugs. There are many who discount any relationship whatever. However, studies and surveys have most definitely documented a progressional relationship. Each study and survey has revealed that the vast majority (usually over 70%) of the heroin addicts first used marijuana. Those that did not use marijuana utilized some other drug. It is a great rarity to encounter a heroin addict who had his initial drug experience with heroin [13]. In addition, there have been studies and surveys made which establish that marijuana users and other drug users develop a pattern of multiple drug use and that this pattern exists throughout the United States. It is this kind of multiple drug use which leads some marijuana users to narcotic addiction. There are some who believe that the misuse of drugs is not the giving up of one drug and moving on to another but generally adding to the number of drugs that are used by one individual. When the drug heroin is added, addiction is the result. Thus it is clear that the progression from marijuana use to heroin addiction is not an inexorable, invariable process. It is rather the result of the marijuana user's immersion in the drug culture where "getting high" is the ultimate goal, where all drugs are obtainable, and friends and associates may be addicts, and where lawlessness is a way of life. The result is the same. A substantial number of marijuana users become heroin addicts.

The nations of the world, many of whom have had to deal with severe marijuana problems on a first-hand basis are in unanimous agreement that marijuana and all of its derivatives are dangerous and damaging drugs warranting strict suppression. Since 1961, marijuana has been under world-wide prohibition under the Single Convention Treaty on Narcotic Drugs. In 1968, the General Assembly of the United Nations voted unanimously to end all illicit or uncontrolled production of *cannabis sativa* in order to shut off illegal trafficking in this drug at its source. Even with this strong feeling and vote by an international body, marijuana and hashish are continuing to be smuggled into the United States and other countries of the world. It has become a highly organized business and the victim is society.

The cost of drug addiction and abuse is astronomical. The average addict will spend $68-70 a day to supply his habit. Using, as an example, an average habit of approximately $50 per day, simple arithmetic clearly establishes that the addicts of the nation obtain $5-6 billion of drugs somewhere on the illicit market annually. Because of the addict's developed physical problem from the use of drugs, he is not capable of holding full-time employment and, in some instances, is not even capable of committing crimes that require skill such as safecracking, fraud, and the like. But the addict does commit thousands of burglaries and robberies each year. A conservative estimate by the United States Department of Justice is that $1.5 billion worth of property is stolen by addicts every year to pay for their addiction. In 1971, Claude Pepper, Chairman of the House of Representatives' Select Committee on Crime, stated that drug abuse and drug dependence are responsible directly and indirectly for 50% of the street crime in the United States. There is also a preponderance of evidence that a high proportion of all criminals arrested are drug abusers or addicts. This evidence is supported by the FBI's computerized records of criminal histories.

As the extent of social impairment and criminality tends to increase because of the drug abuse problem and as some addicts themselves cry for treatment and rehabilitation, it is unfortunate and regrettable that the prognosis for cure of narcotic addicts is poor. In recent years, *methadone* maintenance has been introduced as the panacea for the American drug problem. Methadone maintenance merely substitutes methadone addiction for heroin addiction. When one abstains from methadone, withdrawal symptoms are renewed and there is a desire for heroin. Any irregularity in the administration of methadone can enable an addict to use heroin with the euphoric effect. Furthermore, many drug dealers utilize out-patient methadone maintenance centers as a marketplace for their illicit traffic. Methadone is a highly addictive synthetic opiate drug with virtually the same toxicity as heroin and morphine. Today throughout the nation, it has found its way into the illicit market where it enjoys a good deal of popularity and is easy to obtain. Furthermore, law enforcement has discovered that many addicts have become victims of methadone, having taken overdoses which have killed them.

When a close examination of the literature relating to drug addiction treatment is made, it is clear that most of the voluntary systems of treatment have one thing in common—they do not work. Few drug addicts will seek treatment voluntarily. Those who do usually terminate their treatment before anything resembling cure has been achieved and they immediately lapse back into their previous patterns of addiction.

Compulsory institutionalization and supervision of addicts and drug abusers accomplishes more than the possible rehabilitation of the offender. It serves to prevent narcotic and drug abusers from infecting others with their pernicious habit. It is the opinion of many medical experts that a compulsory program is the necessary first step in any successful treatment program. There is extreme difficulty in achieving abstinence in any environment where drugs are available, and abstinence is an absolute necessity for the cure of drug addiction. Once an individual has been released from an institution, after experiencing successful treatment, there is substantial agreement that intensive supervision is necessary in order to minimize the incidence of relapse by the individual back into his old state of addiction.

Law enforcement efforts have been directed at establishing and maintaining control over the historic affinity that has existed between the Mafia and the traffic in narcotics and other drugs. Organized crime has been powerful and has had an impact in this area because of the magnitude of the profits realized from the sickness and misery of human beings. In recent years, organized crime has relinquished some of their control of the lower echelon drug activity, as a direct result of the enactment of strong and vigorously enforced laws prohibiting such traffic. Prior to their relinquishment, many high-ranking organized crime leaders experienced arrest and some subsequently experienced lengthy prison sentences. Where organized crime has left a void, other criminal organizations have rushed in to continue the operations.

The importing and wholesaling activities of illicit narcotic drugs is in the hands of major criminal organizations and it is organized like a legitimate import-wholesale-retail business. For example, the distribution of heroin requires the movement of this drug through four or five levels from the importer to the street peddler, and, because of the dimensions of narcotic addiction in the drug-abuse problem in the United States, organized criminals who are involved in such illegal trafficking are reaping profits of hundreds of millions of dollars each year. In 1970, federal officers and agencies charged with the responsibility of controlling narcotics and dangerous drugs identified more than 200 criminal organizations with world-wide networks that traffic in drugs. Fifty-eight of these organizations are interwoven into nine major systems which are spread throughout the United States and which reach into almost every large city in the nation. Involving in excess of 1000 identified persons, these systems are the source of 80% of the heroin, nearly 100% of the cocaine, tons of marijuana and millions of dosage units of dangerous drugs used in the United States. The international aspect extends through numerous countries in all parts of the world which have been identified as source points or trafficking routes for drugs destined for the United States.

From that which has been presented on the subject of narcotics and drugs, it is obvious that the "victimless" crimes of narcotics and drug possession, use, and abuse involves hundreds of thousands and possibly even millions of victims. There are those who are debilitated and diseased. There are those who are victims of innumerable burglaries, robberies, and the like, and there is the strong support for these crimes from the vast national and international crime syndicates which prey on society like so many jackals, sapping the essential vitality of our society.

The strong and strict enforcement of all laws prohibiting narcotics and drug violations is necessary for the control and eventual resolution of the drug problem. Enforcement is a proven means of securing aid and rehabilitation for addicts and users, the prevention of the spread of narcotics dependence and drug abuse, and the elimination of illicit drug traffic.

Prostitution

The success of "victimless" crime is due for the most part to its invisibility. "One reason that so widespread and insidious an evil has been able to lurk so often beneath the level of national concern has been the lack of a reliable indicator as to its magnitude or character" [14]. Such a statement is most applicable to organized prostitution. Although organized crime is involved in prostitution, there is no way to accurately estimate the number of criminals involved in, or the vast amount of revenue accruing to them from prostitution. However, it is estimated that this "victimless" crime produces an annual income of some $230 million, much of which goes directly into the hands of organized crime.

Prostitution, as defined by law, is the offering by a female of her time and body for the purpose of engaging in an intimate sexual relationship with a male, for a consideration. There is a very thin line between the amateur who engages in promiscuous behavior and the professional, but the prostitutes who constitute the crime and social problems can be classified according to their method of operation.

As a group, prostitutes are extremely diverse. They range from very intelligent to feeble-minded and from very attractive to homely. For the most part, however, their appearance is less attractive than average. Contrary to popular belief, prostitutes are not oversexed. The fact is, most of them have a very weak appetite for sexual relations and climatic emotion. It is known that many prostitutes are, in fact, lesbians who utilize prostitution as a method to support their girlfriends. But one thing common to all of them is that they each develop a cleverness to avoid, for as long as possible, detection, arrest, and prosecution.

Prostitution is a lucrative business as has been previously discussed. As

FIGURE 14.2. *Street prostitute solicits passerby in vehicle. Courtesy Police Department, San Francisco, Ca.*

a general rule, the prostitute prefers a number of clients each day to only one client and the true professionals are most careful not to contract venereal disease. If she does, she endangers her clients who will become infected and she will surely then be arrested and/or confined and that is the last thing that she wants to have happen to her.

There are a number of different types of prostitutes. The *streetwalker* is a cheap and flashy dresser. She attempts to secure her clients from public places such as sidewalks, parks, bus stations, eating stands, or the passing vehicular traffic. This type is quite diverse in age, ranging from young and inexperienced girls to middle-aged women, and may be found almost anywhere at anytime.

The *bar prostitute* is of several types. The *B-girl* is a female employee of a bar or she may be a tolerated loiterer. Her presence is encouraged for the purpose of soliciting customers to buy drinks in exchange for which she receives a commission on each drink purchased for her. In addition, she serves as bait to lure customers into the bar and if she utilizes the bar to make her contacts for clients, the bartender or owner looks the other way. There is generally no attraction about her except that she is available and will engage in prostitution anywhere and at any time. In addition, there are those women classed as *bar-flies* whose general demeanor is staged to create an attitude of availability; the *bar call-girl* who can be contracted for by telephone if she is not in the bar; and the *housewife* or *working girl* who make contracts for prostitution for extra money for the material things she desires or as a change of pace or type of escape.

Those girls identified as *call-girls* are frequently thought to be something special. They are not, but they usually rank a step or two above those previously discussed. The telephone is the call-girl's second most important piece of equipment. Her method of operation is that she usually works through a telephone answering service to which she subscribes for service.

Other classifications are those known as *creepers, hugger-muggers, house girls, alley workers,* and *teenies.*

Also, very much involved in prostitution, are persons referred to as *pimps.* These people, mostly men, live or derive their support in whole or in part from the earnings of the female's prostitution activities or he may be a person who solicits and thus receives compensation. In addition, there are those known as *panderers* who procure females to become *house girls* in a house of prostitution by promises, encouragement, threats, or violence.

Although prostitutes are involved in organized crime, as a group they are often involved in various crimes in which their clients are the victims. They frequently steal from their customers, assault them, and participate in blackmail and bunco on them. In turn, prostitutes are often victims of various crimes that are committed by their customers, as well as by those who prey on society's rejects because of the reluctance of such victims to make contact with law enforcement authorities. Prostitutes are victims in a much larger sense; they are victimized by the very nature of their illicit activities. "The prostitute is the last link in any chain or 'organization,' whether the organization is limited to a pimp and his stable or whether it extends beyond. By and large, in this context, the prostitute is a victim—obviously a victim of pimps, possibly poverty, of racism and probably a victim of psychiatric abnormality" [15].

Those who argue that legalization of prostitution will eliminate sex crimes are misinformed. The rapist desires only rape; the sadist enjoys only the beating or murdering of his victim and those who molest children lust only after children. Prostitution is a predatory evil. It preys upon society and the prostitute alike. It feeds the insatiable appetite of organized crime, fosters all manner of criminality, spreads venereal disease, and victimizes and depraves the prostitute. Prostitution offers nothing to commend it to society. If it cannot be eradicated, it must be vigorously suppressed. Diligent enforcement of laws prohibiting prostitution activities will provide this suppression and thus a safer, healthier community.

Homosexuality

Homosexuals, male and female, are members of a large minority in the United States. They come from all segments of the society with no race, creed, philosophy, or religion being a barrier. It is conservatively estimated that about 10% of the American male population is homosexual, and this does not even take into consideration the female homosexuals. Included in this minority population is a wide variety of homosexual personalities which range from covert homosexuals who are discreet in their sexual practices to those who publicly proclaim their preferences. It is believed that there are many who are able to lead outwardly normal and productive lives, never engaging in antisocial behavior nor coming to the attention of the police. At the other end of the spectrum are many homosexuals who are emotionally unstable and are prone to violence, who seduce children and participate publicly in indecent conduct. It is also an irrefutable fact that the homosexual is a primary causal factor in the spread of venereal disease, which is an important cause for concern by the total community.

It is not a crime to be a homosexual. It is, however, a crime to practice homosexual or perverted acts. The homosexual is a problem to society as well as to the police because of the types of public locations they most generally utilize as their meeting places. The fact that they are in public and in the presence of other people does not seem to deter or disturb them while they openly participate in their relationships and sexual activities. Many in society view them as a medical or psychiatric problem on which law enforcement should have no opinion, point of view, or policy. Most people have no conception of the problem and its many far-reaching ramifications because they are not in frequent contact with homosexuals, but when contact is made, the average citizen is abhorred and disgusted by what he perceives. The homosexual hangouts and meeting places are under constant complaint from residents in the affected area and also by businessmen who operate in the vicinity. A factor which has deterred effective control of the homosexual society has been the acceptance by many physicians and psychologists of the homosexual's behavior whether it takes place in public or private. This stand thus leads to more open and overt activity which further contributes to the moral decline of society.

Although many strongly deny it, the problem of homosexual crimes against juveniles cannot be minimized. Homosexuals are constantly seeking new and young recruits. There are many who believe, and there is evidence to support the belief, that for a number of homosexual adults, the young teen-aged male represents the primary sexual object.

Sociologists believe that there are grounds for belief that the causal relationship between the seduction of a child by a homosexual and the child's later development into a male prostitute and, ultimately, a confirmed homosexual, is clear. When the profile of the average male prostitute is examined, it is quite likely to discover that he will have been homosexually seduced as a child.

Homosexuals have a compulsive nature and their general promiscuity combined with their apparent attraction to public lavatories and parks creates a severe law enforcement problem of major proportions. The homosexual's *modus operandi* in such places is to approach a likely looking male with a solicitation to engage in perverted sexual activity, and the fact that there may be other people present does not deter him.

Homosexuals show a strong tendency for violence and thus are a continuing enforcement problem. According to Ellis, convicted sex offenders show ". . . a high rate of recidivism, for both sexual and nonsexual offenses" [16]. Much of homosexual-related violence as well as nonsexual crimes stem from male prostitutes whom Cory and Leroy believe to be more numerous than their female counterparts [17].

It is generally proclaimed by experts in the field that homosexuals are psychologically unstable people who have extremely poor control over their sexual impulses and who are not susceptible to any known method of cure. Although some programs have experienced success, the public transgressions of the homosexual demand a continuation of existing enforcement and control. Homosexuals are prone to violence, but they also participate in other forms of criminal conduct, most notably public lewdness and the seduction and molestation of adolescents and children. When one considers the unstable and often criminally compulsive nature of the homosexual it is not unreasonable to suppose that, given the sanction of legality and the aura of respectability, the magnitude of the homosexual problem would proliferate beyond anything now in existence.

Overt homosexual practices, in public places, cannot be considered "victimless" crimes. Individual victims are numerous; victims of molestation, indecent exposure, lewd solicitation, assault, robbery, and murder. Moreover, the homosexual has few peers who equal his ability to spread venereal disease. All of this very effectively victimizes large segments of society.

Within the general policy of law enforcement, all laws prohibiting homosexual activities should be steadfastly enforced. Any other course of action violates the law enforcement agency's responsibility to protect the community. This is especially true in view of the fact that, while homosexuals may or may not be cured of their perversion, legal sanctions are effective in controlling their transgressions against the innocent.

Pornography

Pornography, which is simply obscenity in published or other graphic form, is an area of grave concern for the American public and law enforcement. There has been in recent years a veritable explosion in the United States of the "victimless" crime of pornography and obscenity. The explosion is represented by the seizure of tons of pornographic material, millions of dollars worth of hard core pornographic films, photographs, magazines, and books. All across the nation there has been no area or social group that has not experienced in some way the effect of pornography upon society. The question is often raised as to how one defines pornography, what it is and what it is not. There are three generally accepted guidelines in defining or classifying material as obscene: (a) The material is patently offensive, (b) the material, considered as a whole, has a dominant theme or purpose which appeals to the prurient interest, and (c) it is utterly without redeeming social importance.

Historically, pornography is as ancient as written history and all evidence seems to indicate that there is a relationship between the degree of literacy of the general populace and the degree of concern over obscenity. History reveals that prior to the 1800's, few people knew how to read and that as the rate of literacy increased and education became more common, the first written pornography was produced and at the same time there came the first efforts to outlaw pornographic material. The first laws in America against indecent literature were passed by the state of Vermont in 1821. Today, all fifty states have laws regulating obscene material. In 1865, the Congress

FIGURE 14.3. *Police officers from Public Morals Division of the New York City Police Department conduct a pornographic raid on a 42nd St. store specializing in peep shows and pornographic literature. Courtesy United Press International, New York, N.Y.*

of the United States adopted laws which bar obscene materials from the mails, making the use of the mails in the transmission of pornographic material a criminal offense. The Comstock Law passed by the United States Congress in 1873 still governs obscenity in the mails. Many court decisions in the area of obscenity and pornography have transpired since the enactment of America's first obscenity law, many of which have nullified law enforcement's efforts and working guidelines for arrest and seizure of evidence. Additionally, the court decisions have done nothing to clarify the rules or the standards by which they expect and demand law enforcement to operate. Law enforcement has experienced a good deal of confusion in the manners of approach and procedure because the laws dealing with the areas of obscenity and pornography have been clouded by a lack of consistency on the part of the courts. Recently, however, the United States Supreme Court ruled on June 21, 1973, in *Miller* v. *California* (Vol. 93, U.S. Reporter, p. 2607), that the local population and local juries would decide that which was obscene or pornographic. This landmark decision was a great victory for the general society in their bitter and hard-fought battle to control the availability of pornographic material and to lessen the financial contributions it makes to the world of organized crime. The comments of Judge Robert F. Wagner of Los Angeles regarding the case of *People* v. *Seltzer,* are important to the position which law enforcement has taken in strongly opposing pornography. His comments were also noted by the California Supreme Court and the U.S. Supreme Court prior to the decision of the Miller case. Judge Wagner stated, "History warns us that in the wake of a moral deterioration comes physical deterioration and national destruction. Hence, our interest in the strict enforcement of all laws to prevent the publication and distribution of corrupt literature. As it is the duty of our law enforcing branches of government to enforce with vigor these laws, so it is the correlative function of the courts not to narrow the law's application by accepting tests restrictive of the commonly accepted meaning of the word. Moral standards of thought are not of static or plastic nature. Thought, once accepted, may today be repelled. It follows that the current opinion as to whether or not a publication falls within the prohibition of the section may better be ascertained by a jury of varied occupation and of different experience, yet all in touch with the current views and opinions" [18].

The libertarian supporters and advocates of obscenity are peculiarly ambivalent in their view of the power of books, pictures, films, and plays, to teach, to influence, and to develop. Few of them deny that these mediums exert profound influence on the human mind, but such influences are always seen as being of a beneficial nature. This ambivalence is noteworthy because of the pronounced concern of the civil libertarians among others regarding the visual depictions of violence, sale of toy weapons, war toys, and the like. There is widespread agreement among the social scientists that a continued exposure to acts of violence on television effectively conditions viewers, especially children and adolescents, to violence in real life. In contrast, the pro-obscenity groups steadfastly deny that there is any causal relationship between obscenity, even the most perverted, violent sadomasochistic variety, and socially dysfunctional behavior.

The social scientists are also in agreement that the individual is to a great extent the product of the broad social and cultural context of which he is a part [19]. Sexual behavior is no exception to this socializing process; indeed, some authorities maintain that "sexual socialization in our society has become firmly institutionalized in the adolescent peer groups and the mass media" [20].

Such sexual socialization in the larger environment is seen as outweighing familial influence on the nature of individual sexual behavior. The impact of these extra familial sources may well obliterate the differences developed within the family [21].

A fundamental aspect of pornography and obscenity is the dehumanization of human sexual relationships, the reduction of sex to an animalistic public spectacle of exactly the same nature as the ancient Roman circuses [22]. But even beyond the human degradation involved is the fact that pornography teaches obscenity as a way of life: ". . . It gives a false, lying impression of sex and the way normal civilized men and women behave. The unavoidable fact is that pornography sets up sexually sick people as models of behavior, and emphasizes bestiality, perversion and cruelty . . . as if it were the norm" [23]. The process of sexual socialization internalizes this norm—the norm of mass media and peer groups—in the individual. The norm then becomes the basis of individual sexual behavior. To state it another way, there can be no doubt that if a young person attended a hypothetical college of obscenity for four years, majoring in such courses as "Varieties of Bestiality," "Principles of Pedophilia," and "Advanced Sadomasochistic Violence," he would emerge with patterns of sexual behavior that would be considered other than normal.

Those who purchase the most pornographic material are females 15–20 years of age and males 15–29 years of age. Thus, adolescents and young adults see the most pornography. Those who are engaged in the practice of psychiatric medicine state that to think that we can saturate adults with pornography and effectively isolate their children from it is a fool's dream. It is obviously very much of a fool's dream when it is noted that many millions of pieces of hard-core pornographic material are sent, unsolicited, each year to juveniles through the mails. Another equally dark side to the obscenity industry is that it is in the control of organized criminals. There have been several individuals identified with organized crime who are involved in the large-scale production, distribution, and sale of various forms of hard core obscenity on a nationwide basis. The distribution of such material through retail bookstores nationwide is primarily controlled by men with Mafia connections, and the failure of bookstore owners to satisfactorily cooperate with the dictates of the criminal organizations has brought on retaliatory force in various forms such as bombing, assault, arson, and murder. To some degree, force or threat of force has been used by the Mafia to either extort or take over independent operators in the pornography industry.

As befits the criminal nature of pornography, the people who provide the action—the models, actresses, and actors—are often part of the underworld or its fringes. The records of law enforcement and criminal justice agencies indicate that hard-core performers, whether involved in live obscenity or in the production of pornographic materials, are frequently prostitutes, pimps, homosexuals, drug addicts, and other criminal types, but the main requirement for performers in obscenity is that they must be young and willing to do anything. Experience is no criterion. Thus the pornographer-panderer is always out recruiting, attempting to bring in new talent to this industry which enjoys a gross annual income in excess of $200 million a year, a large proportion of which accrues directly to criminal organizations.

The will of the people is reflected in the statutory law of the federal government, the fifty states, and the District of Columbia which legally restrict production, distribution, sale, and nonprivate possession of obscenity [24].

As a direct result of the Miller case, the United States Supreme Court gave full power to the states to regulate obscenity through local discretion. Justice John M. Harlan of the United States Supreme Court summed up the case against pornography and obscenity as follows: "Furthermore, even assuming that pornography cannot be deemed ever to cause, in an immediate sense, criminal sexual conduct, other interests within the proper cognizance of the state may be protected by the prohibition placed on such materials. The state can reasonably draw the inference that over a long period of time, the indiscriminate dissemination of materials, the essential character of which is to degrade sex, will have an eroding effect on moral standards" [25].

The preponderance of evidence indicates that pornography and obscenity are not only degrading but may also be predisposing factors in sexual deviants and criminality. Victims are clearly involved when children and adolescents are abused for pornographic purposes. The support which pornography gives organized crime directly and indirectly creates numerous victims. The final victimization is society.

Alcohol

Alcoholism is a prevalent and very complex disease which has become a sociomedical problem of enormous proportions, involving far more than the physical condition of the victim. The total personality of the individual is affected pathologically, emotionally, and spiritually. Alcoholism also affects the society in which the victim lives, his family, and the persons with whom he associates. Every leading medical association in the United States has expressed its grave concern over this ever-mounting social problem.

Alcoholism invades the total personality of the individual. These problems affect the total community and every segment of the society, including the police, courts, social agencies, clergy, and the medical experts, all of whom have been called upon to help solve the problem. The alcoholism rate in the United States ranks fourth highest in the world according to the World Health Organization.

Alcoholism is often at the root of family neglect and disorganization, juvenile delinquency, poverty, crime, traffic accidents and fatalities, chronic disease, high hospital costs, acute illness and death, as well as emotional, social, and economic disaster, all of which have profound implications upon the victim and the society of which he is a part. Studies and surveys conducted throughout the United States disclose that 25–35 million persons in the United States are affected by the excessive use of alcohol. Alcoholism's destruction of men, women, and families cannot be measured in money. The permanent degradation, the loss of dignity, the destroyed careers, the emotionally injured children, and the other tragic results of this disease are evidence of a tragedy beyond measure. In addition, the cost of dealing with alcoholism in its various manifestations, ranges in the billions of dollars. A common misconception is that alcoholism is mostly restricted to the so-called "skid-row" bum. In actuality, however, only about 4% of the alcoholics in the United States are found on skid-row. The remaining 96% are individuals from every social and economic strata in the society.

Another misconception is that only the skid-row bum is the one who is a serious criminal threat. Studies and surveys on criminal offenders in relation to drinking involvement clearly establish that the greater percentage of serious criminal offenses are committed by people who are drinking at the time of the offense or immediately prior thereto. Additionally, statistics from the United States Department of Justice indicate that a high percentage of the total arrests made each year are for drunkenness alone, apart from the criminal offenses.

Alcohol, which has been considered both a blessing and a curse to man, has been used by man at least as long as he has recorded history. It cannot be stated with any degree of certainty when and where it was first discovered, but in every society alcohol has played an important role, particularly in the Western cultures, where man incorporated alcohol into his religion, a combination that still exists in some faiths, for example, Indian, Jewish, and

Roman Catholic religions. Many of the pagan religions had their god or gods of wine and beer and, like contemporary Christians and Jews, alcohol invariably entered into their religious ceremonies.

Alcohol has also been extensively used in the field of medicine, sometimes soundly as in the cleaning of wounds, and sometimes unsoundly as in attempts to cure deafness, for dietary reasons, and for pleasure. It is these last two uses that are the most interesting for they indicate how pervasive alcohol has become. As far back as it can be traced, man has always had some kind of problem with alcohol, and drunkenness has always been frowned upon. Possibly the Greeks more than any other group emphasized moderation in the use of this beverage and history furthermore reveals that there was even an age limit of 18 before a person was allowed to utilize alcohol. As one Greek poet said, "To drink much wine is evil; but if one drinks in moderation, wine is not an evil but a blessing."

The Romans were far more strict and harsh with those who drank to excess or drank when they were forbidden. For example, women were forbidden to drink any alcoholic beverage and there are numerous cases where irate husbands killed their wives for taking a drink. This double standard declined along with the Roman Empire. By the last years of the Empire, the Romans had perfected the art of drinking. Their banquets are famous and history records that the host often supplied flamingo feathers for "tickling the mouth to turn the stomach," so more food and drink could be had by all. Possibly the more thoughtful and perhaps more sanitary host supplied special rooms known as "vomitoriums" for this purpose [26]. Some have stated that the decline of the Roman Empire was the result of drunkenness, but this is unfounded. There were many factors which caused its downfall. If anything, the decline led to drunkenness, not drunkenness to the decline.

Man's attitudes toward alcohol have always been confused and ambivalent. There is nothing new about alcohol problems or man's attempt to deal with them. It is unlikely that he will ever be able to do away with all of the problems associated therein and many feel that since it is a part of today's society, its disadvantages along with its benefits must be accepted.

People drink many different types of alcoholic beverages, and people react differently to alcohol. A person may react one way at one time and totally differently another time. When one speaks of the "effects" of alcohol, he is referring to a number of alterations that take place in humans when they become "high" or intoxicated. What causes these changes to take place is the amount of absorption of alcohol which enters the body through the bloodstream. Alcohol is generally absorbed very quickly. The second factor is the individual's metabolism. After absorption, alcohol is distributed by the blood and metabolized or oxidized. A very small amount of alcohol is excreted from the body but around 95% of the alcohol consumed undergoes chemical alteration by the metabolic process. The liver is the principal place where alcohol is metabolized. Thus, the disease, cirrhosis of the liver, is common to those who consume large amounts of alcohol. It is unfortunate, but this disease is frequently fatal.

Alcohol has its most serious effect upon the brain. The intensity to which it is affected, of course, is dependent upon the concentration of alcohol in the blood and brain tissue. Contrary to popular belief, alcohol is a depressant, not a stimulant used to increase a person's activity. Alcohol reduces brain and nerve activity and thus an individual's ability to effectively perform many activities is impaired seriously.

Those in the society who are excessive or heavy drinkers, or who overindulge and develop a true habituation to alcohol, suffer numerous disorders besides the obvious one of alcoholism. There are a variety of disorders associated with the nervous system and digestive system, especially the liver. Examples of such disorders are Wernicke's disease, Korsakoff's psychosis, delirium tremens, and cirrhosis of the liver. Many of these disorders are seen in progressively deteriorating stages. If any of these disorders are discovered early and properly treated, the body will make a positive response. However, if they are allowed to develop, the damage that occurs is often irreversible. It is not clearly known how alcohol contributes to these disorders. However, it has been established that excessive drinkers frequently have very poor dietary habits and that many of the disorders associated with excessive drinking are the result of nutritional deficiencies. Thus, it can be stated with a high degree of certainty that alcohol indirectly causes these and many other disorders. Some drinkers have poor sanitary habits. This, combined with poor eating habits, lowers their ability to resist all forms of illness, and last, an alcoholic is accident prone because of his intoxication. The life span of the alcoholic is shorter than that of the nonalcoholic drinker inasmuch as his death is likely to be the result of complications due to drinking or from accidents. The significant role it plays in the unfortunate and unnecessary loss of life every day in the United States is tragic. There are numerous sociopsychological variables related to the use of alcohol, and the most important factor to remember in this regard is that those who consume it will act differently on different occasions at different places and while in different moods.

The consumption of alcohol is a socially acceptable practice in the United

States, yet 50% of the total arrests made by law enforcement are for drunkenness. Alcoholism is involved in at least 50% of all fatal traffic accidents and each year there are approximately 55,000 lives lost on the highways and close to 2 million people suffer serious injuries. The estimated losses to traffic accidents each year are in the billions of dollars. Industry also has found that the alcoholic represents a billion dollar loss to it each year.

In 1920, when prohibition became the law of the land, it failed to accomplish what the prohibitionists had so strongly hoped for. It is not generally thought that the prohibitionists really represented the majority of the adult population. Prohibition failed and perhaps it was the most disastrous social experiment ever attempted in this country. Millions of law-abiding citizens still desired to drink and flaunted the prohibition law. This experience illustrates the futility of the attempt to legislate out of existence basic social patterns such as drinking, yet this is not meant to imply that all Americans do accept or drink alcohol. In a country that is frequently thought of as a country of drinkers, a surprising number do not drink, or drink very little. It is estimated that only 58% of the adult population in the United States utilize alcohol in some form or another. The drinking patterns of the country are dependent for the most part upon sociological factors such as social class, age, region of the country, and religious affiliation. Yet by themselves these factors mean little. The crucial variable in considering how one drinks is how he is taught to drink. People do not just drink, they learn to drink, and they learn different ways to drink in different groups. An analysis of the European drinking pattern establishes this proposition clearly. Thus it is generally felt that how a person views and uses alcohol is to a greater degree dependent on what his social environment was when he was taught to drink. Because of the view of the American public that alcoholism is a "victimless" crime, they have failed to recognize and identify their responsibility in implementing new medical and social philosophies and programs to deal with this disease. As a result, individuals are still dying every day from chronic alcoholism. When each death occurs one might ask the question: *Who is the victim?*

VICE LAW ENFORCEMENT

Many police agencies across the United States are well organized and structured in a way that enables them to enforce the vice laws of their jurisdiction with alacrity. Sound organizational structure is vital and essential if there is to be an efficient information network and a cooperative attitude and relationship between all officers and agencies concerned with the problems of "victimless" crime. If a law enforcement agency is weak and poorly structured, then, regardless of the individual efforts made by any or all dedicated officers, it will fail in its purpose. When an enforcement agency incorporates a vice control unit into its operation, it may take on, depending upon the size of the agency, an aura of a supersecret intelligence unit. It is generally found in the small police agency that the organizational structure of the vice unit is centralized under the chief of police with the division commander reporting directly to him. In the large centralized vice organizations such as a county sheriff's department, the commander of the vice and the intelligence divisions will have reporting to him the commander of each of these divisions. He in turn reports directly to the county sheriff. In the large, decentralized metropolitan vice organization, the precinct or divisional vice units will generally report through the commander of the patrol bureau who will report in turn directly to the chief of police. There may, however, be within the organizational structure a bureau of special investigation whose leader will be in command over the precinct or divisional vice unit supervisor who will report to him. The central county system consolidating forces for local agencies will by necessity have the chief of the vice operation reporting directly to the chief of police. The types of systems of organizational control described are important for any agency to establish to protect its integrity and to further assure that the officer's efforts are protected by adequate staff planning and internal supervision.

For any law enforcement vice unit to operate successfully, it must have information and a good system for recording the information. Information in law enforcement comes from many sources. How that information is obtained and how it is used are strong indicators of a police agency's effectiveness. Law enforcement vice officers receive information from informants, field officers' reports, concerned citizens, and their own agency's intelligence operations. As the law enforcement officer develops a greater understanding and appreciation for the wide scope of organized crime, he becomes more acutely aware and appreciates to a greater degree the value of information and the value of his contribution as an officer working to disrupt and control the efforts of organized crime.

Intelligence may be divided into two categories: (a) *Tactical intelligence* and (b) *strategic intelligence.* Most police officers better identify with tactical intelligence, for it lends itself to the primary thrust of arrest and prosecution. Included also are "(a) information which is evidence of offenses either substantive or of a conspiracy, (b) information helpful in criminal prosecution,

(c) information helpful in identifying active criminals, (d) information helpful in covering specific areas of criminal activity, and (e) information helpful in identifying *modus operandi"* [27].

Strategic intelligence is a term which is sometimes confusing. It is a type of intelligence that is frequently overlooked and underestimated by the law enforcement officer. Therefore, strategic intelligence is not properly utilized by law enforcement unless the officer has been specially trained to carry it out and make efficient and effective use of it. Strategic intelligence does not lend itself so readily to arrests or prosecutions but nevertheless it is of great value. Strategic intelligence is used for: "(a) Identifying target areas of police concern, (b) contributing to decisions concerning police training and curriculum, (c) contributing to decisions of government which are not directly connected to arrest and/or prosecution, (d) for obtaining legislation which would be helpful in combating organized crime, (e) for public education in the prevention of certain forms of crime, and (f) in obtaining benefits of work performed by professionals in other disciplines, particularly from the academic fields" [28].

Throughout the country there are numerous sources from which intelligence information may be gathered. Of particular strategic importance in this area are the harbor, dock, and waterfront locations, airports and labor unions. Of additional importance are business areas such as those subjected to pressure and influence by syndicate operators such as bars, loan operations, laundries, vending machines, hotels, restaurants, race tracks, sporting events, and conventions.

Much of the information that is collected and utilized by the law enforcement and/or vice enforcement officer is gathered at the local level through his personal contacts with informants, both paid and unpaid, and through the initiation of investigations to gain information and gather evidence for criminal prosecution. In addition, it is essential that the officer be thoroughly familiar with all published information in newspapers, magazines, and correspondence between police agencies regarding the activities of persons participating or suspected of participating in illicit vice activity. Of course, the most effective technique for law enforcement in securing certain types of information is that of placing an undercover police officer in the geographic area where the information is available or that of placing him into the activity taking place. The role that the officer assumes will, for the most part, determine how successful he is in obtaining information. There are many advantages in utilizing the undercover police officer: (a) He is well trained in the law and understands the police function, (b) he is able to observe and report activities, (c) he is able to solicit information and make contacts on the street, (d) he is able to follow up on that which is provided to him in the way of information by surveilling officers as well as by law enforcement patrol officers in the general area in which he is working, and (e) he may be able to seek out or actively engage those who are in the planning stages of criminal activity so that information about their proposed activity may be filtered back to those who are in charge of the investigation.

Every law enforcement agency with a vice enforcement division must keep good records which should be a part of the total integrated criminal justice system. Even records of a confidential nature are more secure in such a system than in a manual record system. The central control, storage, and retrieval of critical information can be protected from indiscriminate inquiry by proper programming, and this will remove any possibility of a remote station making an unauthorized inquiry.

Speed and flexibility are vitally important in a law enforcement record system, particularly a vice intelligence record system. Better investigations and stronger prosecutions will be improved through an information system which can provide history, methods of operation, and current illegal activities to the vice investigator, and the hit-and-miss type of vice violator can be more efficiently dealt with when such information has been computerized. It must be remembered that the vice officer or the vice intelligence officer is only as good and effective as his information. He must therefore be a dedicated and diligent law enforcement officer willing to spend long and tedious hours on sometimes very aggravating, frustrating, and disappointing investigations.

VICE ENFORCEMENT AND THE LEGAL SYSTEM

Law enforcement is charged with enforcing those laws which have been enacted by the various legislative bodies whose responsibility it is to prohibit activity that is not acceptable to society. Whether law enforcement, as an area of public service and trust, endorses or rejects the law is immaterial. In the public interest, it is charged by law with full and impartial enforcement of all statutes enacted by legislative bodies. Throughout the United States the law enforcement profession endorsing this philosophy is committed to the exercise of fair and impartial administration of the law. Unfortunately, as a result of a number of case decisions handed down by the courts, it would appear to the average citizen in this country that the criminal element in the society has greater rights and privileges than the law-abiding citizen. Many of the cases that were so decided involved persons charged with the so-called "victimless" crime and, as a result, the types of "victimless" crime previously described in this chapter have been allowed to take place with only sporadic enforcement.

In order for vice law enforcement to be effective, it must have the full and undivided support and cooperation of the legal system as it is structured. In addition, the police officer must have the assistance of his city administrators and commissions in decision- and policy-making and he must maintain good judicial relations through his agency. In 1968, with the passage of the Omnibus Crime Bill by the United States Congress, for the first time in many areas of the nation, local crime commissions have been formed to support the comprehensive effort to control crime. Such commissions of concerned citizenry conduct investigations to reveal the extent of vice and criminal problems in their area, and to reveal a lack of enforcement or prosecution of vice conditions. Additionally, they hold hearings through which they obtain information they may or may not subsequently furnish to law enforcement. Such information which might not otherwise be forthcoming because of the reluctance of citizens to provide information to a police enforcement agency thus becomes usable. The commissions also conduct investigations into, and research of, organized crime and their various criminal groups and activities. They are therefore better informed as to the nature, type, and volume of crime that is taking place in the community, state, or regional area. Crime commissions also serve an educational role, becoming a medium by which information regarding organized crime and illicit criminal activity taking place within the jurisdiction is transmitted to the local community.

It is commonly believed that crime commissions are invested with great powers and that when one is requested to appear before them, one must do so. But only in such cases wherein the commission has the power of subpoena is an individual required to respond to the commission.

Many people also look upon crime commissions as the watchdog of governmental operations including the grand jury of the county. It should be understood that a crime commission is not usually a governmental agency and as a result, it generally suffers in its efforts to accomplish its tasks because of a lack of funds with which to operate. However, in more recent years, with the assistance of the Omnibus Crime Bill, many agencies which before were not able to establish and operate their own crime commission, have been able to do so because of the availability of federal funding. Frequently police officers from the geographic area are specially assigned and assist the local crime commission.

Police commissions, which are usually a governmental agency and are supported as such, frequently are assisted in the performance of their function by sworn peace officers from the local agency for which the commission is responsible. The members of local police commissions are usually appointed by the mayor, and their general purpose is to establish broad policy decisions for the operation of the police agency. Also, in some jurisdictions throughout the country, the police commission has the sole responsibility for issuing licenses and permits to businesses that are susceptible to control by organized criminal groups. The commission also frequently will sit as an administrative tribunal, hearing appeals from establishments whose licenses have been denied. The commission not only helps to control organized crime but it also serves as an effective medium to keep the citizenry advised of criminal activities and conditions in its geographic area.

Every police officer, particularly the vice and drug control officer, must be acutely aware of and familiar with all of the special court cases that pertain to the legal procedures that they utilize in the enforcement of the law. This establishes for them a framework within which they may operate. For example, they must be familiar with *Katz* v. *United States,* 389 U.S., 347 (1967), which pertains to evidence that is obtained with listening devices; *Mapp* v. *Ohio,* 367, U.S. 643 (1961), which is the exclusionary rule requiring that evidence must be legally seized to be admissible in court; *McCray* v. *Illinois* 386, U.S. 306 (1967), which deals with the use of informers' information; and if the officer is going to use pre- and post-arrest statements as evidence, he must keep particularly in mind *Escobedo* v. *Illinois,* 378, U.S. 478 (1964), which provides that the accused has a right to remain silent and a right to consultation with his attorney. In addition to these and other cases, the officer must be certain that he is not carrying out a local ordinance, invalid because of its attempt to impose additional requirements in a field that is already preempted by state law [29]. Whenever a warrant or a search warrant is served, it is incumbent upon the law enforcement officer to make certain that proper notification as to his position and the purpose of his visit is clear prior to entry [30].

Vice officers also have a responsibility to the community of making the residents aware of their efforts in vice control and the prevention program which the residents should be constantly pursuing. In carrying out such a program, inclusion of the judiciary is not only essential, it is mandatory. The conflicts that result between the judiciary and the vice control officer must be resolved if there is to be effective, efficient, fair and impartial law enforcement in the administration of justice. First of all, both sides must be objective and all personal feelings and issues should be set aside. Because of the individual philosophies of the vice officer and the judiciary, some violations are more stringently enforced than are others. It is likely that if there is a severe difference in philosophy, the judiciary will terminate the prosecution for the public good.

Most frustrating to the law enforcement officer, and especially frustrating to the drug and vice officer in the prosecution of suspects is that frequently the court, the prosecutor, and the defense, forming a triangle, will make arbitrary decisions regarding further prosecution of a defendant, a dismissal, or adjustments of penalty, and never consult with the investigating officer as to the criminal background of the defendant. Conflict and unpleasant experiences with the courts is very discouraging to the law enforcement officer. In order to avoid and/or handle such conflicts, it is suggested by Pace that the officer should: "(a) Disassociate himself emotionally from the case being tried. The sentence imposed or the disposition in a case should be of limited concern to the officer. This does not imply that the officer, through the media available, and as a private citizen, should not actively campaign for necessary change. (b) Prepare cases and reports in such a precise manner that there is no legal question concerning the case. (c) Review notes on each case prior to court testimony. It is easy for an officer handling many cases to become confused over similar incidents. (d) Become acquainted with the prosecutor and his techniques for presenting a case. (e) Not show concern regarding the court's philosophy about vice crimes. (f) Be neutral in his opinions and expressions about certain types of vice violators. The court or jury can detect antagonistic attitudes" [31]. It is thus very important that for quality law enforcement on vice conditions to take place in any geographical area, there must be set forth as general policy statements as to how the personnel of the police agency shall function, and it is also important that all officers function in the same manner and to the same degree. Pace outlines the general guidelines which should be included in every department manual regarding the enforcement of vice law: "(a) All vice laws should be strictly enforced. (b) Vice violations, although different from other crimes, should be an enforcement function of all officers. (c) The techniques of enforcement should be within the rule of law. Sensational or emotional crimes do not justify deviation from the legal laws of arrest. (d) An officer in the field cannot moralize. Statutory laws are explicit and serve as his guide. (e) All violations reported to a department should be reduced to writing. All investigations should be recorded in writing as the investigation progresses. (*f*) Records should be protected but should not be so secretive as to render the information useless" [32].

SUMMARY

It is clear from the foregoing that there is no such thing as a "victimless" crime. The family suffers probably the most from the personal pain and suffering of publicity and notoriety related to these crimes. The parents suffer the pains of searching for their failure in the upbringing of their child; the financial burden of providing bond money, attorney fees, care for the wife and children, of sitting through the trial in the hope that their presence will influence the final verdict. Wherein the male is the accused, the wife suffers all of the foregoing and has the added burden of supporting the children and trying to cut through the shame that they feel. In her efforts to dissuade him from future crime, she has the burden of trying to do what the professionals find impossible—rehabilitating him and making him a valued member of society again. The employer of the gambler, the addict, and the alcoholic suffers too. He suffers from notoriety, from the loss of services, and frequently from theft which accompanies such crimes. And there are the victims of the homosexual, the sex offender, and the gambler.

It is the authors' position that all existing laws prohibiting or controlling activities involved in the so-called "victimless" crimes must be vigorously enforced. When compliance with demands for nonenforcement of such laws is met, the community will be open to a creeping insidious, pervasive corruption that will destroy it and its way of life. The community that is dominated by organized criminals is no more free than is the community dominated by the most odious of dictatorships. The police responsibility is one of protection and service to the community through professional and impartial law enforcement. This responsibility includes the enforcement of all laws coming within the authority of the police, including "victimless" crimes.

ANNOTATED REFERENCES

Attorney General's Task Force on Legalized Gambling and Organized Crime, *Task Force Report on Legalized Gambling,* Sacramento, California, 1971. A good, clear presentation of facts regarding gambling.

Bloomquist, E., *Marijuana: The Second Trip,* Glencoe Press, Beverly Hills, Ca., 1971. This book is probably one of the finest pieces of material ever written on the subject of marijuana. Two points of view regarding marijuana are presented in a clear and unbiased manner. This book is recommended without any reservation to everyone.

Chamber of Commerce of the United States, *Desk Book on Organized Crime,* Washington, D.C., 1969. Organized crime is discussed as it affects the society.

Ellis, A., and R. Brancole, *The Psychology of Sex Offenders,* Thomas, Springfield, Ill., 1956. Highly recommended to those who deal with the sex offender in society.

Pace, D. F., *Handbook of Vice Control,* Prentice–Hall, Englewood Cliffs, N.J., 1971. An excellent handbook discussing all forms of vice and suggested methods and controls to be utilized by law enforcement.

President's Commission on Law Enforcement and Administration of Justice, *Task Force Report: Organized Crime; Task Force Report: Drunkenness; Task Force Report: The Police; Task Force Report: Crime and Its Impact—An Assessment.* U.S. Government Printing Office, Washington, D.C., 1967. Each of the task force reports presents an informative discussion of the various vice crimes, their effects and impact on society.

NOTES

1. *Newsweek,* "Pornography Goes Public," December 21, 1970, p. 28.

2. E. Lumbard, "Local and State Action Against Organized Crime," *The Annals of the American Academy of Political and Social Science,* Vol. 347, May, 1963.

3. R. King, *Gambling and Organized Crime,* U.S. Govt. Printing Office, Washington, D.C., 1969.

4. Lumbard, *op. cit.,* p. 97.

5. V. W. Peterson, "Chicago: Shades of Capone," *The Annals of the American Academy of Political and Social Science,* Volume 347, May, 1963.

6. Chamber of Commerce of the United States, *Desk Book on Organized Crime,* p. 41.

7. The President's Commission on Law Enforcement and Administration of Justice, *Task Force Report: Organized Crime,* p. 3.

8. Attorney General's Task Force on Legalized Gambling and Organized Crime, *Task Force Report on Legalized Gambling,* Sacramento, California, 1971, p. 1.

9. King, *op. cit.,* pp. 11–12.

10. L. F. Hollister, M.D., *Clinical Psychosis,* Thomas, Springfield, Ill., 1968, p. 151.

11. A. Kornhaber, "Marijuana in an Adolescent Psychiatric Out-Patient Population," *Jour. Am. Med. Assoc.,* Vol. 215, No. 12, March 22, 1971, p. 1988.

12. *U.S. News and World Report,* "Latest Findings on Marijuana," February 1, 1971, p. 26.

13. J. Langrod, "Secondary Drug Use Among Heroin Users," *Internat. Jour. Addict.,* Vol. 5, No. 4, Dec. 1970, p. 622.

14. The President's Commission on Law Enforcement and Administration of Justice, *Task Force Report: Crime and Its Impact—An Assessment,* p. 133.

15. San Francisco Committee on Crime, *A Report on Non-Victim Crime in San Francisco,* Part II, San Francisco, 1971, p. 32.

16. A. Ellis, and R. Brancale, *The Psychology of Sex Offenders,* p. 33.

17. D. W. Cory and J. P. LeRoy, *The Homosexual and His Society: A View From Within,* Citadel, New York, 1963, p. 92.

18. *People* v. *Seltzer,* 25 Cal Ap 3rd, Sup. 52.

19. H. M. Clor, *Obscenity and Public Morality,* Univ. of Chicago Press, Chicago, 1969, p. 155.

20. R. J. Udry, "Sex and Family Life," *The Annals of the American Academy of Political and Social Science,* March, 1968, p. 25.

21. *Ibid.,* p. 25.

22. I. Kristol, "On Pornography and Censorship," *Los Angeles Times,* March 28, 1971, Sec. G, p. 2.

23. G. D. Schulz, "What Sex Offenders Say About Pornography," *Readers Digest,* Vol. 98, No. 591, July, 1971, p. 55.

24. C. H. Keating, "The Report That Shocked the Nation," *Readers Digest,* Vol. 97, No. 573, Jan. 1970.

25. *Alberts* v. *California,* 354 US 476.

26. J. D. Rolleston, "Alcoholism in Classical Antiquity," *Brit. Jour. Inebriety,* Vol. 24, 1927, pp. 101–120.

27. D. F. Pace, *Handbook of Vice Control,* p. 9.

28. *Ibid.,* p. 10.

29. *Lane* v. *City of Los Angeles,* 58 Cal. 2d 99 (1962).

30. *Penn.* v. *Newman,* 240 A 2d 795 (1968).

31. Pace, *op. cit.,* pp. 21–22.

32. *Ibid.,* p. 23.

CHAPTER FIFTEEN

Arrest Procedures

Who may make an arrest? In what manner should the arrest be accomplished? Who is exempt from arrest? In this chapter, these questions will be answered and some of the other ramifications of arrest will be discussed, such as arrest with or without a warrant. It is the desire of the authors for this chapter to clarify, inform, and remove many misconceptions and doubts that are possessed by many citizens on the subject of arrest. The subject matter of the chapter should assist and alert the preservice student or new officer to the many facets of arrest that will become a part of his knowledge as he assumes his role in the law enforcement profession.

The position of the law enforcement officer in the light of many recent Supreme Court decisions with regard to arrest, search, and seizure has changed immeasurably, and his task of enforcing the law has been made more difficult. The officer may not make an arrest without reasonable and probable cause to believe that the person being arrested is guilty of committing a violation.

Throughout the world an arrest is considered the taking of a person into official custody, in the manner authorized by law. This same thought prevails today throughout the United States for police officers and citizens alike. The term *arrest* is derived from the French word *arreter,* which means *to stop.* Two well-known definitions might prove helpful in understanding the term *arrest. Cochran's Law Lexicon* states that an arrest is the seizing of a person

346

FIGURE 15.1. *Police officers in the process of capturing a felon take no chances. Courtesy Police Department, San Francisco, Ca.*

and detaining him in custody by lawful authority, and *Black's Law Dictionary* defines it as depriving a person of his liberty by legal authority.

LEGAL PROCEDURE

Manner of Making Arrests

An arrest is made for criminal law violations and, in certain situations, for civil law violations either by the actual restraint of the person or by the person's submission to the custody of an officer. Any person arrested may be subjected to such restraint as is necessary for his arrest and detention. In making the arrest, a police officer must inform the person to be arrested of:

1. Intention to arrest him.
2. Cause of the arrest.
3. Authority to make the arrest.

There are three general exceptions to this procedure. The person making the arrest is not required to comply with the foregoing procedure: *(a) If he has reasonable cause to believe that the person to be arrested is actually engaged in the commission of or an attempt to commit an offense, (b) the person to be arrested is pursued immediately after its commission,* or *(c) after an escape.* The person making the arrest must, on request of the person he is arresting, inform him of the offense for which he is being arrested. Submission to custody is shown when the person to be arrested recognizes the presence of the authority for the arrest, and is advised of the alleged offense. Authority to arrest is shown in two ways: *(a) When the peace officer is in uniform* and *(b) when the person being arrested by the exercise of ordinary care should realize the authority.* Immediate pursuit is not used here in the sense of an escape from custody, but rather in the sense of flight from the scene of a crime. As soon as the complete arrest and restraint is effected by the officer, he must advise the arrestee of his constitutional rights, whether or not he is a citizen of the United States. Every person arrested in the United States enjoys this privilege. It is preferable that there be a witness to the advisement of rights. After the advisement of rights, the arrestee must be asked if he understands his rights. If the answer is affirmative, then and only then may the peace officers begin interrogation of the suspect. If the arresting officer does not desire to question the arrestee, the Miranda admonition is not necessary (*Miranda* v. *Arizona,* 1966).

EXEMPTIONS FROM ARREST

Two classes of people are exempt within certain limits from criminal arrest: *(a) Ambassadors* and other *diplomatic officials* of foreign nations together with their families and members of their official households, except when and where it is necessary to prevent these persons from committing acts of violence; consular officials lack this immunity in the absence of a contrary treaty; *(b) witnesses* who are brought into or are traveling through a state in obedience to a subpoena or order to testify at a criminal or grand jury proceeding in connection with circumstances which occurred before the witnesses entered the state.

On occasion, there have been arrests by peace officers of persons who are immune to arrest. These arrests, when they occur, are voidable and are not an illegal act. The arrestee in these situations must submit to the authority of the arresting officer and later establish his immunity in a judicial proceeding. The classes of persons as listed also are exempt from civil arrest. In addition to these two classes, the following categories of persons are exempt from civil arrest: (*a*) *Witnesses* under court order or subpoena, going to or returning from attendance in court; (*b*) *voters* at, going to, or coming from polls on election days; (*c*) state and federal *legislators;* and (*d*) *state militiamen* at, going to, or returning from their place of military duty.

ARREST BY PEACE OFFICERS WITHOUT WARRANT

A peace officer may make an arrest in obedience to a warrant, or he may arrest a person without a warrant whenever he has *reasonable and probable cause* to believe that the person to be arrested has committed a public offense in his presence. In addition, an officer may arrest a person who has committed a felony not in his presence, and he may arrest a person whenever he has *reasonable cause* to believe that the person has committed a felony, whether or not a felony has in fact been committed. It must be pointed out that a peace officer has certain discretion regarding arrest. He is not required to make an arrest except upon the order of a magistrate or in obedience to a warrant of arrest (*Tomlinson* v. *Pierce,* 1973).

It is a fact that most arrests are made without warrants and therefore they frequently are made in situations where calm, direct, and deliberate action is impossible. As a result, peace officers are obliged to have a thorough and exact understanding of their powers, obligations, and limitations to effect arrests without the aid of a warrant. Why is such understanding necessary? There are four basic reasons: (*a*) *An unlawful arrest may subject an officer to a suit for false arrest;* (*b*) *the arrestee under limited circumstances may have a right to resist the arrest;* (*c*) *any subsequent search is considered unlawful and evidence seized may be suppressed or excluded;* and (*d*) *a confession thereafter is considered to be obtained through duress and coercion and is not admissible.*

Several references have been made to *reasonable cause.* A discussion of this area of arrest procedure is relevant. The peace officer may make an arrest for a felony or misdemeanor without a warrant if he possesses reasonable cause to believe that the person to be arrested has committed the crime in his presence. The term *reasonable cause* is not defined in our legal statutes. Therefore, an officer must understand the meaning to carry out properly, effectively, and justly, his arresting function. To discover the meaning would require an extensive discussion of judicial decisions, which is beyond the scope and purpose of this chapter in acquainting the student and new law enforcement officer with the subject of arrest procedure and technique. It may be summarized, however, that reasonable cause is such a state of facts that would lead a man of ordinary care and prudence to believe and conscientiously entertain an honest and strong suspicion that the person is guilty of a crime.

The term *probable cause* is used interchangeably with reasonable cause by courts throughout the country, except that the probable cause has been defined as supported by evidence that inclines the mind to believe but leaves room for doubt. It does not apply to evidence that would be admissible at a trial on the issue of guilt.

No method exists for determining what is reasonable cause. It depends completely on all the facts and circumstances of each case. Circumstances meriting great consideration include: Any delay that might make it possible for a guilty person to escape; the type and kind of information; the character of the informant; the extent of possible inquiry into the facts and circumstances; and many others. It is vitally important that there be reasonable cause before a search or an arrest is made. If it is absent, the results of the search will be held inadmissible by the courts.

ARREST BY PEACE OFFICERS WITH WARRANT

A warrant of arrest is a written order of a magistrate directed to a peace officer, commanding him to arrest a particular individual and bring him before such magistrate. In obedience to such a command, an officer has no liability and no cause of action shall arise against him. An officer with a warrant, *regular upon its face,* acts without malice and in the reasonable belief that the person arrested on the warrant is the same person referred to in the warrant.

The term *regular upon its face* is important to the officer. He necessarily must have knowledge of the procedure of securing a warrant, and of its form and content. The Supreme Court of the United States has stated that regularity is not to be determined on the basis of scrutiny by a trained legal mind, but that it is sufficient that the warrant upon its face has every appearance of validity in the judgment of an ordinarily intelligent, informed layman [1].

It must be explained further that when an officer serves a warrant he must act in good faith, take precautions to determine that the person about to be arrested is the party against whom the warrant is issued, and be alert to consider information given to him which might reveal that an error is being made. If the officer effects an arrest of the wrong person as a result of his own carelessness or malice, he is civilly liable.

A warrant is initiated by the filing of a written complaint with the county prosecutor. The *complaint,* like an *indictment* or *information,* is an accusatory pleading and it legally constitutes the formal charge to which the defendant must respond upon his arraignment before the magistrate who issued the warrant.

The complaint must contain the same allegations as are required for indictment and information. Criminal complaints frequently are made on the information and belief of the peace officer. This means that a criminal complaint may be issued in situations in which no one is available who possesses absolute knowledge or information on all the facts of the alleged offense. The oath, by the peace officer, on information and belief imparts that the complainant believes that the facts as alleged are true and founded upon information and knowledge which he has actually received.

A warrant may be issued by any magistrate. *Black's Law Dictionary* defines a magistrate as a person having power to issue a warrant for the arrest of a person charged with a specific offense. The term *magistrate* includes justices of the supreme and appellate courts, and judges of the superior, municipal, and justice courts. It is the duty of these justices and judges to issue a warrant of arrest for a person if they in fact are satisfied that the complainant has based his request for a warrant on reasonable information and knowledge that the person named in the warrant committed the crime for which the warrant is requested.

Whenever a judge of a justice or municipal court acts as a magistrate, he has county-wide jurisdiction and is not limited by the territorial jurisdiction of his particular court. It has been a convenient practice for many years for officers to file their felony complaints in the municipal court of the city or in the justice court of the district in which the alleged crime was perpetrated. A justice of the supreme court, whose court has only appellate jurisdiction, may act as a committing magistrate.

There are four special forms of warrants: (*a*) *coroner's warrant,* (*b*) *warrant on writ of habeas corpus,* (*c*) *bench warrant,* and (*d*) *warrant for bail jumper.* The coroner, throughout most of the United States, is thought of as a medical doctor whose task it is to determine the cause of death through examination of human remains. This is true in many areas. He may assume, however, three specific roles—physician, hearing officer, or peace officer. His role as physician has been discussed briefly. As a hearing officer, the coroner presides over inquests into the cause of death. If the coroner's jury, composed of citizens in the area, finds that the death of a person was caused by another under circumstances not excusable or justifiable by law, or that the death was the result of a criminal act by another, and if the subject committing the act is known and not in official custody, the coroner is required to issue a warrant for that person's arrest and detention. The coroner's role as a peace officer may be in the serving of the warrant he himself has issued.

A warrant is issued in lieu of a writ of habeas corpus when it appears to a judge or justice, authorized to issue a writ of habeas corpus, that a person is illegally incarcerated or under detention and may be removed from the jurisdiction of the court or be suffered irreparable injury. The warrant of arrest recites the facts and requires the sheriff, coroner, or constable of the county to bring such person forthwith before the court. In addition, the same warrant may command the apprehension and arrest of the individual responsible for the illegal incarceration or detention. Warrants of this type generally are issued by the court clerk, signed by the judge or justice, and without exception must bear the seal of the court.

To compel the appearance of a witness or the presence of a defendant before the court, a bench warrant is issued by the court clerk upon the direction of the magistrate commanding the appearance or by the magistrate at the request of the prosecuting attorney. If there is no court clerk, then the magistrate issues the warrant directly. These warrants are executed in the same manner and fashion as the warrant of arrest.

A warrant for a bail jumper may be obtained to protect the bondman's investment and a fugitive (on bail) who leaves the state may be arrested on such a warrant. In other words, a warrant for the arrest of such a fugitive can be obtained.

ARRESTS BY PRIVATE PERSONS

Various statutes throughout the United States cover arrests made by private persons. The legal statutes generally provide that a private person may arrest another (a) *for a public offense committed or attempted in his presence*, (b) *when the person has committed a felony although not in his presence*, and (c) *when a felony has in fact been committed, and he has reasonable cause for believing that the person arrested did in fact commit the felony*. It is not necessary that a *citizen's arrest* be accompanied by a warrant of arrest.

An offense is committed "in the presence" of a person when such person can testify to sufficient facts of his own knowledge to show that the offense in question has been committed. If an arrest is made for a crime committed in the presence of a person making the arrest, the powers of arrest possessed by a peace officer or private citizen are equal. The principal difference between the powers of arrest with and without a warrant is that the peace officer may make an arrest for a felony that in fact has not been committed *(reasonable cause)* and the private person may make an arrest only if the felony has been committed. Neither a peace officer nor an individual has the right to arrest without a warrant for a misdemeanor not committed in his presence. It is no justification, as it is in the case of a felony, to prove reasonable cause to believe that the offense has been committed. The only fact justifying such an arrest is that the person arrested in fact committed the offense in the presence of the arrestor.

An arrest for a misdemeanor must be made within a reasonable time. If the arrest is made after the occasion has passed, though committed in the presence of the person making the arrest, it is not justified. A continuous effort to make the arrest must be made by the arrestor. If, instead of making the arrest at the time the violation is committed in his presence, he goes about other matters unconnected with the arrest, the right to make the arrest without a warrant ceases. In this case, to make a valid arrest, a warrant of arrest must be sought.

When a private person makes an arrest, he must conform to the same rules that must be followed by peace officers when making an arrest. An arrest by a private person is made if he merely announces in a clear and audible voice that he is making a *citizen's arrest* even though he does not touch the arrestee or direct the action of a peace officer in detaining the arrestee.

The question often arises, "Can one arrested private person arrest another?" There is nothing in the legal statutes to indicate that the private person loses his privilege to arrest because he himself is under arrest. In a California case, the court said that a private person who is under arrest may arrest another and also that a private person may arrest a peace officer [2]. Opinions of the appellate courts are scarce in the area of lawful arrest. Until a legal statute or a court opinion states in the negative, it should be presumed that a private person who is under arrest may arrest another.

A peace officer has the duty to advise a private person of his powers to arrest and the officer is bound by law to take custody of a person arrested by a private person if the officer believes that the arrest is lawful. The officer should assist the private person with the arrest only when the person to be or being arrested resists such arrest. If the officer believes that the arrest is unlawful, he should so advise the private person, and if the private person continues, it then becomes the officer's duty to aid the person being unlawfully arrested, since a private person has the right to resist an unlawful arrest by another private person.

A private person who assists in the making of an arrest pursuant to the request, persuasion, or order of a peace officer is not liable for a suit for false imprisonment. The appellate courts have stated in the past that it is manifestly unfair to impose civil liability upon the private person for doing that which the varying statutes declare it a law violation for him to refuse to do.

A private person making an arrest is justified in killing a fleeing felon who cannot otherwise be taken, if he can prove that the person is actually guilty of the felony. Deadly force (serious injury or killing) may not be used in effecting a misdemeanor arrest.

For the purpose of protecting his property, the owner of property, in most jurisdictions, may restrain for a reasonable time and for the purpose of investigation one whom he has *reasonable and probable cause* to believe has interfered with or stolen his property. Physically resisting the lawful arrest by a private person is considered in most jurisdictions as the committing of an assault upon the arrestor who is acting in a lawful manner.

It should be kept in mind that resisting arrest by a private person and arrest made by a peace officer differ. A person who resists a peace officer may be guilty of resisting arrest *per se,* of which there are two definite classifications, felony and misdemeanor. Most legal statutes provide that a person may not resist an arrest, lawful or unlawful, made by a peace officer. A person being unlawfully arrested by a private person, however, may use force to resist such arrest. Any person making an arrest may take from the person arrested any offensive weapons that he may have about his person for the protection of himself and those about him. Such weapons must be delivered to the magistrate before whom the arrested person is taken.

A peace officer is not required to accept the custody of an arrested person by a private person if he does not believe the arrest is lawful. The deciding factor in determining the legality of an arrest is the competency of the arresting party. Competency should be seriously considered regarding three population groups:

1. *Children.* Age alone does not determine the competency of a child, therefore it appears that there is no age limit for the arresting person.

2. *Insane or mentally ill.* A peace officer in most cases should not take into custody a person who has been arrested by an insane or mentally ill person since the unstable person is incapable of rendering a sound decision and serving as a competent witness.
3. *Intoxicated persons.* An officer reasonably may assume the arrest to be unlawful if the person making the arrest is under the influence of alcohol or drugs for the same reasons given in group 2.

A vital point to remember is that when any person makes an arrest, he may orally summon as many persons as he deems necessary to aid him. A refusal to respond is morally wrong as well as a violation of law.

SPECIAL STATUTES AUTHORIZING ARREST WITHOUT WARRANT

Eight special statutes found throughout the United States provide for arrest without a warrant. In some states, all eight will be found in the state statutes, whereas in others only a few will be found. Because of the various treatments by the states in the use of the laws, they will be only briefly discussed here.

A magistrate is authorized to order any peace officer or private person to arrest anyone committing or attempting to commit an offense in his presence.

The Uniform Fresh Pursuit Act authorizes that peace officers of one or more states may enter another state in fresh pursuit of a person wanted for a felony in the other state and that they may arrest without a warrant. Their authority is the same as that of peace officers in the state in which the arrest is made. Their arrestees must be taken before a magistrate who is required to determine the legality of the arrest. The magistrate may commit the arrestee for a reasonable time to await extradition.

A felony fugitive or escapee can be arrested at any time or place, and county jail "walk-aways" can be retaken without a warrant.

A bail bondsman or other person who has posted bail with a court for the release of a defendant can arrest without a warrant the defendant for the sole purpose of returning him to custody. A person of suitable age and discretion can be empowered by the bondsman or other person to act in his place. There is, however, one exception. When the fugitive is from another state, a warrant of arrest is required.

Unlawful assembly statutes require that peace officers, city officials, and certain others order persons unlawfully or riotously assembled to disburse. Failure to do so is a criminal violation.

A probationer reasonably believed to have violated the court's terms of his probation may be arrested by a probation officer or peace officer, returned to custody, and produced before the court which granted the defendant his probation.

Another special statute provides that a parolee who leaves the state of his parole, violates the conditions of his parole, or whose parole is suspended or revoked by the granting authority is considered an escaped prisoner and as such can be arrested at any time and any place without a warrant.

Finally, a defendant who is released by a magistrate on his own recognizance can be ordered arrested and returned to custody if he fails to give security or bail if required by the magistrate, or if he fails to appear upon a grand jury indictment or on information filed by the prosecuting attorney charging a felony.

ARREST TECHNIQUES

This section attempts to convey an understanding of the principles and methods pertinent to making both felony and misdemeanor arrests under the various circumstances that will face the officer during every new tour of duty.

The application of "common sense" to the police function in the performance of the everyday duties, particularly in the arrest function, is vital to the accomplishment of the total police purpose. A peril facing every officer is the danger of allowing routine duty to become perfunctory; the subsequent lowering of defenses endangers the officer's life. Arrest can never be routine. An officer with a perfect safety record may be lulled into complacency and may fail to heed warnings and special instructions.

There are arguments for and against the basic suggested methods of arrest. The most practical and proven methods will be recommended, however, for the consideration of the student or new officer.

HUMAN FACTORS

Seven human factors are considered to be the fundamentals to be applied to all types of arrest.

Confidence

Confidence is a prime human factor. An officer's confidence must be accompanied with the ability to act, to be alert and ready to react to any emergency. "To venture is to risk anxiety, but not to venture is to lose yourself," said the Danish philosopher Sören Kierkegaard. Fear is a natural feeling, but one must function in spite of it. An old saying is, "When a brave man encounters fear he admits it, and goes on despite it." An officer, in order to maintain his confidence, must cultivate an attitude of certainty and caution without allowing fear to incapacitate him.

Never underestimate a criminal suspect. A suspect person is usually able to tell if an officer is not confident, and it is even easier to spot an officer who displays overconfidence. Either extreme is dangerous, and an officer should always be alert to these dangers in himself.

Knowledge of the Job

Knowledge of the job, of course, is vital to the successful performance of the police purpose. This knowledge consists of knowing and being able to apply the laws of arrest, search, seizure, and fresh pursuit. For the self-protection and preservation of himself and those about him, the officer must know offensive and defensive tactics, how to provide security and transportation of prisoners, and when the arrest has been completed.

Personality

Personality of the officer also plays a role in the arrest procedure. The task of arrest should be made as easy as possible for all concerned—the arresting officer, his fellow officers, and the person being arrested. Every effort should be made to prevent a clash of personalities. Control of the situation should be maintained at all times. Pleasantness, firmness, and the reflection of confidence and ability should be evidenced by the officer in charge. The officer must be able to sell himself and his job to be effective in his duties.

To become too personally involved, however, is a mistake. An arrest should never become a personal vendetta. Personal feelings should never enter into any arrest, even for the murder of a brother officer. This may appear to be too impersonal, but it should be kept in mind that the officer is a public servant who has the obligation to treat all persons fairly and equally under the law.

Psychology

Systematic knowledge about mental processes and the science of behavior is necessary for the peace officer who constantly deals with human behavior. Initially, however, the officer must be in full command of his own behavior and emotions before he begins to deal with the behavior and emotions of others. When making an arrest, the officer should make every effort to overcome any objection to the arrest by the arrestee and encourage his cooperation. A good rule to remember is "gain advantage of the suspect before he turns the tables."

The peace officer must employ certain routine methods based on experience and training when making an arrest. In the performance of these techniques, he must have humility and sensitivity to the feelings of victims, witnesses, family of arrestee, the arrestee, and the general public.

When making an arrest, a peace officer should never be overtolerant of any situation that is occurring or that is about to occur. If he is overtolerant, he may lose any advantage he may have had, and subsequently he may lose complete control of the situation. Regaining control of the situation is much more difficult than maintaining that control in the first place.

In some instances it may be necessary for an officer to jeopardize his own safety to rescue a victim, to protect a witness, or to protect a suspect from a mob until he can be removed from the crime scene and taken to police headquarters. This the officer does because of the public trust and obligation placed on him by the community he serves. The circumstances of each arrest dictate the method to be used in accomplishing the task. Planning the arrest is vital, however, and the officer should think ahead. It has been said, "People don't plan to fail—they just fail to plan." An officer's planning must be flexible as to method and there should be at least one alternate method open and available to him and those assisting him.

The reputation of the suspect, if known, is important to a peace officer and will assist him in making decisions and plans as to how he should effect the person's arrest. The officer should ask himself:

1. How will the subject react to arrest?
2. What is the suspect's prior criminal record?
3. What other charges are outstanding on this person?
4. Is he a drug addict?
5. What is the person's general reputation in the area?
6. Is the person awaiting adjudication on a pending criminal court case?
7. Is he mentally stable?

After gaining answers to all of these questions, the officer is in a good position to plan and accomplish the arrest of the person, providing the necessary safeguards wherever applicable.

Human Failures

Human failures should be kept in mind when considering the fundamentals of arrest. Lack of knowledge, lack of ability, and failure to use common sense and think ahead are pertinent factors of human failure.

Sympathy for the arrestee should be evidenced with great caution. A suspect under arrest will play upon any obvious manifestation of sympathy and will make every effort to work it to his own advantage. The suspect should be kept under control and constant observation. A favor should never be granted to, or sought from, anyone even remotely connected with the investigation. A good rule to remember is *never make promises unless it is within your power to fulfill them*. A promise made requires an honest and forthright effort to fulfill it.

ARRESTS WITH WARRANTS

Intelligent risk-taking has nothing to do with bravado and foolhardiness, or with impulse and dumb luck. The constructive risk is always based on fact and preparation, and guided by reason [3].

When the law enforcement officer has in his possession a warrant of arrest, and in some cases when he does not, there often is enough time for preliminary investigation of the reported physical and geographical location of the suspect. It would also be advantageous to "check out the suspect" through the police record bureau. Normally, there should be little reason why the arrest could not be planned in minute detail to give the law enforcement officer and his assisting officers the maximum advantage in successfully apprehending the suspect.

"Act or be acted upon," Brigham Young admonished the Mormons who headed west toward the Utah desert. This same choice is faced by the peace officer every day of his life. The officer who is in charge of an arrest operation should keep this in mind, and he should consider the following brief discussion of the details of arrest procedure.

Most important, consideration should be given to sufficient manpower.

Unless it is an emergency, one man alone should never make an arrest. As many officers as are determined to be necessary to execute the job should be assigned and the officers should be stationed so as to ensure complete and maximum coverage. The suspect should always be assumed to be dangerous and the officers' maintenance of full control of the situation is vital until the task is completed and the prisoner is taken to jail.

It is a wise man who assumes that the suspect is armed. In order to discourage a suspect from using weapons he may have on or about his person, an immediate display of the superiority of firearms often has a definite psychological advantage. Thus a suspect may surrender to arrest in a less violent manner than would be possible if he were allowed to gain the advantage. A person who knows he is wanted by the police may be fully prepared to resist arrest; therefore, the police firepower should be carefully planned and the exact location of all firearms should be designated for maximum effectiveness, should it be necessary to use them.

A successful apprehension does not, by any means, require an elaborate plan. Simplicity of method is the key to success. The plan should be exact but simple, and it should provide flexibility. In addition to the operational plan, an alternate plan should be formulated. The officer in charge should anticipate emergencies that might arise after the original or alternate plan has been effected. So that all personnel function correctly in making the arrest, the plan should be completely understood by all persons concerned.

Even the simplest of plans should provide for the coordinated movement of officers and equipment into position quickly and quietly. Positioning the participating officers should be planned very carefully for the following three reasons: (a) To avoid crossfire, should it be necessary to activate weapons, (b) to provide cover for the advance guard, and (c) to provide maximum efficiency.

Preparation of, and provision for, maximum protection for officers and citizens through concealment is also an important factor in developing the plan. The plan should incorporate maximum efficiency and minimum danger. If entry to a building or dwelling is necessary, coverage should be given to the officers making the entry; all entrances and exits also should be covered to prevent the suspect's escape. All positions should be maintained until ordered abandoned.

When the arrest is about to be made, the employment of surprise and speed will prove most advantageous to overcome any possible defense preparations by the suspect. The value of surprise is that the suspect is caught off guard and is less likely to be violent. Most important, however, there is less likelihood of injury to any person present. Coordination of movements is necessary and provides the key to an effective surprise and an uneventful apprehension.

A warrant is complete justification for a law enforcement officer to arrest the person named therein. The officer is merely carrying out the order of a magistrate who has commanded the officer to bring the person named before him. The burden of proof that the arrestee is the right person rests with the officer.

When making an arrest with a warrant, the officer has the right to use only that amount of force that is actually necessary to effect the arrest and overcome resistance to it. Of course, the right of self-protection is evident.

ARRESTS WITHOUT WARRANTS

Arrests made without warrants for crimes committed in the presence of the officer, or with reasonable cause, have been discussed. The previously discussed seven human factors that are fundamental to any arrest should be kept in mind here.

An arrest without a warrant adds danger factors that must be considered because it is not possible to conduct a definite prearrest investigation. It is often necessary to take an intelligent risk on split-second timing. General Omar N. Bradley, former chief of staff of the U.S. Army, points out, "A second-best decision quickly made and vigorously carried out is better than the best decision too late arrived at and half-heartedly carried out."

In arresting without a warrant, the officer will have little or no knowledge of the character, reputation, or prior activities of the person to be arrested. The attitude that arrests for minor violations are not important and can be conducted in a routine manner is both ridiculous and senseless. Such attitudes have cost the lives of many officers. It is impossible, of course, to be prepared for every eventuality, but each serious injury or death can be used as a learning situation to prevent such casualties from ever happening again. Every arrest is important. In addition, knowledge of the job, a serious attitude toward the responsibility entrusted to the officer, willingness to make changes of methods, the following of departmental rules and regulations, adequate training, and the use of good "common sense" will aid further in alleviating danger factors.

The phrase "police brutality" is not new. Unfortunately, during the past few years the phrase has resounded throughout the country. This was espe-

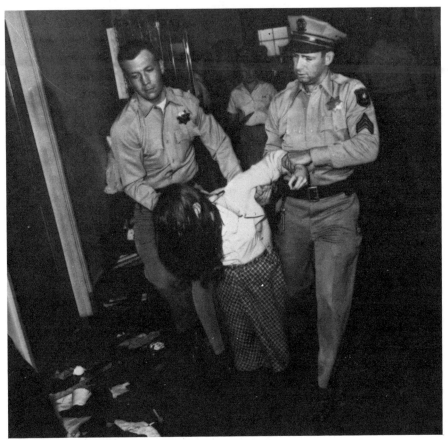

FIGURE 15.2.   *Police officers sometimes encounter difficult circumstances in making arrest and must force unwilling and resisting suspects to accompany them. Courtesy Police Department, Berkeley, Ca.*

cially true during the civil rights riots of the summer and fall of 1964 and during the Democratic convention in Chicago in 1968. These accusations of "police brutality" were leveled at policemen who attempted to quell the riots in the Southern states and New York soon after the Civil Rights Act of 1964 was passed by the United States Congress in July, 1964, and during the Democratic convention riots on the streets of Chicago in the summer of 1968. To prevent these accusations from having any foundation in fact, more and more law enforcement agencies throughout the country are upgrading their entrance requirements for new recruits and are requiring their applicants to take a battery of psychological tests to determine their suitability to law enforcement as a career. It is true that in many cases the charge of "police brutality" has little or no basis in fact and is used to denigrate the officer and maliciously belittle the man who is trying to perform his duty within the law of protecting the life, limb, and property of the citizens of this country. Nevertheless, some of these charges are legitimate and the profession must pursue every avenue to eliminate the problem.

An accusation of "police brutality" should never deter the officer from proceeding with his duties. This includes the duty to make arrests with a minimum amount of force when the need for it occurs.

The brutality charge is a legitimate one when too much force or uncalled-for actions are brought into play by an arresting officer or when a citizen is manhandled by an officer without making an arrest. An officer conducting himself in such a manner is hurting the police image and is committing professional suicide. It is generally held that there is a very thin line separating "all the force necessary to effect arrest" from "too much force used to effect an arrest."

Whenever force is necessary, the officer should be well prepared and should exert the necessary force in as short a time as possible. Such handling of the situation is better for public relations and for the officer, because it is less tiring, less time-consuming, and less damaging to the officer and his equipment.

PROPER METHODS OF APPROACH

On Street

The solo peace officer must be constantly on guard for his own safety and that of those around him. This is especially true when an officer makes an approach to a person on the street for field interrogation or arrest. In advance, the officer should select the place to approach the suspect; he should look for a place that will provide the fewest avenues of escape. The person may be "wanted" or a "fugitive from justice." A good location for field interrogation or arrest is in the middle of a block, close to building walls but not adjacent to doorways. After making the selection, the officer working alone should approach the person from the rear and to his right side in a casual manner, being alert for any furtive action. Since most people are right-handed, approaching from the rear and to the right side gives the officer immediate defensive control of any situation in which he might find himself. In addition, the officer's firearm is protected from and out of the reach of the suspect. When contact is made, it should be friendly, face to face, and in a casual manner until such time as the officer is ready to terminate the interrogation or make the arrest.

If two officers are working together, the approach also may be from the rear but toward both sides of the person; or from the front and rear of the person. The method chosen, of course, should be predetermined by the two officers, and should be the most feasible method for the occasion.

If more than two suspects are to be stopped, it is important to separate them as soon as the contact has been established. This procedure will minimize the likelihood of coordinated assault upon the officers, and the suspects will not have time to establish the same or similar alibis.

In Residence or Building

Peace officers approaching and making contact with suspect persons in a residence or building do so in such cases as *fresh pursuit* from a crime scene or when officers are in possession of information and have established that a suspect is located inside a building. In most situations, it is necessary to force entry into such structures in order to arrest the suspect. Situations differ in that the officer may be acting upon *reasonable cause* or pursuant to a felony or search warrant when making entry. Prior to entering, officers must identify themselves and request admittance. If denied, forced entry then may be made. Rules governing inadmissible evidence in court often make it difficult if not impossible to obtain convictions in such instances. For example:

> Narcotics-squad detectives, armed with a search warrant, are set to raid a house believed to be the headquarters of a heroin ring. Now comes the legally crucial formality that has helped reduce the number of narcotics convictions in many areas. The formality, decreed by the courts, is known as the "knock, knock rule." Before entering the suspect premises, officers must announce who they are, what their authority is and what they want. "If you break down a door without enough shouting and waiting to establish resistance on the part of the suspects," as one detective put it, "your case will go out the courtroom window. If you do bang and shout long enough, your evidence will go out the window right away—or down a toilet, or into an incinerator. These things happen all the time" [4].

Whether entry is gained pursuant to request or forced after denial, there must be adequate cover and protection given to those officers making entry. The same procedures should be followed as outlined previously with reference to making arrests with a warrant. Every precaution should be made to protect innocent parties and brother officers at the scene. It is incumbent upon each officer to aid his fellow officers, to be responsible for their safety and his own, and to avoid being cornered by a suspect who is attempting to flee and who is in a vehement state of mind. Upon contact and during and after arrest, the "human factors" play an important role and should be used to facilitate the success of the entire operation.

In Vehicle

Before halting any suspect vehicle, peace officers (two-man car) should observe the vehicle and its occupants for a few minutes to determine the demeanor of the occupants. At the same time, the driver of the police vehicle should select a location to make the stop which has the least number of avenues of escape, will not be a hazard to traffic, and is in an area not highly populated. The latter is desirable to avoid attracting a crowd that could possibly come to the aid of the suspect and place the officers in a dangerous position. When the officers are in position, the driver should turn on the red lights and sound horn of the police vehicle to attract the attention of suspect persons to be stopped. The passenger officer, in the meantime, should have radioed police communications, advising them as to the location of the stop; the make, model, year, and license number of the vehicle; and the number and brief descriptions of the suspect persons. As the suspect vehicle is rolling to a stop as previously directed, and if it is at night, the police spotlight should be directed into the interior of the suspect vehicle to illuminate the occupants and blind their view of the officers. The passenger officer by this time should be in a covering position to the right rear of the suspect vehicle. The driver officer next should begin his approach in a cautious manner to the driver's side of the suspect vehicle. Upon reaching the vehicle, it is best for the officer driver to stand in such a position as to force the occupants on the left side of the vehicle to look back over their left shoulders in order to see him. The officers then will instruct the suspect persons to leave the vehicle from whichever side is best suited to the situation and location. As the suspect persons come out of the vehicle, they should be ordered into position for a search for weapons.

The foregoing brief description of approaching suspect persons in a vehicle may be used by one officer working alone, with the admonition to use an extra measure of caution and to request a back-up unit to assist with the arrest or questioning.

FIGURE 15.3. *Police patrol officers conduct a vehicle stop and place suspects in a disadvantaged position to provide for their safety while conducting a vehicle search. Notice both suspects have been required to place their hands where the officers may see them at all times. Courtesy Police Department, Berkeley, Ca.*

If a suspect is going to take any offensive action, he usually will make his move either before he is placed under arrest or while he is in the process of being arrested.

A peace officer may save himself both grief and hardship if he will be alert in all situations to the demeanor of the suspect. Briefly, the officer might ask himself these questions in regard to the suspect person: *Is he belligerent? Is he relaxed and not at all worried about the prospect of going to jail? Does he show any evidence of shifting feet or is he moving his eyes around looking for a possible avenue of escape?* Keeping alert at all times while treating the suspect with respect and courtesy is a good procedure. For the officer's safety and well-being, as well as those about him, a search of a suspect should always be conducted for the possible possession of some offensive weapon.

SPECIAL PROBLEMS

Constitutional Rights

The law enforcement philosophy expressed in Chapter Three recognized a general distinction between *apprehending* law violators and *punishing* law violators. Although both the police and the courts share a mutual responsibility of *preventing* law violations, the police apprehend the violators whereas the courts punish or otherwise dispose of cases involving accused persons. Various U.S. Supreme Court decisions in recent years, however, make this philosophical distinction between police and court more difficult to incorporate in practical law enforcement matters. Distinguishing between these philosophical functions has been difficult in that the court has undertaken not only rulings that judge the court's function but also rulings that judge the police function. Much of the basis of the increasing Supreme Court assessment of police practice is the fourth, fifth, and sixth constitutional amendments and, to some degree, the ninth amendment. Additionally, they have given a good deal of attention to the *due process* clause of the fourteenth amendment. The implications of the fourth amendment to the police function have received more than adequate concern in the literature [5]. Nonetheless, a brief review of the highlights of the more significant court decisions may serve to clarify this.

In 1914, the U.S. Supreme Court ruled in the *Weeks* v. *United States* case that a federal court could not accept evidence that was obtained in violation of "search and seizure" protection guaranteed by the fourth amendment. In 1963, the Supreme Court·ruled on the appeal case of *Gideon* v. *Wainwright.* The effect of this ruling, based on the sixth amendment, was that new trials could be demanded by anyone convicted of crime without legal counsel. Moving closer to the function of police, in 1964, a decision was handed down in the case of *Escobedo* v. *Illinois.* This decision, based also on the sixth amendment and with a vote of 5–4 majority, secured the constitutional right of an indigent to be provided with legal counsel at the time of police interrogation. In June of 1966, again by a 5–4 majority, the court ruled on the case of *Miranda* v. *Arizona.* The "Miranda Decision" based on the fifth and sixth amendments, had the effect of providing legal counsel for persons suspected of crimes during police questioning. In 1968, the case of *Terry* v. *Ohio,* the Supreme Court defined a "stop" as opposed to an arrest, and a "frisk" as opposed to a search, and ruled that the idea of "protective search" by police officers is a lawful technique. In 1970, the United States

Supreme Court ruled in the case of *Chimel* v. *California* that the scope of a search incidental to an arrest to the person of the arrestee and the area within his immediate control, and within which he might reach a weapon, or reach and destroy evidence, would be all that would be permitted. This case essentially ruled that law enforcement must, whenever practical, obtain prior judicial approval of searches and seizures which necessarily requires that a search warrant be issued. Since this and the previous rulings have been made on the basis of constitutional rights, law enforcement has found itself compelled to regard many traditional investigative methods as unconstitutional. If constitutional rights are violated by certain heretofore accepted and practiced police methods, the question becomes one of alternate approaches.

As alternate methods of retaining efficiency, the literature has offered many fine proposals well worth consideration. Of course, any of the proposals no doubt would improve the effectiveness of police attempting to function within the legal framework currently in existence. To many agencies, however, such proposals are somewhat remote as prospects. For many agencies, increasing the size of their department, like obtaining funds for training and equipment, is beyond the average enforcement budget potential of many police agencies. However, this situation has been somewhat alleviated in more recent years with financial support and encouragement from the Law Enforcement Assistance Administration of the U.S. Department of Justice. This agency, acting under the authority of the Omnibus Crime Bill of 1968, has provided law enforcement and the entire criminal justice system with new avenues of development that never before would have been possible. The assistance provided by the agency has been largely that of financial support, but the agency has also provided outstanding leadership and qualified technicians to assist the many agencies that comprise the criminal justice system.

More readily available for prompt use, however, are proposals such as developing effective treatment of juvenile offenders, more meaningful adult court sentences, increasing police morale, and arousing public interest. But regardless of how available proposals of this type are for prompt use, they nevertheless tend to become complicated through the lack of agreement on methods of implementation. For instance, treatment of juveniles beyond proper police methods or procedures discussed elsewhere in this text, becomes a matter for juvenile courts rather than police. Treatment, rehabilitation and "sentencing" are matters better left to the juvenile court. The sentencing of adults similarly is removed from police control. And the very removal of treatment methods from police control in some instances further complicates morale problems beyond the difficulties previously discussed. This brings up the final proposal: Arouse public interest.

Public support has been presented throughout this book as a primary police goal. Now, in the context of retaining police efficiency within the context of increasing concern for constitutional rights, public support is presented as absolutely imperative. Great philosophical differences divide police thinking on the correctional treatment of both juveniles and adult offenders—at least in terms of reducing crime or increasing police efficiency. And yet police thinking, regardless of how divided, should be a significant consideration in the determination of appropriate correctional treatment of both juveniles and adults. Public support of police, as such support presents itself through the laws passed by the legislatures, brings police thinking to bear on the treatment process. The court's administration of correctional treatment functions, after all, by law. And most if not all courts would welcome *enlightened* legislation more squarely aligning law enforcement with correctional treatment—enlightenment of course stemming from the sophisticated research that an aroused public can generate.

All things being equal in terms of the problems presented in Chapter Nine, police morale under conditions of public support would appear assured of improvement. And with respect to police morale, it may well be that public support goes beyond the obvious legislative influence and comes to bear on the proposals of larger departments and better equipment and training—considerations of major importance to police morale.

The role of human relations has become crucial in this "era of constitutional rights."

Selected Problems

A number of problems confront police agencies which are special not because they are unique but rather because of the unique manner in which they combine with other problems. A brief mention of a few such problems may prove helpful.

One problem confronting any department with growth potential is the question of *specialization.* How large the department becomes often determines how long a policy remains for "all men to perform all duties." Patrol, traffic, identification, and detective work may be either broad specialties or promotional considerations. But narcotic investigations, vice-squad activities, specialized records, and criminalistics including fingerprinting usually evolve into specialties as the department grows.

Frequently, *training* becomes another problem affecting specialization. The funds available usually determine how far training can go "beyond the pistol range" as well as often determining the educational background of candidates. And since the educational background of candidates tends to dictate the need for most forms of police training, *recruitment* of candidates with good educational background is frequently a special problem.

Related to training and educational background of candidates is the problem of good police reports and good records. In spite of constant improvements in central, federal, and state record systems, most police agencies depend on local record information to deal successfully with routine (often domestic and juvenile) law enforcement problems that differ from criminal investigations.

An additional problem dealt with universally by police agencies is the female offender. The differential treatment given "the weaker sex" until recently has escaped satisfactory examination in the literature. An introductory textbook, however, is hardly the place to correct this deficiency in the literature, particularly since recent works are very definitive and comprehensive [6].

SUMMARY

The legal procedure that must be strictly adhered to in any arrest and the various techniques of taking a suspect into custody are vital to every police officer sworn to enforce the law equally among all men. In the accomplishment of the physical arrest, it often is necessary to use force, yet a peace officer must carry out his arrest and restraint of a suspect within the framework of the law and in compliance with the edicts which have been handed down to him by appellate court decisions called *case law*.

What persons are exempt from both civil and criminal arrest, what the requirements are for an arrest with and without a warrant along with the types of warrants, who may issue them and who may carry them out are important facts to every peace officer and should be considered part of his fundamental knowledge. In addition to these, the peace officer must know his role in the arrest, as legally authorized under certain conditions, by a private person of another.

Discussed at length in the chapter were *seven human factors* pertinent to the arrest procedure. The procedure in making arrests in most jurisdictions with or without a warrant varies somewhat in legal procedure and in the necessary groundwork before the actual arrest is consummated.

This chapter discussed constitutional rights in terms of recent Supreme Court rulings that affect police work. Police methods that jeopardize constitutional rights are unacceptable. But in instances where concern for constitutional rights affect law enforcement effectiveness, alternate methods of maintaining police efficiency must be adopted. Various proposals geared to creating the needed increase in effectiveness are presented with continuing emphasis given the value of *public support.*

ANNOTATED REFERENCES

Applegate, R., *Kill or Get Killed,* Stackpole, Harrisburg, Pa., 1961. A good reference on self-protection and most effective procedures in handling criminal suspects.

Fricke, C. W., and A. L. Alarcon, *California Criminal Law,* 9th ed., Legal Book Store, Los Angeles, 1965. An excellent reference on California law and its provisions; explanations in easy-to-understand language.

Hall, Livingston, and Y. Kamisor, *Modern Criminal Procedure,* 2nd ed., West, St. Paul, Minn., 1966. An excellent reference of correct procedure, legal terms, definitions, and implications, applicable to all systems of justice in the United States.

Kerper, H. B., *Introduction to the Criminal Justice System,* West, St. Paul, Minn., 1972.

LaFave, W. R., *Arrest,* Little, Brown, Boston, 1965. An outstanding discussion on the subject of arrest and its varied ramifications throughout the United States. This reference is a must for every student and law-enforcement officer.

Weston, P. B., and K. M. Wells, *The Administration of Justice,* 2nd ed., Prentice–Hall, Englewood Cliffs, N.J., 1973.

NOTES

1. *Vallindras* v. *Massachusetts etc. Ins. Co.,* 42 Cal. 2d 149, 265 P. 2d 907 (1954).
2. *Lorenz* v. *Hunt,* 89 Cal. App. 6, 1967.
3. J. K. Lagemann, "Rewards of Risking It," *Christian Herald,* January 1967.
4. F. Sondern, Jr., "Take the Handcuffs Off Our Police!" *Readers Digest,* Vol. 87, No. 508, Sept. 1964.

5. E. L. Barrett, "Personal Rights, Property Rights and the Fourth Amendment," *1960 Supreme Court Review,* Chicago Univ. Press, Chicago, 1961, p. 65. See also C. R. Sowle (ed.), *Police Power and Individual Freedom,* Thomas, Springfield, Ill., 1962; and W. H. Parker, "Birds Without Wings," *The Police Yearbook,* International Chiefs of Police, Washington, D.C., 1965.

6. T. C. Esselstyn (ed.), *The Female Offender,* Spartan Bookstore, San Jose State College, San Jose, Ca., 1966; R. Ruskin, *An Investigation of the Police and the Female Offender,* Spartan Bookstore, San Jose State College, San Jose, Ca., 1966.

CHAPTER SIXTEEN

Crime Prevention

The three preceding chapters have dealt with what crime "is" and *one thing* that police can do about crime: Control crime by making arrests. This chapter deals with another thing that can be done about crime: Attempt to prevent it.

Of course not *all* crime is preventable, but certainly it is possible to prevent *some* crimes. And being able to prevent *any* crime on a systematic basis probably begins with understanding the nature of police *priorities.* Consider the following quotation:

Every year, in cities all over America, a small number of policemen are presented medals for outstanding achievement, often for shooting it out with an armed and dangerous robber. To the police and most Americans, these medals and the indisputably brave deeds they stand for are the sum of law and order [1].

In terms of police priorities, consider the implications of the phrase in this quotation, *"sum* of law and order." Whether the implications of such a comment are accurate, this chapter will cover many areas in which law and order *can* be "expanded"—expanded to encompass the prevention of crime.

PREVENTION AS A CONCEPT

Lejins delineates a clear distinction between the *control* of crime and the *prevention* of crime: "Prevention is a measure taken *before* a criminal or

373

delinquent act has actually occurred for the purpose of forestalling such an act; control is a measure taken *after* a criminal or delinquent act has been committed. Both prevention and control should be viewed as sub-categories of society's negative attitude and action against crime and delinquency" [2].

In this context, routine police activities discussed throughout this volume can be judged in a given circumstance as *either* preventive *or* controlling, depending upon the particular circumstance.

But *prevention* on a priority basis suggests a far greater commitment to the "measures taken before a criminal or delinquent act" [3]. In this regard, Lejins goes on to present three major "types" of prevention: (*a*) "Punitive prevention," (*b*) "corrective prevention," and (*c*) "mechanical prevention" [4].

1. *Punitive prevention* is, theoretically, at least part of the rationale for criminal sanctions. Fear of punishment is presumed to prevent the individual from committing a crime. As more and more becomes known about the human behavior discussed in Chapter Five (criminal behavior), more and more recognition is given the reality that punishment may prevent *some* individuals from committing *some* crimes.
2. *Corrective prevention* is, again theoretically, an effort to eliminate influences toward criminal behavior. These influences may be economic, sociological, psychological, political, perceptual, or in the thinking of a number of contemporary writers, a combination of all these considerations inside certain social institutions that make up a broad definition of the environment [5].
3. *Mechanical prevention* is the type that involves fences, locks, guards, lighting, alarms, and a host of other "physical" efforts to prevent crime from occurring "in the first place."

Each of these three types of prevention form a major part of the *concept* of *preventing* crime—a concept distinctly different from the concept of *controlling* crime. *And even though the very nature of the police function relates primarily to the "punitive prevention" category, all three categories will nonetheless be discussed as conceptually appropriate for police.*

POLICE AND CRIME PREVENTION

The first type of prevention to be considered is the type defined as *punitive prevention.* With the particular emphasis on use of such a term in the *technical* and *theoretical* sense, only brief comment is required. The brevity of the discussion relates primarily to the fact that virtually all police procedures are designed, in part, to symbolize the potential of a negative or "punishing" experience from law violations.

As already noted, however, it may be that the "threat" of punishment may prevent *some* individuals from committing *some* crimes, but by no means prevent all individuals from committing criminal acts. In this regard, consider the following [6]:

> Although there are some that argue that tolerating any form of law violation serves as an encouragement of other forms of antisocial or criminal behavior by the violators, some research in this area suggests precisely the opposite. A series of studies of approximately 300 young Black people who engaged in a series of acts of civil disobedience were undertaken in a western city. On the basis of their observations, the author concluded: "There have been virtually no manifestations of delinquency or antisocial behavior, no school drop-outs, and no known illegitimate pregnancies. This is a remarkable record for any group of teen-age children of any color in any community." . . . The evidence is insufficient to demonstrate that acts of civil disobedience of the more limited kind inevitably lead to an increased disrespect for law or propensity towards crime. In fact, some experts have argued that engaging in disciplining civil disobedience allows people to channel resentment into constructive paths, thereby reducing the propensity for engaging in antisocial behavior. . . . Disobedience to law does not appear to adversely affect the attitudes of the people who engage in it. . . . For such conduct does have a serious adverse effect both upon other people in the society, and most importantly of all, upon the system of laws which society must inevitably depend. . . .

It is hopefully clear that the implications of this commentary go far beyond the "simple civil disobedience" cited. Put in the context of *punitive prevention,* then, another way of saying the same thing is to note that even though "fear of consequences" may not seem to deter *some* individuals from *some* crimes, this does *not* establish a rationale for abandoning the vital "preventive" function that police serve in this regard generally.

The grossly oversimplified arguments to the contrary are usually articulated by those who *expect* police to respond and use whatever authority is required when "other laws" are being violated—particularly when the other laws that are violated happen to be against the person of one of those who argue against the *punitive prevention* function of police.

This facet of crime prevention, overlapping heavily into crime control as it does, is extremely significant even though not elaborated in depth at this point—not elaborated because virtually *all* police activities in some way relate to this type of crime prevention.

FIGURE 16.1. *Peaceful demonstration should not be discouraged by police. This does not mean, however, that nonpeaceful demonstrations should be tolerated. Courtesy Police Department, San Francisco, Ca.*

Police and Corrective Prevention

In many ways, the discussion of police-community relations that will follow later in Chapter Eighteen encompasses much of what is being referred to in this chapter as *corrective prevention*. This is true if for no other reason than the economic, sociological, psychological, and political influences already mentioned tend to *form* the community to which police "relate."

But including this broader definition of crime prevention within police role is by no means easy to *do,* even though it is relatively easy to *say* [7]:

Throughout history those finding themselves in the role of police have tended to think of their work in terms of either apprehending or in some other way dealing with criminals. Although the complexity of modern law has increased the proportion of individuals who technically be labeled "criminal," the police tend to see their role as it relates to law violation—particularly police who define their duties as *law enforcement.* Certainly no valid criticism can be leveled at such a tendency. But . . . certainly there is indicated a substantial broadening of the police role to include not only control of crime, but influence over the disruptive tensions in the changing society as well.

The basis of the need for this role expansion is extremely complex and the subject of an entire volume [8]. But in relatively simple terms, consider the following [9]:

The problems of crime control, in general, and law enforcement in particular, are always related to changes in the social scene. The dimensions and substance of community life are undergoing such wholesale and radical transformation in our time that it behooves us to pause and reflect upon the influences that are sharply modifying the conditions in contemporary community life and posing new problems for the agencies of law enforcement.

There are basic changes going forward in the community, and these are transforming the problems which confront law enforcement officials. . . . If there are those in America who expect groups in our society to act differently than they currently do, they should realize that this will happen only if the necessary conditions come about. The view law enforcement has of minority groups is a necessary condition of the attitude these groups take toward law enforcement. And if law enforcement sees them only as persons who are troublesome and difficult and have shortcomings, without reference to the conditions which have formed their behavior, then police officers will not be disposed to act in such ways as to invite any kind of response other than hostility, anger, and indeed, outright violence.

As the implications of the above citations suggest, attempting to condense so complex a subject into a single chapter as one of many principles of law enforcement leaves a great deal more unsaid than said—particularly in this specific area of expanding police role. And yet a great deal is being said in the above citation. For one thing, the obvious yet frequently overlooked observation is made that law enforcement is "always related to change in the social scene."

For another thing, the conspicuous problems of "change *per se*" is related to the not so conspicuous problem of "attitude"—both police and public attitude. These two considerations alone afford ample conceptual approach to considering police "strategies" to *corrective prevention*.

Amos and Wellford suggest seven categories of prevention, one of which is *directly* related to police [10]:

1. Prevention through the family.
2. Prevention through religion.
3. Prevention through the school.
4. Prevention through recreation.
5. Prevention through the economic structure.
6. Prevention through the police.
7. Prevention through the judicial process.

Obviously, some of these categories have activities more related to *punitive prevention* than to *corrective prevention*. Also obviously, some categories are even more involved in *control* of crime than *prevention* of crime. Not quite so obviously, however, *all seven* categories could be a part of a master police strategy to adopt programs of *corrective prevention*—simply a matter of police initiative.

To greater or lesser degree, police are already involved in each of all of the categories. By building constructive programs around the area of involvement, a strategy for *corrective prevention* can get underway.

And it matters not whether the particular area of a given involvement is necessarily "crime related." Even minimal police participation in the service clubs of local businessmen can, in such areas as cooperation on recreational needs, develop a powerful influence in a given local jurisdiction. Collaboration with social agencies or religious groups that serve families that have frequent law enforcement contact has "obvious yield" but perhaps no more than the yield available through collaboration with the probation agency serving the judicial process. And so it could go.

Corrective prevention, insofar as police involvement is concerned, might be summed up as follows [11]:

. . . Human relations has been defined in terms of the goal: "police participation in any activity that seeks law observance through respect other than enforcement."

Police interest in human relations of course relates to behavior that requires police action. These behaviors, whether or not the causes are known (i.e., childhood experience; poverty, neglect; etc.), seem to dictate that police examine the relationship between the behaviors and those *influences* on which police have impact. For it is these influences that relate most often to the problems most susceptible to *prevention,* rather than "cure." Successful community relations programs deal with these influences as they relate to behavior and the *human relations* segment of the program seeks to facilitate a community attitude of accepting this police role (the police image). For the citizen who is convinced that police are brutal is reluctant to participate in the broader community relations program. And the *validity* of the belief matters less than the *strength* of the belief.

The wisdom of recognizing that the *validity* of a belief is far less significant to police than the *strength* of a belief probably remains the core of any *corrective prevention* programming for police.

Police and Mechanical Prevention

The preceding discussion of corrective prevention summarized what has been called the "community's most enduring protection against crime . . . to right the wrongs and to cure the illnesses that tempt men to harm their neighbors" [12]. With re-emphasis on the cursory nature of that brief discussion, attention is now turned to what was identified earlier as "mechanical prevention."

Before proceeding with a discussion of the fences, locks, lights, guards, alarms, and similar "security measures" that make up part of "mechanical crime prevention," some thought will be given to police preventing crime *directly*—preventing crime simply by "being there."

In this context, new methods of accomplishing police business is "prevention" in the sense that it makes possible the release of more officers to be "in the field" more of the time.

As an example, consider the following [13]:

Through use of a computer-lined microfilm system, the Baton Rouge (La.) Police Department has eliminated a major paperwork problem and released five patrolmen for line duty.

Information-filing and retrieval involves the addition of more than 10,000 pieces of paper per month in eight record-keeping areas. Before we went to microfilm, the files were jammed to capacity with more than 3.5 million documents dating back to the early 1950's.

Of course in an era of ever-increasing automation and cybernation, this is but one of myriad labor-saving methods that hopefully increase the actual number of policemen in the field. In addition to automating such things as criminalistic data, crime files, identification, and related records, police man-power can be "stretched" toward this style of prevention in other ways.

Consider, for example, the following [14]:

> Since its inception, the National Institute of Law Enforcement and Criminal Justice, the research arm of the Law Enforcement Assistance Administration, has been interested in the use of helicopters in routine police patrol. Its predecessor agency, the Office of Law Enforcement Assistance, funded a helicopter demon-stration/evaluation for the Los Angeles County Sheriff's Department, Project Sky Knight, in Lakewood, California. The project resulted in a decrease in incidence of certain types of crimes. It also served to interest police departments throughout the country, plagued by rising crime rates, in the part that a helicopter could play in reducing crime.

While it is *not* being suggested that this example, any more than any other example serves to prevent crime alone, it *is* being suggested that conceiving of methods to increase the actual number of policemen in the field (or in this case, in the air) will tend to prevent certain varieties of crime.

With this as the background consideration, attention is returned to the specific prevention of crime through security—through *mechanical preven-tion* [15]:

> The third concept, mechanical prevention, again refers to something entirely different than the first two. Here obstacles are placed in the way of the potential offender to make it difficult if not impossible for him to commit an offense. Such preventive action does not involve the personality of the individual: no attempt is made to influence his intentions by threatening punishment or by changing his motivation; hence the suggested term mechanical prevention. An increase in police protection in neighborhoods known for the certainty of criminal acts is a typical example. The increased difficulty of committing the offense—for in-stance "rolling a drunk"—because of intensified police supervision may well prevent impressionable youths from following the example of their more advanced gang companions. Various security measures, such as dependable locking sys-tems, bars on tellers windows, signaling systems to be used in case of attack, may serve as further examples of mechanical prevention intended to forestall criminal acts by making their execution more difficult. It should be kept in mind that mechanical prevention, just as punitive and corrective prevention, also has its counterpart in the crime-control area. There it appears as incapacitation of an offender whose criminal career it seeks to interrupt; for instance, by keeping him confined in some kind of preventive detention system.

Police involvement in establishing neighborhood programs on increased security tend to blend with corrective prevention already considered. More-

FIGURE 16.2. *Oakland Police Officer conducts a traffic safety educational program for elementary school children in an attempt to establish greater traffic safety. Courtesy Police Department, Oakland, Ca.*

over, this "blend" occurs in the police-community relations to be discussed in Chapter Eighteen.

For example, the relationship between local businessmen and police constitute one of many areas in which *corrective prevention* can be practiced. But in exactly the same context, *mechanical prevention* can also be practiced.

Businessmen conferring with police on improving community conditions that seem to generate crime is one facet of *corrective prevention.* These same businessmen at the same conference can be taught modern security methods, which of course include *mechanical prevention.*

Perhaps this particular example suggests further elaboration.

Consider a police department confronted with a steadily climbing rate of commercial-store burglaries. Patrol is fairly adequate in the business district involved but the reporting pattern of these burglaries tends to be the morning following the crime.

One approach to *mechanical prevention* might be the police chief addressing service clubs or Junior Chamber of Commerce about "Community Conditions," and closing with an offer to have his detectives provide security training to store owners upon request.

Businessmen accepting the chief's offer would hopefully hear the advantages and disadvantages of such things as:

Audible alarms	Night watchmen and "door shakers"
Silent alarms	Increased lighting
Locking systems	Video equipment
Fences/gates	Cameras
Dogs	Warning signs

Mechanical prevention of shoplifting might also prove useful for businessmen considering security for the daylight store operation (i.e., such things as mirrors, etc.).

Following the same model, residential security might be dealt with by the chief extending the same type of invitation to homeowners at the conclusion of an address to the PTA or other school functions—or possibly some religious function addressed by the chief.

Homeowners accepting the chief's invitation would hopefully hear from the detectives or patrolmen various precautions to take when away from home:

Light at night automated	Window security
Light in bathroom	"Hiding place" for keys,
Removal of newspapers	as a "myth"
Removal of milk and	Neighbor awareness
other deliveries	Dogs
Removal of mail	Identity of callers
Lock adequacy	

Schools, through meetings with school officials, might be extremely impressed with security measures being developed against vandalism—a growing problem confronting many law enforcement jurisdictions.

In much the same manner that a fire marshall or fire chief may inspect for fire hazards, a police chief can offer similar security inspections to detect security hazards. Even if staffing or other local situations preclude such security inspection, many large insurance firms would doubtless respond favorably to a police invitation to provide such a service.

The *control* of crime also affords an opportunity to introduce *mechanical prevention.* A department policy can be adopted that patrolmen and detectives give property-crime victims a security analysis as part of the investigation. Such an analysis would hopefully include specific recommendations for security improvement. If handled in a positive, constructive manner, such advice stands little risk of being misinterpreted as an accusation, and may even become an essential part of the community-relations program of the department.

In the sense that ultimately *all* police activities must become part of the community-relations program, it might be useful to think of *mechanical prevention* in a larger context [16]:

That we permit conditions of ill health to prevail among millions is perhaps the most devastating, contemporary, commentary on our character. We could end this in a few short years. Malnutrition, brain damage, retardation, mental illness, high death rates, infant mortality, addiction, alcoholism—these are principal causes of crime. But crime is a small part of the pain they inflict on society. Health is a key measure of the human condition. There is little chance for quality in life with poor health. Doctors, nurses, medicines, vaccines, clinics, hospitals, research, counseling and physical fitness facilities, clean air and water, some quiet and reasonably orderly environment are essential to reducing violence. We can supply them abundantly if we care. We can build 20 million housing units in five years if we want to, and tear down the ugliness of the slums where crime is cultivated.

While this may encompass a great deal more than the police function in society, and relate more directly to *corrective prevention* where it does relate to police, it is worth noting that ultimately *mechanical prevention* can succeed no better than the *corrective prevention* implied by this quotation. Moreover, it may well be that neither form of prevention can ultimately succeed unless both are developed by police within the context of the implications of this quotation.

Whether there is agreement with any particular critic of American criminal justice, one consensual point of many critics seems worthy of consideration [17]:

American democracy has survived largely because it is a patchwork system. If one batch fades, or is cut or burned out, another can usually be put in its place without much difficulty, and although the new piece may not fit exactly or may not carry out the surrounding pattern fully, no one seems to notice for long, because the complexity of the overall design conceals changes in it. This is never more apparent than when the greatest change of all occurs—during the transfer power over the executive branch of the government from one party to another. The United States has peacably, even placidly, undergone such change seventeen times since 1789 marks it as a nation that believes in the rule of law. And that the process has been conducted each time with decency and purpose, even if sometimes none too cordially, marks the society as one that trusts itself. But part of the explanation for what might appear to be an extraordinary kind of public adaptability is that, despite the bitterness of any contest for Presidency, the expectations which always accompany the transfer of authority from one President to another, not many patches in the quilt are actually changed.

The idea that "not much has changed" refers of course to the overall lack of profound change in American life-styles—a "deficiency" often at the heart of many criticisms of American criminal justice.

Again without agreement or disagreement within the particular criticism of American justice, the *validity* of the assertion that profound changes do not occur is worth consideration.

For if *mechanical prevention* of crime depends in large measure on successful *corrective* programs which in turn depend upon social changes, it may well be that *all* crime prevention including police efforts relate to the ability to make changes—perhaps profound changes.

Definition of Changes

In the ideal, such change is not a matter of responding to a particular criticism or group of criticisms. Ideally, changes that might be regarded as profound would occur on the basis of experience—conscientiously interpreted experience.

Police implementing combinations of *corrective* and *mechanical prevention* programs directly encounter the precise areas in which change is needed —and encounter it in such a way that experience conspicuously supersedes speculation and theory.

This is not to reduce the *value* of an independent criticism. Interpreted properly, criticism can be "a rifle instead of a shotgun" approach to "zeroing in" on what it takes to prevent crimes in terms of specific change. Indeed, in some instances, criticism may prevent "change for the sake of change."

But emphasizing police experience in moving into efforts to prevent crime is the point of this discussion. Such experience, occurring simultaneously with police efforts to *control* crime, affords an ideal context for any *needed* changes to occur. *The only risk is police unable to perceive such need.*

SUMMARY

This chapter introduced the concept of preventing crime in terms of police priorities. These priorities were elaborated within the context of the general perception of law and order.

Prevention was introduced as distinctly different from control of crime in that *prevention* relates to efforts *before* a crime is committed, and *control* refers to police efforts *after* a crime is committed.

Control, nevertheless, was presented as serving one of the three prevention categories discussed: Punitive, corrective, and mechanical. The relationship between control and punitive prevention was discussed in terms of deterrence.

With emphasis on the theoretical context of "punitive" the deterring nature of *all* police activities was discussed.

Corrective prevention was related to community-relations programming that will be discussed in Chapter Eighteen. This relationship was presented in terms of the influences that generate criminal behavior to which both corrective prevention and community-relations programs are usually addressed.

Mechanical prevention was related to corrective prevention in the sense that ultimately, both must succeed if either is to succeed. Within this context of the ultimate relationship, mechanical prevention was presented in terms of various physical security methods applying to the community business sector, private sector, schools, and other special interests. The general context of corrective prevention that relates to family, religion, school, recreation, economic factors, and judicial process underpinned the discussion of efforts to bring mechanical prevention to bear on community crime problems.

The overall context of crime prevention was related to social change as a possible requisite. Emphasis was given police experience in determining such change, but not to the exclusion of criticism.

ANNOTATED REFERENCES

Amos, W. E., and C. T. Wellford (eds.), *Delinquency Prevention*, Prentice–Hall, Englewood Cliffs, N.J., 1967. A fine collection of subject-relevant articles.

Campbell, J. S., J. R. Sahid, and D. P. Stang, *Law and Order Reconsidered*, Bantam Books, New York, 1970. A good context for what was presented in this chapter as the "priorities."

Clark, R., *Crime in America*, Pocket Books, New York, 1971. Elaboration of what was presented in this chapter as the "value of criticism."

Coffey, A., E. Eldefonso, and W. Hartinger, *Human Relations: Law Enforcement in a Changing Community,* Prentice–Hall, Englewood Cliffs, N.J., 1971. In-depth elaboration of rationale for expanding police role.

Harris, R., *Justice: The Crisis of Law, Order and Freedom in America,* Avon Books, New York, 1970. Excellent example of what was presented in this chapter as criticism of American justice.

NOTES

1. D. Burnham, "Special Introduction," *in* J. S. Campbell, J. R. Sahid, and D. P. Stang, *Law and Order Reconsidered,* p. xii.

2. P. P. Lejins, "The Field of Prevention," *in* W. E. Amos and C. F. Wellford (eds.), *Delinquency Prevention,* Prentice–Hall, Englewood Cliffs, N.J., 1967, p. 2.

3. *Ibid.*

4. *Ibid.,* pp. 3–5.

5. See, as a typical example of this approach, C. R. Jeffery, *Crime Prevention Through Environmental Design,* Gage, Beverly Hills, Ca., 1972.

6. H. W. More, Jr., *Critical Issues in Law Enforcement,* Anderson, Cincinnati, Oh., 1972, p. 204.

7. A. Coffey, E. Eldefonso, and W. Hartinger, *Police-Community Relations,* Prentice–Hall, Englewood Cliffs, N.J., 1971, p. 75.

8. A. Coffey, E. Eldefonso, and W. Hartinger, *Human Relations: Law Enforcement in a Changing Community.*

9. *Ibid.,* p. 28.

10. W. E. Amos, and C. T. Wellford (eds.), *Delinquency Prevention,* Chapters 5–11.

11. Coffey, Eldefonso, and Hartinger, *op. cit.,* pp. 224–25.

12. R. W. Winslow (ed.), *Crime in a Free Society,* Dickinson, Belmont, Ca., 1968, p. 370.

13. J. B. Firmin and E. B. Morel, "Microfilmed Records Free Five Officers," *Law and Order,* Aug. 1971, p. 54.

14. M. D. Maltz, "Evaluation of Police Air Mobility Programs," *The Police Chief,* April 1971, p. 34.

15. Lejins, *op. cit.,* p. 5.

16. R. Clark, *Crime in America,* p. 322.

17. R. Harris, *Justice: The Crisis of Law, Order and Freedom in America,* p. 9.

CHAPTER SEVENTEEN

Ethics

What are ethics? What do we mean by ethics in law enforcement? The late J. Edgar Hoover, former Director of the FBI, once stated that "the public has a right and a duty to demand unimpeachable integrity from its public servants." So we might begin by defining ethics in law enforcement as unimpeachable integrity from public law enforcement servants. Ethics more formally stated are:

A system of conduct recognized in respect to a particular class of human actions or a particular group, culture, etc. or that branch of philosophy dealing with values relating to human conduct, with respect to the rightness and wrongness of certain actions and to the goodness and badness of the motives and ends of such actions [1].

It is natural for man to ask thoughtful questions about what he should and should not do. Man does not have to make a choice about who his parents are or whether he should take a breath, but he does have to ask himself how he should treat his family or whether he should accept a bribe. Some of man's actions are not determined for him but fall within his moral choice.

Ethics involve man's moral ideals and goals, motives of choice, and his patterns of good and bad conduct, and it is a science of right living. A

387

code of ethics thus gives us some general practical knowledge, but man must still make personal decisions in applying this knowledge to particular cases. He should not only do right, he should know *why* he should do right.

Man is not always sure about what moral principle should govern a particular decision. For example, a young man may face the question of whether to continue his education, go to work to help support the family, or enter into the service of his nation. Any of the three could be the moral choice for his situation. Ethics develops a way of probing these difficulties and reaching a systematic general doctrine on moral life.

Each profession should have a code of ethics by which it regulates its actions and sets standards for its members. When a profession establishes a code, it is done in an attempt to assure high standards of competence, strengthen relationships of its members, and promote the welfare of the whole community. No professional code will automatically assure that these goals are achieved, but it most certainly will aid in serving as a reminder or guide. Many recognized and established professions have produced codes of ethical conduct which clearly serve to define the ideals and principles for their members. Witness the Hippocratic oath of the medical profession. An ethical code does not solve problems, but merely aids the professional in meeting and handling the everyday questions of right and wrong that arise in his work and responsibilities.

In the professional standards of the American criminal justice system, exemplary behavior and unimpeachable conduct must be constantly observed. Commenting on this subject prior to his death in 1972, J. Edgar Hoover stated, "Public trust is built on respect and confidence inspired by outstanding service. In discharging its responsibilities, law enforcement can follow the objectives and ideals of professional police standards of service to avoid a breach of this trust."

The general public in America has a common attitude that the criminal justice system as it exists is capable, efficient, effective, and dedicated. Men and women in law enforcement who have lived and worked honestly and morally have earned this public trust. But let newspaper headlines proclaim POLICEMAN ARRESTED FOR BURGLARY OF SMALL BUSINESS and the public is infinitely more incensed than they would be from the arrest of a private citizen. Or, as another example, a situation develops whereby an agency such as a municipal police department fails to maintain its standards or fulfill its responsibilities, and the public rancor rises and the agency in question and other similar agencies near and far are subject to the condemnation that ensues. Any agency may acquire the public support necessary to function with professional efficiency if it establishes and maintains high standards and an unequivocal adherence to an adopted and clear-cut code of ethics.

In his discussion of ethics in the police service, John L. Sullivan, retired Special Agent, FBI, Washington, D.C., has stated:

> There is no question that a code of ethics is essential in a profession. Without such a code a profession could not exist. Moreover, the rules and regulations selected must reach the highest standards. There must be no opportunity for compromise. Professional ethics dictates the application of such absolutes as "always" and "never." To be effective, the code must cover all areas of endeavor, leaving no questions of right or wrong unanswered. Naturally, it is admitted that no code could, when phrased only in words, encompass every possible circumstance. However, within the confines of reason, a sensible, attainable set of rules can be formulated.

A code of ethics should include all fundamental and material objectives. The late D. L. Kooken of Indiana University in his book *Ethics in Police Service* sets forth six such law enforcement objectives:

1. To elevate the standing of the profession in the public mind, and to strengthen public confidence in law enforcement.
2. To encourage law enforcement officers to fully appreciate the responsibilities of their office.
3. To develop and maintain complete support and cooperation of the public in law enforcement.
4. To ensure the effectiveness of the service by encouraging complete cooperation of its members for their mutual benefits.
5. To strive for full coordination of effort in all official relationships with other governmental bodies.
6. To consider police work an honorable profession and to recognize in it an opportunity to render a worthwhile service to society [2].

The foregoing objectives are praiseworthy in every respect. In order that these objectives might be realized and given the stature they most certainly deserve, many law enforcement and criminal justice agencies across America and throughout the world have adopted codes of ethics. In the United States such notable policing agencies as the Federal Bureau of Investigation, the National Conference of Police Associations, the International Police Association, the International Narcotic Enforcement Officers Association, the International Association of Chiefs of Police, and National Sheriff's Association, to name a few, have adopted the Law Enforcement Code of Ethics. This code of professional ethics was developed and first adopted in 1956 by the Peace Officers' Research Association of California. In 1957, the International Association of Chiefs of Police gave the Code formal recognition and it was unanimously adopted by the Association at their annual conference. In the same year the IACP also adopted the Canons of Police Ethics. Many criminal justice and law enforcement organizations strictly adhere to both codes in their daily operations.

LAW ENFORCEMENT CODE OF ETHICS

AS A LAW ENFORCEMENT OFFICER, my fundamental duty is to serve mankind; to safeguard lives and property; to protect the innocent against deception, the weak against oppression or intimidation, and the peaceful against violence or disorder; and to respect the Constitutional rights of all men to liberty, equality, and justice.

I WILL keep my private life unsullied as an example to all; maintain courageous calm in the face of danger, scorn, or ridicule; develop self-restraint; and be constantly mindful of the welfare of others. Honest in thought and deed in both my personal and official life, I will be exemplary in obeying the laws of the land and the regulations of my department. Whatever I see or hear of a confidential nature or that is confided to me in my official capacity will be kept ever secret unless revelation is necessary in the performance of my duty.

I WILL never act officiously or permit personal feelings, prejudices, animosities or friendships to influence my decisions. With no compromise for crime and with relentless prosecution of criminals, I will enforce the law courteously and appropriately without fear or favor, malice or ill will, never employing unnecessary force or violence and never accepting gratuities.

I RECOGNIZE the badge of my office as a symbol of public faith, and I accept it as a public trust to be held so long as I am true to the ethics of the police service. I will constantly strive to achieve these objectives and ideals, dedicating myself before God to my chosen profession . . . law enforcement.

CANONS OF POLICE ETHICS

Article I: Primary Responsibility of Job

The primary responsibility of the police service, and of the individual officer, is the protection of the people of the United States through the upholding of their laws; chief among these is the Constitution of the United States and its amendments. The law enforcement officer always respects the whole of the community and its legally expressed will and is never the arm of any political party or clique.

Article II: Limitations of Authority

The first duty of a law enforcement officer, as upholder of the law, is to know its bounds upon him in enforcing it. Because he represents the legal will of the community, be it local, state, or federal, he must be aware of the limitations and proscriptions which the people, through law, have placed upon him. He must recognize the genius of the American system of government which gives to no man, groups of men, or institutions, absolute power, and he must ensure that he, as a prime defender of the system, does not pervert its character.

Article III: Duty to Be Familiar with the Law and with Responsibilities of Self and Other Public Officials

The law enforcement officer shall assiduously apply himself to the study of the principles of the laws which he is sworn to uphold. He will make certain of his responsibilities in the particulars of their enforcement, seeking aid from his superiors in matters of technicality or principles when these are not clear to him; he will make special effort to fully understand his relationship to other public officials, including other law enforcement agencies, particularly on matters of jurisdiction, both geographically and substantively.

Article IV: Utilization of Proper Means to Gain Proper Ends

The law enforcement officer shall be mindful of his responsibility to pay strict heed to the selection of means in discharging the duties of his office. Violations of law or disregard for public safety and property on the part of the officer are intrinsically wrong; they are self-defeating in that they instill in the public mind a like disposition. The employment of illegal means, no matter how worthy the end, is certain to encourage disrespect for the law and its officers. If the law is to be honored, it must first be honored by those who enforce it.

Article V: Cooperation with Public Officials in the Discharge of Their Authorized Duties

The law enforcement officer shall cooperate fully with other public officials in the discharge of authorized duties, regardless of party affiliation or personal prejudice. He shall be meticulous, however, in assuring himself of the propriety, under the law, of such actions and shall guard against the use of his office or person, whether knowingly or unknowingly, in any improper or illegal action.

In any situation open to question, he shall seek authority from his superior officer, giving him a full report of the proposed service or action.

Article VI: Private Conduct

The law enforcement officer shall be mindful of his special identification by the public as an upholder of the law. Laxity of conduct or manner in private life, expressing either disrespect for the law or seeking to gain special privilege, cannot but reflect upon the police officer and the police service. The community and the service require that the law enforcement officer lead the life of a decent and honorable man. Following the career of a policeman gives no man special perquisites. It does give the satisfaction and pride of following and furthering an unbroken tradition of safeguarding the American republic. The officer who reflects upon this tradition will not degrade it. Rather, he will so conduct his private life that the public will regard him as an example of stability, fidelity and morality.

Article VII: Conduct Toward the Public

The law enforcement officer, mindful of his responsibility to the whole community, shall deal with individuals of the community in a manner calculated to instill respect for its laws and its police service. The law enforcement officer shall conduct his official life in a manner such as will inspire confidence and trust. Thus, he will be neither overbearing nor subservient, as the individual citizen has neither an obligation to stand in awe of him nor a right to command him. The officer will give service where he can, and require compliance with the law. He will do neither from personal preference or prejudice but only as a duly appointed officer of the law discharging his sworn obligation.

Article VIII: Conduct in Arresting and Dealing with Law Violators

The law enforcement officer shall use his powers of arrest strictly in accordance with the law and with due regard to the rights of the citizen concerned. His office gives him no right to prosecute the violator nor to mete out punishment for the offense. He shall, at all times, have a clear appreciation of his responsibilities and limitations regarding detention of the violator; he shall conduct himself in such a manner as will minimize the possibility of having to use force. To this end he shall cultivate a dedication to the service of the people and the equitable upholding of their laws whether in the handling of law violators or in dealing with the law-abiding.

Article IX: Gifts and Favors

The law enforcement officer, representing government, bears the heavy responsibility of maintaining, in his own conduct, the honor and integrity of all governmental institutions. He shall, therefore, guard against placing himself in a position in which any person can reasonably assume that special consideration is being given. Thus, he should be firm in refusing gifts, favors, or gratuities, large or small, which can, in the public mind, be interpreted as capable of influencing his judgment in the discharge of his duties.

Article X: Presentation of Evidence

The law enforcement officer shall be concerned equally in the prosecution of the wrongdoer and the defense of the innocent. He shall ascertain what constitutes evidence and shall present such evidence impartially and without malice. In so doing, he will ignore social, political, and other distinctions among the persons involved, strengthening the tradition of the reliability and the integrity of an officer's word.

The law enforcement officer shall take special pains to increase his perception and skill of observation, mindful that in many situations his is the sole impartial testimony to the facts of a case.

Article XI: Attitude Toward Profession

The law enforcement officer shall regard the discharge of his duties as a public trust and recognize his responsibility as a public servant. By diligent study and sincere attention to self-improvement he shall strive to make the best possible application of science to the solution of crime and, in the field of human rela-tionships, strive for effective leadership and public influence in matters affecting public safety. He shall appreciate the importance and responsibility of his office, hold police work to be an honorable profession rendering valuable service to his community and the country.

FBI PLEDGE FOR LAW ENFORCEMENT OFFICERS

Humbly recognizing the responsibilities entrusted to me, I do vow that I shall always consider the high calling of law enforcement to be an honorable profession, the duties of which are recognized by me as both an art and a science. I recognize fully my responsibilities to defend the right, to protect the weak, to aid the dis-tressed, and to uphold the law in public duty and in private living. I accept the obligation in connection with my assignments to report facts and to testify without bias or display of emotion, and to consider the information, coming to my knowl-edge by virtue of my position, as a sacred trust, to be used solely for official purposes. To the responsibilities entrusted to me of seeking to prevent crime, of finding the facts of law violations and of apprehending fugitives and criminals, I shall give my loyal and faithful attention and shall always be equally alert in striving to acquit the innocent and to convict the guilty. In the performance of my duties and assignments, I shall not engage in unlawful and unethical practices but shall perform the functions of my office without fear, without favor, and without prejudice. At no time shall I disclose to an unauthorized person any fact, testimony, or information in any pending matter coming to my official knowledge which may be calculated to prejudice the minds of existing or prospective judicial bodies either to favor or to disfavor any person or issue. While occupying the status of a law enforcement officer or at any other time subsequent thereto, I shall not seek to benefit personally because of my knowledge of any confidential matter which has come to my attention. I am aware of the serious responsibilities of my office and in the performance of my duties I shall, as a minister, seek to supply comfort, advice, and aid to those who may be in need of such benefits, as a soldier, I shall wage vigorous warfare against the enemies of my country, of its laws, and of its principles, and as a physician, I shall seek to eliminate the criminal parasite which preys upon our social order and to strengthen the lawful processes of our body politic. I shall strive to be both a teacher and a pupil in the art and science of law enforcement. As a lawyer, I shall acquire due knowledge of the laws of my domain and seek to preserve and maintain the majesty and dignity of the law; as a scientist, it will be my endeavor to learn all pertinent truth about accusations and complaints which come to my lawful knowledge; as an artist, I shall seek to use my skill for the purpose of making each assignment a masterpiece; as a neighbor, I shall bear an attitude of true friendship and courteous respect to all citizens; and as an officer, I shall always be loyal to my duty, my organization, and my country. I will support and defend the Constitution of the United States against all enemies, foreign and domestic; I will bear true faith and allegiance to the same, and will constantly strive to cooperate with and promote cooperation between all regularly constituted law enforcement agencies and officers in the performance of duties of mutual interest and obligation.

GENERAL RULES OF OFFICIAL CONDUCT [3]

I

Policemen shall be habitually courteous; they shall recognize their responsibilities as public servants and shall be particularly attentive to citizens seeking assistance or information or who desire to register complaints or give evidence.

II

They shall accept their responsibility to the public by being punctual in their engagements and expeditious in the performance of their duties.

III

They shall regard their office as a public trust and in the discharge of their duties, be constantly mindful of their primary obligation to serve the public, efficiently and effectively.

IV

They shall administer the law in a just, impartial and reasonable manner; and shall not accord to some more reasonable treatment than to others. They shall recognize the limitations of their authority and at no time use the power of their office for their own personal advantage.

V

They shall be true to their obligation as custodians of public property and shall bear in mind that the misuse and waste of public property is equally as reprehensible as the misuse of money from the public treasury.

VI

They shall not limit their effectiveness in the administration of their office by accepting gratuities or favors from citizens or corporations with whom they may have official dealings.

VII

They shall cooperate fully with all other public officials to the end that the safety and general welfare of the public will be assured. They shall not permit jealousies or personal differences to influence their cooperation with other agencies.

VIII

They shall add to their effectiveness by diligent study and sincere attention to self improvement. They shall welcome the opportunity to disseminate practical and useful information relating to matters of the public's safety and welfare.

They shall so conduct their public and private life that the public will regard them as examples of stability, fidelity, and morality.

IX

They shall bear faithful allegiance to their government, and be loyal to their profession. They shall accept as a sacred obligation their responsibilities as citizens to support the Constitution of the United States; and as public officials they shall consider the privilege of defending the principles of liberty as defined in our Constitution and Laws, the greatest honor that may be bestowed upon any man.

It is paramount in the American criminal justice system, particularly in law enforcement, that the foregoing codes of ethics be meaningful. Too often such resolutions become just so many words, pious and smug. For these codes to be of value they must be understood and accepted by everyone—no exceptions—and they should be applied to the environment in which one performs his public service. When such codes are understood, accepted, and applied there is a decrease in abuses, particularly in law enforcement. The late O. W. Wilson, who probably contributed more to the law enforcement and general criminal justice profession in the area of professionalism and ethics than any other single person puts the case clearly:

Police administrators and supervisors must develop a high degree of "intestinal fortitude." We must have the strength within our agencies to run a "tight ship," and to detect and correct our own weaknesses. We should not have to wait for public pressures and newspaper exposés to call these matters to our attention. Too many of us—abiding by a false sense of camaraderie—conceive our function as being that of protecting our fellow officers. It is one thing to aid a man in combat; to cater to our sick; to care for the families of police officers; and to support a man in the rightful performance of his duties. It is another thing to cover up wrongdoing or the commission of a crime by one of our members. Friendship can be gained by being tolerant of such conditions, but friendship alone does not result in good administration or in the advancement of law enforcement. True leadership can be gained only by an intolerance of wrongdoing by police officers. Unless we abide by the very highest standards among ourselves, we have no business enforcing the law upon others [4].

ETHICS AND EMPLOYMENT POLICIES

To prevent unethical activity on the part of an employee requires very careful and judicious screening and selection of new personnel. In addition, a sound program of practical training which stresses public relations and acceptable ethical conduct is necessary. If it is ascertained through an effective evaluation and through supervision that there are employees in the system who will not abide by the rules and regulations set forth at the time employment was commenced, then swift and certain dismissal of those employees is mandatory.

SUMMARY

Law enforcement strides toward professionalization through internal controls which include an ascription to a code of ethics which each sworn law enforcement officer is pledged to observe. Police officers become professionals not by proclamation, but by recognition as such by the public and the nation's leaders, including the courts. The field of law enforcement has achieved this recognition in the United States, and law enforcement throughout the world is following its example. Aside from advanced educational standards, probably the one greatest factor responsible for achieving this professional status has been the development of, and strict adherence by, law enforcement to a code of ethics encompassing professional standards and performance, the end result of which is a behavior and integrity that is exemplary.

ANNOTATED REFERENCES

Kooken, D. L., *Ethics in Police Service,* Thomas, Springfield, Ill., 1957. A general discussion on police ethics.

Wilson, O. W., *Parker On Police,* Thomas, Springfield, Ill., 1957. Very interesting reading because it enables one to understand how the late W. H. Parker was such a successful police chief in a large American city. Discusses his administrative responsibilities, problems, philosophy, patience, diplomacy, judgment, and his unusual moral courage and emotional strength.

Wilson, O. W., *Police Administration,* McGraw–Hill, New York, 1972. An excellent discussion of police administration including views on ethical conduct and standards.

NOTES

1. *The Random House Dictionary of the English Language,* Random House, New York, 1967.

2. D. L. Kooken, *Ethics in Police Service,* p. 19.

3. *Ibid.,* pp. 19–20.

4. O. W. Wilson, Address to the Annual Meeting of the International Association of Chiefs of Police, Montreal, October 3, 1961.

CHAPTER EIGHTEEN

Police-Community Relations

What will be presented in this, the concluding chapter of the book, is the relationship that exists (or fails to exist) between law enforcement and the community served by law enforcement. As a background for this concluding chapter, consider the following [1]:

> Law enforcement and the equal administration of justice have become major national concerns in recent years. The rapid growth of our cities—with attendant problems in housing, education, employment, and social welfare services—has accentuated these concerns and has been highlighted by the increasing urban concentration of minority groups.
>
> Crime rates have generally been higher in these areas where poverty, family disintegration, unemployment, lack of education, minority group frustration, and resentment in the face of social and economic discrimination—the ghetto syndrome—are manifest. The expectations, excitements, and additional frustrations engendered by the civil rights movement have compounded the difficulties in law enforcement and the administration of justice.
>
> Foremost among these difficulties are the relationships among police, minority groups, and the general community. There is increasing evidence of deterioration in these relationships, particularly between police and Blacks. There are widespread charges of "police brutality" and demands for greater assertion of civilian control over police actions. On the other hand, many police officials decry the growing disrespect for law, public apathy, mollycoddling of criminals by the courts, and political influence on the law enforcement process. Some police continue

398

to view civil rights groups as troublemakers, disruptive of the law and order the police have sworn to uphold, while at the same time, some Blacks and Puerto Ricans hold a stereotyped image of the policeman. These misconceptions severely hamper cooperative relationships.

While many believe that increasing awareness of the implications of the above reduce part of the problem for police, few would argue that community relations is *not* a continuing major problem for police around the nation. Indeed, it has been stated in the literature that there are "restrictions imposed on law enforcement by government in general and *constitutional government in particular*" [2]. These "restrictions," in large measure, are those influences that impinge directly on police through their relationship with the community. And they are *restrictions* that have made the "complexity of enforcing law increase steadily throughout history beginning with the Magna Carta, Bill of Rights, fourth amendment, and other rulings molding the foundation of modern constitutional government" [3]. Indeed, within the context in which these restrictions will be discussed, police-community relations are perhaps the most significant of *all* principles of law enforcement. Community relations, then, is of major concern to police, and will be presented in that context.

In discussing the philosophy and history of law enforcement, Chapter Three set forth a virtual requirement that law be enforced if society is to survive—at least survive in a civilized manner. Requiring the enforcement of law prevents society from completely depending on simple persuasion to induce law observance. The term *enforcement,* and indeed the very nature of man, implies the potential use of force. This potential to wield force then is necessarily a part of the police image. But the manner in which this potential is viewed by the public often determines whether the police image is good or bad. And because good police image and similar influences tend to affect favorably the individual's willingness to observe the law voluntarily, police retain a vital interest in a good image. Police interest in a good image is vital for a number of reasons, but one reason in particular that is singularly practical is that the greater the voluntary law observance the less the need for forceful enforcement. So the question becomes: What can be done to promote the understanding and use of social influences to encourage voluntary law observance?

The various crime theories reviewed in Chapter Five make clear the lack of agreement among biologists, anthropologists, criminologists, sociologists, and psychiatrists concerning the causes of crime. Yet these behavioral scientists generally agree that societal influences both encourage and discourage crime. Influence, as it relates to criminal behavior, is merely a power to affect human willingness to conform to law. And so the question of influence becomes a consideration of forces with enough power to encourage voluntary law observance.

The manner in which the public views the police method of enforcement has already been indicated as one such force. Another force, and perhaps more fundamental, relates to the manner in which children are raised. The old saying, "As the twig is bent so grows the tree," has particular significance in a free society. The citizen who holds little respect for law enforcement goals may merely reflect the values learned as a child. Racial tensions, economic conditions, and various physical and emotional deprivations contribute to the failure to acquire respect for the law. But the main contribution to this failure might be early and unfortunate experience with police. The detrimental and sometimes lasting effect of such unfortunate experience will be discussed later in this chapter. For now, unfortunate experience of this nature will serve merely to introduce the subject of *human relations.*

Evidence that police increasingly are involved in human relations can be found in such references as the April 6, 1967, *New York Times* article describing the high percentage of courses devoted to this topic at the New York Police Academy. For purposes of pursuing human relations further, however, a definition of the term might be in order.

HUMAN RELATIONS DEFINED

The literature increasingly reflects an implied definition of human relations in terms of "avoiding police brutality" [4]. A further definition includes police discretion or decision making in terms of "police attitudes" [5]. Going beyond these rather narrow considerations, a definition of law enforcement human relations might be: Police participation in any activity that seeks law observance through respect rather than enforcement. This definition will be clarified and elaborated further as the chapter progresses.

Regardless of how human relations is defined, however, police interest in the subject should be related in some way to the "causes" of crime. It has been noted already that behavioral scientists fail to agree on the causes of crime. A cause or even a group of causes (such as alcoholism, poverty, broken home, and parental neglect) can be isolated which seem to turn one individual and yet not another to crime even when both are subjected to precisely the same causes. Even such an extensive catalog of human characteristics as the Yale University Human Relations File (originally the

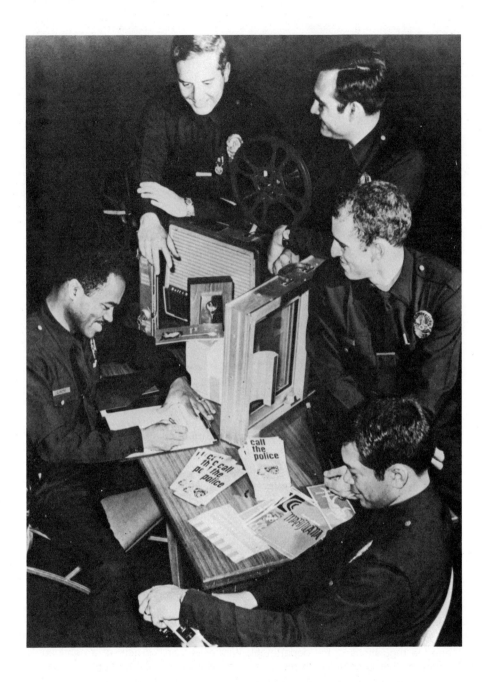

FIGURE 18.1. *A specific program to improve police image in the community. Courtesy Police Department, Los Angeles, Ca.*

cross-cultural survey) fails to clarify how cultural causes affect different people in different ways.

But whether or not behavior science can agree on crime causes, law enforcement practitioners tend to agree that there appears to be a relationship between at least some kinds of crime and certain community influences. These influences more often than not relate to combinations of problems such as poverty, racial tensions, parental inadequacies, and others. An additional influence already indicated is the police image held by the community.

Because the community's attitude toward police (or the police image) is one of the primary influences with enough force to encourage voluntary law observance, this influence or force is of primary concern to law enforcement. For the individual citizen who is convinced that police are, say, brutal, will probably find it difficult to respect police goals—particularly if the brutality is believed to be directed toward only certain minorities. And as a practical matter, the *validity* of the belief may matter less than the *strength* of the belief. The individual functions on the basis of what is believed regardless of the validity of the belief.

HUMAN RELATIONS AND ETHICS

It might be said then that the use of the principles of human relations by police should begin with an attempt to eliminate or at least reduce influences contributing to a bad image. Creating and maintaining a good police image, for the majority of the community, requires little more than conscientious adherence to the standard *Law Enforcement Code of Ethics:*

> As a Law Enforcement Officer, my fundamental duty is to serve mankind; to safeguard lives and property; to protect the innocent against deception, the weak against oppression or intimidation, and the peaceful against violence or disorder; and to respect the Constitutional rights of all men to liberty, equality, and justice.
>
> I will keep my private life unsullied as an example to all; maintain courageous calm in the face of danger, scorn, or ridicule; develop self-restraint; and be constantly mindful of the welfare of others. Honest in thought and deed in both my personal and official life, I will be exemplary in obeying the laws of the land and the regulations of my department. Whatever I see or hear of a confidential nature or that is confided to me in my official capacity will be kept ever secret unless revelation is necessary in the performance of my duty.
>
> I will never act officiously or permit personal feelings, prejudices, animosities, or friendships to influence my decisions. With no compromise for crime and with

relentless prosecution of criminals, I will enforce the law courteously and appropriately without fear or favor, malice or ill will, never employing unnecessary force or violence and never accepting gratuities.

I recognize the badge of my office as a symbol of public faith, and I accept it as a public trust to be held so long as I am true to the ethics of the police service. I will constantly strive to achieve these objectives and ideals, dedicating myself before God to my chosen profession . . . law enforcement.

Personnel selection, training, and supervision geared to maintaining strict adherence to this code usually ensure public respect, because strict adherence eliminates marginal practices such as accepting gratuities for individually selective enforcement methods and related activities that generate disrespect for police. And needless to say, strict adherence to the code eliminates the more obviously corrupt practices as well.

As the late FBI Director J. Edgar Hoover, stated in the January 1966 *FBI Law Enforcement Bulletin:*

Public trust is built on respect and confidence inspired by outstanding service. In discharging its responsibilities, law enforcement can follow the objectives and ideals of professional police service to avoid a breach of this trust.

But in spite of high ethical standards and conscientious performance of duty by police, certain members of the community often require further persuasion, or "selling," to eliminate a bad police image in their minds.

Obviously, the press continues to retain all of the significance implied in Chapter Nine. The question of whether the press creates or reflects the police image cannot be ignored. For the purpose of discussing image in terms of human relations, an unknown degree of influence by the press will be assumed while still other influences are being examined.

In returning to the subject of promoting or "selling" respect for police goals to certain members of the community, some consideration might be given the apparent reasons for this disrespect. It seems reasonable to assume that a person brutally mishandled by one policeman may have difficulty in "seeing" how helpful most policemen really are. This possibility alone should afford convincing argument for the elimination of force wherever possible. Behavior scientists believe a kind of "selective perception" sets in which causes an unjustly abused individual to look for and "see" only those incidents that "prove" that the police are brutal. Years and years of looking for and seeing such incidents, combined with reassurances from other persons doing the same thing, of course, create a bad police image.

REWARDING MISBELIEF

As professionals, police are charged with the responsibility of trying to prevent the incidents "that are being looked for" which in turn worsen police image. This does not suggest a reduction in police efficiency. Indeed, the ultimate respect that accrues to a good police image demands vigorous and conscientious performance of all duties. But such respect further demands sensitivity to all sources of a bad image.

In recent years a traditionally Freudian psychiatrist, Eric Berne, developed a new theory of human relations and named his method "transactional analysis" [6]. In describing the reasons why people behave as they do, Berne offers a piece of human understanding that is of singular value to law enforcement. He identifies the "rewards" that motivate people as "payoffs"—a notion that Berne elaborates in terms of rewards not necessarily appearing as rewards except to the person being rewarded.

Borrowing from this psychiatric explanation of motivation, it could be speculated that an individual who violates laws for no outwardly apparent reward or reason nevertheless feels that he is rewarded with a payoff. The payoff may be the reward of "proving" earlier beliefs about how unfair the world is or how brutal policemen are. If proving that their beliefs are correct is rewarding to humans, then perhaps some individuals have sufficient need for this reward to "create" situations that *provoke* proof.

Continuing this speculation, an individual might be able to "prove" a belief that police are brutal simply by behaving in a manner that requires police to use force. A similar reward might be gained (through supporting one's beliefs) by "proving" that police are racially prejudiced through isolation of racial issues in a situation demanding police action. In both cases, the "proof" is rewarding in terms of the confidence gained in one's beliefs and one's judgment whether or not the beliefs are valid. It must be remembered, of course, that a policeman who believes that someone is criminally inclined also may feel rewarded if this judgment is "proved" correct.

But since these examples are mere speculation, most or even all crimes may not be motivated in this manner. And yet these kinds of influences may very well determine the degree of respect for police held by certain groups in the community. And to whatever degree respect for law enforcement goals affects voluntary law observance, police concern for understanding these aspects of human relations is completely justified. But understanding human relations is one thing whereas implementing this understanding may prove quite another matter.

The notion of criminal behavior being rewarded may provide a starting point for the understanding of human relations needed to repair "bad police image" in areas where the image has deteriorated.

HUMAN-RELATIONS PROGRAMS

The community itself traditionally approaches problems, particularly social problems, through some kind of "council." Councils usually function to coordinate the activities of groups or social agencies that would otherwise operate on the philosophy ". . . agencies exist to provide distinct services to groups able to accept them. . ." [7]. A variety of opinions exist regarding how involved the "coordinating" should become with broad community problems outside specific neighborhoods. But the central idea nevertheless remains to bring the combined forces of various agencies to bear on defined problems [8]. In an era in which a bad police image increasingly stimulates consideration of civilian police review panels [9], law enforcement could scarcely ignore this obvious method of implementing the principles of human relations.

An example of police participation in a community program designed to "improve image" is reflected in a publication by Watson, entitled "The Fringes of Police Community Relations" (Police Administrator's Conference, Indiana Univ. Medical Center, June 29, 1966). Another such example is reflected in the following "handout":

The basic purpose of these talks is to develop a more positive relationship between the young people of the community and the police, and to foster a greater degree of social consciousness on the part of these young people. Rather than dealing simply in what the law is and how it affects young people, which tends very often to be somewhat sterile, we dwell more on motivating good behavior in general. We attempt to define a role for the vast majority of young people who do not get into trouble but at the same time assert little influence if any on those that do. This represents the first phase of the presentation.

The second phase of the presentation is devoted to a colored slide program showing Juvenile Hall, the ranches and a Youth Authority Institution. What we are striving to do is to take the glamour away from young people who go to these facilities. Very often they come back to school and become leaders because the rest of the young people think that this is some sort of achievement after listening to the stories fabricated by these individuals. Also we found that most of the questions by students previously were directed to the nature of these facilities and the slides provide the closest thing to a guided tour.

The third phase of the program is devoted to answering any questions that the students might have. This interaction hopefully develops the positive nature of the contact between these students and someone who represents the Police Department. It is with this in mind that we desire to keep presentations at the classroom level to develop the highest degree of communication and interaction.

This handout is presented to teachers prior to addresses at schools by officers assigned to the community-relations unit of the San Jose, California Police Department. Although the handout deals primarily with improving police image with youth, it seems reasonable to assume that this activity may gain the respect of the community at large. Even citizens completely satisfied with conventional police services will be likely to respond favorably to the program.

Still more relevant to programs geared to improving police image, specifically among groups ordinarily resentful of police, is the message of the following letter:

Mr. Nat Shaffer
Council of Community Services
431 6th Street
Richmond, California

Subject: Relation of Police-Community Relations Aides to
        Police-Youth Discussion Group Program

Dear Sir:
   There has been exhibited throughout the nation a dislike, distrust, and, in some cases, hatred of police by a large segment of our Negro citizens. The City of Richmond, with one-fourth of the population Negro, falls into the national pattern. I shall not attempt to go into the "whys" of this situation at this time. I would rather accept this situation as a fact and seek solutions.
   It is my strong conviction that in today's society, we must attempt to reach the youth with a concentrated effort to establish more meaningful lines of communication between them and the police. In particular, with Negro youth. We must try to bring about a better understanding, a deeper appreciation for one another and our problems.
   We have in the City of Richmond taken steps to reach the Negro youth through a series of Police-Youth Discussion Groups. Our method of setting up such groups is quite simple. Take a small geographical area of the city, seek out the youth who have exhibited antisocial behavior, get them to a meeting with selected police officers. At such meetings, the youth are encouraged to speak their minds, regardless of how hard it is on the police. On the other hand the police are to answer all questions, avoiding none. They explain the responsibility, the law and the policy with which the police must govern themselves. I hasten to add that such a meeting is not attempted on the basis that all ills or misunderstanding will be cleared

away at a single meeting or a dozen meetings. However, we have, through discussion groups, brought about far better understanding between these two forces. This is demonstrated by a lessening of crimes committed by those youth who have participated and by many, having been school dropouts, having returned to school.

Much of the success of the Police-Youth Discussion Groups can be attributed to the work and dedication of the five Police-Community Relations Aides. It is they who go out into the community and invite the youth to the group meeting. They pick them up at their homes (or wherever they can be located), bring them to the meetings and take them home at the close. Further, the personal contacts with the youth in their homes oftentimes bridges the gaps of communication, counsels both the youth and their parents.

At the present time, the Richmond Police have conducted two twelve-week Police-Youth Discussion Groups within the Negro community. Both groups are continuing as structured clubs. Just during the past two weeks, three new Discussion Groups have been formed. We cannot, at this time, even offer a guess as to the number of groups that might form within the next six months. Regardless of the number now or in the future, we can see the Police Community Relations Aides as a very important part of a program that shall have a present and lasting value to those in the various groups, their families and the community.

Very truly yours,

C. E. Brown /S/
Chief of Police

Again it might be noted that although youth seems to be the primary subject, the entire community stands to gain by this human-relations activity.

HUMAN RELATIONS WITH "PRECRIMINALS"

Recalling the significance of the saying, "As the twig is bent so grows the tree," it does not seem surprising that many human-relations programs in fact do focus on the subject of youth. For indeed, "bending the twig" in the direction of respect for police goals yields results that cannot be measured throughout the ensuing noncriminal adult life. But more than human-relations programs are required for such ideal crime prevention. Also needed is a sensitivity to the profound impact on children who come into contact with police authority.

The problem, of course, is two-fold: First, there must be the special police sensitivity just implied, and second, there also must be sufficient firmness to justify the child's respect. A recent book on this topic, *Law Enforcement and the Youthful Offender,* outlines the general functions juvenile law enforcement must fulfill in this regard [10]. With particular regard to the question of firmness, the author states:

> Juveniles are not exempt from the enforcement of the law. They must be held to answer for their wrongs against society. Tender years, immaturity, irresponsibility are not excuses for theft, vandalism, or violence. The fact that a person is an adult does not permit police always to use force in arresting him; nor does the fact that one is a juvenile per se, require that no force is used. What is unnecessary or excessive force is determined by the extent of the circumstances, of which age is but one factor. This is not to say that there are no differences in handling juveniles and adults. However, insofar as the realization of basic objectives is concerned—the vigorous and successful completion of the job given the policy by society—there are no fundamental philosophical or policy differences. There are adaptations of philosophical concepts which, while they do not in any way modify the basic objectives, result in procedural differences in the handling of juveniles as compared to adults [11].

The author goes on to clarify the use of reasonable force in such terms as the distinction between an 11-year-old candy thief and a 17-year-old assault rapist.

FIGURE 18.2. *Programs such as the Police Athletic League instill respect and understanding for the role and function of police officers in the field. Courtesy Phil Crawford, Police Athletic League, San Jose, Ca.*

But the important point, perhaps the crucial point, is ". . . the arresting officer must so conduct himself in all cases as to promote and encourage reform and nothing must be done that would tend to cause a juvenile to continue his criminal behavior. . ." [12]. Encouraging reform may require sensitivity to the child's needs along with respectable police conduct. Respectable conduct is that combination of "firmness with fairness" that tends to engender confidence in police judgment. Respectable conduct as it relates specifically to juveniles will include holding the juvenile accountable for delinquent behavior even when the juvenile cannot be held criminally responsible.

Even the child who is truly a "victim of his environment" can develop lifelong respect for law enforcement goals when his arrest experience has been a firm but fair insistence by police that he account for behavior even when his age precludes his being held criminally responsible for his behavior.

As already noted, no known method exists to measure the reduction in the crime that occurs when children reach their adult years with a healthy respect for law enforcement goals developed through respect for police officers with whom they have been in contact. And of course the increase in crime attributed to children reaching adult years with fear and hatred of police can scarcely be measured either. But measurable or not, the challenge to human relations in law enforcement is clear, and far more than police image may be at stake. For in spite of tremendous public concern over crime [13], law enforcement appears to have reached an era in which public respect, even among those seeking only conventional police service, can no longer be taken for granted.

PUBLIC SUPPORT

If it is correct that law enforcement has reached an era in which citizen respect can no longer be taken for granted, then it might be said further that at least one police goal is now in jeopardy. Chapter Nine identified this goal as an administrative responsibility to gain public support for police activities. The problems reviewed concerned determining whether the press reflected or caused public opinion. Other administrative problems relating to the interpretation of public opinion also were reviewed. But the message of Chapter Nine regarding public support was that police need all the support they can get—at least in a democratic society.

Being unable to take citizen respect for granted [14], and further faced with a need to persuade at least part of the community that "bad image" is inappropriate, the police task may seem rather tremendous and yet rather uncomplicated. Regrettably, the actual task is just as complicated as it is tremendous.

Among the many police agencies currently involved in successful community programs such as those described earlier in this chapter, few if any could honestly claim success without at least some help from community leadership. Community leadership, whether it be the mayor, the president of a PTA, a neighborhood organization director, the head of a service club, or a clergyman, either directly assists or influences others to assist in most successful police-sponsored programs. In many instances, gaining this type of support is relatively easy—merely a matter of showing the need. The difficulty then often is not whether community programs can be undertaken by police, but rather *who* the programs influence and *how*.

If the term *public support* meant simply a majority of citizens, most police-sponsored community programs would enjoy the success of public support. If, however, public support includes the support of all the minority groups or neighborhoods that pose the greatest problems, then many so-called "successful" programs fall short of the police goal of gaining public support.

This indictment must be examined in terms of the "payoff" or rewards discussed earlier in this chapter. If the law violator finds a "reward" in "proving" that policemen "hate" because policemen arrest (even if the arrest has to be provoked), then it might be possible to gain further rewards by proving that policemen sponsor programs only for those that policemen do not hate or want to arrest. And in the case of misbehaving until "confirming" the belief that police "hate" enough to arrest, the "proof" that police-sponsored programs are meant for someone else is merely a matter of showing disinterest or actually disrupting the programs until police patience and tolerance is exhausted—thereby supplying the desired proof.

Here then is a dilemma. If, as recommended earlier in this chapter, police seek to understand what efforts are needed to remedy a bad image, they are likely to recruit the aid of community leadership in whatever human-relations program is undertaken. Such aid is a virtual requisite to successful program promotion. But if the groups for whom the image change is designed prefer to view community leaders merely as police collaborators rather than real leaders, then much reward accrues to proving the program is for someone else (by simply forcing police rejection).

The solution to this problem varies greatly depending on the unique characteristics and social resources of the community. But in communities in which respect for law enforcement has deteriorated with a segment of the population, efforts almost invariably are needed to ensure the confidence of that segment that program planning and operation involves leaders from both the segment involved and the community at large. Even in police agencies where a sensitive understanding of how a bad image is reinforced exists, however, it proves anything but easy to combine the often divergent views of leadership from both areas of the community. This difficulty is singularly significant when years of resentment between the two segments has fostered the belief that "the other guy cannot be trusted."

But easy or not, the effort invariably proves justified in terms of strengthening respect for law enforcement. And because respect for law enforcement can contribute to preventing crime, using the principles of human relations to promote this respect is not only appropriate, but imperative.

SUMMARY

Chapter Eighteen introduces the subject of police image in terms of the manner in which the public views the potential use of police authority. In spite of the absence of a valid scientific theory of crime cause, behavior science is cited as being in agreement on the presence of various social influences affecting crime rates. Establishing and maintaining a favorable police image (public respect) is presented as one of the more effective influences toward encouraging voluntary law observance which in turn is presented as crime prevention.

A favorable police image is created to some degree through the press as indicated in Chapter Nine. More amenable to direct police effort, however, is a favorable police image developed through observing ethical standards and through applying the principles of human relations—where human relations is defined as police participation in any activity that seeks law observance through respect rather than enforcement. Chapter Eight notes examples of police participation geared to attain public support, stressing in particular judicious use of force, the long-range effect of police contact with juveniles, and the value of combining leadership from all interested segments of the community in meeting problems. Possible problems that tend to reinforce unfortunate misbeliefs that hinder development of favorable police image also are presented. Methods of avoiding problems presented in both this and the previous chapter were considered—considered in the context of being absolutely imperative.

ANNOTATED REFERENCES

Challenge of Crime in a Free Society, A Report by the President's Commission on Law Enforcement and Administration of Justice, U.S. Government Printing Office, Washington, D.C., 1967. An excellent overview of the dimensions of human dynamics in police problems.

Coffey, A., E. Eldefonso, and W. Hartinger, *Human Relations: Law Enforcement in a Changing Community,* Prentice–Hall, Englewood Cliffs, N.J., 1971. A comprehensive in-depth coverage of the entire subject range of this chapter.

Coffey, A., E. Eldefonso, and W. Hartinger, *Police-Community Relations,* Prentice–Hall, Englewood Cliffs, N.J., 1971. Also comprehensive elaboration of the entire subject range of this chapter but not to the depth of the above-cited reference.

Kooken, D. L., *Ethics in Police Service,* Thomas, Springfield, Ill., 1957. A discussion of nonregulated but expected police conduct.

Sowle, C. R. (ed.), *Police Power and Individual Freedom,* Thomas, Springfield, Ill., 1962. A discussion of the title subject with emphasis on potential impact of authority.

Westley, C., "Violence and the Police," *Am. Jour. Sociol.,* Vol. 59, No. 34, 1953. A good discussion of the title subject from a perspective of causal relationships. Still a "classic" study. In this context, the "image" of police is further elaborated in Rankin, T. L., "Fact or Farce," *Police Chief,* March 1971. See also Freeman, N. W., "Building a Better Public Image," *FBI Law Enforcement Bulletin,* Feb. 1971.

NOTES

1. A. Coffey, E. Eldefonso, and W. Hartinger, *Police-Community Relations,* p. 1.

2. A. Coffey, E. Eldefonso, and W. Hartinger, *Human Relations: Law Enforcement in a Changing Community,* p. 52.

3. *Ibid.*

4. See, for example: L. E. Berson, *Case Study of a Riot: The Philadelphia Story,* Institute of Human Relations Press, New York, 1966; C. Westley, "Violence and the Police," *Am. Jour. Sociol.,* Vol. 59, No. 34, 1953; E. H. Sutherland and D. R. Cressey, *Principles of Criminology,* 6th ed., Lippincott, Philadelphia, 1960, p. 341; D. R. Rolph, "Police Violence," *New Statesman,* Vol. 66, No. 102, 1963.

5. J. H. Skolnick, *Justice Without Trial: Law Enforcement in a Democratic Society,* Wiley, New York, 1966.

6. E. B. Berne, *Games People Play,* Grove Press, New York, 1966.

7. H. H. Stroup, *Community Welfare Organization,* Harper, New York, 1952, p. 305.

8. A. Dunham, *Community Welfare Organization,* Crowell, New York, 1962, p. 31.

9. A. C. Germann, F. D. Day, and R. J. Gallati, *Introduction to Law Enforcement,* Thomas, Springfield, Ill., 1962, pp. 187–88.

10. E. Eldefonso, *Law Enforcement and the Youthful Offender,* 2nd ed., Wiley, New York, 1972, Chapters 7–9.

11. *Ibid.,* pp. 87–88.

12. *Ibid.,* p. 88.

13. *The Challenge of Crime in a Free Society,* President's Commission on Law Enforcement and Administration of Justice, U.S. Government Printing Office, Washington, D.C., 1967, pp. 49–50.

14. *Crime and Law Enforcement,* Special Analysis, College Debate Series, No. 16, Oct. 6, 1965, The American Institute of Public Policy Research, Washington, D.C., p. 81.

APPENDIX A

Criminal Process and Court Structure

A police officer should have a general idea of the various steps in the criminal process. The following outline is a simplification of these steps and also a brief survey of the major rules pertaining to the protection of the defendant in criminal cases. Although California's State Constitution is often cited as an example, most State's Constitutions are somewhat similar.

Also included in this outline is a brief description of the various courts, their make-up, and function.

CRIMINAL PROCESS AND PROCEDURE (GENERAL)

The following steps take place in the criminal process:

I. Arrest
   A. There is no difference between the right of a private citizen and a police (peace officer) to make an arrest without a warrant (with one exception).
   B. Both may make an arrest when a misdemeanor is committed in their presence. A private citizen may make an arrest when a felony has in fact been committed, and it is reasonable to believe the arrested party did commit the felony. A police officer may make an arrest when he has reason to believe (not that it actually has been committed) a felony has been committed and reason to believe the arrested party was the offender.

414

C. Note neither a peace officer or a citizen has the right to make an arrest without a warrant for a misdemeanor unless committed in his presence.

II. Complaint

A. An accusation in writing filed before a magistrate.

B. Private citizen may go before the district attorney and swear to facts indicating that defendant has committed a crime against him. The district attorney may then have a judge issue a warrant for defendant's arrest.

C. Citizen or peace officer making arrest without a warrant must then file a complaint before the district attorney.

III. Arraignment, Lower Court

This is held in the lower court to inform the defendant of the charges made against him, presenting him with a copy of the complaint against him, to advise defendant of his rights, to get his plea, and to set a date for trial.

A. Following arrest, the defendant must be taken before the court for arraignment within a "reasonable" length of time, generally 48 hours.

B. Court reads the complaint, identifies the defendant by asking his name, informing defendant of his right to counsel and setting bail if such has not been done.

1. IF OFFENSE IS MISDEMEANOR

a. At the arraignment the defendant may plead guilty to the charge and be sentenced at this time.

b. Defendant may request continuance before entering his plea to obtain counsel, or a continuance for a valid reason.

c. Defendant may plead not guilty. A date may then be set by the court for trial. This may be by jury or by judge. Defendant has a right to have the trial in 30 days, if not then, the charge is dismissed. Defendant may waive this 30 day requirement.

2. IF OFFENSE IS A FELONY

a. At the arraignment of the lower court, the defendant may plead guilty to the felony charge.

b. Lower court has no jurisdiction to hear or to sentence in the felony matters.

c. Lower court in not less than 2 or more than 5 days must order defendant to appear in the Superior Court for sentence. Reason: Lower court cannot sentence for felony.

d. Defendant then appears in Superior Court to be sentenced.

e. If defendant pleads not guilty—date set for preliminary.

IV. Preliminary Examination

A. At arraignment in the lower court, the defendant may enter a plea of not guilty. The magistrate must then have the preliminary examination within 5 days. Postponements may be allowed at defendant's request.

B. Defendant must then have a preliminary examination in the lower court. The purpose is to determine if there is reasonable grounds to believe the offense committed is a felony, and there is reason to believe the defendant committed it. However, the defendant may waive right to preliminary examination and be sent direct to Superior Court.

C. This is not a trial and the District Attorney need not give his case away by presenting all his evidence. Just enough evidence is presented to "tie the defendant" with the felony. This preliminary is a "screening" of cases so that the Superior Court will not waste its time hearing cases where it is obvious that the prosecution does not have a case, or where in fact the offense is not a felony.

D. The lower court may dismiss case against the defendant, if there is not sufficient evidence to indicate a felony has been committed, or that even if there was a felonious act that defendant can not be connected with its commission.

E. At this preliminary examination, it may be discovered that the offense is really only a misdemeanor. Defendant may then be ordered to stand trial on this.

F. If at the preliminary, the judge finds a felony has been committed, and there is reason to believe the defendant may have been the culprit, the defendant is "held to answer," which merely means that the defendant will go into the Superior Court for trial. The defendant can not be deprived of this preliminary examination.

G. In some jurisdictions, the custody of the defendant is transferred from the city jail to the county jail. The reason is that lower courts (Municipal Courts) are in large areas city courts under the city police, while the Superior Court is a State Court and the County Sheriff has jurisdiction over the prisoner.

Note: At this point the law provides that persons awaiting trial (not convicted of anything at this point) are not to be placed in custody with persons serving sentences for conviction of crimes.

V. Filing Information

A. The written accusation charging a person with a crime, the jurisdiction of which lies in the Superior Court, is signed by the District Attorney after examination (the lower court discussed) and is committed by the magistrate.

B. This is simply the transcript of the testimony of the preliminary examination held in the lower court signed by the District Attorney. The defendant is charged with a felony.

C. This "information" must be filed in the Superior Court within 15 days after the preliminary examination or the case is dismissed. The offense charged must be stated and signed by the District Attorney.

VI. Arraignment Superior Court

A. The information (transcript from the preliminary examination in the lower court) is filed in the Superior Court.

B. The defendant is then again arraigned in the Superior Court. The charges are read to him, he is informed of his rights to counsel, and the day for trial is set.

C. The defendant, of course, may plead guilty at any point, and receive his sentence, or ask for continuance.

D. Defendant has a right to be brought to trial within 60 days after the arraignment in Superior Court, unless he requests continuance and waives this right. Date for trial is set.

    E.   At every stage of the proceedings, defendant is entitled to counsel of his own choice and, if he can't pay for counsel, the court must provide him with appointed counsel.

VII. Trial in the Superior Court

    A.   If defendant pleads guilty at the arraignment in the Superior Court, his case is normally continued for 2–4 weeks for the probation officer's report. Date set for sentence at this point.

    B.   If defendant has a trial (by judge or jury) and is found guilty, again date for sentence is put over 2–4 weeks for probation officer's report. Date set for sentence.

    C.   Defendant then sentenced when probation officer's report submitted to the court.

VIII. Information and Indictment

    A.   All offenses must be prosecuted in the Superior Court by indictment or information except:

        1.   Removal of state officers.

        2.   Offense in the militia.

        3.   Misdemeanor which jurisdiction has been conferred upon Superior Courts sitting as Juvenile Courts.

        Thus there are only two methods to get most cases before the Superior Court.

    B.   INFORMATION: As previously discussed. Merely, the transcript of the preliminary examination is signed by the District Attorney and an order of the examining magistrate clearly stating the offense.

    C.   INDICTMENT: An accusation in writing presented by a grand jury to a competent court charging a person with a public offense.

IX. Grand Jury

    A.   Each county has a grand jury of 19 citizens, drawn from the jury panel.

    B.   They may inquire into all public offenses committed, which may be tried, within the county and present them to a competent court by indictment.

    C.   They are not responsible to the courts or the District Attorney and may make their own investigations. They may also inquire into all county officers and county expenditures. They may examine all accusations made to them by private citizens, public officials, and their own members.

    D.   The District Attorney usually presents the cases to the Grand Jury when he seeks an indictment. Twelve of the nineteen jurors must concur.

Note: When there is a felony indictment against a defendant, the first court proceeding is the arraignment in the Superior Court. No arraignment or preliminary examination in the lower court. At the arraignment the defendant must be presented with a copy of the Grand Jury's transcript.

 X. Why Grand Jury Indictment Instead of Complaint—Information Procedure:

    A.   When defendant is "missing," indictments may be made without defendant being present. He must be present in a preliminary examination in order to file the information.

B. When there are many defendants involved and if the prosecution started charging or trying some of them, others may flee. Best to secretly indict them all at once.

C. No complaint necessary. No complaining witness.

D. The prosecution may wish to avoid "tipping its hand" in the preliminary examination. Thus, get indictment and avoid preliminary.

E. Sometimes easier to get grand jury indictment than to withstand a preliminary examination. Defendant need not be present at grand jury but must be at preliminary.

XI. Distinction between Felony and a Misdemeanor (California)

A. Penal Code Section of Respective State Defines Distinction

1. A felony is a crime which is punishable by death (if falling within the January 1, 1974 "guidelines" of acts which may carry the death penalty), or confinement in a State Prison.

2. When a crime is punishable by State Prison OR County Jail, it is deemed a misdemeanor for all purposes after a judgement other than imprisonment in the State Prison.

3. If committed to the Youth Authority, the crime is a felony.

B. A commitment to the Youth Authority is a Felony, unless

1. After the ward is discharged from the Youth Authority, he has not been placed in a State Prison by the Youth Authority (D.V.I. is not a State Prison).

2. The committing court, on the person's application, makes an order determining that the crime for which he was convicted was a misdemeanor. Section 1772 W. & I. Code provides the same procedure except the defendant must have an honorable discharge (meaning good record on parole) and then the court may set aside the verdict of guilty and dismiss the accusation or information and release him from all penalties and disabilities. Thus no conviction at all.

PRACTICE: This may be done by the Probation Department, District Attorney, Public Defender, Private Attorney, or the ward himself by obtaining:

a. A certified copy of his discharge.

b. An affidavit reciting subject was not placed in a State Prison signed by the Clerk of the Youth Authority.

c. Placed on the calendar of the committing court.

d. Oral or written motion made praying that offense be declared a misdemeanor; or under 177 W. & I. that the verdict of guilty be set aside.

3. The implication of the above section seems to mean that if the Youth Authority places a ward in a State Prison during its control, that the ward like an adult authority felon must meet the requirements of Penal Code Sections 4850–4853 in order to have his commitment set aside through pardon.

SUMMARY OF COURT STEPS (CALIFORNIA)

I. Arrest, Complaint
II. Arraignment, Lower Court
    A. Misdemeanors
        1. Sentence if guilty plea to misdemeanor.
        2. Not guilty plea—trial for misdemeanor.
    B. Felony
        1. Guilty plea—referred to Superior Court for sentence.
        2. Not guilty plea—put over for preliminary examination.
III. Preliminary Examination, Lower Court
    A. Guilty plea at this time—put over for sentence.
    B. Finding a felony committed and reasonable grounds that defendant committed it. Defendant held to answer in Superior Court.
IV. Arraignment, Superior Court
    A. Guilty plea—put over for sentence.
    B. Not guilty plea—put over for trial.
V. Trial, Sentence

DEFENDANT'S CONSTITUTIONAL AND STATUTORY RIGHTS WHEN CHARGED WITH A CRIME (GENERAL)

The person charged with a crime has certain protections set up by the constitution and by code provisions. The United States Constitution is the protector of the people against the Federal government, and generally the first ten amendments (known as the Bill of Rights) do not apply against the State. The "due process" clause of the United States Constitution has by inclusion and exclusion covered some of these rights of the people against the State.

Thus, it is necessary to look to the "State Constitution," which is the document that gives the people right against their own State Legislative acts, to determine what these protections are. Various code sections and common law rules of evidence also gives the defendant every guarantee of a fair trial.

An officer of the law should have a general knowledge of these rules so that he is not placed in a position whereby misunderstanding occurs. The following are a few of these major rules.

I. Right to a Jury Trial, State Constitution
    A. Every defendant may have a common law jury of 12 to decide the disputed facts of his case. The defendant may waive a jury trial, if he

fully understands the nature of the waiver. He may also waive the number and be tried by less than 12 in misdemeanor cases.

B. To sustain a conviction all jurors must agree. If less than all agree then it is a hung jury and defendant may be tried again. No limit to the number of times defendant may be tried.

C. Defendant can have the judge hear the case without jury.

II. Double Jeopardy, State Constitution
Simply means no one can be tried for the same crime more than once.

A. A hung jury is not an acquittal, and a retrial for the same offense is not double jeopardy.

B. Same act may be an offense under two jurisdictions and thus may be tried for both.
EXAMPLE: Auto theft in San Francisco. Drove car to Nevada. Two crimes:
1. State law violation.
2. Federal law violation, Dwyer Act. Defendant may be charged and convicted of both, one in State Court, the other in the United States Court. This is not double jeopardy.

C. Same act may be more than one crime. Unless merged, defendant may be tried on both.

III. Right to Bail—None Excessive Bail—State Constitution

A. Prior to conviction defendant always has a right to bail.

B. Capital offense. Discretionary with judge and not a right. Any offense punishable with death is capital.

C. After conviction and pending appeal, bail is discretionary with judge and not a right. Same rule applies to Youth Authority Commitments from Superior Court; judge may allow defendant out on bail pending acceptance of case.

D. If defendant does not have funds to put up for bail, he may be retained in custody, but cannot be put in with those convicted of a crime.

IV. Right to Speedy Trial—State Constitution

A. Right to be brought before a magistrate after arrest in a reasonable time, 48 hours.

B. Defendant entitled to have his case adjudicated in an expedient manner. He may always waive this right in an open court.

C. In Superior Court, defendant must be brought to trial in 60 days after indictment by grand jury or filing of information by District Attorney. If not brought to trial, there is a dismissal and a bar to further prosecution for that offense.

V. Right to Counsel—State Constitution

A. Defendant has a right to counsel of his own choice at every stage of the proceedings.

B. California Constitution: "If defendant desires counsel and cannot pay a fee, the court must appoint counsel to defend him. Court should so inform defendant of his right."

C. Defendant may always waive his right to counsel. Court cannot force counsel on defendant as he always has the right to act as his own attorney.

VI. Right Not to Testify against Self—Self-Incrimination—State Constitution
   A. Defendant need not testify against himself. There is always the presumption of innocence, and he need not declare such. Burden of proof always on the prosecution. Defendant need not sign or make any statement to the police.
   B. Defendant never needs to take the stand and declare his innocence or to answer any questions at all. The rule applies to "testimony" and does not apply to fingerprinting, standing to be identified by witness, putting on coat, hat, etc. worn by culprit.
   C. California allows judge and District Attorney to comment to jury that defendant has not taken the stand to deny the charges or to offer testimony as to his innocence (Contra rule in most States).
   D. District Attorney cannot mention defendant's prior felony conviction unless defendant takes the stand. If defendant does, District Attorney may impeach his credibility as a witness by showing a prior felony conviction.

VII. Right to be Confronted by Accuser—State Constitution
   A. Defendant always has a right to have witness against him testify in his presence.
   B. Defendant, or his counsel, has a right to cross-examine the witness against him, to seek the truth, and to impeach the witness to show he may be lying, mistaken, hostile, prejudiced, etc. The jury must weigh the credibility of the witness.

VIII. Statute of Limitations
   These statutory requirements simply mean that within the prescribed period of the statute, an indictment, a complaint, or information must be filed. The time requirement does not run when the defendant is out of the State. The purpose is to allow a defendant to get his defense together, and it would be unjust not to set some limitation on the time that a person could be charged with a crime. This rule is of course meant to protect the innocent, but many times an asset to a clever criminal. His crime may be outlawed by that time and then nothing the police can do if he subsequently admits it.
   A. Felonies: Crimes so specified as felonies have a three year statute of limitations from time information filed, NOT from filing of complaint.
   B. Misdemeanors: One year statute of limitations from time complaint filed. When these time limits have expired, the defendant cannot be tried for the committed offense. This is jurisdictional and a conviction after statute has run is void, even if the defendant does not plead this as a defense. The time starts to run from date of crime's commission.
   C. Acceptance of bribe by a public official or employee—6 years.
   D. No statute of limitations for murder, embezzlement of public money, or falsification of public records.

IX. No Common Law Crimes in Some States (e.g., California)

- A. There can be no crime committed unless such is so designated by statute and a penalty is prescribed.
- B. The statute must be clear and not vague as to what is prohibited. The statute must be in plain English (no Latin medical terms). People must be able to understand what the statute means.
- X. No Cruel and Unusual Punishments (State Constitution)
   - A. Prisoner must be treated as a human.
   - B. Interpretation of "cruel and unusual" changes with the time and the sociological make-up of the Supreme Court. Death penalty by hanging, shooting, or gas held NOT CRUEL. Beating not permitted in California now, but is in Southern States.

RULES OF EVIDENCE WHICH PROTECT THE DEFENDANT (GENERAL)

The purpose of the rules relating to presentation of evidence is to get to the truth. To exclude testimony or demonstrative evidence that confuse the issues and to admit that which seeks to show the true facts. Obviously we can only discuss a few of the major highlights with which the police officer should be familiar.

- I. Establishing the Corpus Delicti
   In every criminal case the corpus delicti must be proved before any other evidence as to guilt may be presented.
   - A. Corpus Delicti—the elements of a crime; called the body of the crime. It must be shown that a criminal act took place, i.e., a car was stolen, a store was burglarized, a person was robbed, etc.
   - B. The identity of the person committing the crime is not a part of the corpus delicti.
   - C. Hollywood leads you to believe one cannot prosecute for murder without "producing the body." Corpus (body) delicti has nothing to do with production of a body. You can show the corpus delicti of a homicide by circumstantial evidence—the corpse not necessary.
   - D. Thus, usually if one cannot get the complaining witness in robbery, burglary, etc., to testify, no proof of corpus delicti and no prosecution.
   - E. Proof that a crime has been committed must be shown before the extra judicial confession or admission of the defendant are admissible in evidence. However, admission in open court is enough.
- II. Competency of Witness
   - A. Every witness may be competent except young child, insane or feeble-minded. All witnesses may be cross-examined to test their credibility or competency.
   - B. Wife not a competent witness against her husband who is charged with a crime. Not so when the crime the husband is charged with is against

wife or child. Merely old Common Law rule that husband and wife are one. Neither husband nor wife alone can waive this rule of competency and thus one cannot testify against the other. After divorce each may testify against the other, subject to the rules of privileged communication discussed below.

III. Privileged Communications
  A. Certain communications are privileged and the defendant can refuse to waive—thus the other party cannot testify against the defendant.
      1. Husband—Wife. Not to be confused with competency of husband or wife to testify against one another. Privileged communication is only that which took place during the marriage, not any communications which took place before marriage. Thus, once divorced, may testify to anything communicated prior to marriage, however, during a valid marriage husband or wife cannot testify at all against one another.
      2. Attorney—Client
      3. Clergyman—Priest-Confessor
      4. Newspaper reporter may refuse to disclose source of information.
      5. No such privilege between doctor-patient in criminal case.
  B. No privileged communication between probation and parole officer and client. A duty of parole or probation officer as a peace officer to disclose any information they have as to a crime commission to proper authorities.

IV. Illegally Obtained Evidence
  A. Federal Courts will not admit evidence against a defendant which has been obtained illegally, i.e., unlawful search without search warrant, stolen evidence, wire tap, etc.
  B. California and twenty-two other States will admit any evidence regardless of how obtained if it is otherwise admissible.
  C. Defendant may civilly sue the police officers, but evidence will still be admitted.

V. Hearsay Evidence Rules (At Least Twenty Exceptions)
  A. Simply means that the testimony offered rests on the veracity of some other person other than the witness.
  B. The law requires that the witness testify to those facts only which he gained by his own perceptions—not what some one else has told him.
  C. The law demands that the person who actually saw the act, or heard (if that is the fact to be proved) testify, not the third person who gained the information from someone else.
  D. Exceptions are numerous. A few important ones in criminal cases are:
      1. Admission of silence, conduct, flight, etc.
      2. Confessions must be freely and voluntarily given.
      3. Dying declaration may only be used in connection with naming the person who killed the dying victim.
  E. Testimony to facts only, not opinions. Exceptions are numerous.
      1. Expert witnesses (medical, scientific, blood tests, handwriting, etc.).

2. Opinions as to color, height, speed, weight, etc., and imperfect describable event.

VI. Conviction with Only Uncorroborated Testimony of Accomplice

A. An accomplice is one who may be prosecuted for the same offense as defendant.

B. Mere knowledge of a crime is not an accomplice.

C. A child under 14 cannot be an accomplice, because law presumes one under 14 incapable of committing a crime unless CLEAR PROOF SHOWN THAT HE KNEW THE WRONGFULNESS OF THE ACT.

D. Parties to a crime.

1. Principal: One who participates in a crime directly, or who aids and abets, or who, not present, advises and encourages its commission. The act of one principal is the act of them all. The same rule applies to conspirators.

2. Accessory: Every person who conceals or aids a person after a felony has been committed with the intent to help him escape is an accessory. This means more than mere silence, there must be some overt act to make one an accessory.

COURT STRUCTURE (EXAMPLE CALIFORNIA)

I. Supreme Court

Chief Justice, six associate justices. Two departments, three in each. Appointed by governor with approval of Judicial Council. They are then elected for 12 year terms. No opposition but running on their record. A yes or no vote.

A. Highest Court of Appeal in State.

B. Cases come up from District Court of Appeal or Superior Court. All death cases reviewed.

C. May order any case in District Court of Appeal up to them on questions of law alone. No jury.

D. Issue writs of Habeas Corpus everywhere in State (except Federal cases).

E. Final review unless U.S. Constitutional question involved.

II. District Court of Appeal

There are four districts with each district having at least one division:

San Francisco—two divisions

Los Angeles—four divisions

Sacramento—one division

San Bernardino—one division

There are three justices to each division including a presiding justice. Three justices sit on each court. No jury.

A. Same procedure for appointment and term of office (12 years) as in Supreme Court.

B. Appellate jurisdiction on all criminal cases in their district prosecuted by indictment or information (felonies), except where judgement of death rendered.

C. Issue writs of habeas corpus for persons in custody within the district.

III. Superior Court

Number vary in different county—set by legislature.

A. Elected for 6 year term.

B. Highest trial court—tries all felonies. May issue writ of habeas corpus in respective county.

C. Accepts appeals from lower, inferior courts.

D. Juvenile Court—original jurisdiction for 702 W. & I. cases even if only a misdemeanor.

IV. Municipal Courts (Court Reorganization January 1, 1953)

Each county divided into Judicial Districts by Legislature—try misdemeanors.

A. Over 40,000 population, Municipal Court formed.

B. Under 40,000, Justice Court.

C. Where Municipal Court exists, there are no Justice Courts.

D. Justice Court is a court for a township—a political subdivision of a county.

E. Police Court is a City Court.

V. Judicial Council

A. Composed of Chief Justice of Supreme Court, one Associate Justice, three Justices of District Court, four judges of Superior Court, one judge of Municipal Court, and one judge of Inferior Court, all chosen by Chief Justice for 2 year terms.

B. FUNCTION: Advising and coordinating body for improvement of the administration of justice. Assigning of judges from one county to another when calendars heavy. Prescribes rules for practice and procedure on appeals. Make recommendations to Governor and Legislature regarding improvement in the judicial branch of government.

APPENDIX B

History of Law Enforcement

2370 B.C.	Sumerian King Ura-Ka-Gina controls oppression.
2130	Sumerian King Nammu issues code of laws.
2100–1900	Kings Lipit-Ish-Tar, Eshnunna, and Hammurabi standardize offenses of much of the unwritten *lex talionis.*
1900	Roman Law; Hammurabi's "Great Code"; The Mosaic Code; Plato's Philosophy on Punishment; Emperor Augustus' Praetorian Guards.
	Rome—Fifteenth Century A.D.—Feudal Laws—Heresy Enforcement.
1607	Jamestown creates parish constable as in England.
1629	Dutch West India Company appoints "schout-fiscal" to keep peace in Nieu Amsterdam (New York).
1631	April 12, Boston court orders that watches be set.
1634	September 1, Boston elects a constable.
1636	February 27, Boston town government assumes control and appointing powers over the watch.
1649	Jamestown sheriff empowered as the King's representative to keep peace.

426

1692	Philadelphia creates a watch for daytime only.
1693	July 8, New York watch wears first uniforms.
1699	Massachusetts standardizes procedure for establishing watches throughout its province.
1700	July 1, Philadelphia begins a new system of drafting citizens to serve on the watch.
1712	Boston establishes pay for watchmen.
1785	April 17, Boston appoints first inspectors of police.
1807	March 10, Boston establishes first police districts.
1823	Texas Rangers organized.
1833	December 26, Philadelphia establishes first police force as well as first daytime police.
1836	Congress authorizes postal agents to investigate mail depredation.
1838	May 21, Boston appoints first permanent day watch.
1844	New York City is first to establish a permanent day and night police force.
1850	Allen Pinkerton organizes private detective agency to deal with rail robberies.
1851	First public American execution in San Francisco: John Jenkins for burglary.
1851	Boston uses first detective division.
1852	New Orleans and Cincinnati organize police departments along Peel lines.
1853	Baltimore establishes police department under control of mayor.
1855	New York ordinance passed requiring use of police badge.
1856	San Francisco replaces marshal's office with chief of police.
1857	Trend toward state control of police begins.
1858	Boston and New York City install first police telegraph systems.
1860	Secret Service created as a bureau of treasury.
1861	Congress appropriates money to investigate crimes against the United States.

1863	Nevada City "vigilantes" formed.
1867	First use of call boxes for patrolmen.
1868	Internal Revenue Service gets twenty-five detectives.
1871	Wild Bill Hickok appointed Abilene marshal.
1876	Wyatt Earp made chief deputy marshal of Dodge City.
1881	Sheriff Pat Garrett kills Billy the Kid.
1893	National Chiefs of Police Union formed (later called International Association of Chiefs of Police).
1900	Trend toward returning control of police to local authorities.
1905	Pennsylvania establishes first state police force.
1908	New York police use wireless telegraph on patrol boats, and appoint first woman detectives.
1918	Prohibition law enacted.
1921	September 4, first police radio broadcast made in St. Louis, Missouri.
1924	J. Edgar Hoover organizes the Federal Bureau of Investigation.
1929	Eliot Ness appointed head of Prohibition Bureau (later identified with "The Untouchables").
1930	Bureau of Narcotics formed.
1933	July 10, first radio police car put into service by Eastchester, New York.
1934	Federal kidnapping, banking, and interstate-compact laws passed.
1935	July 29, FBI establishes a training school for police officers.
1953	Peace Officer's Research Association formed in California under acronym, "PORAC."
1960	October, California forms the Commission on Peace Officers' Standards and Training.
1965	New York Police Department begins converting fingerprint records to magnetic tape.
1967	The President's Commission on Law Enforcement and the Administration of Justice releases task force reports.

APPENDIX C

Pertinent United States Supreme Court Decisions

Much of the basis of the increasing Supreme Court assessment of Police practice is the *fourth amendment,* and to some degree the *ninth amendment* (see Appendix E). The implications of the *fourth amendment* to the police function have received more than adequate concern in the literature. Nevertheless, a brief review of the highlights of the more significant court decisions may serve to clarify these implications.

Weeks v. United States (1914)

The U.S. Supreme Court ruled that a federal court could not accept evidence that was obtained in violation of search and seizure protection, which is guaranteed by the *fourth amendment.*

Mallory v. United States (1943)

The U.S. Supreme Court declared that only the courts can decide to deprive a person of liberty. In the absence of a judicial warrant or probable cause, "there can be no lawful arrest; illegal detention for 'investigation' may invalidate an otherwise legal confession." The U.S. Supreme Court stated "*. . . We cannot sanction this extended delay, resulting in confession, with-*

429

out subordinating the general rule of prompt arraignment to the discretion of arresting officers in finding exceptional circumstances for its disregard.''

Mapp v. Ohio (1961)

The U.S. Supreme Court overruled a conviction in the State of Ohio declaring that the *fourth amendment* prohibited "unreasonable searches and seizures." The prohibition will be enforced and the convictions based on procedures contrary to the *fourth amendment* though consistent with State law will be overruled. In reversing the Ohio State Supreme Court ruling, the U.S. Supreme Court stated ". . . *All evidence obtained by searches and seizures in violation of the Constitution is by the same authority, inadmissible in a State court.''*

Gideon v. Wainwright (1963)

The U.S. Supreme Court established the precedent that a person charged with a felony shall have counsel even if he is too poor to pay for it. (Essentially, this meant that the State must pay for defense counsel for accused felons.) The effect of this ruling was that a new trial could be demanded by anyone convicted of a crime who did not have legal counsel.

Escobedo v. Illinois (1964)

This decision held it the constitutional right of an *indigent* to be provided with legal counsel at the time of *police interrogation.*

Miranda v. Arizona (1966)

This U.S. Supreme Court decision made it mandatory that a person be forewarned about his rights under the Constitution. The Miranda decision has the effect of providing legal counsel during *police questioning* for persons *suspected* of crimes. The person must be informed of his constitutional rights to counsel and his right to remain silent. Absence of such warnings will result in making a confession inadmissible.

Gault v. Arizona (1967)

The Gault decision gave minors many of the rights that adults enjoy in the court process such as: NOTICE (i.e., charges or claims against the defendant—complaint); RIGHT TO A LAWYER, PROTECTION AGAINST SELF-INCRIMINATION, CONFRONTATION (i.e., right to confront the witnesses against him, to hear their testimony, to have them under oath, and to cross-examine them); RULES OF EVIDENCE; WAIVER OF RIGHTS (intelligent waiver); POLICE INTERROGATION (i.e., Miranda warning); and, TRIAL TRANSCRIPT OF HEARING. It should be noted that the U.S. Supreme Court did not reverse (a) jury trials, (b) public trials, (c) public access to records, or (d) appeal as a right; nor did it so much as suggest a contradiction of the Juvenile Court philosophy or method other than to confer on children the basic Constitutional rights enjoyed by adults.

APPENDIX D

Glossary of Legal Terms

ABET Encouraging or inciting a crime. Abet usually applies to aiding an individual in the violation of a law.

ACCESSORY Person who has knowledge of a law violation (felony) which has been committed and assists the perpetrator to avoid arrest, trial, or punishment.

ACCOMPLICE Individual who is *equally* responsible for an offense considered a violation of a law.

ACCUSED Term for a defendant in a criminal case. Often used interchangeably with "prisoner" or "defendant."

ADMISSION Acknowledgement of the existence of an act or a fact.

AFFIANT Refers to a person who constructs and signs an affidavit.

AFFIDAVIT Written statement made under oath, usually before a notary public or another authorized person.

AFFIRMATION Positive declaration or assertion, but not under oath, that the witness will tell the truth.

AGGRESSOR One who aggresses; a person who initiates a quarrel, or fight, making an unprovoked attack.

AID AND ABET Any assistance rendered by encouraging words, acts, support, or presence.

ALIAS   Fictitious name sometimes used by fleeing felons.

ALIBI   Excuse; the accused person was elsewhere than at the alleged scene of the offense with which he is charged.

ALIEN   Foreigner; a foreign-born resident of this country who has not become a naturalized citizen.

ALLEGATION   Assertion without proof but which its advocate proposes to support with evidence.

AMICUS CURIAE   Friend of the court. Usually an attorney who volunteers to assist the court in whatever manner deemed necessary.

ANARCHIST   Person who proposes the overthrow of the government by creating disorder and violence.

ANIMUS   State of mind, intention, and will.

ANIMUS FURANDI   Fully intending to commit a theft (state of mind at the time the theft is committed).

ANNUL   Invalidate; void and cancel. Commonly used in annulment of marriage.

ANONYMOUS   No name known or acknowledged; unsigned letter, note, etc.

ANTHROPOMETRY   Having to do with the measurement of the human body to determine differences in races; comparison with corresponding measurements of other individuals.

APPELLATE   Relating to appeals; person who appeals to a higher court; appeal from the decision of the lower court to a higher court.

APPELLATE COURT   Court that has the power to review appeals from another jurisdiction and affirm or reverse the decisions of lower courts.

APPELLEE   *Person appealed against;* often times referred to as the "respondent."

ARRAIGNMENT   Bringing a person before a court of law to answer an accusation.

ASPORTATION   Taken away; moving of items from one place and "transporting" said items to another. Removal of such goods is extremely important when considering an offense of larceny.

ATTAINDER   Loss of civil rights, inheritance, property, etc. Such loss of civil rights occurs after a person has committed treason or felony and received a sentence of death for his crime.

ATTEST   To bear witness and testify under oath or signature.

AUTOPSY   Examination and dissection of a dead body to discover the cause of death.

BALIFF   Sheriff's assistant who serves processes and officer who has charge of prisoners and guards the jurors in court.

BAILMENT   Provision of bail for an arrested person.

BENCH WARRANT   Order issued by a judge or law court for the arrest of a person charged with a contempt of court or criminal offense.

BROTHEL   Establishment which commonly functions as a house of prostitution.

BUNCO GAME   Act or trick contrived to gain the confidence of the victim who is then defrauded. This form of theft is handled by a special investigative unit in most police departments.

CADAVER   Corpse; a person who has been dead over a period of time.

CAUSA CAUSANAS   Immediate cause and the last link in the change of causative factors (Black's Law Dictionary).

CAVEAT EMPTOR   Under this particular rule, it is incumbent upon the buyer to examine the goods and determine any malfunctions or defects. Often termed as "let the buyer beware" or "take care."

CERTIORARI   Review; the higher court issuing a writ directing the lower jurisdiction to forward all records and proceedings for *review* or trial of issues in question.

CHANGE OF VENUE   Suit which is initiated in one county or district may be changed to another county or district for trial purposes. Referring to criminal cases, a good example of change of venue would be the Angela Davis trial and John Linley Frazier trial transferred from its county of initial jurisdiction to the County of Santa Clara.

CHATTEL   Item, article, or piece of property which is somewhat personal and transferable.

COLLUSION   Secret agreement for fraudulent or illegal purposes; conspiracy.

COMMITMENT   Consignment to state prison; commitment by means of a court order or warrant of a person to a particular facility for incarceration.

COMMON LAW   Unwritten law of the country based on custom, usage, and decisions of law courts, as contrasted with *statute law*. Common-law marriage is not solemnized by religious or civil ceremony but effected by an agreement to live together as husband and wife; cohabitation.

COOL BLOOD   Crime not committed in a fit of anger; this is a term utilized in cases relating to homicides in which there is an absence of emotion or violent passion: "The crime was executed in cold blood."

CORONER   County officer whose function is to inquire into the circumstances and causes of any violent or sudden death (with suspicion) occurring within his jurisdiction. Often referred to as "the coroner's inquest."

CORPORAL PUNISHMENT   Type of punishment which is physical as distinguished from "punishment by a fine."

CORPSE   Dead body, commonly of a human being.

CORPUS DELICTI   Substance of the crime; the essential elements of a violation of law—*not* a dead human body.

CORROBORATING EVIDENCE   Confirmation by further evidence; seconding or confirming initial evidence.

DEADLY WEAPON   Weapon which is designed for the destruction of life or inflicting an injury: "A deadly weapon likely to produce death or severe bodily harm."

DEBAUCHERY   Excessive hedonistic pleasure; usually in the sense of sexual immorality or the unlawful excessive indulgence of lust in the form of sexual activity.

DELIBERATELY   Deliberately committing a law violation; premeditation, intentionally, willfully; as previously stated "in cold blood."

DEMURRER   Plea for the dismissal of a law suit on the grounds that even if the statements of the opposition are true, they do not sustain the claim because they are insufficient or otherwise legally defective.

DICTUM   Formal statement made by the judge; a judge's statement or opinion on some legal point other than the principle issue of the case. Such a statement usually is utilized as illustration or argument.

DOMICILE   Customary or permanent dwelling place, home, residence. Taken in a legal frame of reference, domicile refers to "one's official or legal residence."

DURESS   Coercion or compulsion: as confession signed under *duress.*

EMANCIPATION   Rendered free or set at liberty by his parents, guardian, or master. "A child emancipated from his parents."

EMBEZZLEMENT   Fraudulent appropriation of money or goods entrusted to one's care.

EMINENT DOMAIN   Government's power to take private property for public use.

ENTRAPMENT   Deceiving or tricking a person into committing a crime not contemplated by the individual; entrapment does not imply the mere act of a police officer furnishing a person the opportunity to violate the law, where the criminal intent was already present.

EVIDENCE   Represents any question of fact; the procurement of facts to substantiate the violation; the gathering of facts which would constitute sufficient evidence to prosecute.

EXPARTE   Action in behalf of one party only.

EX POST FACTO LAW   Under the Constitution of the United States, the states cannot pass any *ex post facto* laws. This is a law which is passed after the occurrence of an act.

EXTORTION   Use of coercion, force, or fear, property is obtained from others with his consent.

EXTRADITION   Fleeing of a felon to another state and the surrender of a felon by the state where he is found to a receiving state for prosecution of a crime committed in the state from which the felon fled.

FACSIMILE   *Exact* copy of the original.

FALSE ARREST   Unlawful physical restraint upon an individual of another's liberty; such restrictions could occur in prisons, jails, or other maximum security facilities.

FELONIOUS   Malicious intent to commit a crime; an important element here is "intent."

HABEAS CORPUS   In Latin, habeas corpus refers to "you have the body." Habeas corpus is a term accorded to a variety of writs. These writs serve as instruments for bringing the accused party immediately before a court or judge. In law, a writ or order requiring that a prisoner be brought before a court at a stated time and place to decide the legality of his detention or imprisonment. In other words, the right of *habeas corpus* safe-guards one against illegal detention or imprisonment.

HOLOGRAPH   Instrument, usually a deed or will, written entirely by a person without the benefit of an attorney or any kind of legal advice. It is written in his own hand and is accepted by courts throughout the land as his last testament.

INDICTMENT   Accusation or charge in writing by a Grand Jury; specifically, a formal writing, accusation, charging of one or more persons with the commission of a crime, presented by a Grand Jury to the court when the jury has found, upon examining the prosecutor's statement of the charge (Bill of Indictment), that there is a valid case.

INFANTICIDE　Murder of an infant immediately *after birth*. The actual birth of the infant distinguishes this particular act from "procuring abortion." Abortion, naturally, is the destruction of the *fetus in the womb*.

INFORMATION　In law, information is an accusation of criminal offense, not by indictment of a Grand Jury, but by a public officer such as the District Attorney. It is an accusation in the nature of an indictment, differing from the Grand Jury indictment in that it is presented by a competent public officer on his oath of office.

INJUNCTION　Writ or order from a court prohibiting a person or a group from carrying out a given action, or ordering a given action to be done. An injunction enjoins, binds, or commands a person to refrain from a particular act.

INQUEST　Judicial inquiry, especially when held before a jury, as a coroner's investigation of a death. "The coroner's inquest" investigates the manner of death and is authorized to bring forth a verdict of such an inquiry.

INSANITY　Legally there are numerous tests of insanities such as the Duran and the McNaughton Rules. It is a state of illness or derangement and, specifically in law, any form or degree of mental derangement or unsoundness, permanent or temporary, that makes a person incapable of what is regarded legally as normal, rational conduct or judgement. Such a state, legally, prevents a man from comprehending nature and the consequences of his acts or from distinguishing between right and wrong conduct.

INTENT　"A state of mind." Formulating a design or a resolve to do a particular act. Some crimes necessitate that there be a concurrent act and intent to commit said act.

JURIDICAL DAYS　Days in which courts are in session.

JURISDICTION　Territorial range of authority; "jurisdiction of the court." The administration of justice; authority or legal power to hear and decide cases. The power to adjudicate or exercise any judicial power over a person within "the jurisdiction of the court."

JURISPRUDENCE　Science or philosophy of law or system of laws; a part or division of a law.

JURIST　Expert in law; scholar or writer in the field of law.

JURY　In legal terms, jury refers to a group of people sworn to hear the evidence and inquire into the facts in a law case, and to arrive at a decision in accordance with their findings. "The right to be judged by a competent jury of his peers."

KLEPTOMANIAC   One who continues to involve himself in thefts of items because of an irresistible, persistent, and abnormal impulse or tendency to steal.

MALADMINISTRATION   Insufficient or corrupt conduct of public affairs.

MALA IN SE   Acts considered morally wrong; according to Black's Law Dictionary, "wrongs in themselves; offenses against conscience."

MALFEASANCE   Misconduct in handling public affairs; an official who is found guilty of taking graft.

MALICE AFORETHOUGHT   Intentionally committing an unlawful act; a deliberate intention and plan to "commit a violation of law—as murder."

MALICIOUS   Spitefully and maliciously causing the injury of someone; an intentional mischievous, or harmful act.

MALIGN   Person who plots to deceive; a malignant influence causing harm to one's reputation (slander).

MALUM IN SE   Wrong in itself; the very nature of the act is illegal based upon principles of natural, moral, and public law. (Black's Law Dictionary).

MALUM PROHIBITUM   Act expressly prohibited by law. The act need not be considered immoral, but by the very nature of the fact that the law forbids such an act it is "malum prohibitum."

MENS REA   "State of mind;" a criminal intent.

MOTIVE   Refers to any impulse, emotion, or desire that moves one to action (i.e., greed was his only *motive* for stealing; his *motive* for murdering his grandfather was for the inheritance); motive is an inner drive, impulse, or intention that causes a person to do something or act in a certain way. In order to allay any confusion, the distinguishing factor between "motive" and "intent" is that *motive* is, as previously stated, an inner drive impulse emotion, etc. that moves one to action to obtain a definite reward or result; *intent,* in contrast, is the desire to use a particular "tool" to create, effect, or produce such a result.

MURDER   Unlawful and malicious or premeditated killing of one human being by another. Murder can also be viewed as such when in the course of committing a felony such as rape or robbery, a human being is killed by another. "To kill (a person) unlawfully with malice."

NOLO CONTENDERE   Noncontested issue (Latin: "I will not contest it.") A plea in a criminal action which may have the same legal ramifications as a plea of guilty—insofar as all proceedings on the indictment, and on which the defendant may be sentenced by the court. It may not be used as an admission elsewhere, such as in a civil case whereby the victim attempts to obtain civil remedy for any losses sustained (automobile accident, restitution for damages occurred).

PRECEDENT   Previous decision by a court which may serve as an example or authority for a similar case.

PRIMA FACIE   From the first disclosure or at first sight; "we will put on a prima facie case."

RECIDIVIST   Person who continues to commit criminal acts—a habitual criminal (repeater).

STARE DECISIS   Upholding precedence; resting upon the principle that any law by which government seeks to govern its people should be unfluctuating, definite, and of common knowledge. Laws cannot be changed unless changed by competent authority.

SUBPOENA   Order by the court compelling a person to appear in court (as witnesses). The subpoena (subpoena duces tecum) may also require the party to bring with them all documents, records, evidence, which may be in their possession.

SUBSTANTIVE LAW   Codified law, that particular part of law that creates and defines and regulates rights, as opposed to remedial law, which prescribes a particular method of obtaining redress for their violations.

SUMMONS   Official order to appear in court; a writ, directed to a public servant, usually a sheriff, to notify the person named that an action had been taken against him in court, and require him to appear on the date and time named in the writ. In order to answer the complaint and the action in question.

TORT   Wrongful act, injury, or damage (not involving a breach of contract) for which a civil action can be brought.

TRANSCRIPT   Official description of a court hearing; proceedings in court are recorded by an official court reporter, thereby making the proceedings available to anyone interested in a judgement or other pertinent information in court.

TRAUMA   Injury or wound violently produced and the condition of neurosis resulting from such a wound; psychiatrically speaking, an emotional experience, or shock, which has a less than psychic effect.

TRIAL   Act or process of trying, testing, or putting to proof; a formal examination of the facts of a case by a court of law to decide the validity of a charge or claim.

VENIRE FACIAS (Venire) Writ or order issued by a judge to a sheriff or coroner, instructing him to summon persons to serve as jurors (cause to come).

VENUE Specific place in which a case is tried—"the court has jurisdiction of the case." The county or locality in which the cause of action occurs or where the crime is committed and the locality in which a jury is drawn and the case is tried. Venue is that part of a declaration in an action that designates the county in which the trial is to occur . . . "Change of venue" in law, the substitution of another place of trial, as when the jury or court is likely to be prejudiced.

WRIT OF CERTIORARI Writ utilized by a high court directing the lower court to send all the available information (records) of a proceeding in order that it be reviewed by the higher court. All cases on appeals usually involve the writ of certiorari.

WRIT OF ERROR CORAM NOBIS Procedure in which the record of the trial court proceedings may be embellished or expanded with evidence other than what was used for the initial court hearing—such evidence may still be reviewed by the appellate court although the required time for appeal expires.

WRIT OF EXECUTION Such a writ may be issued to confiscate property to satisfy a civil judgement.

WRIT OF HABEAS CORPUS Any person responsible for the confinement of another individual may be required by order of the court to immediately present the person before the court in order that the judge can ascertain the legal reasons for such a confinement. If the court is of the opinion that such a confinement is illegal, the judge orders the person so confined to be released. Such a writ may be directed to police officers, prison officials, sheriff (responsible for jail incarceration), or, with unusual circumstances, a private citizen. Such a writ orders the person responsible for the confinement of another to present the prisoner before the court immediately and assign a time and place for such adhering.

WRIT OF MANDAMUS Writ which in essence is a command or order. It is a writ issued by a court ordering some official to execute the specific act described in the writ. The writ of mandamus is an unusual remedy for a situation and, therefore, will not be issued by the court if the official to whom it is directed has the authority to refuse to perform such an act.

APPENDIX E

Laboratory of Criminalistics

The objective of the Laboratory of Criminalistics is to provide scientific support to law enforcement in the County of Santa Clara in connection with physical evidence examination and evaluation [1].

CHARACTERISTICS

It is characterized by a modern laboratory employing those instruments and resources of chemistry, physics, and other related basic sciences which find application in the peculiar physical evidence problems of law, law enforcement, and the administration of justice.

Personnel of the criminalistics profession are characterized by special training in the basic disciplines of science and their application in the consideration of law enforcement problems. Specific applications include examination, analysis, and evaluation of objects of physical evidence as well as consulting and advice to peace officers and trial attorneys.

Personnel habitually remain abreast of new developments by reading professional journals and attending periodic scientific meetings, symposia, and seminars.

Capital outlay is limited to instruments which are used sufficiently to more than repay the cost of leased or per case-fee consulting of commercially

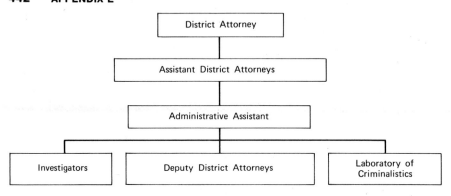

available facilities. When the need arises for professional work beyond the scope of County facilities, it is engaged on a contractual or fee basis.

ORGANIZATION

The Laboratory of Criminalistics is a division of the Department of District Attorney, and is related as indicated by the organization chart above. As laboratory operations grow in accordance with the forecast of population increase, the laboratory operations will develop and will have to change from time to time to meet new requirements.

The work of a criminalistics laboratory is characterized by the fact that the director and criminalists have the primary responsibility of case work. In order to accomplish the case work systematically and in time for law enforcement application, it is necessary to assign the staff administrative functions to suit the particular abilities and special areas of knowledges of available personnel without regard to grade of criminalist.

Staff assignments of other special projects and studies are made from time to time for training and development.

There is a cooperative interplay and administrative support among the staff on all case work; however, the responsibility for administrative functions of a continuing nature is clearly fixed by the organizational chart and the staff supervision chart.

NOTE

1. Adapted from: *California Criminal Justice Cost Project,* Phase I. Prepared by Public Systems Inc., Sunnyvale, Ca., Aug. 1971 (mimeograph). For California Assembly Rules Committee, Sacramento, Ca.

APPENDIX F

Purpose of the District Attorney's Office

The purpose of the District Attorney's office is to carry out the duties imposed by law upon the District Attorney [1]. The principal functions of the District Attorney's Office are as follows:

Public Prosecutor.   The District Attorney is the Public Prosecutor.

Preparation and Trial of Criminal Cases.   The district attorney prepares complaints upon which warrants are issued for the arrest of people charged with or reasonably suspected of committing public offenses. He draws all indictments and informations, and conducts the trial of criminal cases. He may grant immunity to witnesses. After felony conviction, the district attorney files with the Clerk of the Superior Court his views with respect to the defendant and his crime for transmittal to the Department of Corrections, and he assists the Attorney General on appeals from criminal convictions. He obtains civil judgment against bonding companies arising out of bail forfeiture. The district attorney investigates and reports to the Superior Court on all applications for rehabilitation and pardon.

Advises Grand Jury.   The district attorney is the legal advisor to the Grand Jury.

Trial of Accusations Against Public Officials.   The district attorney conducts the trial of accusations against public officials.

443

Conducts Civil and Criminal Actions for Nonsupport of Children. The district attorney is specifically required to prosecute criminal violations for nonsupport of children. In nonsupport matters, he also brings civil actions to determine paternity, and conducts civil actions for nonsupport under the Uniform Reciprocal Support Act.

Abates Public Nuisances. The district attorney conducts civil and criminal actions to abate public nuisances.

Commitment and Trial of Mentally Ill, Drug Addiction, and Inebriacy Cases. The district attorney prepares commitments for the mentally ill, the mentally deficient, and the feeble-minded, narcotic addicts, and persons addicted to habit-forming drugs and inebriates. He also conducts the trials of these cases.

The district attorney prosecutes all violations of state law and county ordinances. He does not prosecute violations of federal statutes or violations of city ordinances.

To assist the district attorney in performing these functions, he has a staff of assistant and deputy district attorneys, criminal and nonsupport investigators, clerical personnel, and the Laboratory of Criminalistics (see Appendix E).

PREPARING COMPLAINTS

Requirements

As Public Prosecutor, the District Attorney prepares complaints for the arrest of people charged with or reasonably suspected of committing public offenses. In addition, he draws all indictments and informations. There are four tests which should be applied in every case before a criminal complaint is prepared. They are as follows:

1. Has a public offense been committed?
2. Is the identity of the perpetrator known?
3. Can the offense be proven beyond a reasonable doubt?
4. Should there be a prosecution under all the circumstances?

No complaint should be authorized unless each of the above four questions is answered in the affirmative.

While the prosecutor owes a duty to the people of the State of California to prepare complaints in proper cases, he also owes a duty to the accused to prove his case beyond a reasonable doubt. The prosecutor should never forget that an arrest is a serious matter, particularly to the individual arrested. Every arrest constitutes a criminal record which, in most instances, will remain with the arrested person for life.

When a complaint is prepared, the proper ultimate charge should be selected at the outset. The practice of authorizing one charge and later reducing the case to a lesser charge or increasing to a greater charge should be studiously avoided.

Authority

Misdemeanors.   All deputies are authorized to prepare misdemeanor complaints when the basic requirements for a criminal complaint have been met.

Felonies.   In California, the Assistant District Attorneys and Attorneys IV and III (more experienced senior D.A.) are authorized to prepare felony complaints.

The senior deputies assigned to courts (Municipal) may authorize felony complaints for the respective police department in each jurisdiction. When the deputy assigned to these courts is not a senior attorney, he should insofar as is practicable, review each felony complaint prepared with an Assistant District Attorney.

Drafting

In General.   Complaints may be stated in the ordinary and concise language of the statute. The time at which the offense was committed may be pleaded at any time within the statute of limitations before filing the complaint. A single complaint may include two or more different offenses of the same class of crimes or two or more different offenses connected together in their commission.

Signing and Filing

Complaints may be sworn to on information and belief in both misdemeanor and felony cases. All felony complaints should be signed by a peace officer. Misdemeanor complaints should be signed by a peace officer whenever possible. Deputy District Attorneys should not sign complaints except in instances where a stipulated reduction complaint is filed in a municipal or justice court.

Generally, complaints should be filed in the Municipal or Justice Court having jurisdiction of the place where the offense was committed. An exception may be made in certain nonsupport cases and certain cases involving State regulatory agencies where all of the parties involved in the action.

When misdemeanors committed in another judicial district are filed in the county seat, the complaint should show on its face where the offense occurred.

Citizen Complaints

Felonies. All citizen complaints concerning the commission of felonies should be referred to the police agency having jurisdiction of the place where the offense occurred. A felony complaint requires preliminary examination, production of witnesses at preliminary and trial, and extensive investigation which a private citizen is not able to perform. In addition, court notices for preliminary examination and trial are sent to the parties signing the complaint. Peace officers know what to do upon receipt of these notices. Private citizens usually do not know what to do upon receiving the notices.

Misdemeanors: Investigated Complaints. Where the police have investigated the commission of a misdemeanor, and a citizen appears in the office with a copy of the police report seeking a complaint, he should be fully questioned to determine if the four requirements for preparing a complaint have been met. If it appears that a complaint should be authorized, and if the police report contains a statement of the accused regarding his side of the matter, then deputy district attorneys may prepare a complaint.

When it appears the four requirements for preparing a criminal complaint have been met, but the police report contains no statement from the accused as to his side of the matter, a complaint should not be prepared until the deputy district attorney has given the accused a chance to state his side of the case. The complainant should be advised that the accused will be given an opportunity to state his side of the matter and a future date should be set when the complainant can be informed of the results of our interview with the accused and what action we then propose to take.

Prior to preparing a complaint, the complainant should be informed of the seriousness of a criminal action. He should further be informed that once the action is instituted, only the district attorney can move the court to dismiss it. He should be clearly informed that *he* cannot "drop charges" after the action has begun.

It is generally better practice to move slowly in authorizing citizen complaints. Trials are usually conducted many months after a complaint is issued.

Most citizen complainants will no longer wish to come to court over the matter after a few weeks' time has elapsed. Deputy district attorneys should be particularly cautious about approving criminal complaints where family or neighborhood disputes are involved. Many of these disputes are primarily civil in nature where a separation, divorce, civil injunction, or a move away from the undesirable neighborhood is the only real solution to the problem. A criminal complaint rarely solves the basic problem in these cases. Usually, the citation method of handling the dispute will be more successful than authorizing a criminal complaint.

Misdemeanors: Noninvestigated Complaints. In cases where there has been no police investigation of the citizen's complaint, excepting very minor criminal matters, the complainant should be referred to the police department having jurisdiction of the offense so that the complaint may be investigated. When the investigation is complete, the case should be handled as an investigated complaint described above. The district attorney's office is not an investigative agency and has neither the personnel nor authority to conduct investigative work which should be done by police agencies.

Minor criminal complaints involving only the complainant and the accused may be investigated by the deputy district attorney, using the citation method. A noninvestigated citizen complaint should never be authorized without first hearing what the accused has to say.

POLICE AGENCY COMPLAINTS

Complaints prepared for police agencies must meet the same four requirements as any other complaint outlined in "Requirements" above. Prior to authorizing the complaint, the deputy district attorney should assure himself that all necessary police investigation has been completed. If the investigation necessary to prove the case beyond a reasonable doubt has not been completed, the complaint should not be authorized until such investigation is complete. The fact that a man is already in custody is no justification for issuing a criminal complaint where, because of incomplete investigation, the case cannot be proved beyond a reasonable doubt.

If a complaint meets the four requirements and is authorized for a police agency, a copy of the complete police report should be attached to the office copy of the complaint. At the time the complaint is authorized, the officer in charge of the investigation should be clearly advised of any follow-up investigation which will be required prior to trial.

At the time the complaint is authorized, the officer should be advised which witness and what evidence will be required for the preliminary examination. The officer should further be advised that the preliminary examination will be held within five days and that the witnesses and evidence must be present in court at that time.

Deputy District Attorneys should resist any tendency to authorize a complaint either greater or lesser than the planned ultimate charge and disposition of the case. The practice of filing a greater charge with the idea in mind of taking a reduction at a later date is not acceptable.

NOTE

1. Adapted from: California Criminal Justice Cost Project, Phase I. Prepared by Public Systems Inc., Sunnyvale, Ca., Aug. 1971 (mimeograph). For California Assembly Rules Committee, Sacramento, Ca.

Index

Accessory, 424
Accomplice, 424
Adams, 66
Addiction, 444
Administration, 175, 190–191
  management, 191
  operation, 191
  services, 191
Alarcon, 371
Amendment, 429
Amos, 385
Analyze, 138, 190
Ancillary, 182, 188–189
Anthropologist, 109
Anxiety, 15, 168
Apathy, 36
Appeal, 116, 424
Applegate, 244, 371
Applicants, 137, 143, 147
Apprehension, 7, 10, 27
Apparatus, 5
Arraignment, 118–119, 414, 416, 419
Arrest, 11, 15, 118, 124–125, 414, 419
  approaches, 363

Arrest (continued)
  by private persons, 352
  exemption, 348
  false, 124–125
  human factors, 356
  human failures, 359
  laws, 36
  manner, 347
  on street, 363
  psychology, 358
  procedures, 346
  residence or building, 364
  special statutes, 355
  special problems, 367
  techniques, 356
  vehicles, 365
  with warrant, 350, 359
  without warrant, 349, 361
Assault, 42, 46
Attitude, 169
Authority, 445

Bail, 13, 118, 125–126, 420
Bailey, 149

Bailiff, 189
Baldwin, 155
Barnes, 24, 51, 66, 113
Baughman, 149
Beat, 142
Beattie, 38
Behavior control, 27, 57, 102, 105
Block, 24, 97
Bloomquist, 344
Blum, 171, 172
Board, 143–144
Bond, 125–126
Bradford, 281
Brancole, 344
Bristow, 194, 244
Budget policy, 206
Bureau, 193
Burger, 18, 24, 161
Burglary, 42, 46, 422

Cadets, 136
Cahn, 127
California Highway Patrol, 155
Campbell, 385
Causation, electic, 110
Chapman, 66
Civil, 116, 123–125, 444
Clark, 385
Clergymen, 423
Coercion, 34
Cline, 244
Coffey, 24, 127, 173, 215, 385, 412
Columbus, 215
Command, 175
  horizontal, 179
  vertical chain of, 175–176
Communication, 33, 99
  privileged, 176, 189, 423
Complaint, 415, 418, 444–448
  authority, 445
  drafting, 445
  filing, 445
  requirements, 444
  signing, 445
Constitution, 419–421, 424
  rights, 367
Contact, 8
Control, 27
  coercive, 33
  persuasive, 34
  role, 36
Coordination, 22, 174, 181

Corporate, 116
Corpus delicti, 422
Correctional apparatus, 3
Corrections, career in, 6, 15–16, 21, 160
  advantages, 165
  challenge, 165
  disadvantages, 165
  juvenile, 6
  promotion, 167
  salaries, 165–166
  security, 165
Counsel, 5, 420
Courts, 20
  Appellate, 11, 19, 117–118
  Civil, 123
  Criminal, 117
  District, 424
  Judicial, 425
  Juvenile, 43
  Lower, 117
  Municipal, 416, 425
  structure of, 414, 424
  Superior, 117, 416–417, 425
  Supreme, 18, 22, 83, 125, 424
Cressey, 51, 113
Crime, 42–46
  challenge of, 172
  extent of, 42, 46, 99, 100
  index, 49
  prevention, 238
  reports, 42–43
Crime laboratory, 266, 441–442
  documents, 275
  fiber and hair, 272
  fingerprint, 269
  firearms examination, 268
  local, 267
  metallurgical and petrographic, 272
  neutron-activation, 273
  personnel, 267
  photographic, 274
  radiological, 274
  regional, 267
  serological, 271
  spectrograph, 269
  toxicological, 272
Criminal, 98, 100–101, 106, 108–109, 115
  description of, 5
  justice, 5
  lower class, 105
  organization, 5
  problems, 16

Criminal *(continued)*
  process, 5, 414
  white collar, 105
Criminalistics, 263
  history, 264
  need, 264
  pioneers, 264
  purpose, 265
Cross-examinations, 421
Cummings, E. I., 51
Cumming, L., 51
Custody, 416

Daly, 82
Day, 51, 66
Davis, 215
Defense, 19–20
Delinquency, 39, 99–100, 103–104, 106
  limitations on measurements, 39, 41
Department of Justice, 155
Dependent, 13
Derbyshire, 34, 51
Detaining, 13–14
Devlin, 32, 51
Dienstein, 261
Differential association, 105
Disasters, 240
District, 192
District Attorney, 443
Division, 192
Donald, 159
Dugdale, 109
Dwyer Act, 420
Dysfunctional, 19

Earp, 428
Ectomorph, 110
Edell, 51
Education, 36, 135, 137–138
Edwards, 17, 24, 38
Efficiency vs effectiveness, 213
Ego, 108
Eldefonso, 24, 127, 173, 385, 412
Endomorph, 110
Ellis, 344
Elson, 88
Embezzlement, 421
Employment opportunities, 153, 162–163, 168
  disadvantages, 167
  in communities, 167
  pressure, 167
Enforcement, 176

Enforcement *(continued)*
  American philosophy of, 54–55, 58
  development of American, 63
  functions, 29
  opportunities, 176
  technical aspects, 176
Escobedo, 43, 83
Esselstyn, 127
Ethics, 387, 391
  code, 389
  employment policy, 396
  FBI pledge, 393
  human relations, 402
  law enforcement code, 390
  rules of conduct, 394
Evidence, 260, 422, 430
  heresay, 423
  illegal, 423
Examinations, 147

Fabian, 97
Federal Bureau of Investigation, 85, 88, 147,
    155, 166, 189
Felony, 12, 117–118, 124, 414–416, 418–419,
    445–446
Fingerprint, 77, 189, 258–259
Fiscal policy, 206
Fitzgerald, 261
Fragmented, 3, 5, 20
Frank, 166
Freedom, 50
Freud, 107
Fricke, 262, 371

Gallati, 66
Gammage, 154, 172–173
Garabedian, 173
Garrett, 428
Gault, 18, 430
Geis, 24
Germann, 66, 215
Gideon, 18, 430
Glasser, 163
Glossary, 432–440
Gluck, 107
Goddard, 109
Goggin, 171–172
Gourley, 244
Griffin, 52, 215

Habeas Corpus, 13, 424
Hall, 371

Hammurabi, 426
Harris Survey, 30
Hart, 128
Hartinger, 173, 385
Hedonistic, 104
Hickok, 428
History, 59, 61
Hoover, 46, 48, 68, 77, 80, 84–89, 94, 264, 428
Hooton, 109–110

Id, 108
Identification, 257
Immigration Border Patrol, 155
Imbau, 262
Incrimination, 421, 431
Indictment, 12, 118, 417
Information, 416–417
In-service, 137–138
Intent, 123
International Association of Chiefs of Police, 8, 23, 94–96, 138, 142
Interrogation, 252, 431
Interview, 252
Investigation, 7, 10, 246–247, 251

Jail, 416
Jamestown, 426
Jeopardy, 420
Jones, 280
Jukes, 109
Jury, 120, 415
    Grand, 12, 118–119, 126, 417, 443
    Petit, 119
Juvenile proceedings, 14

Kamisor, 37
Kallikak, 109
Kavaraceus, 113
Keeler, 68, 78, 92–94
Kerper, 24, 371
Kirk, 280–281
Kolbrek, 262
Kooken, 397, 412

LaFave, 371
Larceny, 42, 46
Larsen, 215
Larson, 78
Lavine, 97
Law, 115–116, 421
    accusatorial, 115

Law *(continued)*
    aspects of, 116
    inquisitional, 115
    substantive, 116
Law enforcement career, 149
    advantages, 149, 151
    challenge, 149
    disadvantages, 151–153
    disrespect, 151
    frustration, 152
    hostility, 153
    promotion, 149, 151
Laws, 54–55, 57, 59–60, 242
Leadership, 68, 203
Leonard, 194, 215
Liabilities, 117, 123–125, 143–144
Limitations, 421
Lombroso, 109
Los Angeles, 134–135
    Police Department, 90

Magistrate, 415
Mallory, 18, 429
Management, 206
    functions, 205
    philosophies, 204
Manpower, 21, 163, 169
Mapp, 18, 430
Mens rea, 123
Mentally ill, 444
Mesomorph, 110
Metropolitan Police Act, 62, 71
Miller, 113
Miranda, 18, 430
Misconceptions, 98–100
Misdemeanor, 117–118, 124, 415, 418–419, 421, 445–447
Misunderstanding, 100
Modus operandi, 77–78
More, 67, 214
Mores, 26, 101
Mosaic Code, 60, 426
Moral character, 141
Municipal, 178
Myths, 100

Neglect, 184
Ness, 428
Nixon, 88–89
Nonsupport, 444
Nuisances, 444

Obligatory Act of 1856, 63
Offenses, 41
O'Hara, 262, 281
Order, 8
Organization,5,21,144,174–177,179–181,190
  characteristics of, 180
  descriptions of, 192
  physical aspects, 179
  principles, 181
  psychological, 179–180
  ranking officer, 179
Osterburg, 262

Pace, 344
Parker, 68, 83, 89–92, 97, 172
Parole, 159–163
  role of officers, 160
Parties, principal, 424
Pathology, 106
Patrol, 8, 185, 221
  aircraft, 229
  automobile, 226
  bicycle, 225
  canine, 227
  evolution of, 218
  electronic, 236
  foot, 222
  horse, 224
  marine, 231
  motorcycle, 226
  objectives, 220
  plainclothes, 235
  private, 237
  saturation, 233
  special, 232
  team, 234
Payton, 244
Peace Officers' Standards and Training, 139
Pearlman, 48
Peel, 68–70, 80
Penology, 150, 162, 169
Personal Safety, 55
Personnel, 134, 164
  shortages, 164
  specialists, 164
  technicians, 164
Peters, 113
Physical agility, 142–143
  condition, 143
  coordination, 143
  testing, 143

Photography, 258
Pinkerton, 68, 72–74, 97, 427
Plaintiff, 123–124
Platoon, 192
Plea bargaining, 12, 118–119
Police, 31, 155
  administrative, 182, 188, 197, 212
  and crime prevention, 374
  awareness, 31
  community relations,8,31,152,398,400,405
  definition, 27
  discipline, 211
  ethics, 387, 402
  fragmentation, 198
  morale, 210
  organization, 209
  patrol, 217–218, 220–222
  power, 27
  precriminals, 407
  psychological role, 31–33
  public support, 27
  qualifications, 159
  rewarding misbelief, 404
  services, 181–182, 188
  women, 155, 157–159
Policy, 203
Polygraph, 78, 93, 276
Post-trial, 13
Post, 192
Poverty, 151
Power, 34
Preliminary, 119, 415–419
President's Commission, 19, 21, 24, 44, 134,
    143, 145, 153, 163, 169, 171, 172
Prevention, 7–8, 27, 373
  and police, 374
  concept, 373
  mechanical, 379
Priest, 423
Pressure groups, 209
Prima facie, 119
Primary, 7
Probable cause, 124–125
Probation, 21, 145, 159, 161–163, 417
Probate, 116
Probationary period, 147
Processes, 5–8, 11, 13–16, 18–19, 22,
    117–118, 166, 414
Programs, 10
Property security, 56
Psychosis, 107

Psychiatrists, 107
Psychological factors, 27–28, 30, 106–109
  approach, 107
  research, 108
Prosecution, 5, 12, 19–20, 118, 120, 443
Punishment, 57
Public disorders, 240
Public opinion, 207

Rape, 42, 46
Recognizance, 3
Recruit, 137, 145, 147
Reid, 262
Rights, 419
  legal counsel, 431
Robbery, 42, 46, 422
Roucek, 100–101
Route, 192
Rubin, 24

Sahid, 385
Salaries, 147–149, 162
  benefits, 148
  bonus, 148
  fringe, 148
Schizophrenia, 107
Scientific aids, 259
Section, 193
Sector, 192
Selection, 147
Sentence, 11
Sheldon, 110
Smith, 32, 195
Sociological factors, 102
Socioeconomic, 17
Soderman, 262
Sowle, 412
Specialization, 182–188
Speck, 82
Standards, 134, 139–140, 153, 159
Statistics, 37–39, 42, 48–49, 71, 135, 138
Statute of limitations, 421
Stihchcomb, 172
Stone, 77, 85
Sullivan, 24, 67, 127
Superego, 108
Supervisor, 192
Support, 27
Suppression, 7–8
Surveillance, 256
Survey of corrections, 160, 163

Sutherland, 104, 113
Symbol, 33–34
Systems, 3, 5–6, 18, 21–22
  fragmented, 3, 20

Taft, 113
Tamm, 94–96
Tappan, 24, 67, 128
Task Force Report, 72, 169
Taylor, 78
Teeters, 24, 51
Testimony, 119–121, 416, 421, 423–424
Tests, 143
Texas Rangers, 427
Theft, 42, 46, 420
Theoretical approaches, 101
Theory, 111
Toch, 33
Tort, 123
Traffic, 8
Traffic enforcement, 242
Training, 137–139, 163
  emphasis on, 135
Traits, 144
Transcript, 417
Trial, 11, 13–15, 415–417, 419–420
Truth, 119–120, 122
Turner, 281

Undercover work, 255
Uniform Crime Reports, 41, 47
U.S. Childrens Bureau, 42, 48–49

Victimless Crime, 310
  alcohol, 332
  gambling, 314
  history, 311
  homosexuality, 326
  legal system, 339
  narcotics and drugs, 318
  pornography, 328
  prostitution, 323
  scope of, 312
  types of, 314
  vice enforcement, 336, 339
Voice print, 278
Vollmer, 68, 75, 81, 83, 113

Wainwright, 430
Waiver, 420, 431
Ward, 13

Warrants, 118, 124–125, 415
Warren, 100–101
Weeks, 429
Wells, 262, 371
Wellford, 385
Weston, 262, 371
Westley, 412
Wilson, 68, 78–84, 90, 97, 149, 172, 181, 192–193, 195, 215, 245, 397

Whisenand, 244
Whitmore, 171–172
Witness, 120, 122, 124, 422
Work furlough program, 166
Writs, 424

Yablonski, 113
Youth Authority, 418